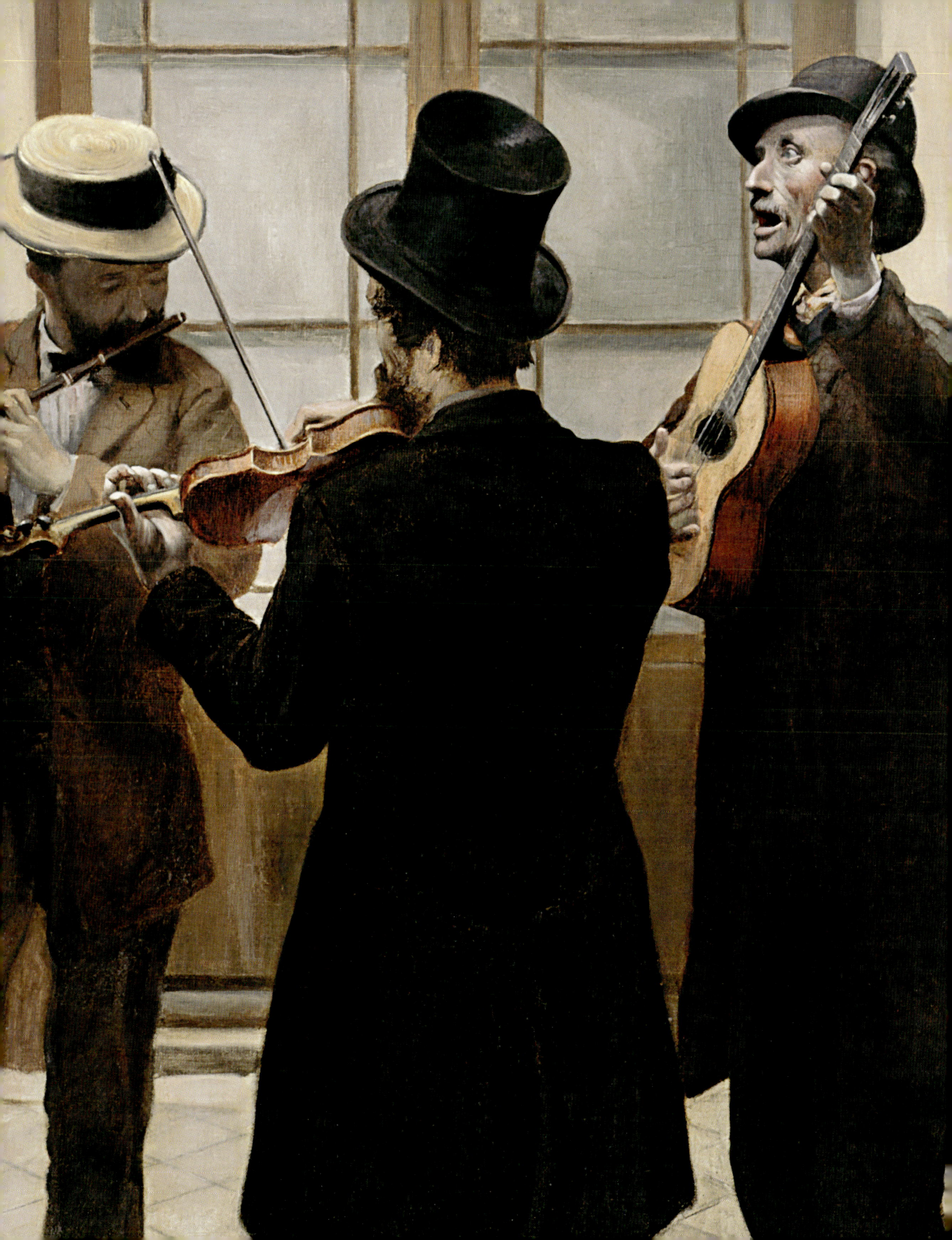

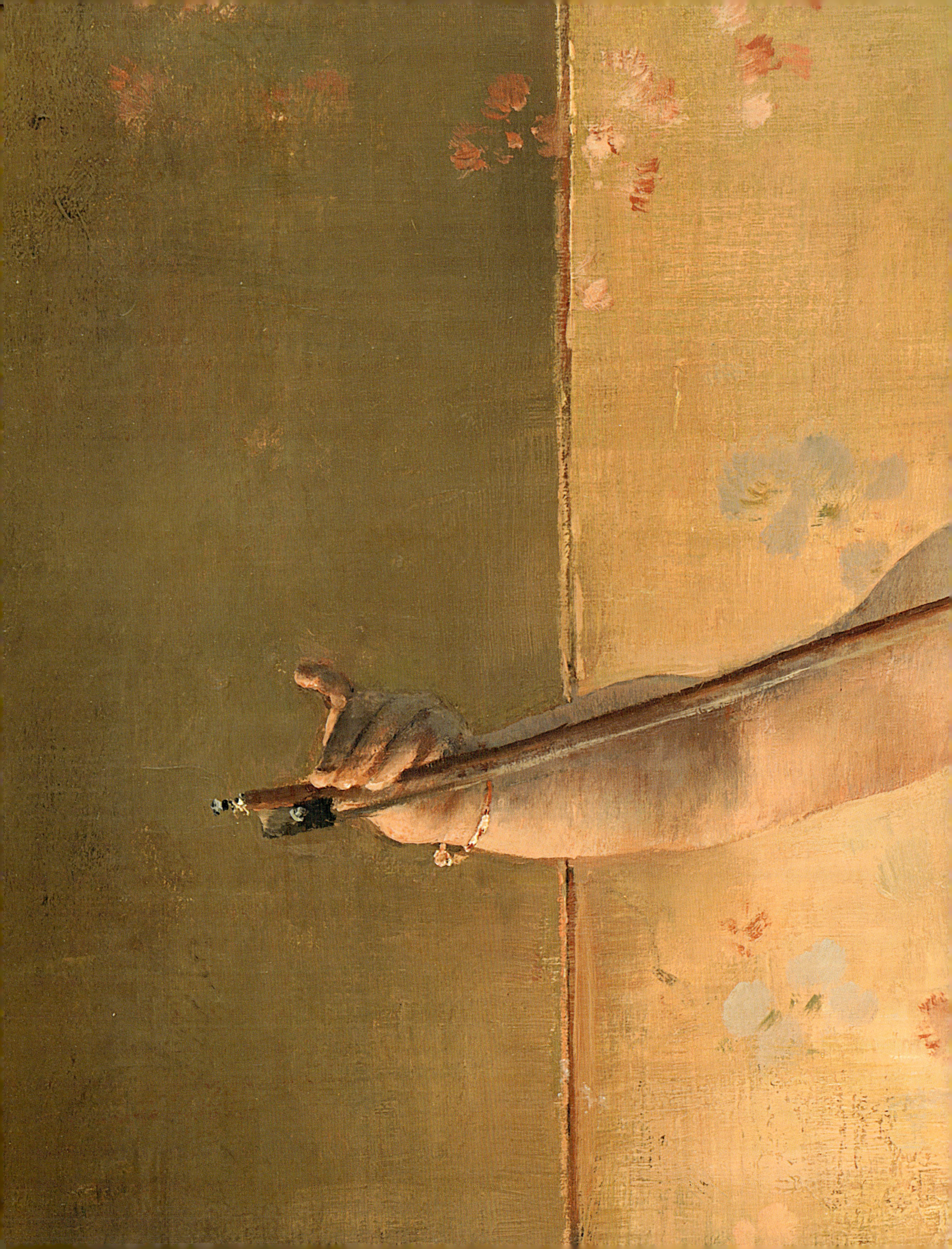

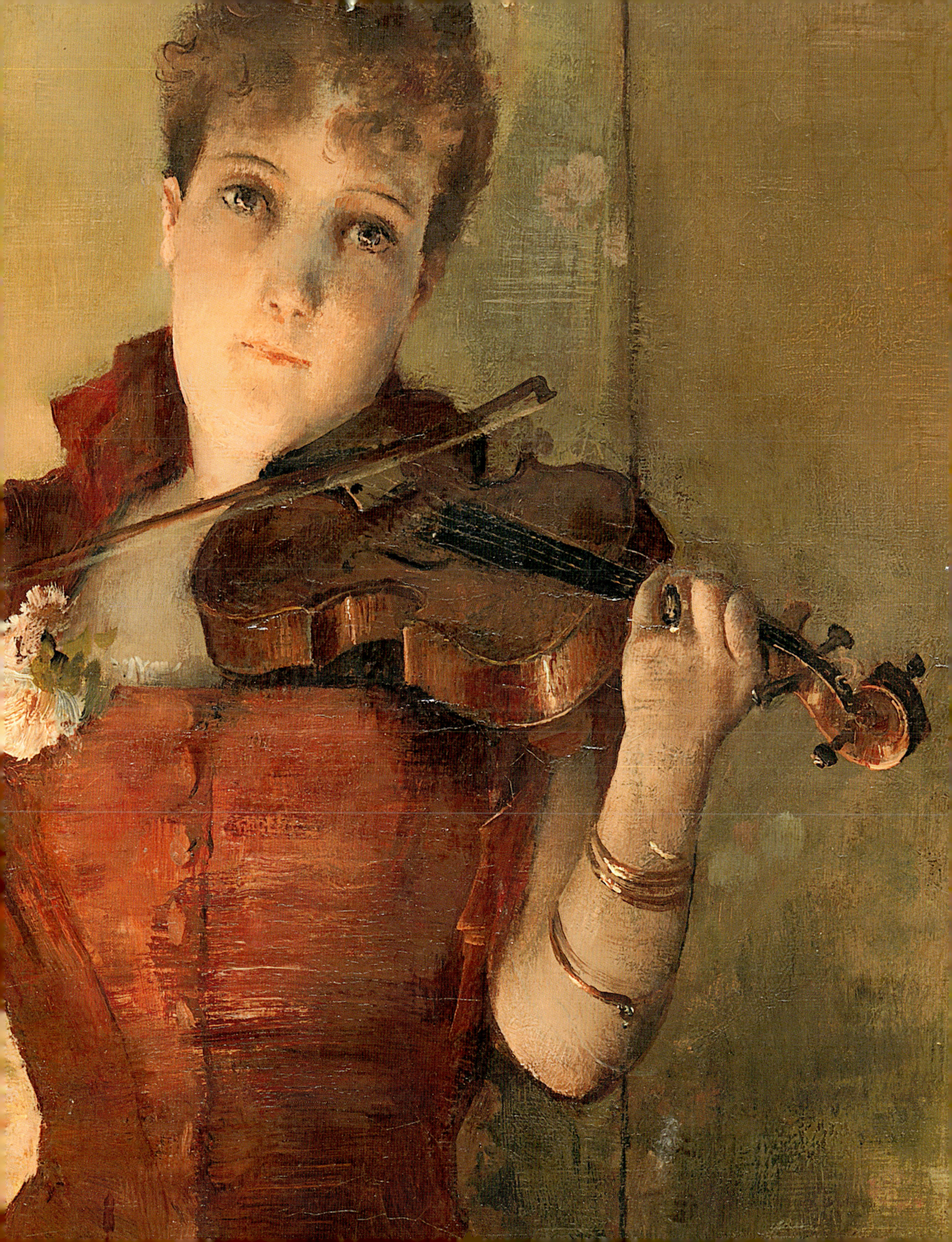

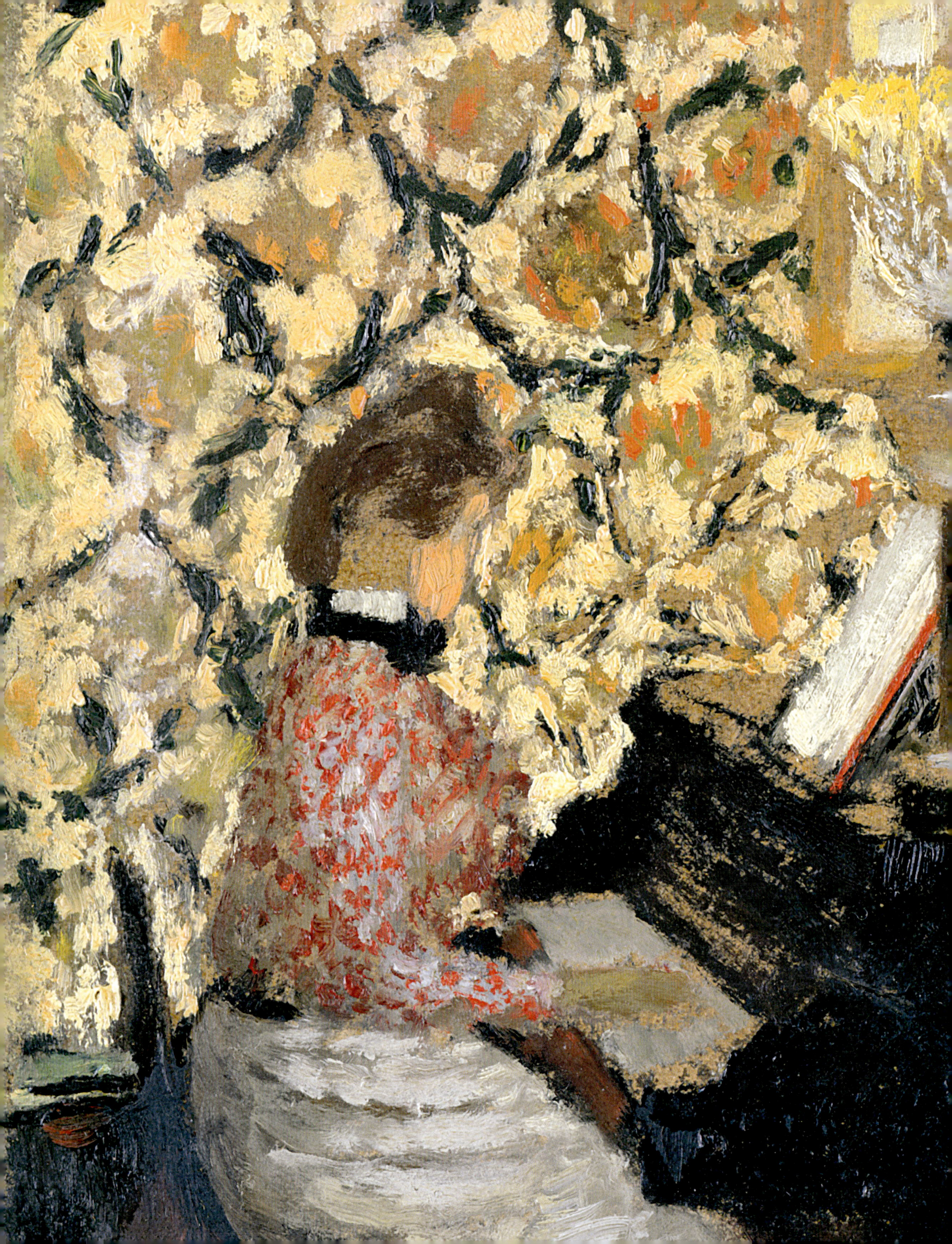

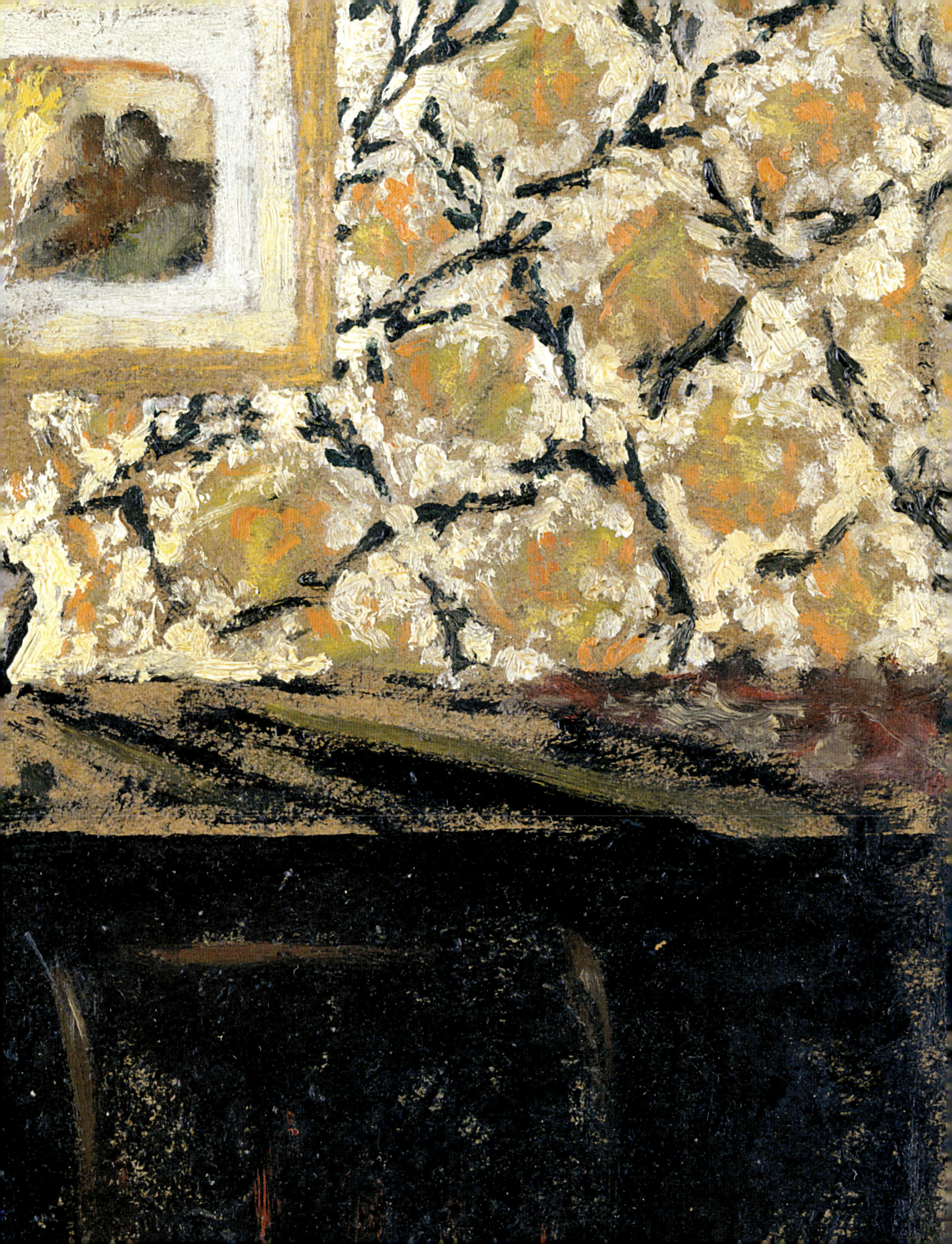

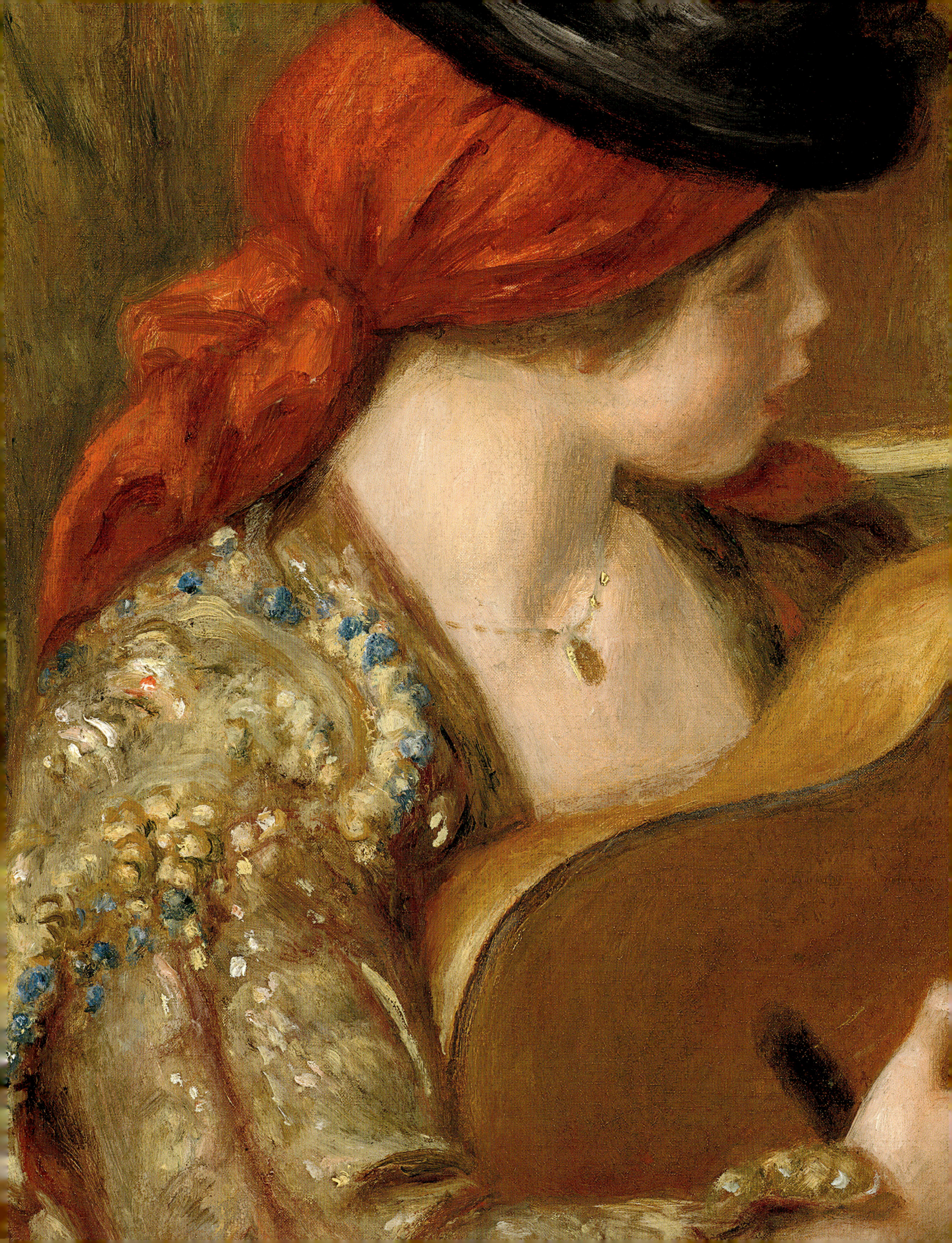

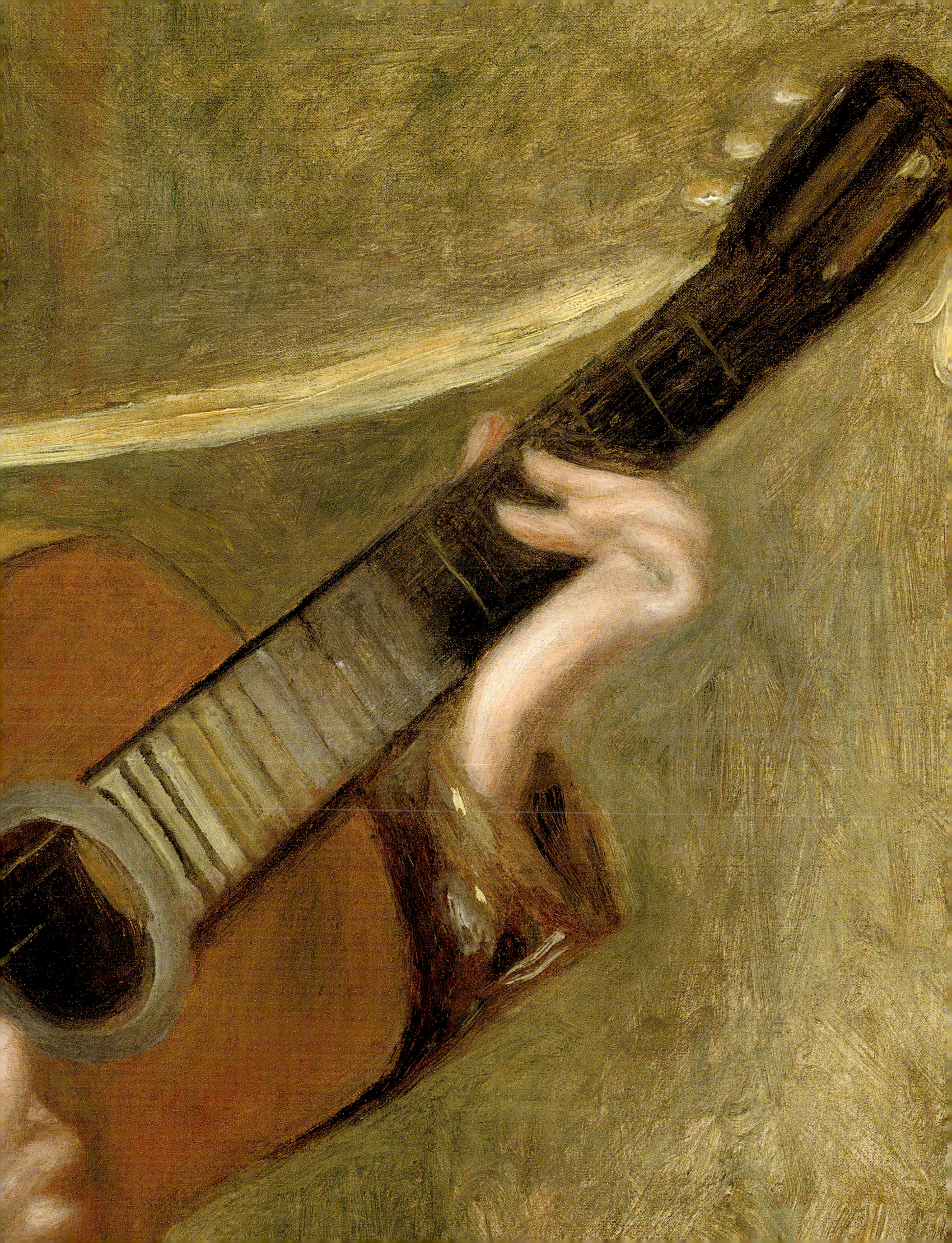

in concert!

musical
instruments
in art
1860–1910

in concert!

musical instruments in art

1860–1910

Edited by
Frédéric Frank and Belinda Thomson

Contributions by Lolita Delesque, Frédéric Frank,
Anne Leonard and Belinda Thomson

Distributed by Yale University Press, New Haven and London

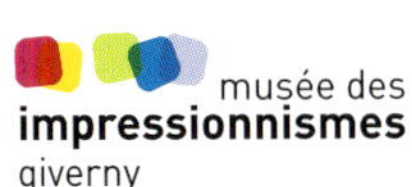

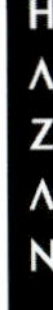

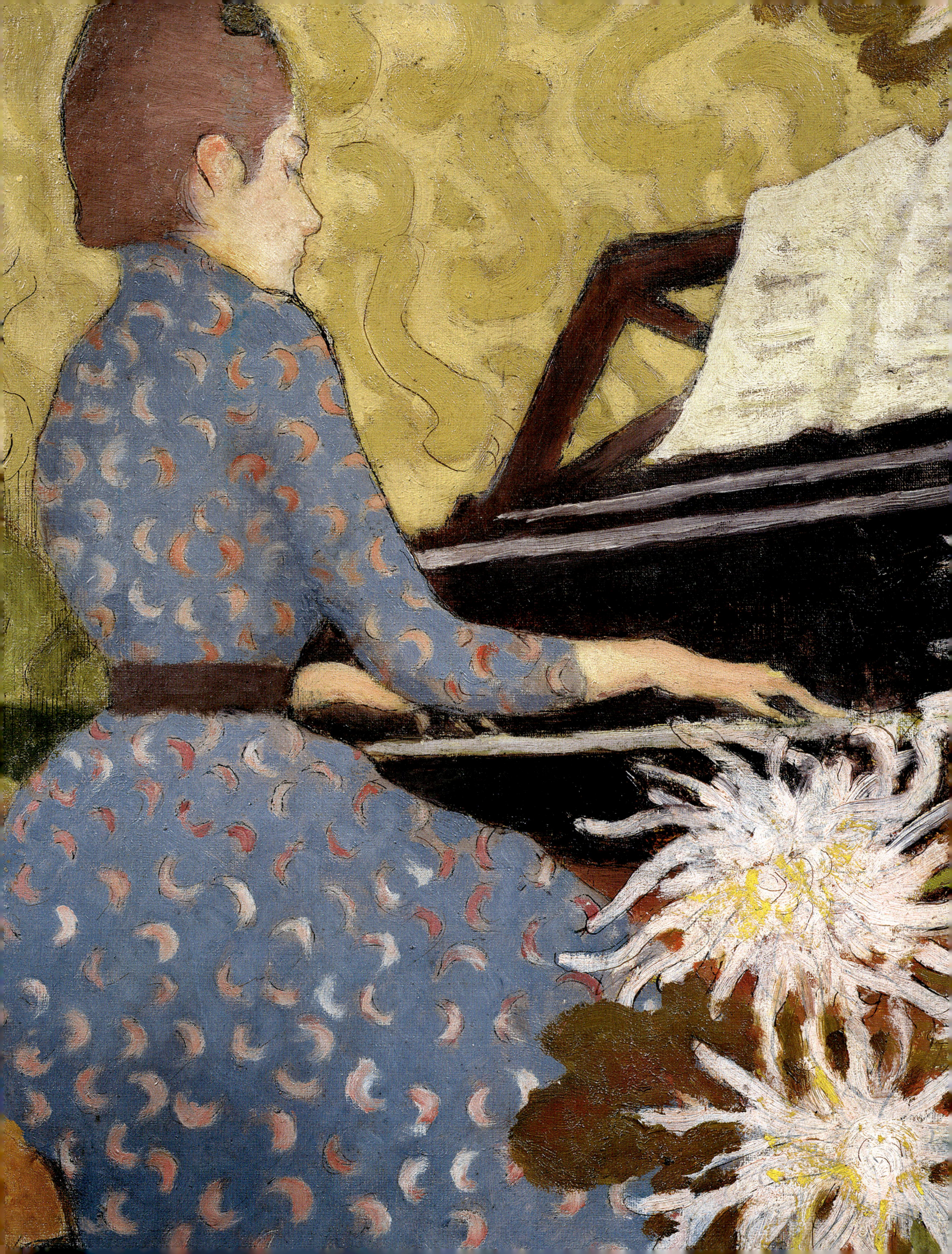

This catalogue is published on the occasion of the exhibition '**In Concert! Musical Instruments in Art, 1860–1910**' organised by the musée des impressionnismes Giverny from 24 March to 2 July 2017

With the exceptional support of the Musée d'Orsay and the Musée de l'Orangerie

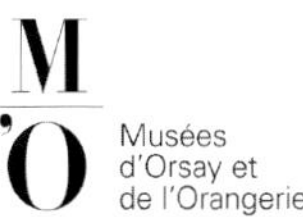

The Caisse d'Épargne Normandie is the main partner of the musée des impressionnismes Giverny

Founding members of the musée des impressionnismes Giverny

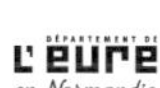 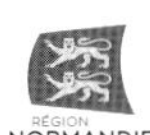 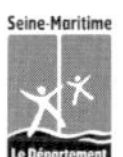 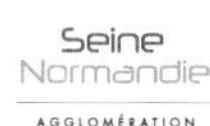 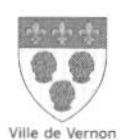 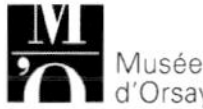 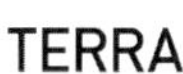

Jacket: James McNeill Whistler, *At the Piano*, 1858–1859 (detail, cat. 22, p. 92)
p. 1: Albert Bartholomé, *The Musicians*, also known as *Musicians in a Courtyard*, 1883 (detail, cat. 4, p. 72)
p. 2–3: Alfred Stevens, *The Violinist*, c. 1875 (detail, cat. 32, p. 103)
p. 4–5: Édouard Vuillard, *Misia at the Piano*, 1895 or early 1896 (detail, cat. 29, p. 99)
p. 6–7: Auguste Renoir, *Young Spanish Woman with a Guitar*, 1898 (detail, cat. 45, p. 118)
Facing page: Pierre Bonnard, *Young Woman at the Piano*, 1891 (detail, cat. 50, p. 125)

exhibition

Curators

Frédéric Frank
Director general, musée des impressionnismes Giverny

Belinda Thomson
Honorary professor, University of Edinburgh, Chevalier dans l'Ordre des Arts et des Lettres

musée des impressionnismes giverny

Sébastien Lecornu
President

Guy Cogeval
Vice-president

Frédéric Frank
Director general

Marina Ferretti
Director of Research and Scientific Affairs

Vanessa Lecomte
Associate Curator

Camille Larroumet and Valérie Reis
Exhibition organisers

Céline Mittelette
Registrar

Véronique Roca
Conservator

Denis Atanné, Didier Guiot, Laurent Lefrançois, Pascal Mérieau, Olivier Touren
Installation

Marie Delbarre, Charlotte Guimier, Hélène Furminieux, Laurette Roche
Public programme

Keren Bensalmon, Géraldine Brilhault
Communication (Giverny)

Anne Samson
Communication (Paris)

Annaïck Aubry, Christelle Lampérier, Xavier Poc
Administration

Frédérique Aude Blondiaux
Bookshop

catalogue

Musée des impressionnismes Giverny

Vanessa Lecomte
Editorial coordinator

Éditions Hazan

Jérôme Gille
Editorial director

Anne-Isabelle Vannier
Editorial coordinator, assisted by Manon Clercelet

Sylvie Milliet
Catalogue design

Claire Hostalier
Production

Charles Penwarden
Translation into English

Bernard Wooding
Copy-editor

lenders

We would like to express our deep gratitude to the lenders who generously contributed to this exhibition.

Dobra Collection

Belgium

Brussels, Belfius Art Collection
Brussels, Bibliothèque Royale de Belgique
Brussels, Musées Royaux des Beaux-Arts de Belgique
Ostende, Mu.ZEE
Ville de Liège, Musée des Beaux-Arts de La Boverie

Denmark

Odense, Brandts Museum of Art & Visual Culture

France

Albi, Musée Toulouse-Lautrec
Blérancourt, Musée Franco-Américain du Château de Blérancourt
Cergy-Pontoise, Collection Conseil Départemental du Val-d'Oise
Giverny, Bibliothèque du musée des impressionnismes
La Couture-Boussey, Musée des Instruments à Vent
La Rochelle, Musées d'Art et d'Histoire
Paris, Bibliothèque Nationale de France
Paris, Institut National d'Histoire de l'Art, Bibliothèque, Collection Jacques Doucet
Paris, Les Arts Décoratifs
Paris, Musée de l'Orangerie
Paris, Musée d'Orsay
Paris, Musée d'Orsay, on permanent loan at the Musée d'Art et d'Histoire de Saint-Denis
Paris, Musée Marmottan Monet
Paris, Petit Palais, Musée des Beaux-Arts de la Ville de Paris
Toulouse, Fondation Bemberg
Saint-Germain-en-Laye, Musée Départemental Maurice-Denis
Ville d'Avignon, Fondation Calvet
Ville de Clermont-Ferrand, Musée d'Art Roger-Quilliot
Villeneuve-sur-Lot, Collection Musée de Gajac

Germany

Hamburg, Hamburger Kunsthalle

Netherlands

Amsterdam, Van Gogh Museum (Vincent van Gogh Foundation)

Switzerland

Geneva, Association des Amis du Petit Palais

United Kingdom

City of London, Guildhall Art Gallery
London, Tate

United States

Baltimore, The Baltimore Museum of Art
Boston, Museum of Fine Arts
Chicago, Terra Foundation for American Art
Cincinnati, Taft Museum of Art
Cleveland, The Cleveland Museum of Art
Indianapolis, Indianapolis Museum of Art
New York, The Metropolitan Museum of Art
Sarasota, The John & Mable Ringling Museum of Art
Washington, Hirshhorn Museum and Sculpture Garden, Smithsonian Institution
Washington, National Gallery of Art
Washington, Smithsonian American Art Museum

As well as private collectors who preferred to remain anonymous

curators' acknowledgements

Frédéric Frank would like to point out that this exhibition project owes a great deal to the encounter with Belinda Thomson, whose passion for the piano and music and tremendous erudition regarding those major artists Maurice Denis, Pierre Bonnard, Édouard Vuillard, Vincent Van Gogh and Paul Gauguin he found constantly inspiring and a considerable enrichment to the theme.

For her part Belinda Thomson wishes to offer her heartfelt thanks to Frédéric Frank, with whom it has been a pleasure to work, for his generous and irresistible invitation to get involved in this project, and the opportunity it offered of making a long-held dream of a musical exhibition become a reality. She also wishes to thank her husband Richard for his unstinting encouragement and her mother Easta for her enthusiastic interest and forbearance.

The curators give special thanks to Marina Ferretti, Guy Cogeval and Xavier Rey, who always followed and supported this project with great benevolence.

The friendly help of the following individuals assisted us in the conception of this exhibition and this catalogue. We met with a remarkable reception all over the world when looking for works, contacts and ideas:

Paola Aeschlimann-Rebstein, Alexandra Allen, Guillaume Ambroise, Lynne D. Ambrosini, Sylvain Amic, Dita Amory, Stéphane Aquin, Seth Armitage, Beatrice Avanzi, Nienke Bakker, Edwin Becker, Claire Bernardi, Markus Bertsch, Jane Block, Katherine Bourguignon, Bénédicte Bouton, Deborah and Iain Boyd Whyte, Sylvain Boyer †, Sylvie Brame, Ian Brearey, Carol Brodie, Elizabeth Broun, Élisabeth Buxtorf, Isabelle Cahn, Lisa Cain, Thomas Campbell, Patrick de Carolis, Annette Carruthers, Laurence des Cars, Emma Chambers, Stéphanie Chardeau-Botteri, Éric de Chassey, Cyril Chazal, Elizabeth Childs, Melissa Chiu, Corrine Chong, Michael Clarke, Isabelle Collet, Caroline Collier, Gordon Cooke, Kitty Corbet Milward, Marlyse Courrech, Philippe Cros, Elizabeth Cumming, Mads Damsbo, Sylphide de Daranyi, Peter Dayan, Lolita Delesque, Pascale Delmaere, Veerle De Meester, Claire Denis, Huguette Devriendt, Danièle Devynck, Roger Diederen, Nilufer Dobra, Michel Draguet, Marina Ducrey, Ann Dumas, Christophe Duvivier, Ellen Egemose, Alexander Eiling, Deborah Emont Scott, Laurence Engel, Mark Evans, Charlotte Eyerman, Jérôme Faucheux, Shari Felty, Jay Fisher, Frances Fowle, Martina Fusari, Olivier Gabet, Isabelle Gaëtan, Hubertus Gaßner, Gilles Genty, Claude Ghez, Elizabeth Glassman, Sylvie Gonzalez, Meg Grasselli, Gloria Groom, William M. Griswold, Anna Gruetzner-Robins, Estelle Guille des Buttes-Fresneau, Stéphanie Guiraud-Chaumeil, Valérie Haerden, Margrit Hahnloser-Ingold, Katie Hanson, Karin Hellwig, Steven High, James Holloway, Claude Holstein, Timo Huusko, Karoline Hvalsøe, Leïla Jarbouai, Kimberly A. Jones, Sir Mark Jones, Ellen Josefowitz, Philippe Junod, Guillaume Kazerouni, Marine Kisiel, Victoria Kleiner, Eirini Koutsouroupa, Felix Kraemer, Hélène Lagès, Paul Lang, Claire Leblanc, Ellen M. Lee, Géraldine Lefèbvre, Robin Lelijveld, Heather Lemonedes, Antoinette Le Normand-Romain, Anne Leonard, Christophe Leribault, François Lespinasse, Béatrice Lescossois-De France, María López Fernandez, Yann Lorang, Marleen Madou, Dominique Marechal, Lady Marks, Marianne Matthieu, Armelle Maugin, André Mayer, Déborah Mayer, Dan Mayer, Matthew McLendon, Virginia Mecklenburg, Thierry Mercier, Olivier Meslay, Asher Miller, Charlie Minter, Jocelyn Monchamp, Janet Moore, Elaine Mordaunt, Mary Morton, Jenny Nex, Jolanda van Nijen, Annick Notter, Eva Nygårds, Christophe Olivereau, Frances Palmer, Ivonne Papin-Drastik, David Park Curry, Amanda Partridge, Denis Patouillard, Katherine Pearce, Sandra Pisot, Isolde Pludermacher, Sandra J. Poole, Earl A. Powell III, the late The Rt Hon Lord William Prosser QC, Vanessa Prosser, Rodolphe Rapetti, Béatrice Recchi-Altarriba, Régine Rémon, Cathy Ricciardelli, Christopher Riopelle, Anne Robbins, Fleur Roos Rosa de Carvalho, Anders Rosdahl, Katy Rothkopf, Françoise Rouart, Jean-Marie Rouart, Yves Rouart, Nathalie Roux, Martin Royalton-Kisch, Axel Rüger, Tatiana Ruiz Sanz, Willem O. Russell, Laurent Salomé, Juan San Nicolàs, Mathilde Schneider, Véronique Serrano, Karen Serres, Murray Simpson, Claude Sorgeloos, Fabienne Stahl, Emmanuel Starcky, Sarah Stauderman, Meg Steer, Susan Stein, Valérie Sueur-Hermel, Bertrand Talabardon, Sarah Talbot Cape, Joanna Tapp, Alain Tarica, Matthew Teitelbaum, Anne Terrasse, Richard Thomson, Céline Tranquille, Tamara Trodd, Phillip Van den Bossche, Élisabeth Verbecq, Marie-Paule Vial, Charles L. Venable, Charles Villeneuve de Janti, Éric de Visscher, Malcolm Warner, Barbara Weinberg, Sylvia Yount.

In Giverny, this exhibition could not have happened without the unfailing support of the Conseil Départemental de l'Eure, and in particular of Sébastien Lecornu, Élise Brigand, Philippe Gustin, Orlane Jauregui, and all the teams.

The members of the board of administration of the musée des impressionnismes Giverny showed their fidelity and their trust.

We also wish to thank the club of corporate patrons of the musée des impressionnismes Giverny, and more particularly the Caisse d'Épargne Normandie, for its constant support, and the Société des Amis du Musée.

At the musée des impressionnismes Giverny: Denis Atanné, Annaïck Aubry, Keren Bensalmon, Emmanuel Besnard, Frédérique Aude Blondiaux, Géraldine Brilhault, Marie Delbarre, Hélène Furminieux, Charlotte Guimier, Didier Guiot, Christelle Lampérier, Vanessa Lecomte, Laurent Lefrançois, Pascal Mérieau, Céline Mittelette, Xavier Poc, Valérie Reis, Véronique Roca, Laurette Roche, Olivier Touren.

—

Frédéric Frank and Belinda Thomson

If painting and music are sister arts, their connections were particularly close in the last third of the nineteenth century. During the Second Empire a new society took shape, driven by an entrepreneurial bourgeoisie that was increasingly confident of its values. It now looked to the model of aristocratic education, in which painting and drawing were taught alongside music, singing or dance, but at the same time modernised its forms by introducing new instruments and, even more importantly, allowing a new freedom that was conducive to invention. The technical revolutions that had gone hand in hand with the social transformations of the nineteenth century not only spawned a new kind of painting, soon to be known as 'Impressionism', but also led to unprecedented changes in musical life. This entered a veritable golden age in which – with the gramophone soon to make its appearance – it became increasingly common to learn a musical instrument and attend concerts, whether private or public. Like travel and sporting activity, going to the opera and to concert halls became emblematic of modern life. Families of artists with complementary talents began to replace the old lineages in which the trade was passed on from father to son and uncle to nephew. The Impressionist painters naturally depicted musicians – and their instruments – since these were an integral part of their everyday life.

In the Degas family, the father, Auguste, was a passionate music lover who organised musical Mondays in the family apartment. The only portrait of him left by his son Edgar shows him with a musical score, open behind him, framing his head as he listens with rapt attention to the guitarist Pagans. Martial, the brother of the painter Gustave Caillebotte, was a composer, and the older son painted his sibling absorbed in reading a score. Édouard Manet married a piano teacher, Suzanne Leenhof, whom Baudelaire described as 'a very fine artist'. Her husband, who loved to listen to her play, represented her with her hands on the keyboard, engrossed in her music. This family tradition continued with the painter's niece, Julie Manet, who was often depicted playing the violin, the mandolin, the flageolet or the piano by her mother, Berthe Morisot. Perhaps there was some reference here to Julie's godfather, Auguste Renoir, who painted so many young girls at the piano.

In the Bonnard family we must begin with the painter's brother-in-law, the composer Claude Terrasse. Looking set for a very serious career as an organist and chapel master, he became famous for his Belle Époque operettas. Andrée Bonnard, his wife, was an excellent pianist and they used to organise concerts together. Writing to Andrée of his planned visit to his friend Terrasse, when the couple were still only engaged, Pierre told his sister that he was making ready to hear the waves of music that would escape from his home, the Villa Bach in Arcachon. 'I am taking my box of colours', he added, 'and waves of green, blue and yellow will also flow in turn.' But that did not prevent him from producing some superb drawings for Andrée's husband, including the delightful *Petit Solfège illustré*.

There are numerous examples of the stimulating cohabitation between painting and music in the Impressionist period. Think, among many other instances, of the Sèthe sisters, who were raised 'in the cult of music and the arts': all three were fine musicians. Their talent came to attention at the concerts organised to accompany the Salon des XX in Brussels. Their friend Théo van Rysselberghe painted remarkable portraits of each one: Irma poses with her violin, Maria, who married Van de Velde, is shown seated at the harmonium, while the portrait of Alice announced the artist's adoption of the Neo-Impressionist method.

The more subtle correspondences between music and painting were evoked in the exhibition 'Debussy, la musique et les arts', organised at the Musée d'Orsay in 2012. Today, the musée des impressionnismes Giverny is presenting a joyous visual concert to recall the remarkable richness of musical life in those days and to show how it affected painters both in their everyday life and in their art.

Sébastien Lecornu
President of the musée des impressionnismes Giverny

Guy Cogeval
Vice-president of the musée des impressionnismes Giverny

Marina Ferretti
Director of Research and Scientific Affairs
of the musée des impressionnismes Giverny

The Caisse d'Épargne Normandie has made its partnership with
the musée des impressionnismes Giverny the main focus of its
cultural and artistic patronage. We consider the work carried out
by this museum to be remarkable in every respect, a fact reflected
in the huge success of its exhibitions and its ranking among
museum institutions. The museum's activities make an important
contribution to the cultural life of the region and to promoting the
heritage of Normandy. These are two objectives that the Caisse
d'Épargne Normandie fully shares as a cooperative bank seeking
to play an active role in the life of its region. Moreover, each
new project by this museum exemplifies the values of attentiveness,
responsibility and boldness that guide our own action. Historically
rich with its twofold economic and humanist dimension, the
Caisse d'Épargne Normandie is particularly proud to have been
the museum's official partner for over six years now.

'In Concert!' offers a magnificent exploration of musical
instruments in art. Linking art and music was bound to please us,
given our interest in the musical world and support for new music.
The wind of modernity and freedom blowing through the two arts
during the period of Impressionism can still be felt in our everyday
lives today. I wish this exhibition every success.

Joël Chassard
Chairman of the Board of Directors
of the Caisse d'Épargne Normandie

preface

Frédéric Frank

Painting is an art of space – or 'surface' to be more exact – music, an art of time. This observation, made on countless occasions by artists, art historians and philosophers,[1] immediately raises the question of the relationship between the 'sister arts' and, at the same time, of the seemingly insoluble problem of their synthesis. The term 'sister arts' goes back to Leonardo da Vinci[2] and has been associated with art history ever since, notably in the work of Paul Gauguin.[3] It evokes both a theory of similarities or analogies and a desire to create this convergence (the *Gesamtkunstwerk*) or synthesis of the arts. The aphorism 'Ut pictura musica'[4] (As with music, so with painting) recurs endlessly in the writings of artists from both disciplines.

The relationship between painting and music is, without doubt, a subject of growing interest today, as can be seen from the number of exhibitions, publications, talks and symposia in recent years.[5] Looking beyond this impressive corpus, we asked ourselves two questions: what might an exhibition of this kind bring to the musée des impressionnismes in Giverny, and why not talk about the musical instruments themselves?

To reflect on the interest this subject could have for Giverny meant, in effect, questioning the specificities of Impressionism. Ultimately, this movement in painting did not represent such a radical break in art history, and its relation to academic art was more porous than is commonly imagined. This premise, admittedly now more widely held, is one that it seems to me the present exhibition and catalogue confirm. The prism of music makes it all the more tangible by bringing together works of different periods and different styles, paintings that engage not only with 'classical music' but with a set of practices and divertissements from popular music. The iconographic approach we have adopted reveals the existence, at this period, of a continuum between all the different facets of musical life. Artists like Manet, Degas and Béraud embraced the whole musical gamut. If on the one hand 'classical' composers, from Liszt to Ravel and Dvořák to Satie, introduced popular, folk or traditional music into their works, on the other the tunes from 'great music' could also be heard in cafés and theatres or on the street. That is why we thought it would be interesting to show how the painting produced between 1860 and 1910, the period that witnessed the development of concert venues, brass bands, orchestras and conservatoires, bore witness to these trends, and to note the role played by this rich musical output and its greater accessibility in the context of the emergence of new themes in art and the heightened sensibility of painters to all forms of musical expression.

Why, we asked, had musical instruments been so largely overlooked as a subject, apart from their symbolic or allegorical

dimension – David's harp, Saint Cecilia's organ, the virginal favoured
by the seventeenth-century Dutch? For their ubiquity and diversity
reflect major developments that tell us a great deal about the period
and its artists. Their technical evolution during the crucial period
of the nineteenth century had an impact upon the way they were
represented. Their forms fascinated, like that double-bass head, for
example, which is like a leitmotiv in so many works by Manet, Degas,
Seurat and others. The evolution of instrument-making also radically
changed the music scene, and therefore the visual subject. Hundreds
of patents were registered for musical instruments, especially wind
instruments, guitars and pianos.[6] From 1800 to 1900 they ceased
to be luxury objects beyond the reach of the average purse and
became relatively widespread, mass-produced commodities whose
manufacture was standardised.

This meant that it was easier to be a musician and that
instruments were more varied. It was also easier for painters to have
musical instruments in their studios or in their living rooms, while
musical subjects were more accessible generally. It was for all
these reasons that the modern piano began to appear in paintings.
In seeking to evoke the variety of musical practices represented
by artists at the fin de siècle, it was impossible, at some point, not
to take into consideration the materiality of the objects that actually
produced the sounds, objects that were later a great source of
fascination for artists of the avant-garde.[7]

Finally, music in art introduces the question of time, both
passing time and contemporaneity. This allusion is certainly not
new in the history of painting: in still lifes, mandolins sit beside
candles and skulls to evoke the brevity of time (*tempus fugit*)
and, by the same token, the finite nature of all things. But the
question of time became a crucial challenge at this period, whether
in the shock effect provoked by Manet's genre scenes with their
emphasis on contemporary reality, or in Monet and Pissarro's
atmospheric series of paintings evoking the passage of time, or in
the echoes of chronophotography in the framing and composition
of works by Caillebotte or Degas. Painters were no longer concerned
with timelessness, rather they sought to pinpoint the moment,
asserting their presence in and *of* their time, and even letting
their techniques reveal the artist 'in action'. All these factors make
musical instruments apt symbols of that modernity which Baudelaire
described as 'the transient, the fleeting, the contingent',[8] not only
because they evoke the passing of time but because the way they
were made and played inscribes them into their contemporary world.
They form a subject that allows the idea of modernity in painting to
be given its full resonance.

[1] Adorno contrasts painting, which 'has pathos
in that which is', with music that 'purports a
becoming'. Theodor W. Adorno, *Philosophy of Modern
Music* (1947), London, Bloomsbury Publishing, 2007,
p. 138.

[2] 'Music is not to be regarded as other than the
sister of painting,' in *Leonardo on Painting*, New
Haven and London, Yale University Press, 2001, p. 34.

[3] 'Painting too should be in a separate category;
Sister of music, it exists through forms and colours.'
Cahier pour Aline, 1892–93, translated in *Art
Criticism*, Stony Brook, NY, Stony Brook University,
1991, p. 78.

[4] Philippe Junod, *Contrepoints, Dialogues entre
musique et peinture*, Geneva, Contrechamps, 2006,
pp. 9–18.

[5] 'Vermeer Suite: Music in 17th-Century Dutch
Painting', Dallas Museum of Art, 2016; 'Vermeer
and Music: The Art of Love and Leisure', The National
Gallery, London, 2013; 'Looking and Listening in
Nineteenth-Century France', Smart Museum of Art,
The University of Chicago, Chicago, 2007–2008;
'Debussy, la musique et les arts', Musée de
l'Orangerie, Paris, 2012; 'Allegro Barbaro. Béla Bartók
et la modernité hongroise 1905–1920', Musée d'Orsay,
Paris, 2013–14; 'Marc Chagall. Le triomphe de
la musique', Philharmonie de Paris, 2015–2016;
eds. James Rubin and Olivia Mattis, *Rival Sisters, Art
and Music at the Birth of Modernism, 1815–1915*,
Burlington, VT, Ashgate, 2014.

[6] See 'L'évolution du piano au XIXe siècle: histoire,
facture et caractéristiques techniques', by Jean-Claude
Battault, forum recorded at the Cité de la Musique,
Paris on 20 May 2000.

[7] Notably in the Analytical Cubism of Picasso,
Braque and Juan Gris.

[8] Charles Baudelaire, *Le Peintre de la vie
moderne* (1863), Paris, Calmann-Lévy, 1885, chap. 4,
'La Modernité', p. 70.

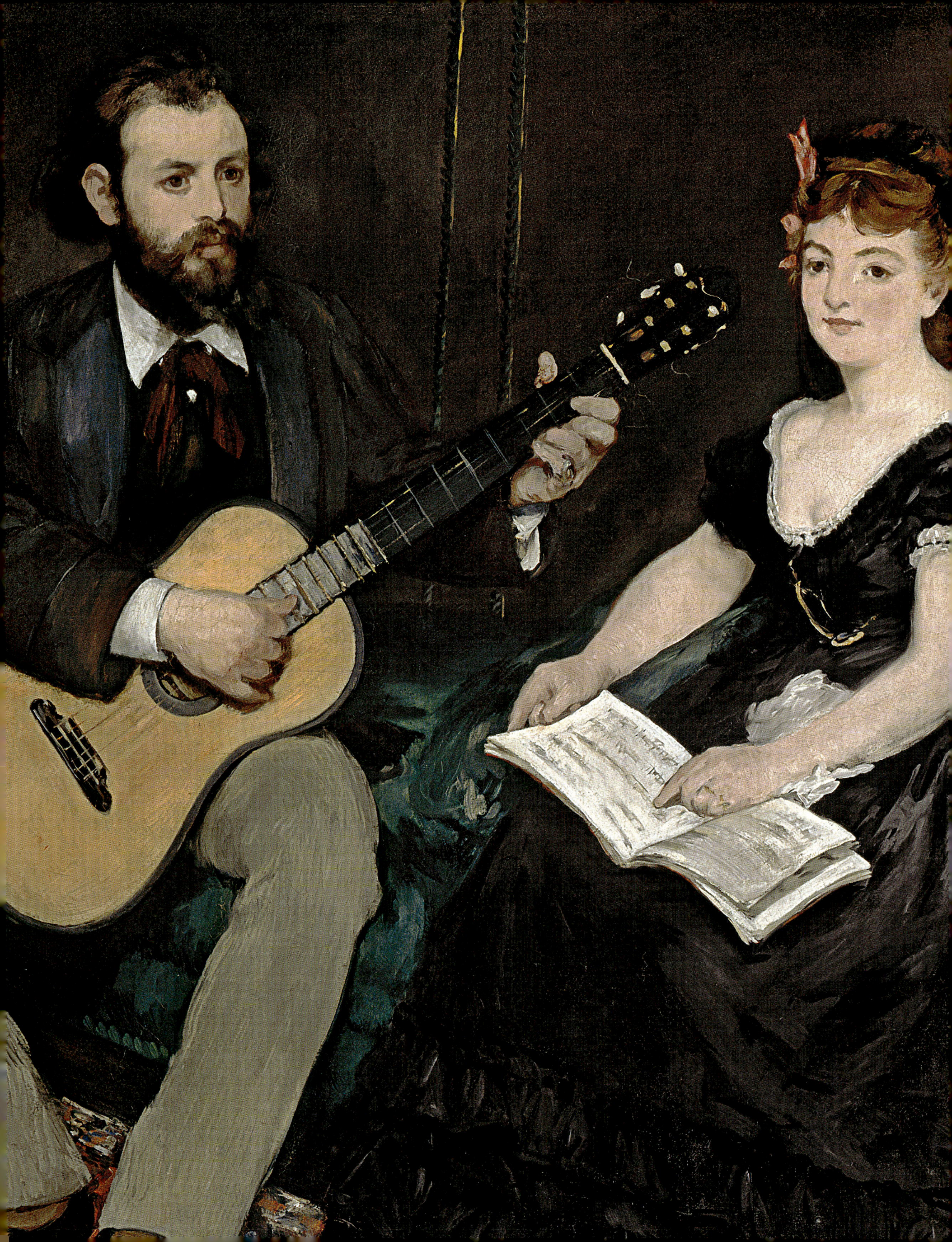

contents

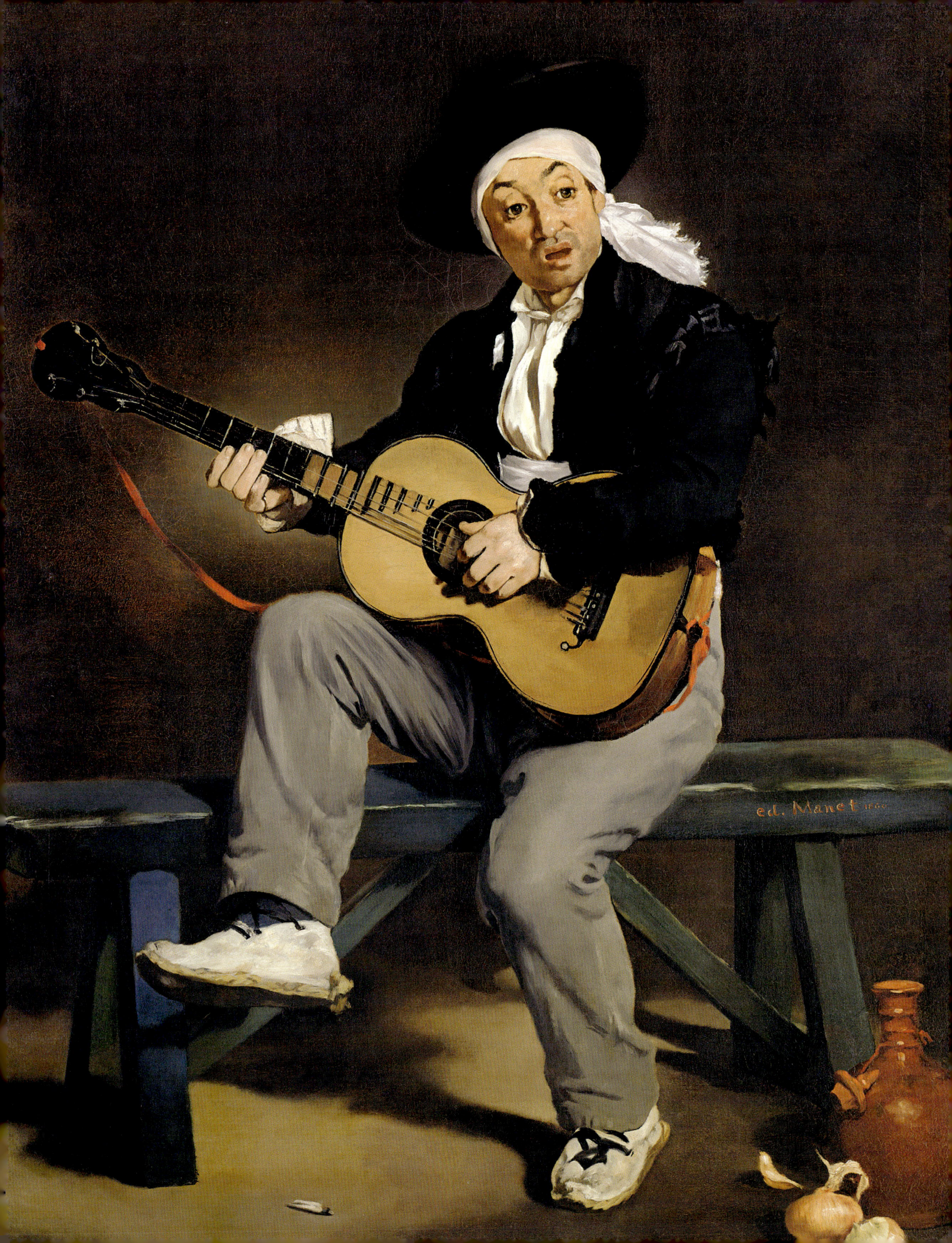

ed. Manet

musical instruments in the works of gauguin and manet: tradition reinvented

Frédéric Frank

GAUGUIN AND MUSIC, IN THE WAKE OF COROT AND COURBET

At the very start of his career, Paul Gauguin painted *Study of a Nude*, also known as *Suzanne Sewing* (fig. 2), which features a mandolin. Twenty years earlier, Édouard Manet had made his career debut with *The Spanish Singer* in which a guitar likewise features (fig. 1). Gustave Arosa, who was Gauguin's guardian from 1871 to his death in 1878, owned a collection that included canvases by Camille Corot, Eugène Delacroix, Jean-François Millet and Gustave Courbet, and these made a strong impression on his ward.[1] Gauguin owned the catalogue of the engravings,[2] executed in a limited edition by Arosa himself, that accompanied the catalogue for the posthumous sale of his collection at Drouot.[3] Among the works reproduced was Corot's *Seated Italian Woman Playing the Mandolin* (1865–70, Sammlung Oskar Reinhart 'am Römerholz', Winterthur). Gauguin later cut this out and stuck it in his *Notebook for Aline* (fig. 3). It is therefore not unreasonable to suggest that the masters in this collection influenced his work, even if the only artistic model he acknowledged in his writings was Camille Pissarro. The similarities between Corot's *Italian Woman* and *Suzanne Sewing*[4] are striking: the expression, the gestures and the composition, in which only the mandolin has changed position, reveal a clear connection. The instrument is the iconographic element that establishes the link between the two works. Gauguin produced three still lifes on the same subject (*Mandolin on a Chair*, 1880, private collection; *Dahlias and Mandolin*, 1883, private collection; and *Still Life with Mandolin*, 1885, Musée d'Orsay, Paris). Whereas Manet[5] took Courbet's *Woman with a Parrot* (1866, The Metropolitan Museum of Art, New York) and clothed her in his painting of the same title (also 1866, The Metropolitan Museum of Art),[6] Gauguin undressed the model in his nod to Corot (in a previous canvas he had already depicted his wife, Mette, clothed, in a composition that was very close to Corot, but without the mandolin).[7] In his commentary on *Suzanne*, written in 1881, Huysmans evokes Courbet, inappropriately in my view – and also in Gauguin's[8] – for his remarks concentrate on the nudity[9] and completely miss the allusion to Corot.

That said, Courbet does seem to have influenced two works by Gauguin on musical themes, if we consider the importance of the Arosa catalogue as an artistic source for his own painting and the undoubted impact of the works by the Master of Ornans that he saw at the Musée Fabre in December 1888.[10] In early 1894, Gauguin seems to have painted two artistic friends, and, going by the similarity of the colours in the setting to those in *Portrait of the Artist* (1893–4, Musée d'Orsay, Paris),[11] this was probably in his Parisian studio in the rue Vercingétorix. The musician Fritz Schneklud is represented as a cellist (*Upaupa Schneklud*, fig. 5) and the sculptor and collector Paco Durrio as a guitarist (fig. 6). The latter painting has often been dated to 1900 or 1902. Now, Durrio was in Paris in 1894 and spent a fair amount of time with Gauguin and their circle of mutual friends (Gauguin was in metropolitan France between 1893 and 1895), but there is nothing apart from the style itself to support the hypothesis that Gauguin painted this portrait in Papeete or Atuona. It seems reasonable to consider that these two works were not only painted at the same time but that they were also conceived as companion pieces.[12] Once one views them in these terms, they can be compared to three youthful paintings by Courbet: on the one hand, to the *Young Man in a Landscape*, also known as *The Guitarrero* (fig. 7), a portrait of his violinist friend Alphonse Promayet,[13] and to its pendant, the self-portrait *The Sculptor* (1845, private collection);[14] and on the other, to *The Cellist* (fig. 4), another self-portrait.[15] This idea that Gauguin was copying Courbet's practice of painting portraits of his artistic friends as companion pieces, including one moreover in the role of a guitarist, seems like a relevant hypothesis, all the more so since the portrait of Schneklud was long considered a self-portrait. Only the title dispels this doubt because the Schneklud we see in a photograph taken at around this time looks very different.[16] As for Courbet's *The Cellist*, it too belonged to Arosa's collection, and the related print had been cut out by Gauguin and kept for many years in his 'portable imaginary museum'.[17] Although there is no obvious parallel with Courbet in *Upaupa Schneklud*, it does repeat the posture, the composition and the framing of *The Cellist*, with the hand holding the bow touching the edge of the canvas. Given these correspondences between the two works, the ambiguous relationship between portrait and self-portrait, mentioned above, may not be a coincidence.

These two portraits shed light on a little-known dimension of Gauguin's work: his passion for music. Apart from the canvases already discussed, the only paintings of his to feature musical instruments are *Interior of the Painter's House in Paris, Rue Carcel* (1881, Nasjonalgalleriet, Oslo), *The Flageolet Player on the Cliff* (cat. 38), *Arearea / Joyeusetés I* (1892, Musée d'Orsay, Paris) and *Pastorales tahitiennes* (1892, State Hermitage Museum, Saint Petersburg). Gauguin

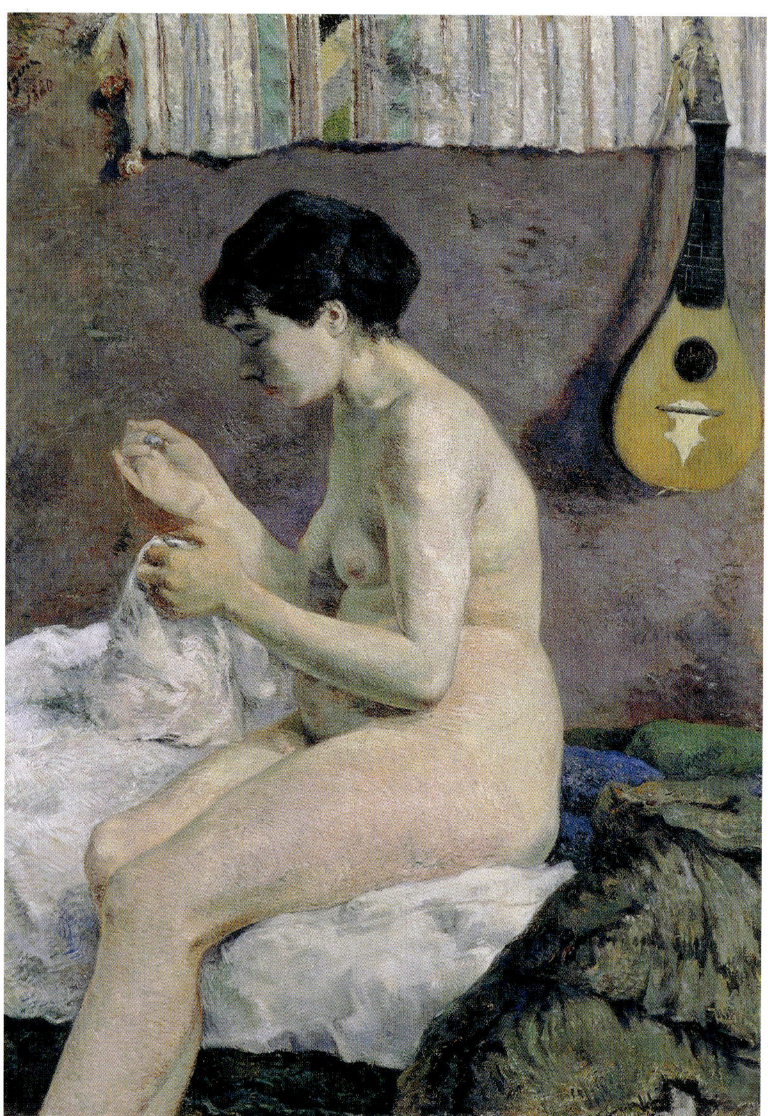

Fig. 2

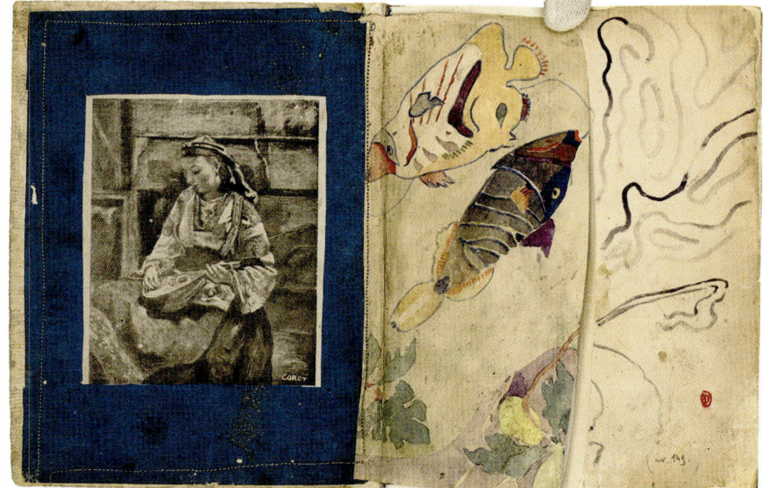

Fig. 3

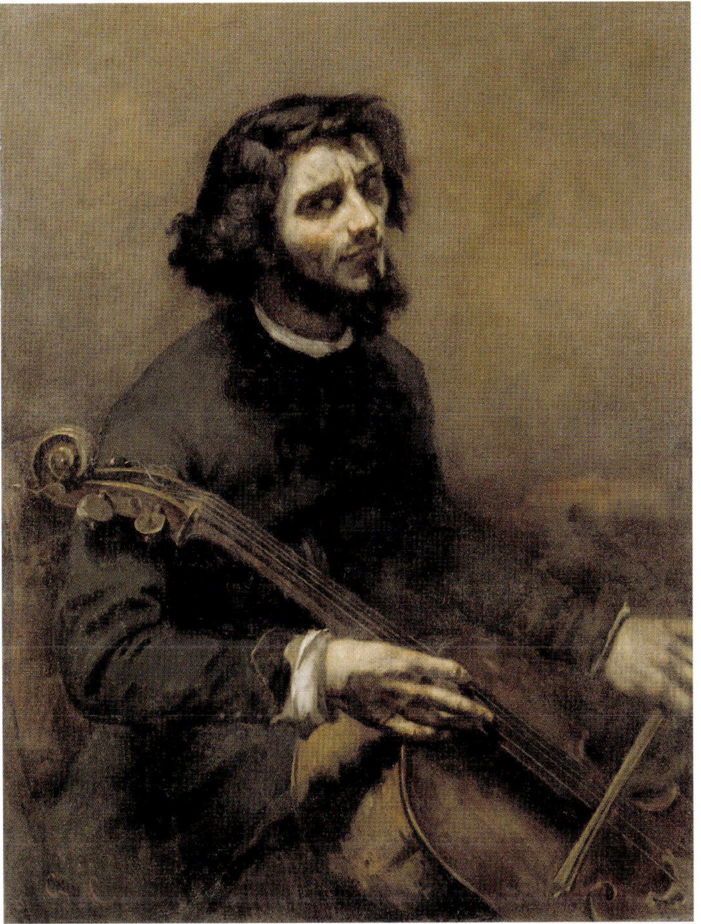

Fig. 4

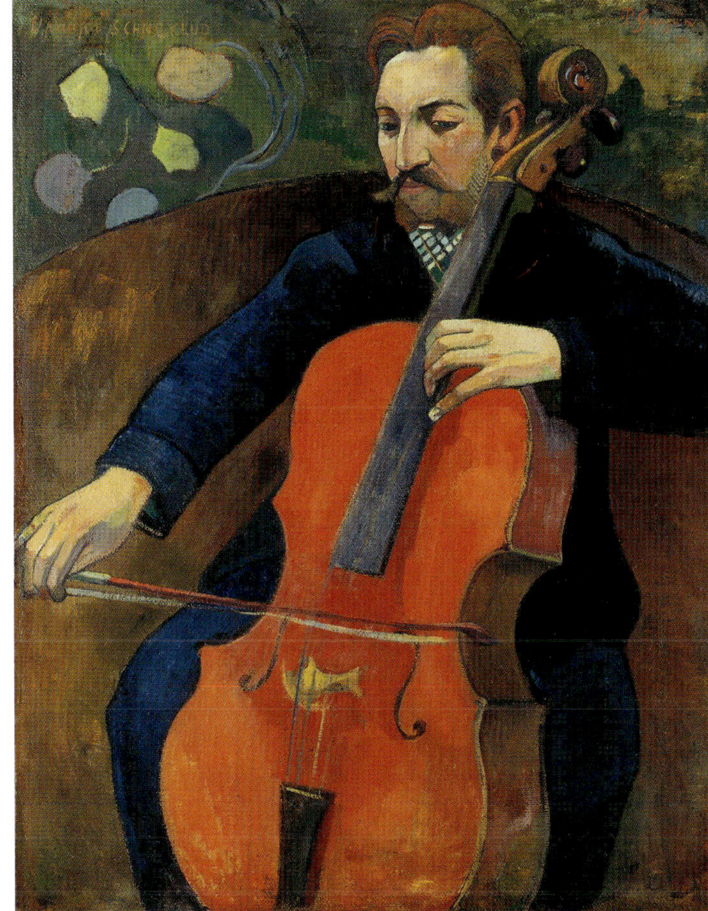

Fig. 5

Fig. 2. Paul Gauguin
Study of a Nude or *Suzanne Sewing*, 1880
Oil on canvas, 111.4 × 79.5 cm
Ny Carlsberg Glyptotek, Copenhagen,
SMK 3453

Fig. 3. Paul Gauguin
Notebook for Aline, 1893
Manuscript illustrated by the artist,
watercolour and collage
Institut National d'Histoire de l'Art,
Collection Jacques Doucet, Fonds
d'Estampes d'Artistes, Paris,
cote NUM MS 227

Fig. 4. Gustave Courbet
The Cellist, Self-Portrait, 1847
Oil on canvas, 117 × 89 cm
Nationalmuseum, Stockholm, Donated
by Nationalmusei Vänner, 1936,
NM 3105

Fig. 5. Paul Gauguin
*Upaupa Schneklud
(The Player Schneklud)*, 1894
Oil on canvas, 92.7 × 73.3 cm
Baltimore Museum of Art,
Given by Hilda K. Blaustein, in memory
of her late husband, Jacob Blaustein,
1979.163

himself played various instruments: the bandoneon, the accordion, with which he is sketched in a small drawing by Paul Sérusier (Musée d'Orsay, Paris),[18] but also sometimes the guitar or the harmonium.[19] Gauguin portrays himself as a mandolin player in *Self-Portrait with a Mandolin* (1889, private collection, New York). This work, contemporaneous with *Bonjour, Monsieur Gauguin*, combines the idea of the self-portrait as musician from Courbet's *Cellist* and the bucolic setting of his *Guitarrero* with the posture (head and eyes lowered) and sibylline smile of Corot's *Italian Woman*.

Gauguin, in his paintings with musical subjects, had clearly assimilated the influence of Corot and Courbet. And although neither the musical motif nor the theory of correspondences were the focus of his pictorial approach, they are important in helping us to understand it and its relation to Manet, his admiration for whom can be seen from the copy of *Olympia* he made in 1891 (private collection).

Thus the idea of the *Gesamtkunstwerk*,[20] the synthesis of music and painting, carries weight in both Gauguin's art

and writings. In his *Notes synthétiques* (1885), for example,
he argues: 'Painting is the most beautiful of all the arts. . . . A
complete art that sums up all the others and completes them.
Like music, it acts on the soul through the intermediary of
the senses: harmonious colours correspond to the harmonies
of sounds. But in painting a unity is obtained which is not
possible in music, where the chords follow one another, so
that the judgment experiences a continuous fatigue if it
wants to reunite the end with the beginning. . . . The hearing
can only grasp a single sound at a time, whereas the sight
takes in everything and simultaneously simplifies it at will.'[21]
In a letter of August 1901 to Daniel de Monfreid, he wrote:
'There is, in short, more point to looking for suggestion than
description in painting, as is also the case with music.' And
later: 'Bonnard, Vuillard, Sérusier, to mention some young
artists, are musicians, and you can be sure that coloured
painting is entering a musical phase.'[22]

MANET AND COURBET: THE 'SEMINAL' *GUITARRERO*

Manet's passion for music was more obvious, both in his life
and in his work. He was close to Chabrier, Cabaner, Offenbach
and Rossini, and his paintings marked the beginning of a
period when art engaged comprehensively with modern
musical life. *Music in the Tuileries Gardens* (1862, National
Gallery, London), *Madame Manet at the Piano* (cat. 47),
The Old Musician (1862, National Gallery of Art, Washington),
Corner of a Café-Concert (1878–80, National Gallery,
London), *The Fifer* (1866, Musée d'Orsay, Paris), *The Spanish
Singer* (1860, The Metropolitan Museum of Art, New York),
The Music Lesson (1870, Museum of Fine Arts, Boston),
Jean-Baptiste Faure as Hamlet (1877, Folkwang Museum,
Essen) and *Masked Ball at the Opera* (1873, National
Gallery of Art, Washington), as well as other works, form
a complete musical panorama that many other artists
would echo between the 1860s and 1910s.

His *Spanish Singer* (1860, The Metropolitan Museum
of Art, New York) manifestly connects him also to Courbet,
with whom he shared numerous sources.[23] Indeed, *Guitarrero*
was the title Manet gave to engraved versions of this work
(cat. 39) in 1861. The host of titles and themes that
Manet took up from Courbet[24] show the two men to have
been interested in identical subjects. The two *guitarreros*
by Courbet and Manet are seminal representations in
their respective artistic careers, reflecting different influences
– medieval for Courbet[25], in whose work the costume is
a reference to the *Troubadour*[26] by Thomas Couture, Manet's
master (1843, Philadelphia Museum of Art),[27] and Hispanic

for Manet – while hinting at a parallel between painter and
guitarist. For both artists, too, their painting was closely
associated with a self-portrait: *The Sculptor* (1845, private
collection) for Courbet and *The Absinthe Drinker* (1859, Ny
Carlsberg Glyptotek, Copenhagen) for Manet.[28]

The two works clearly warrant comparison from this
point of view. Each canvas, moreover, points to an analogy
with the position of the painter. For Manet, *The Spanish
Painter* (fig. 1) was almost an act of provocation with regard
to his bourgeois background. His family did not want him
to become a painter and his father, a magistrate, was harsh
in his condemnation of gypsies and performers.[29] Manet's
painting of a Spanish guitarist is thus an outright statement
of opposition.[30] The dandy Manet's most ambitious paintings
also suffered widespread vilification by his contemporaries.
The figure of the gypsy, free but often despised by the crowd,
can be related to this position, as indeed can the status of
any guitarist: such musicians were outsiders in France where
classical music and official recognition were concerned.[31] In
addition, Manet set out to paint the immediacy of the real, and
the guitar, especially the flamenco guitar,[32] was one of the
main instruments involved in the growing fashion for musical
improvisation at the end of the century. Improvisation, too,
implies immediacy. Moreover, Manet's rejection of finish
in his paintings is paralleled by the risks of wrong notes
implicit in improvisation, as opposed to classical music, in
which everything is (purportedly) thoroughly laid down and
meticulously annotated.

In short, how can we not see this analogy between the
painter and the guitarist as a meditation on the specificity
of artistic creation, given that the main difference between
the musician and the painter is that the former is heard while
he is performing his work whereas the painter's work is in
essence supposed to be seen only after it has been produced?
For someone like Manet, who does not trouble to erase
the traces of the creative process, this parallel seems fairly
pertinent. We can say that Manet presents his paintings
on musical subjects as if they were concerts. In this *mise-
en-abyme*, the painter behaves a bit like the guitarist on the
canvas, and in this way gives the viewer the chance to observe
him in the midst of the creative act.

THE GUITAR IN MANET'S WORK:
BOURGEOIS, SPANISH AND BOHEMIAN

If *The Spanish Singer* appears to be foundational, this is
not only by virtue of its meaning, but also because the guitar
is the musical instrument that appears most frequently

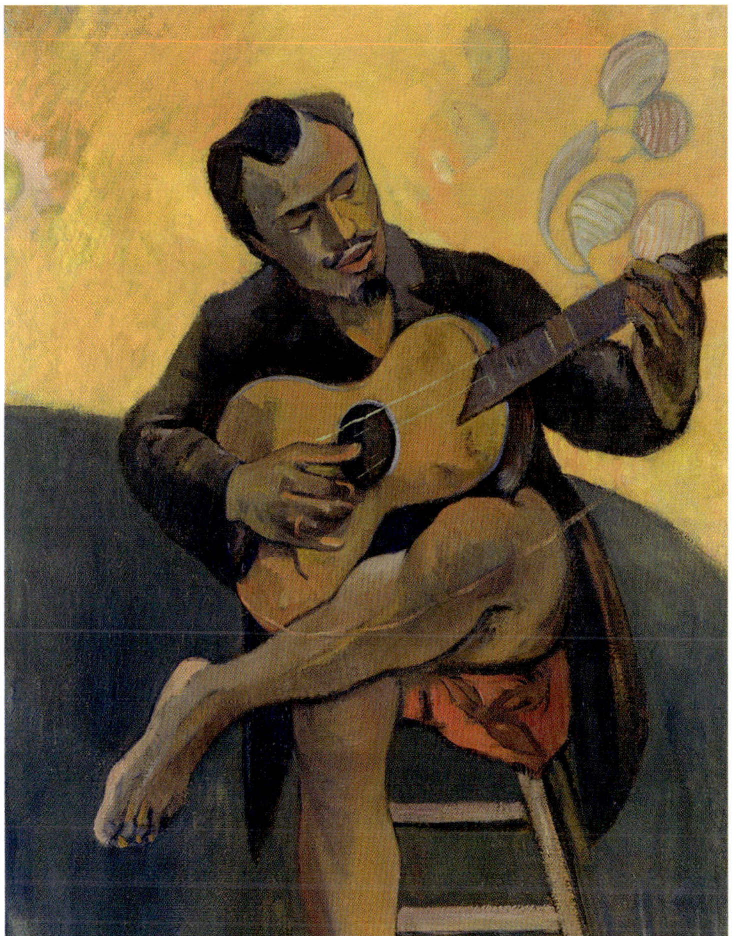

Fig. 6

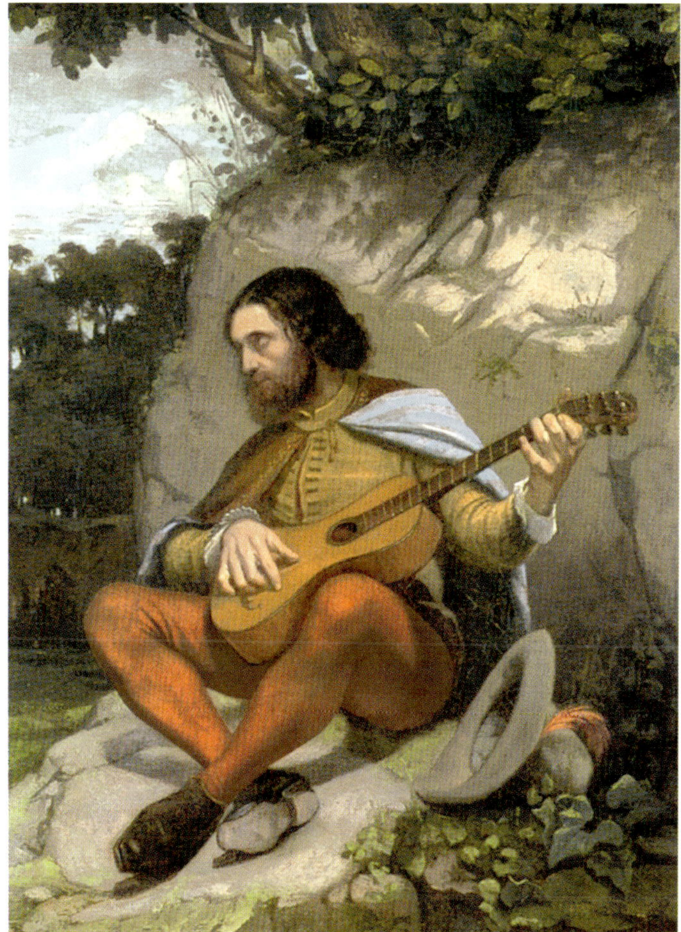

Fig. 7

In Manet's paintings. It is featured in no fewer than eight works: in addition to *The Spanish Singer*, it appears in *The Gypsies* (1862, of which only three fragments remain: *The Bohemian* and *Still Life with Bag and Garlic* at the Louvre Abu Dhabi and *The Water Drinker* or *The 'Régalade'* at the Art Institute of Chicago), *The Spanish Ballet* (1862, Phillips Collection, Washington), *The Street Singer* (1862, Museum of Fine Arts, Boston), *Still Life – Hat and Guitar* (cat. 1), *The Guitarist* (1866, Hill-Stead Museum, Farmington, CT), *Portrait of Zacharie Astruc* (1866, Kunsthalle Bremen, Bremen) and

———   ———

Fig. 6. **Paul Gauguin**
The Guitar Player, c. 1894
Oil on canvas, 90 × 72 cm
Private collection

Fig. 7. **Gustave Courbet**
Young Man in a Landscape, also known as *The Guitarrero*, 1844
Oil on canvas, 55 × 41 cm
Private collection

Music Lesson (cat. 16). This omnipresence in the 1860s is no coincidence if we consider his artistic approach and his sources, both contemporary and past.

The nineteenth century, the century so associated with the piano, was also the century of 'guitaromania'. The fad for this instrument peaked in the 1850s. Manet was first and foremost a painter of his times and his guitars reflect this, especially the ones in *The Guitarist* and *The Lesson*. The bourgeoisie, which was increasingly influential in shaping new musical tastes, was especially fond of the instrument. The guitar came from a less aristocratic tradition, and it was also a symbol of modernity, making it an indispensable accessory for fashionable homes in the 1860s.[33] In around 1874, the so-called 'modern' classical guitar appeared for the first time in Spain, replacing the 'baroque' and 'romantic' models, in the workshop of Spanish instrument maker Antonio de Torres Jurado.[34]

Manet, who died in 1883, and whose guitars all predated 1870, did not paint this modern guitar, which was rare and costly, but the models chosen for his paintings are nevertheless of interest. The guitar in his *Spanish Singer*, for example, is a romantic model made by Jean-Nicolas Grobert in the 1830s. This type of instrument was common at the time – it was used, notably, by Berlioz[35] and Paganini.[36] The same accessory no doubt served again (we can see only the head, a guitar's identity card) in *The Gypsies* (1862).[37] Such a prop would have been easy to find, since many bourgeois homes had such instruments in the 1840 and 1850s.

In addition to guitaromania, it is the wider influence of Spain that informs Manet's representations of these instruments. With the development of flamenco in Andalusia in the late eighteenth century, the guitar had become emblematic of Spain itself. Second Empire France was ardently Hispanophile,[38] and in the figure of Eugénie even had a Spanish empress. Manet, who made his first trip to the country in 1865, was very much steeped in this culture, which had infiltrated all areas of life, especially music.[39]

Francisco de Goya y Lucientes was one of the Spanish masters who inspired Manet and the guitar motif can be found in works of his such as *The Blind Guitarist* (1778, Museo Nacional del Prado, Madrid). The setting and composition of *The Old Musician* and *The Gypsies* inevitably bring to mind this kind of work. It is true that Goya's painting was located in the Spanish royal palace until 1870, when it was transferred to the Prado, but Manet knew Goya's work from the prints. The influence of Spanish painting on Manet's work is one example of the picturesque vision of Spain found in many a painting produced between 1860 and the 1900s, when Spain supplanted Italy as the destination for the cultural tourist. In such images, the pathetic figure of the beggar (in the great Spanish tradition – we need think only of Murillo here) sits beside a more luminous figure of the Spaniard, the flamenco guitarist, who gradually became dominant.[40] This figure thus embodies Hispanism in painting, his emblematic status and exotic character comparable to odalisques in Orientalism and geishas for Japonism. Manet's guitarists and guitars made him the bard of Hispanism.

Alongside the violin, the guitar also became the favoured instrument of street musicians and acrobats (*saltimbanques*). We find it in Manet's *Street Singer* and *Bohemian*. These two types of figures, together with the *Spanish Singer*, show how blurred the frontiers were between street musician, café artist, *saltimbanque*, gypsy (a vision often imported from eastern Europe, via the music popularised by Liszt)[41] and Spaniard. This pictorial archetype, summed up in the term 'bohemian', is in essence ambiguous in that it refers simultaneously to gypsies, the Roms of eastern Europe, the Spanish *gitanos*, and the Romantic idea of the poor, doomed artist,[42] the beggar and *saltimbanque*. The motif of the bohemian with the guitar is thus at once Romantic, naturalist and Hispanicising.

In these eight works, Manet made palpable this twofold status of the guitar as an instrument both bourgeois, reflecting his social background, and Spanish and bohemian, embodying his aesthetic influences. The first associations, of family and respectability, are in evidence in *Still Life*, *The Guitarist*, *Portrait of Zacharie Astruc* and *Music Lesson*, while the second connotations, exotic and popular, appear in *The Spanish Singer*, *The Gypsies*, *The Spanish Ballet* and *The Street Singer*. Setting aside questions of pictorial handling and technique, it was no doubt in capturing this zeitgeist[43] that we see Manet at his most modern.

<h3 style="text-align:center">WATTEAU AND MANET: FROM THE GUITAR OF LOVE TO LOVE OF THE GUITAR</h3>

Manet also reinvented two older forms of painting that were being rediscovered at the time: seventeenth-century Dutch genre painting, but also, and above all, eighteenth-century French painting. He seemed to derive not only formal ideas from these works but also a predilection for certain motifs. For example, their buffoons (Frans Hals) and *commedia dell'arte* characters (Antoine Watteau) were the forerunners of the street singers, *saltimbanques* and circus artists favoured by Manet. His paintings constitute a transposition of these sources, as well as other, more recent ones, such as his master Thomas Couture,[44] into modernity, notably in musical matters.

The guitar brings to mind three figures from the seventeenth and eighteenth centuries: Johannes Vermeer, Watteau and Jean-Baptiste Greuze. Of these, Watteau undoubtedly had the greatest influence on Manet, but the tone was set even earlier, in the seventeenth century, by Vermeer's *The Guitar Player* (1670–2, Kenwood House, London). This unusual theme stands out among genre scenes by virtue of its composition: the elbow out of the frame, the vibration of the strings, the manifest yet enigmatic emotion of the young girl in the middle of playing. The painting hanging in the background has been identified as a landscape by Pieter Jansz. van Asch, and already shows the linking of an interest in painting and an interest in music. It provides an early suggestion of a relationship between the representation of this instrument and ideas of freshness, lightness and freedom.

Antoine Watteau was no doubt the most music-loving of the French masters then being rediscovered.[45] Analysis of the score[46] in *The Scale of Love* (fig. 8) and of the fingering of the guitar players in his works generally shows him to have had considerable knowledge of music. Manet did not, nor

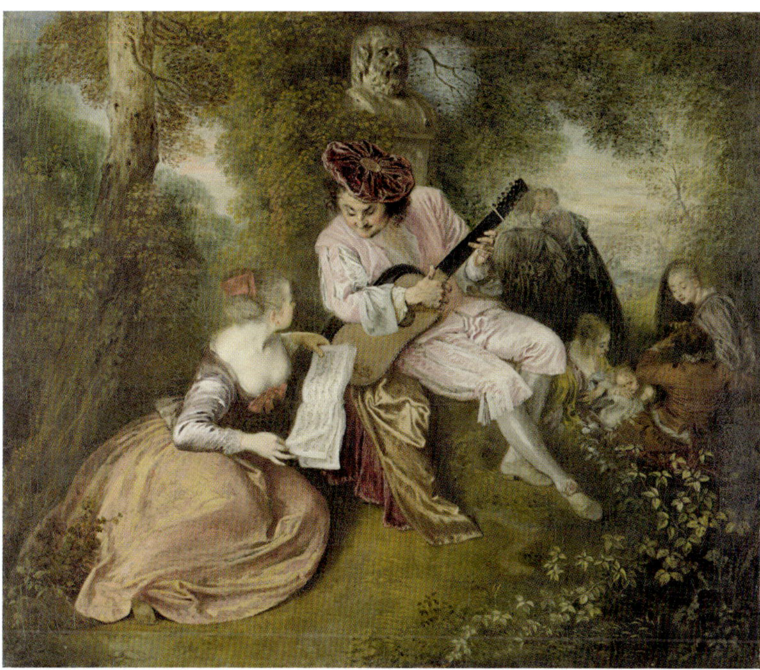

less sentimental light. The shift in dominant cultural influences – from Italy in Watteau's day to Spain in Manet's – reinforces this change in representation. The contrast is striking if we compare, say, *Mezzetin* (fig. 9) with *The Spanish Singer* (fig. 1). In the first, the Venus in the background with her back turned, signifying love denied, refers to ancient Rome; in the second, the still life with a carafe and onions recalls *bodegones*, the still lifes of Diego Velázquez and Francesco Zurbarán.

In *The Scale of Love* (fig. 8), the guitar is part of a gallant scene in which the young woman sitting at the guitarist's feet is holding the score for him. In *Music Lesson* (cat. 16), Manet certainly reprises the idea of the duet, but his two figures are both on the same level and their gazes do not meet. All sense of seduction has gone from the scene: they are not looking into each other's eyes but looking at us, exposed to our gaze. Zacharie Astruc, Manet's model for the male figure here, is described by Françoise Cachin as striking a 'Titian-like pose'.[50] The point of this, according to Duret, was to avoid meeting with 'the mockery that had greeted *The Balcony* at the previous Salon'.[51] Moreover, the lesson would appear to be a singing lesson with guitar accompaniment, which hardly arouses the same kind of ardent relationship as in *The Scale of Love*, where the characters are totally at one, as the man reads the score held by the woman. What Manet reinvents from his source is an image devoid of artefacts, allusions and hidden signifiers. Astruc (whose portrait by Manet already included a guitar) and his student seem to be elsewhere. All that counts is the gaze of the spectator, witnessing a scene that is both typical of bourgeois musical education and slightly Hispanicising as regards the student's costume and the choice of the guitar. Here there is no still life on the floor, no decoration apart from the carpet. Manet does not tell a story but, as simply as possible, gives us something to see, and perhaps even to hear. Thanks to the complete absence of a narrative dimension, the gaze is drawn to the playing of the guitarist, which is the only signifying element in this pared-down reality. We are invited to 'listen with the eyes' and nothing more. This work, which has never aroused much enthusiasm from critics,[52] might gain in interest if reread from this point of view.

It was Paul Mantz who revived interest in Antoine Watteau with an article published in *La Revue française* in 1859.[53] And it was Pauline Lyne-Stephens, née Duvernay, who owned *The Scale of Love* in the 1860s, when it hung in her Parisian home. A number of her friends also knew Manet well, among them Carolus-Duran and Henri Fantin-Latour, and it is therefore possible, although unconfirmed, that through them he may have come to see the Watteau in her apartment. He certainly knew *The Scale of Love* from the engravings executed by Le Bas (c. 1735, Jean de Jullienne, *Œuvre gravé,*

did this particularly worry him. When his friend Renaud de Vilbac pointed out that his *Spanish Singer* was holding his guitar the wrong way round he still could not be bothered to retouch his canvas.[47]

The guitar has a very special place in Watteau's work. The one that appears so frequently in his gallant scenes (*The Serenader*, c. 1715, Musée Condé, Chantilly, *The Scale of Love*) and *commedia dell'arte* episodes (often held by Mezzetin) is a baroque guitar by Jean-Baptiste Voboam,[48] a fragile instrument that was given scant regard by the major composers of the day, its role being limited to accompanying romances, ballads and comical plays. In Watteau's work, it is associated with seduction and sensuality. It was held tight, its strings made to vibrate, while its curves evoke feminine forms. In Manet, only *The Street Singer* (which has the same spontaneous feel found in Vermeer) carries a possible erotic allusion in the form of the cherries.[49]

Manet's appropriation of the Pierrot, Harlequin and Mezzetin figures playing in Watteau shows them in a new,

---

Fig. 8. **Antoine Watteau**
The Scale of Love, 1715–8
Oil on canvas, 50.8 × 59.7 cm
The National Gallery, London, Bequeathed
by Sir Julius Wernher Bt, 1912,
NG2897

known as *Recueils Jullienne*), which were widely reproduced
in the wake of Mantz's article. Baron Edmond de Rothschild
and many others began collecting these works in the 1860s
and 1870s. Edmond de Goncourt completed the catalogue
raisonné of Watteau's work in 1875.[54] This connection
between Watteau and Manet is evinced by the explicit
quotation of Watteau's *Pierrot* (1718–9, Musée du Louvre,
Paris) in the figures of *The Old Musician* (1862, National
Gallery of Art, Washington, Chester Dale Collection), a work
whose many references range from Schlesinger (*The Stolen
Child*, 1861, Bibliothèque Nationale de France, Paris)[55] to
Scheffer (*The Three Magi*, 1844, private collection).[56] It looks,
too, as if Manet himself was the model for the figure in the
top hat, itself an echo of *The Absinthe Drinker*.

This comparison gives an insight into Manet's musical
interests. We realise that Watteau's central concern is
sentiment, which is evoked by the narrative, symbols and
allusions, whereas for Manet music and painting are
central and self-sufficient. At the same time as he makes
an emphatic reference to obvious sources, Manet radically
shifts the meaning of the musical motif.

As we have seen, both Manet and Gauguin modernised
their sources. Their musician figures carry a hint of the
self-portrait and speak of the analogy between painting and
music, contributing to the emergence of a form of painting
that was individualist, subjective, free and independent.
Ultimately, painting was placed on the same level as music
and freed of the obligation to represent nature or beauty. It is
painting and music themselves that have the central role in
what these canvases say to us, and the former draws on the
latter in order to be no longer limited to offering colour and
light, but to offer sound, tones and harmony. The way was
open to other forms of exploration. The guitar, which would
later become popular with the Cubists, played a fundamental
role in this radical transformation.

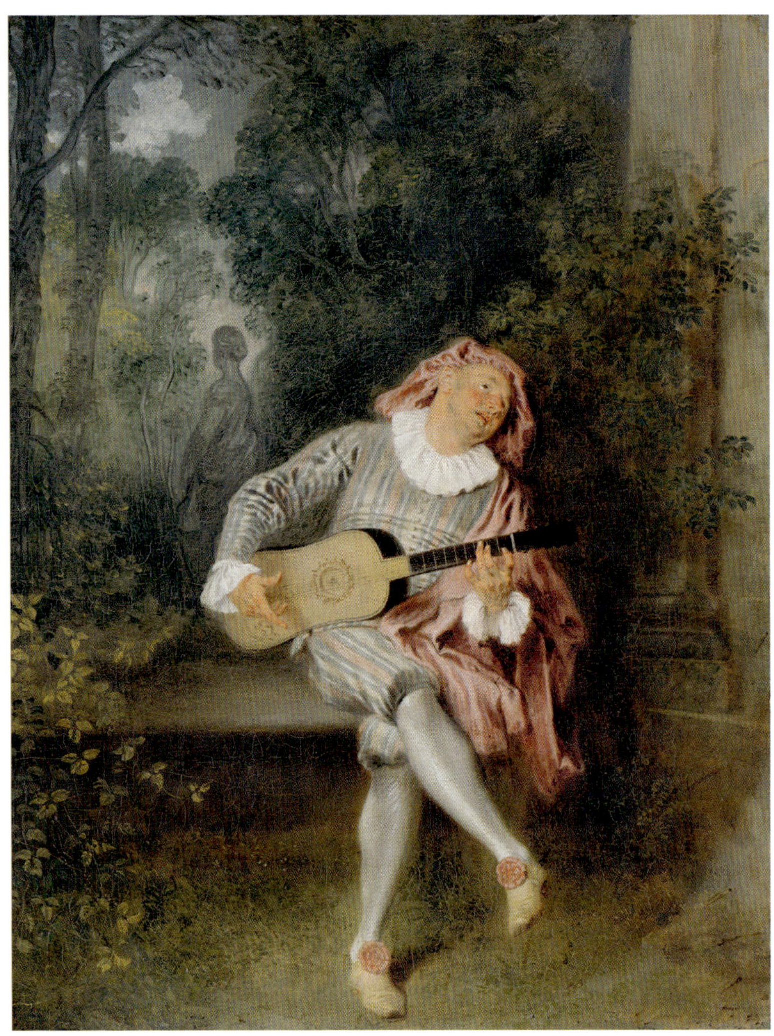
Fig. 9

Fig. 9. **Antoine Watteau**
Mezzetin, c. 1718–20
Oil on canvas, 55.2 × 43.2 cm
The Metropolitan Museum of Art, New York,
Munsey Fund, 1934,
34.138

[1] See Belinda Thomson, 'Paul Gauguin: Navigating the Myth', in *Gauguin: Maker of Myth*, ed. Belinda Thomson, exhibition catalogue, London, Tate, 2010, pp. 21–23.

[2] *Tableaux modernes. À l'appui du catalogue Arosa par son procédé personnel a publié à très petit nombre, un Album de 56 planches photogravures exécutées à l'aide d'un procédé nouveau exploité sans grand succès par M. Arosa : 25 février 1878*, Paris, Bibliothèque de l'Institut National d'Histoire de l'Art (now known as INHA).

[3] *Catalogue, vente de la collection de M. G. Arosa, Hôtel Drouot, Paris, le 25 février 1878*, no. 65, Bibliothèque de l'INHA.

[4] Evoked by Françoise Cachin in *Gauguin*, Paris, Flammarion, 1988, pp. 16–8.

[5] To whom Claire Frèches-Thory compares Gauguin in her entry on the work in the volume by Richard Brettell, Françoise Cachin, Claire Frèches-Thory and Charles F. Stuckey, *The Art of Paul Gauguin*, exhibition catalogue, Washington, National Gallery of Art, 1988, p. 52.

[6] *The Guitarist*, 1866, Hill-Stead Museum, Farmington, CT, also uses the parrot motif.

[7] *Mette Gauguin*, c. 1880, Stiftung Sammlung E. G. Bührle, Zürich.

[8] Gauguin wrote to Pissarro: 'Not for one minute did he [Huysmans] understand Manet . . . I see that he is charmed by the anecdotal detail of my nude woman and not by the painterly aspect.' *Correspondance de Paul Gauguin 1873–1888*, Paris, Fondation Singer-Polignac, 1984, p. 48.

[9] In J-K Huysmans, *L'Art moderne*, Paris, Stock, 2nd ed., 1902, pp. 262–4.

[10] *Bonjour, Monsieur Courbet* (1854, Musée Fabre, Montpellier) directly inspired *Bonjour, Monsieur Gauguin* (1889, two versions: Hammer Museum, Los Angeles, and Národní Galerie, Prague).

[11] See the article by Richard Brettell in *The Art of Paul Gauguin, op. cit*, pp. 312–4.

[12] Ibid., p. 314 – their dimensions are indeed identical.

[13] Hélène Toussaint quoted by Sylvain Amic in Laurence des Cars, Dominique de Font-Reaulx, Gary Tinterow and Michel Hilaire, *Gustave Courbet*, Paris, Réunion des Musées Nationaux, 2007, p. 96.

[14] See the entry by Sylvain Amic, ibid., pp. 96–97.

[15] This was pointed out by Philippe Burty in 1878 in the introduction to the catalogue of the Arosa sale, *op. cit.*, p. 6.

[16] See Brettell, *The Art of Paul Gauguin, op. cit.*, p. 312.

[17] See Belinda Thomson, 'Paul Gauguin: Navigating the Myth', in *Gauguin: Maker of Myth*, p. 21.

[18] Paul Sérusier, *Paul Gauguin in Breton Costume Playing the Accordion*, 1890, RF 38796.

[19] Gauguin's last letter to Daniel de Monfreid in April 1903 confirms the presence of this instrument in the Marquesas: 'It is true that the women often come and see me for a while . . . especially to try to play my harmonium.'

[20] This expression was coined by the German Romantic painter Philipp Otto Runge.

[21] Translated in ed. Herschel B. Chipp, *Theories of Modern Art*, Berkeley, Los Angeles and London, University of California Press, 1968, p. 61.

[22] In *Racontars de rapin*, Paris, Mercure de France, 2003. Quotation from the facsimile of 1987, éditions Avant et Après, Papeete, p. 16.

[23] Laurence des Cars, 'Le vrai en héritage, la référence à Courbet de Manet à Cézanne', in *Gustave Courbet, op. cit.*, pp. 64–7.

[24] Laurence des Cars, ibid., p. 65: *The Bath* and *The Bathers*, *Luncheon on the Grass* and *The Hunting Meal*.

[25] Coincidentally, Courbet's painting was executed in the year that the Musée de Cluny, the Parisian museum of the Middle Ages, opened.

[26] Interest in the legendary figure of the troubadour, the medieval travelling musician, was revived by François Raynouard in *Des troubadours et des cours d'amour*, Paris, Didot, 1817, and *Nouveau choix des poésies originales des troubadours*, Paris, Crapelet, 1836–44.

[27] See Therese Dolan, 'Strums the Word: Manet's *Spanish Singer*', in eds. James Rubin and Olivia Mattis, *Rival Sisters, Art and Music at the Birth of Modernism, 1815–1915*, Burlington, VT, Ashgate, 2014.

[28] According to Antonin Proust in *Édouard Manet. Souvenirs*, Paris, L'Échoppe, 1988 (originally published in 1913), the rejection of this work led to the creation of the *Guitarrero*, in keeping with Baudelaire's injunction to 'be yourself'.

[29] Nancy Locke, *Manet and Family Romance*, Princeton and Oxford, Princeton University Press, 2001, p. 17, quoted in Therese Dolan, *op. cit.*

[30] At the Salon of 1861, the *Portrait of M. and Mme Auguste Manet* (Musée d'Orsay, Paris) was hung opposite *The Spanish Singer*.

[31] The guitar was not accepted at the Conservatoire de Paris until 1969, whereas the trumpet, for example, was accepted in 1895.

[32] Manuel Cano, *La guitarra. Historia, estudios y aportaciones al arte del flamenco*, Universidad de Córdoba, Servicio de Publicaciones, 1986.

[33] See the satirical article on musical instruments in the journal *Le Tintamarre*, 11 June 1871, pp. 1–2.

[34] See Alain Miteran, *Histoire de la guitare*, Paris, Zurfluh, 1997; Harvey Turnbull, *The Guitar from the Renaissance to the Present Day*, New York, Scribner's, 1974.

[35] It is given a whole chapter in Berlioz's *Grand traité d'instrumentation et d'orchestration modernes* (1844). Berlioz composed on the guitar.

[36] See the Grobert guitar at the Musée de la Musique, Philharmonie de Paris (fig. 35, p. 172).

[37] Other props from *The Spanish Singer* were used in later works, notably *Mademoiselle V. in the Costume of an Espada* (1862, The Metropolitan Museum of Art, New York).

[38] We see it in literature (Gautier, Baudelaire, Hugo, Mérimée, Dumas, etc.), travel (Germond de Lavigne), fashion (ribbons, the crinoline, etc.), music (Chabrier, Bizet) and the visual arts (following the opening of the Louvre's Spanish gallery by Louis-Philippe in 1838, the Spanish influence can be noted in Géricault, Bonnat, Gérôme, Corot, Courbet, Carolus-Duran, Legros, Fantin-Latour and Whistler, among others).

[39] See Gary Tinterow and Geneviève Lacambre, *Manet/Vélazquez. The French Taste for Spanish Painting*, exhibition catalogue, New York, The Metropolitan Museum of Art, 2003, and Mena Marques, *Manet en el Prado*, exhibition catalogue, Madrid, Museo del Prado, 2003.

[40] Hispanism in painting went well beyond musical themes: consider *Mademoiselle V. in the Costume of an Espada* and all the way up to *Ambroise Vollard Dressed as a Toreador* by Renoir (1917, Nippon Television collection, Tokyo).

[41] On Liszt's influence, see Ewing Campbell, 'Manet, Liszt and *The Old Musician*', in eds. Rubin and Mattis, *Rival Sisters, op. cit.*

[42] This originated in *Scènes de la vie de bohème* by Henry Murger in 1851.

[43] This word was coined by Herder (1769) and used by Hegel in the nineteenth century.

[44] See Ewing Campbell, 'Manet, Liszt and *The Old Musician*', in eds. Rubin and Mattis, *Rival Sisters*.

[45] Due in part to Edmond de Goncourt's passion for the artist.

[46] The conductor William Christie reflects on this in Frederick Wiseman's film *National Gallery* (2014).

[47] Quoted in Proust, *op. cit.*, p. 28.

[48] See the 1708 model kept at the Philharmonie de Paris, Musée de la Musique (E.999.15.1).

[49] Manet described to Antonin Proust his vision of a singer coming out of a café in Rue Guyot. She refused to let him paint her, so he had to recreate the scene with Victorine Meurent (Proust, *op. cit.*, p. 28).

[50] In *Manet, 'J'ai fait ce que j'ai vu'*, Paris, Gallimard, 1994, p. 70.

[51] Théodore Duret, *Histoire de Édouard Manet et de son Œuvre*, VisiMuz digitised edition, 2014 (repr. of the second revised edition, Paris, Bernheim-Jeune, 1919), p. 60.

[52] See ibid.

[53] In 'L'École française sous la régence, Antoine Watteau', *Revue française*, 5th year, vol. 16, 1859, pp. 263–72, 345–53.

[54] Marie-Catherine Sahut and Florence Raymond, *Antoine Watteau et l'art de l'estampe*, Paris, Musée du Louvre éditions and Le Passage, 2010.

[55] James Rubin, *Manet*, Paris, Flammarion, 2011, p. 47.

[56] Ewing Campbell, 'Manet, Liszt and *The Old Musician*', in eds. Rubin and Mattis, *Rival Sisters*, p. 170.

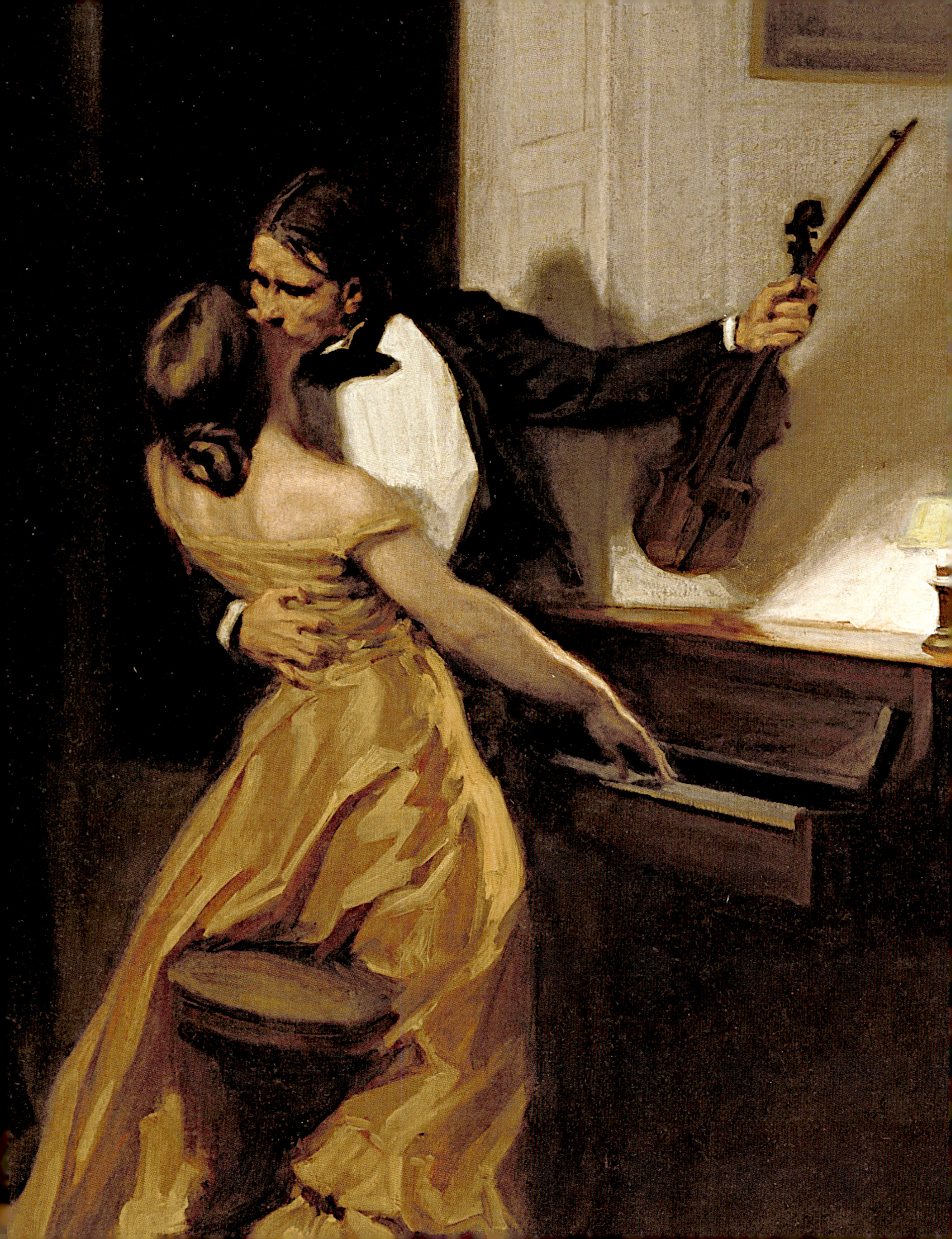

moments musicaux: paintings of pianists, from the 1860s to the 1910s

Belinda Thomson

In 1866 Frédéric Bazille submitted his first major figure painting to the Paris Salon. He had invested considerable time and money in it, renting a larger studio, hiring an attractive green satin dress and engaging a model to wear it, getting a male friend to pose as a listener. For the large-scale modern life subject he had chosen to paint was a *Young Girl at the Piano*. Despite all his efforts and hopes of making a splash, his 'very simple' painting was rejected by the Salon jury. Until recently we only knew of its existence from Bazille's letters, which speak about it at length. Indeed, he proceeded with it in a public way, keeping open studio and receiving welcome encouragement from Gustave Courbet, although others were evidently more critical.[1] Following Bazille's untimely death in 1870, there was no trace of the work concerned, although the splendid green dress lived on, his friend Claude Monet having availed himself of it for an over life-size portrait of his future wife.[2] Following recent technical investigations, it is now clear that Bazille had assuaged his disappointment by painting over his large piano canvas with a biblical composition, again intended for the Salon.[3]

The case of Bazille's *Young Girl at the Piano* is not just an intriguing mystery now solved. The artist's choice of subject, in 1866, was significant on both a personal and a cultural level. Bazille himself was a proficient pianist who liked nothing better for relaxation than to play duets with fellow *mélomane*, the critic Edmond Maître, typically sight-reading piano transcriptions of new operas or symphonies.[4] This was the standard way in which music from the classical repertoire permeated down through society in the nineteenth century, in some cases becoming the popular air whistled on the street.[5] But personal inclination aside, as an ambitious avant-garde artist Bazille opted for a modern theme favoured by numerous realist painters in the 1860s.[6] His unhappy experience with his 'Young Girl at the Piano' subject would have been known to two close friends who pursued musical subjects in later years: Auguste Renoir (cat. 21 and 45) and Henri Fantin-Latour (cat. 60).

Cat. 30
René Prinet (1861–1946)
The Kreutzer Sonata, 1901
(detail, cat. 30, p. 101)

This essay will explore the reasons why the piano and the pianist became so prominent in the portraiture and genre painting of this period, in particular why the young woman at the piano was such a popular choice of subject.[7] A number of questions and paradoxes surround this iconographic phenomenon. What did artists make of the theme and how musically attuned were they? To what extent were the ranks of pianists really dominated by young women? A quick glance at the art of the time would lead one to assume that the piano was exclusively played by women yet it was chiefly male composers who wrote piano music, reams of it, and chiefly male virtuosi who performed it in public. Moreover, the example of Bazille and Maître is proof positive that the piano was played at an amateur level by men as well. Why were so few of them thought suitable subjects for the painter? Should we take at face value the 'information' provided by the sheer number of representations of women at the piano?[8]

A GENDERED OCCUPATION?

One simple reason for the presence of so many pianos in paintings during the period covered by the exhibition is recognition of a sociological truth: the piano was the dominant instrument of the nineteenth century. The piano's ubiquity and central role both in private and public entertainment demanded that it be represented. Home-grown, popular domestic musical entertainment centred upon the instrument, although by the turn of the century there were already signs of its coming demise. As for explaining the wealth of images of female piano players, both social and artistic factors have a part to play. *Musique d'Amateurs*, an *image d'Épinal* dating from the 1840s, gives a clear indication of the gender bias concerning the relative attraction of the sexes to different instruments. Women are shown singing or playing the piano, guitar and harp, while all the other instruments, from strings to woodwind, brass and percussion, are played by men. The underlying assumption must be that a lady could scarcely maintain her femininity whilst blowing into the mouthpiece of a tuba or straddling a cello, whereas strumming a lute, guitar or harp or touching the notes of a piano keyboard were suitably decorous activities. Over the course of the century that bias began to change, and by 1907 there were increasing numbers of female players and teachers of the violin, although female cellists were a rarity.[9] Meanwhile the preponderance of women among the teachers of singing and the piano is undeniable. Whether the inevitable visual association between women and amateur piano playing reflected a reality or was in part an

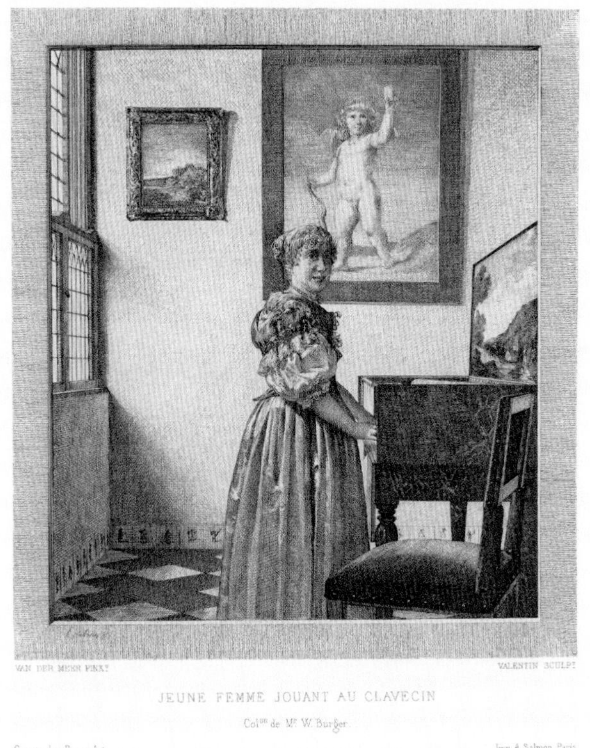

Fig. 10

idealised myth, the visual cliché was inescapable; it was commonly used in advertising and fashion plates. But one should remember that in fin-de-siècle France, all consumer products, from champagne to toothpaste, were advertised by associating them with flirty young women.

The artistic connection between women and keyboards has a long history. In one survey of the secular imagery of keyboard players across Europe, three quarters of the eighty or so paintings and prints assembled show female players.[10] And yet the anthology, like this exhibition, omits mythological subjects and religious art. It is as though the image of Saint Cecilia, patron saint of music, conventionally shown seated at the organ, lingered on as a stereotype in artists' minds following the Reformation. The art of seventeenth-century Protestant Holland abounds in images of women at the virginals or harpsichord. These discreet images of domestic music making, brought to delicate perfection in the work of Johannes Vermeer, were much admired by French realist artists of the nineteenth century. Johannes Vermeer's name had been all but forgotten until his rehabilitation as a great master by the French critic Théophile Thoré, alias William Bürger.[11] The intense interest in Vermeer in France thus

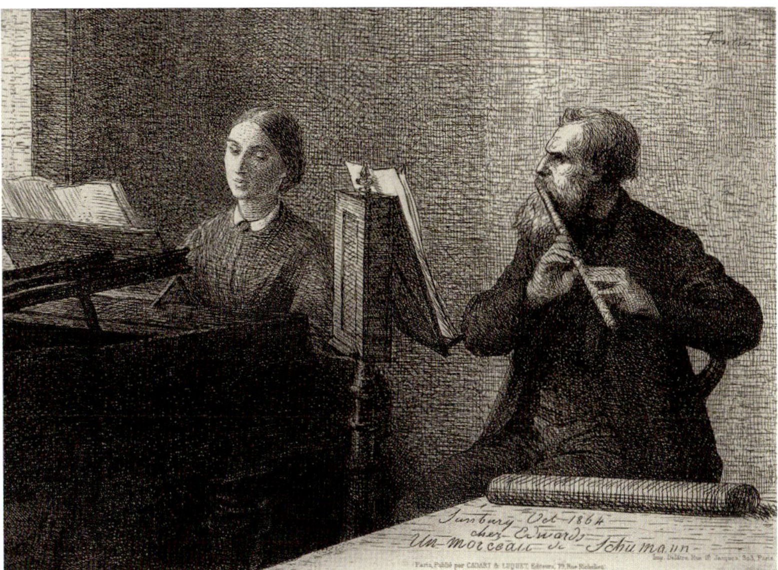

Fig. 11

coincided with, and arguably influenced, the early careers of the artists in Bazille's circle who were so drawn to the piano subject in the 1860s.

One painter swept up in this vogue was the American, James McNeill Whistler, and it is fitting that he should have produced one of the most seminal images of the keyboard subject. *At the Piano* (cat. 22), begun in London and finished in Paris in 1859, depicts Whistler's half-sister Deborah, who was married to the English doctor and printmaker, Seymour Haden. She is shown in shallow relief against a geometric arrangement of picture frames, playing a grand piano that had been shipped, at considerable cost, to London from Saint Petersburg in 1849, after her father's death. Its rich mahogany case, along with the red carpet and green dado, provide the main colour notes in an otherwise monochrome composition, the pianist making a triangular form of black balanced by her attentive daughter, in white. Nothing

Fig. 10. **Johannes Vermeer**
A Young Woman Standing at a Virginal as reproduced in the *Gazette des Beaux-Arts*, vol. XXI, 15 October 1866, p. 327 accompanying William Bürger's article 'Van der Meer de Delft'

Fig. 11. **Henri Fantin-Latour**
A Piece by Schumann, with the inscription *'chez Edwards, Sunbury, Oct 1864'*, etching, 18.7 × 27.7 cm. Printed by Cadart and Luquet, plate 142 from *Eaux-fortes modernes*, 1865, National Gallery of Australia, Canberra, 84.188.142

distracts from the simplicity of the arrangement – no raised piano lid, no anecdotal details such as musical scores or exchange of glances. Perhaps due to its absence of narrative, the painting was rejected from the Paris Salon of 1859, but Whistler showed it in François Bonvin's Paris studio instead, alongside works by fellow realists who had also suffered rejection, Fantin-Latour, Legros and Ribot. There it was seen and admired by Courbet among others. At the Royal Academy of 1860 it was poorly hung but well received. Seven years later, in a typical spirit of defiance and with Fantin's encouragement, Whistler submitted the painting once more to the Paris Salon jury and this time, in the year of the Exposition Universelle, it made a triumphant appearance. Thoré was quick to spot a parallel to Vermeer in this work by an artist of the younger school. He wrote to Édouard Manet in 1867: 'You are on good terms, I believe, with Whistler. What a lovely painting: *At the Piano*, no. 1561! Oh, how I'd love to own that . . . If the price isn't beyond the means of an artist like me, I'll try to make myself a present of this painting which would look so good hung with my van der Meer of Delft.'[12] In fact, Whistler's picture was not for sale. It returned to the collection of the Hadens, its first owner, the British painter and lover of Velázquez and Spanish painting, John Phillip, having just died. But what a tantalising mental image this must have conjured for Whistler, his calm and restrained painting hanging next to one of the poised and delicate interiors by the revered Vermeer (fig. 10).

For more recent art historians, Whistler's 'piano painting', as he called it, bequeathed in 1962 to the Taft Museum, Cincinnati, looks forward to the artist's subsequent 'emphasis on music as the epitome of impersonally pure art', an emphasis that his later titles would repeatedly evoke – *Nocturne, Arrangement, Symphony, Harmony* – despite their subjects having nothing to do with music-making per se.[13] But at the time of its inception too, it arguably inspired the paintings of pianists by Stevens, Bazille, Manet, Degas and Cézanne. *At the Piano* must have held a special meaning for Fantin-Latour as well (fig. 11). It was in 1859, spending a memorable evening with the Hadens in Chelsea, to whom he had an introduction from Whistler, that he experienced the kind of epiphany that helped to foster a lifelong passion for music. 'In the evening we go to the drawing room,' he wrote to his parents, 'where Mme Haden is playing. I stand near the door. Through the window I see the backdrop of the dark garden . . . In this semi-obscurity, I see Mme Haden wearing white crepe with black and pink ribbons gently running her fingers over the piano keys, she plays the famous Barcarolle from Oberon; where does one go to in such moments? what an experience music is, oh! Art . . .'[14] Apart from Weber, as Fantin went on to explain, his hostess's repertoire also ran to Mozart, Beethoven, Mendelssohn, Schubert and Chopin.

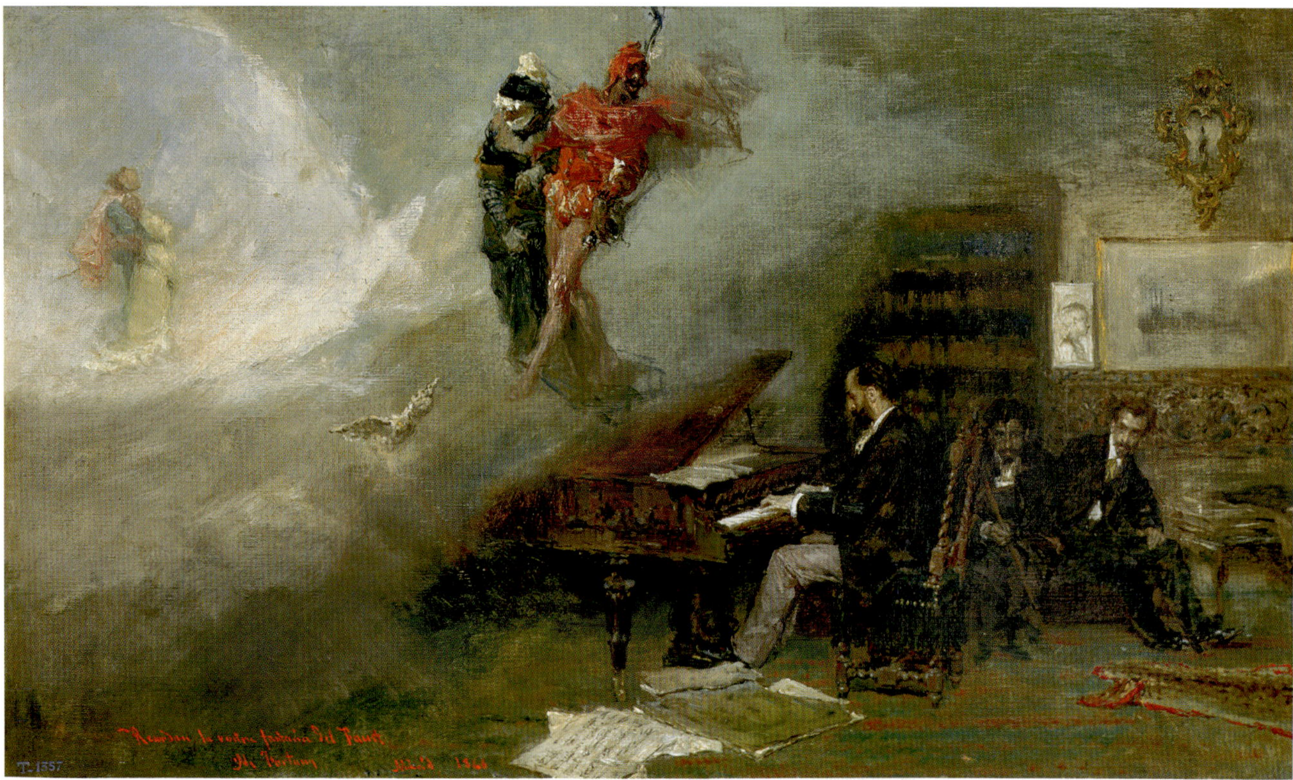

Fig. 12

In later years, Fantin's musical reveries would mostly find form in lithographed subjects inspired by the imaginary world of Wagner's operas, the evoked music floating free of the material source of the sound. It is rare to find a nineteenth-century artist attempting to bridge, in a single image, the dichotomy between the musical instrument and the images it could conjure for the sensitive listener: Mariano Fortuny's attempt to do so, with reference to Gounod's *Faust*, is thus something of a curiosity (fig. 12).

There were notable exceptions among the Impressionists to the rule that painters exclusively represented female piano players. One was the painting by Gustave Caillebotte of his composer brother Martial, shown at the 1876 Impressionist exhibition (fig. 13). Louis Edmond Duranty had it in mind when, in his pamphlet 'La Nouvelle Peinture', he cited the subject of the man at his piano as a template for modern genre painting. Using an arrestingly foreshortened perspective, Caillebotte presents Martial as a serious musician playing an Érard grand: we even see the type of music he was playing, including a score by his noted Conservatoire piano teacher Antoine Marmontel. At the 8th Impressionist exhibition of 1886, an unidentified interior scene by Federico Zandomeneghi, which featured a young man sight-reading

at the piano while a young woman idly listened, was described appreciatively by several critics.[15]

But if playing the piano was an option for young men, for young women musical accomplishment was imposed as a duty if she was to stand a chance on the marriage market. Bazille, doubtless feeling a certain pressure to find a wife, had mixed feelings of attraction and repugnance at the prospect of getting hitched to just such a suitable 'young woman (well brought-up, accomplished musician, that's the formula)'.[16] The eligible young woman entertaining potential suitors from the piano is a stock character in nineteenth-century fiction. Once wed, unless she was truly talented, she could safely put her *solfège* lessons to one side. Dorothea Brooke, the intelligent heroine of George Eliot's *Middlemarch* (1874), realises with

Fig. 12. **Mariano Fortuny**
Fantasia on Gounod's Faust, 1866
Oil on canvas, 40 × 69 cm
Museo del Prado, Madrid,
P02605

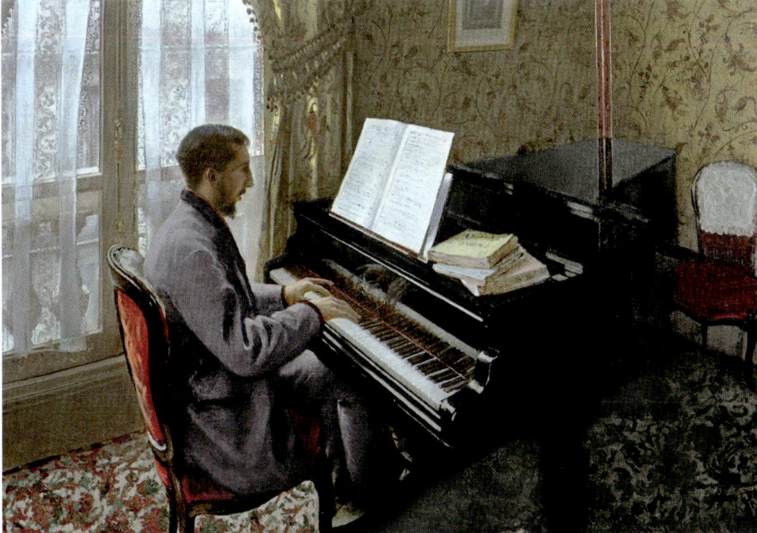

Fig. 13

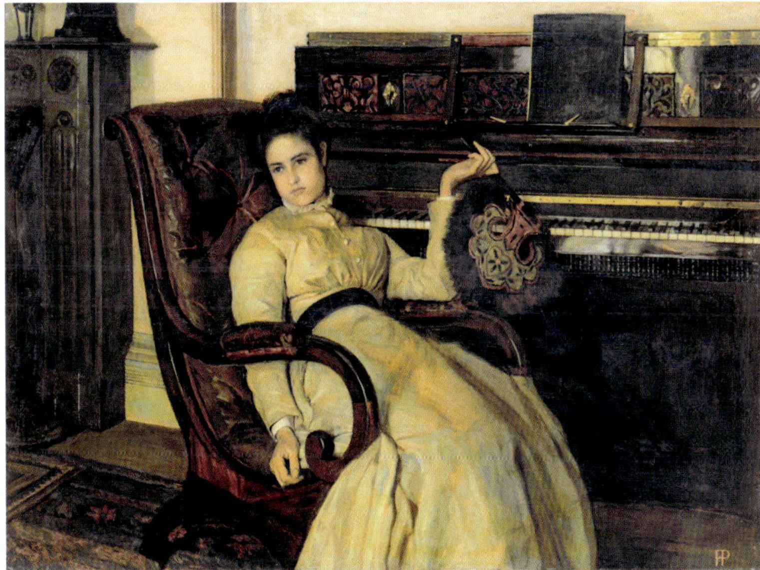

Fig. 14

Fig. 13. Gustave Caillebotte
Young Man Playing the Piano, 1876
Oil on canvas, 80 × 116 cm
Bridgestone Museum of Art, Tokyo,

Fig. 14. Frank Huddlestone Potter
Girl Resting at a Piano, c. 1880
Oil on canvas, 51.4 × 71.4 cm
Tate Britain, London,
N04617

relief as soon as she becomes a wife that she can 'leave off learning morning lessons and practising silly rhythms on the hated piano'.[17] Occasionally, such conflicted feelings find their way into painting too. Frank Huddlestone Potter's *Girl Resting at a Piano* captures something of the constraint and distaste felt by the unmusical victim of this social convention; in his painting a languid young woman turns her back on the piano and the tedious practice it involves (fig. 14). A similar ennui seems to characterise the woman in Zacharie Astruc's *Parisian Interior*, shown at the first Impressionist exhibition of 1874 (Musée de l'Ancien Évêché, Évreux). In *At the Piano* (fig. 15), a clear-eyed view of petit bourgeois moeurs painted by Frédéric Cordey, friend of Renoir and Caillebotte, we see a pianist surely doing her best to impress her intended, however faltering her playing may be. He, forced into the position of listener, appears more constrained than enraptured, hence the whimsical title, *A Captive Audience*, which may well have been added at a later date. But for more adept pianists such as Renée Mauperin in the Goncourts' novel of that name (1864), the piano became a useful emotional sounding board, a solitary solace, and in paintings such as Theodore Robinson's *At the Piano* (cat. 23) the instrument appears to be an absorbing intellectual challenge for a proficient female player.

PARIS AS MUSICAL HUB

The importance of Paris as the centre of a pianistic musical tradition is another factor relevant to the outcrop of piano imagery. Just as would-be painters from the provinces, Europe and America flocked to the French capital to perfect their techniques, aspiring musicians headed to Paris to complete their studies or, like Offenbach, to make their name. Chopin, Liszt and Wagner all had important relationships with the French public, in the latter case passing from absurd hostility in mid-century to absurd adulation in the 1880s. In 1871 the Société Nationale de Musique was established by Camille Saint-Saëns and Romain Bussine to support the national tradition and resist the dominance of Germanic music. This initiative helped to foster a new generation of composers, with such names as Ernest Chausson, Gabriel Fauré, Claude Debussy and Maurice Ravel, many of whom moved in painterly circles, just the most familiar of a brilliant period in French musical history. Alongside classical music, the climate for popular music was flourishing too, with a constant demand for catchy chansons with simple piano accompaniments or easy piano pieces. Certain composers, Erik Satie most famously, but also Emmanuel Chabrier, Gabriel Fabre and

Désiré Dihau, divided their time between the two spheres, playing piano accompaniments at café concerts or composing popular chansons in order to subsidise their more serious musical activities.

An awareness of this background helps to some degree with the interpretation of the musical content of images. Some artists give a specific indication, as in Fantin-Latour's etching *A Piece by Schumann* (fig. 11), which records a musical enthusiasm he was keen to share with his English friends, Edwin and Ruth Edwards, at a time when Schumann's music was still relatively rarely heard. (Incidentally, the piano and flute look strangely back-to-front because Fantin, a non-practising musician and inexperienced print-maker, had not bargained for the way the printing process would reverse his drawn image, a problem that recurs in other prints of musicians, cat. 62.) Schumann's intensely romantic, pictorial and playable piano music was revered by Gauguin, and the Belgian painter Fernand Khnopff, Félix Vallotton and Odilon Redon all paid him artistic homage.[18] German music of a very different order is celebrated in Cézanne's *Overture to Tannhäuser* (fig. 16), its emphatic repetitions and baroque swirls perhaps seeking to echo the overture's character. Although Wagner is usually said to be the unifying genius behind Fantin-Latour's *Around the Piano* too (1884, Musée d'Orsay, Paris), it is the French composer and art-lover Chabrier, renowned for the brilliance of his piano playing despite the shortness of his arms, who presides at the piano. At the time Chabrier, like other composers, was enamoured of Spain: might not a contest between Hispanophile and Wagnerian musical forms be at issue in this painting? The score open on the piano has been variously identified as by Bizet or Brahms, but surely one of Chabrier's own difficult piano compositions is a more likely candidate, its shimmering character transmitted, perhaps, to the febrile hatchings we see in Fantin's drawn study (cat. 60).[19] In July 1882 Chabrier made a trip to Spain that resulted in his orchestral work *España*, and in 1884 he composed *Habañera* at the prompting of his music publishers, Enoch frères, to offer something readily playable by the amateur pianist. Replete with clichés from Spanish folk music, particularly guitar-like arpeggios in the left-hand, it is dedicated to Mademoiselle Marguerite Lamoureux, the conductor's daughter. Although Fantin evidently posed his models elsewhere, Chabrier would have composed *Habañera* with Manet's last great masterpiece, *A Bar at the Folies-Bergère* (1882, The Courtauld Gallery, London), within view. Having acquired it at his great friend's posthumous sale, he hung it over his piano.

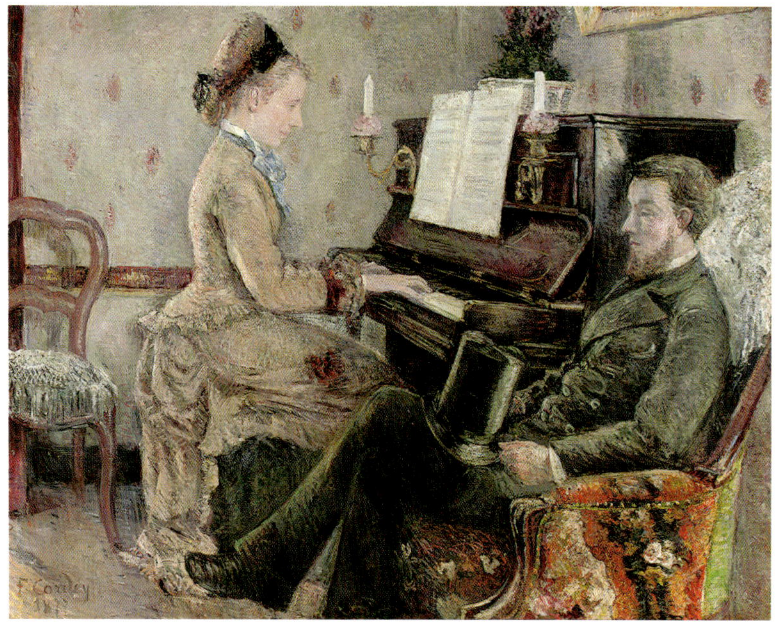

Fig. 15

MUSIC LESSONS AND DUETS

The theme of the music lesson involving two figures around the keyboard was taken up by several of the Impressionists. It had a long heritage, particularly in Dutch painting: artists like Vermeer and Gerrit Dou habitually played on the dialogue between master and pupil and the erotic associations of music making. That playful trope was kept alive in the eighteenth and early nineteenth century by satirists like Rowlandson in England, and Gavarni and Daumier in France. Indeed, for nineteenth-century viewers, the very idea of the *Music Lesson* automatically conjured images of amorous dalliance, although the realities of how music was taught forced a gradual change in perception. Learning the piano was still a chiefly bourgeois pursuit, and teaching it, especially to children, was one of the few respectable career paths for single women, a way to achieve economic independence. Vast numbers of piano teachers were to be found advertising lessons and women were prominent among them. Bazille regretted that such 'maîtresses de piano' of conservative tastes dominated the audiences of the Conservatoire concerts he attended.[20] Some 400 or so are listed in the *Annuaire spécial des artistes musiciens* for 1863, but many more were probably unlisted. Whether all women advertising piano lessons were to be taken at face value (some were a cover for prostitution) was a question that did not fail to raise mirth when the

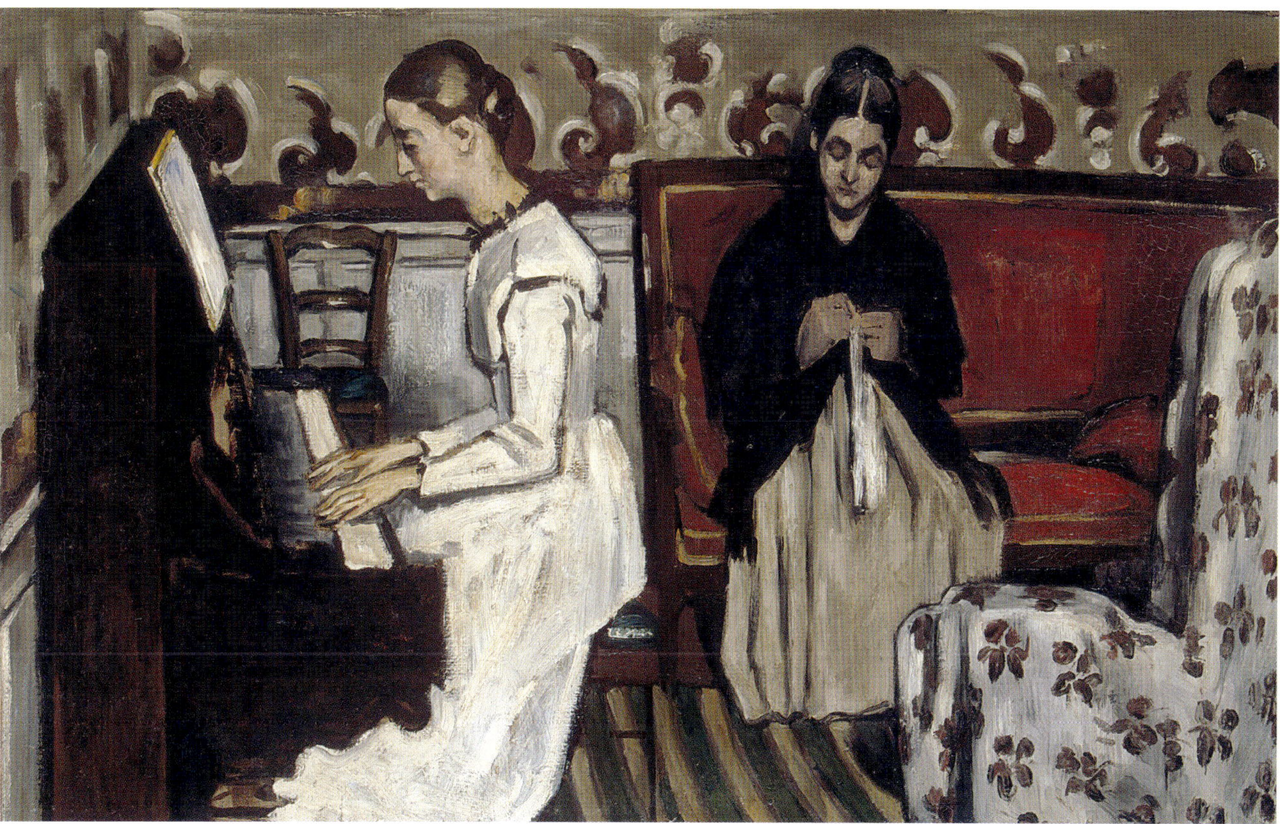

Fig. 16

Chambre des Députés reviewed the idea of a piano tax and its implementation. One of the clinching arguments for the tax's opponents was that it would be anti-democratic: 'Since for the last fifteen years musical activity has greatly spread among the lower classes, it follows that this plan to impose a tax is increasingly anti-democratic, and consequently contrary to the spirit of this Parliament.' So wrote the journalist of the weekly musical journal *Le Ménéstrel*, echoing views expressed in 1874 and 1877 when the benefits of piano playing as a means of keeping young people entertained at home, away from more harmful distractions, were

Fig. 15. **Frédéric Samuel Cordey**
At the Piano or
A Captive Audience, 1877
Oil on canvas, 114.3 × 146.7 cm
Private collection

Fig. 16. **Paul Cézanne**
Girl at the Piano
(The Overture to Tannhäuser),
c. 1868
Oil on canvas, 57.8 × 92.5 cm
The State Hermitage Museum,
Saint Petersburg,
9166

acknowledged.[21] It was indeed Third Republic policy to promote musical education, and a stipulated number of hours on the school curriculum for girls and boys alike were devoted to singing and to mastering the *solfège*.

Individual music lessons were de rigueur for the well brought up young person, and ideally should begin young, but not too young, according to the author Félix Le Couppey, whose piano primer was one of the most popular in France, appearing in multiple editions.[22] For this liberal-minded tutor, the pupil needed to be able to read and to show some spontaneous interest in music. He deplored the obligatory tutoring of young girls whatever their aptitude. Many artists found the subject of children practising the piano an appealing one (cat. 24). Lessons were encouraged not only for the young, but also for the adult learner, as Caillebotte's charming *Piano Lesson* (cat. 20) reveals. The subject is given a modern, realist slant. Eschewing all the past risqué associations of the music lesson, Caillebotte focuses instead on the models themselves, seen close to, in profile or *profil perdu*, dignified independent women enjoying a mutually beneficial transaction. The painting is thought to represent Alice Hoschedé, who was to become Claude Monet's second

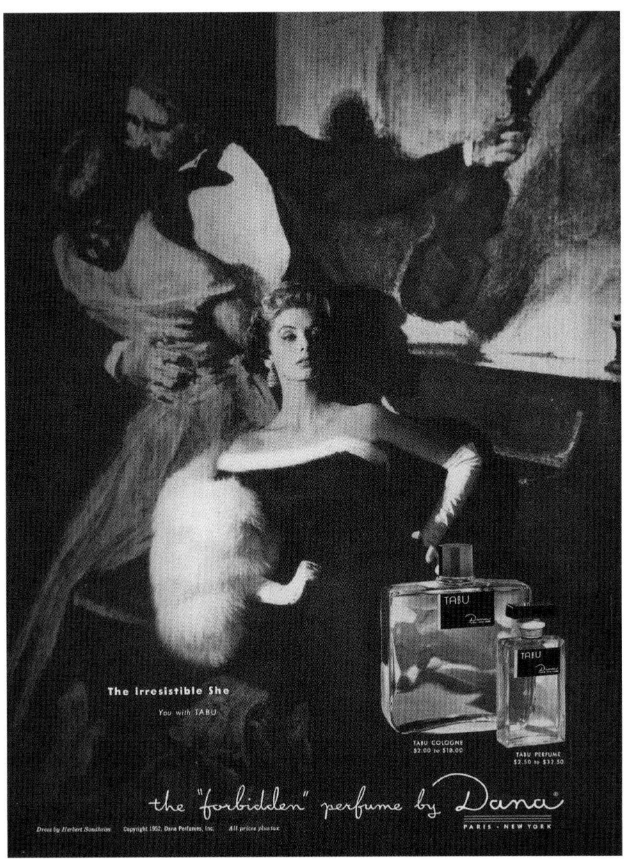

Fig. 17

woman standing by a piano, but does the title allude to her yearning for a lover or to the piece of music she is thinking of playing?[23] A gentle erotic charge underlies many paintings of female pianists playing under male supervision: Albert Besnard's double portrait of the composer Ernest Chausson and his wife at the piano, for instance (private collection), or Rusiñol's of the composer Erik Satie and his lover Suzanne Valadon, *A Romance* (fig. 18). Things get thoroughly out of hand in the duet being performed in René Prinet's *The Kreutzer Sonata* (1901, cat. 30), its title referencing both Beethoven's violin and piano sonata and Tolstoy's short story. The painting was sold initially to the Prince Regent of Bavaria, and later Javier Serra, director of Dana Perfume, who would use it in a series of advertising images (fig. 17).

PIANO SOLOS AND PIANOS IN THE STUDIO

The late nineteenth century produced some of the most enduring music of the piano repertoire as well as quantities of meretricious compositions. As Le Couppey lamented, 'Today everyone writes for the piano. The result of this manic over-production is a surfeit of mediocre music.'[24] Painted tableaux are, by definition, not only two-dimensional but also mute. Nevertheless, certain artists' images help us to discern the character of the music or the quality of the performance. The situations in which music is being produced together with the associated body language give important clues: tentative sight-reading in Guillaumin's *Piano Practice* (cat. 24) or anxious struggle with a difficult piece in Theodore Robinson's *At the Piano* (cat. 23); relaxed and confident playing in Stevens's *Eva Gonzalès at the Piano* (cat. 59). One can distinguish between the amateurish picking out of a new melody with one hand in Renoir's *Young Girls at the Piano* (cat. 21) and the vigorous technical bravura and professionalism in Toulouse-Lautrec's *Mademoiselle Dihau at the Piano* where the pianist lifts her hands high above the keys. The model's professionalism as a teacher is also indicated in the surrounding scores (cat. 53). Playing has the look of a pleasant solitary distraction for Lucie Cousturier in Maximilien Luce's rapidly executed study of his artist friend (cat. 58), as we know it was for other painters who were also talented musicians, John Singer Sargent for instance, who liked to break off from portrait sessions with diverting interludes of piano-playing, as several of his sitters recorded.[25] He introduced Madame Subercaseaux, the subject of one of his first major piano portraits, to the music of composer Gottschalk, enthusing about the composer's creole and Hispanic rhythms.

wife, but whether she is in the role of teacher or pupil is unclear. Indeed, it is not clear whether the teacher is giving a lesson on her own premises, as many did, or in the home of her pupil. The former seems the more likely, since the woman in street attire sits squarely in front of the piano and the woman without the hat, seated slightly to the side, seems to take the role of instructor marking time with her finger. At any event, when Caillebotte gave the painting to Monet he hung it in his bedroom in Giverny.

Eroticism was difficult to dissociate from the image of the pianist, particularly when so much music – whether classical or popular in style – played on the cliché of the romance. Musical composers themselves were scarcely innocent in this regard, often evoking sentimental themes in their titles. Both Schubert and Debussy wrote piano duets with cross-hand passages that enforced a sometimes awkward intimacy upon their players. Indeed, there is much overlap, if not confusion, between the titles of paintings and of musical compositions: such evocative themes as *Simple Aveu*, *Tristesse* or *L'Absence* were much in vogue. The latter is the title of an 1862 painting by Alfred Stevens showing a melancholic young

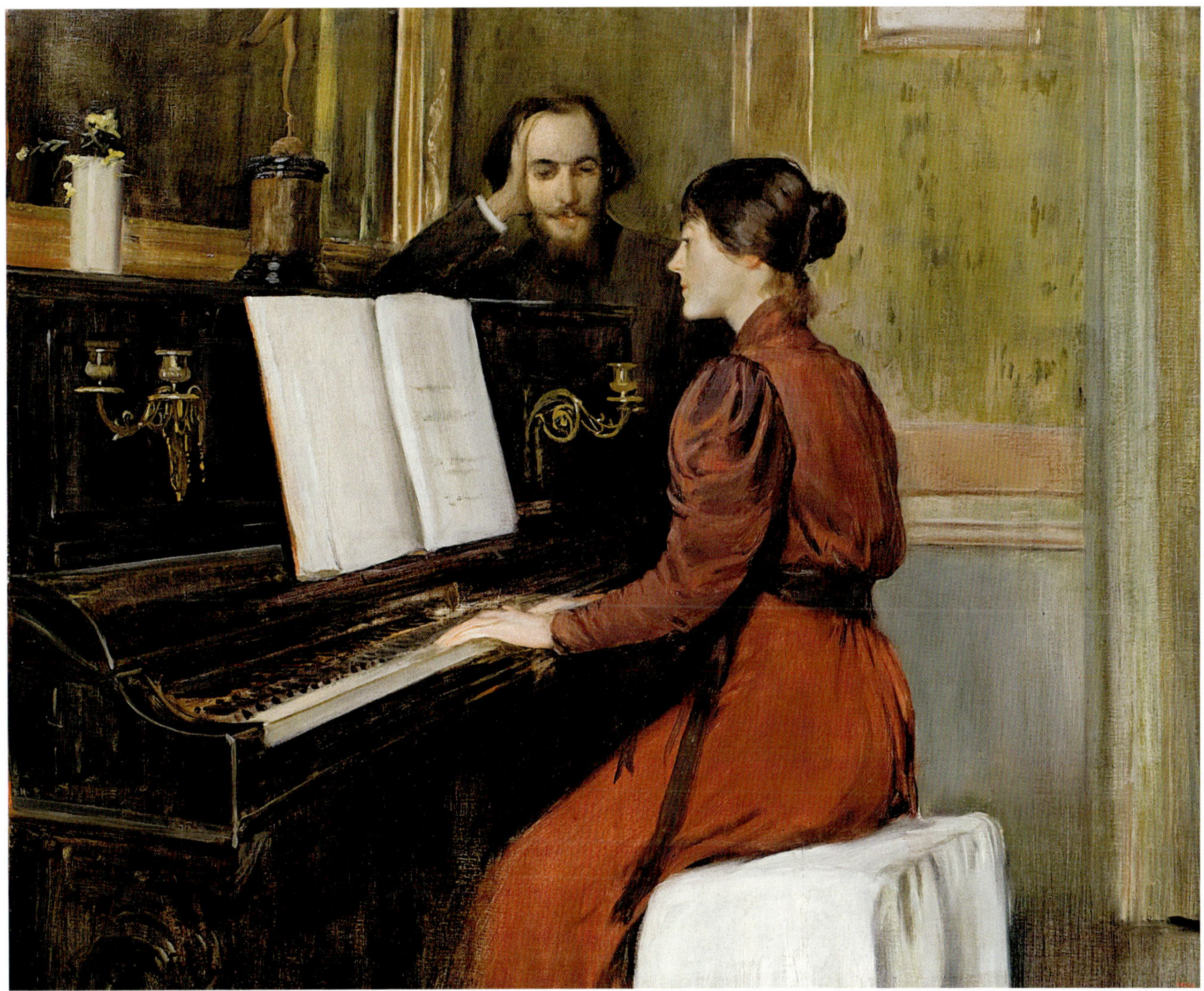

Fig 18

If there was an intrinsic elegance to the activity of piano playing that doubtless recommended it to both portraitist and sitter, the realities of fixing upon the right viewpoint posed problems. It has to be acknowledged that the upright piano itself lacks picturesque charm. A further difficulty was to include both the face and the player's hands on the

keys. Pianos had none of the tactile grace of the stringed instruments, and few players owned an elegant instrument such as the family heirloom played by Deborah Haden. Most upright pianos were boxy, funereal monstrosities of dark wood, which had little to recommend them visually apart from their reflective surface and twisted candle sconces. When the player was seated at a grand, the obvious angle to view from was profile, which usually meant truncating the queue, but an oblique viewpoint was often more successful. Renoir, for instance, who chose a piano subject for his one state commission in 1892, adopted a rear view in his first roughly indicated sketch for *Young Girls at the Piano*.[26] He posed the models in his studio, using the rosewood Érard upright he had given his wife as a wedding present, whose light tone complements the reds and golds of the girls' hair, dresses

Fig. 17. Advertisement for Dana perfumes, featuring René Prinet's *The Kreutzer Sonata*, 1901, from *Vogue*, 15 November 1952. Courtesy Condé Nast Archive Collection

Fig. 18. Santiago Rusiñol *A Romance – Erik Satie and Suzanne Valadon*, 1894 Oil on canvas, 89.5 × 111 cm Museu Nacional d'Art de Catalunya, Barcelona, 011422-000

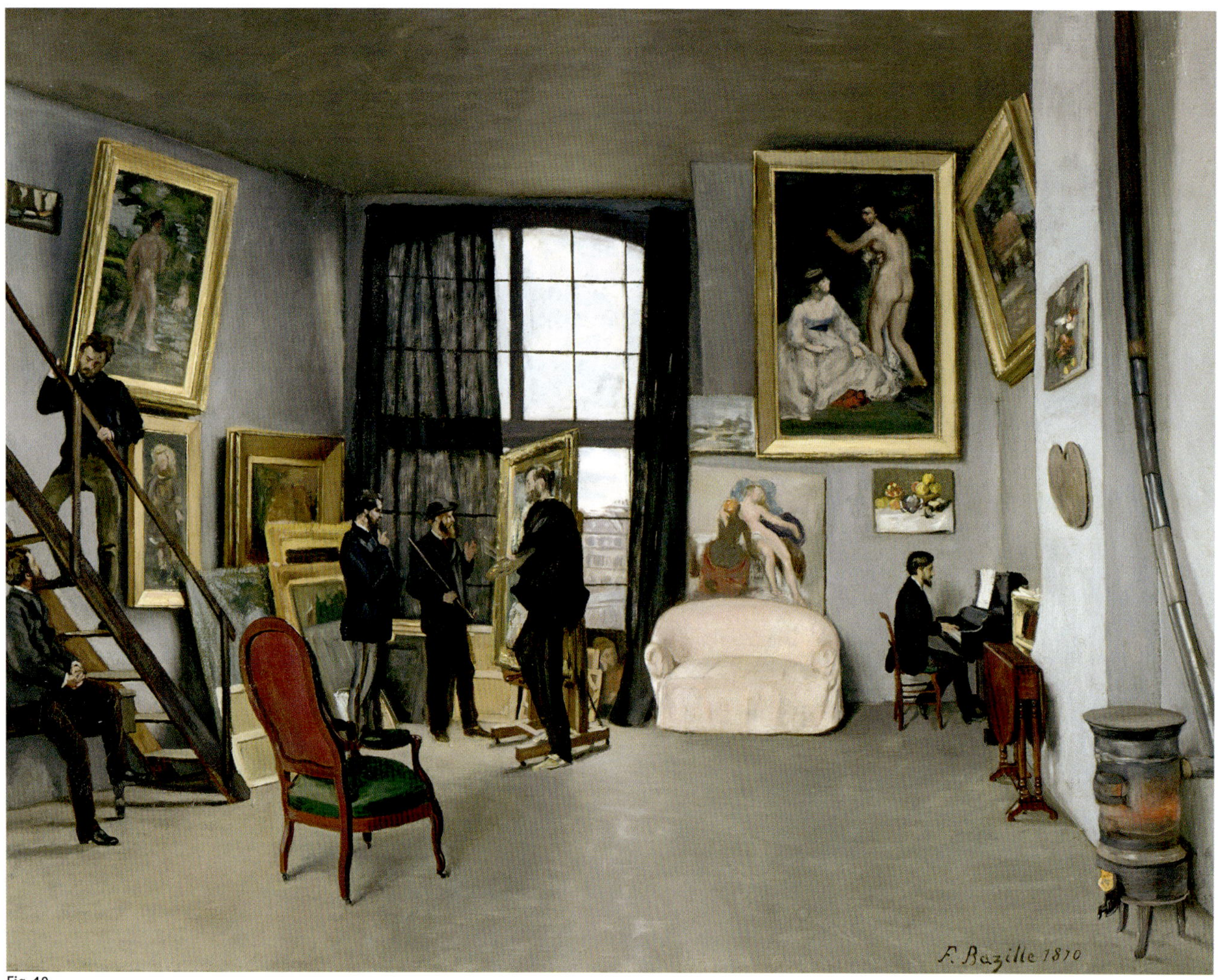

Fig. 19

and decor. By switching to the profile viewpoint, he was able
to play upon the charming warmth of their interrelationship.
While the avoidance of precision in his first version of *Young
Girls at the Piano* is harmonious and 'musical', when the
piano's details and the setting assumed greater importance as
he progressed with the composition, the picture undoubtedly
lost something, as he himself acknowledged.[27] Degas, in
his portrait of his friend the pianist and teacher Marie Dihau,
solved the compositional conundrum by showing Dihau's
left hand only poised on the keys of what looks like a Pleyel
upright, and having her turn to face him, a solution which, for
all its spontaneity, somewhat defeats the purpose of having
her at the piano (cat. 52). Two decades on, Toulouse-Lautrec
adopted the more animated *profil perdu* viewpoint for his
portrait of the same sitter, which respectfully incorporated

Degas's earlier painting hanging on the wall. He used abrupt,
comma-like brushstrokes throughout the composition,
perhaps in emulation of the rapidity of her piano technique.
Seeing it at the 1890 Salon des Indépendants inspired
Vincent van Gogh to paint a similar portrait of Mlle Gachet.

The turning pose was used repeatedly and we cannot
assume, as in Huddlestone Potter's genre painting, that
it denoted distaste. Denis adopted it for his portrait of his
fiancée Marthe at the piano (fig. 21). Sargent, in his stylish
portrait of Catherine Vlasto, posed her standing but slightly
leaning into an upright piano, his own (cat. 27). An inventory
and photographs of his London studio show that he had
a Bechstein upright, as, incidentally, did Debussy. We do
not know whether Catherine Vlasto, who died soon after
this portrait was made, was musical. One might conjecture

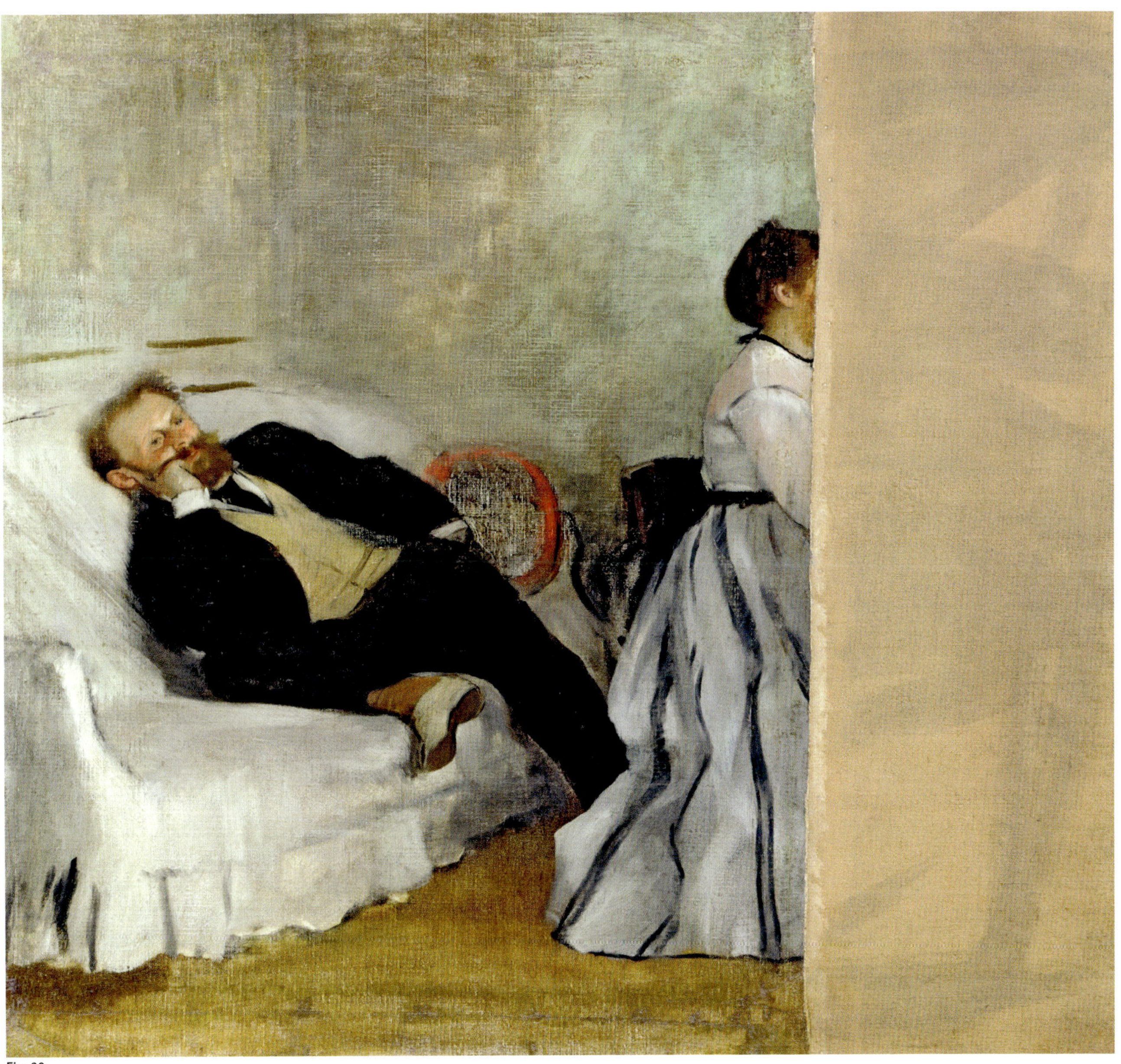

Fig. 19. **Frédéric Bazille**
*Studio in the rue
La Condamine*, 1870
Oil on canvas, 98 × 128 cm
Musée d'Orsay, Paris,
RF 2449

Fig. 20. **Edgar Degas**
Édouard Manet and Mme Manet,
1868–9
Oil on canvas, 65 × 71 cm
Municipal Museum of Art,
Kitakyushu

not, for the notes she is distractedly depressing with her right hand would in fact, were we to hear them, sound a high-pitched discord. One wonders how Sargent arrived at this composition, which certainly shows off the subject's elegant white dress to advantage in contrast with the ebony piano case – many artists chose to portray pianists in white dresses for the same reason. Perhaps Catherine Vlasto's tense yet statuesque pose was suggested by another fixture in Sargent's Tite Street studio, his famous portrait of *Madame X (Madame Pierre Gautreau)* (The Metropolitan Museum of Art,

New York), whose scandalous reception at the Salon of 1884 had so enhanced his career.

As Sargent's case shows, by the latter part of the century the piano had become one of the essential accoutrements of the artist's studio. George du Maurier's popular novel *Trilby*, published in 1894 but mostly set in the Paris of the 1850s and based on his personal experience as an art student there, describes the expensive installation in the protagonists' shared studio of a Broadwood grand brought over from London. It is on this instrument that his demonic character Svengali plays Chopin and Schubert to mesmerising effect. The upright piano that Bazille installed – seen in the corner of his *Studio in the rue La Condamine* (fig. 19) – had been conveyed to Paris from his home in Montpellier.[28]

If the artist did not expect to remain at the same address for long, it made sense to hire rather than buy, and piano rental firms sprang up to cater to this need. Whistler, who to'ed and fro'ed between Paris and London, left a legacy of piano rental agreements and angry demands for overdue payments. Artists who installed pianos, presumably having hired them, include the Italian Giovanni Boldini and the Norwegian Harriet Backer. For musically inclined Parisians, pianos could even be hired for the length of a summer *villégiature*. Émile Bernard had to hire one for his sister Madeleine so that she could keep up her practice when she joined him in Saint-Briac in Brittany in 1891.[29] Her playing of Bach, Beethoven and Mendelssohn provided the background accompaniment to his confused artistic reveries that summer. A similar requirement was made the following year by Paul Sérusier's musical brother, Henry, when visiting the artist in the remote Breton village of Huelgoat.[30] Sérusier, as a chorister with the Euterpe chorale in Paris, doubtless knew his way around the piano, but he lacked the intuitive aptitude for music he envied in his artistic mentor Gauguin who, when in Le Pouldu, installed a bargain piano he had spotted in Lorient.[31] Doubtless it was this instrument that led him to draw an intriguing pianistic analogy when defending his recent works against uncomprehending criticism. He bitterly contrasted the unfavourable circumstances in which he had produced them – like a virtuoso playing in a café on a honky-tonk piano – to Degas, who was like a performer playing to a rapt and select audience on an Érard.[32]

CHAMBER MUSIC

The piano, of course, played an essential support role in social music-making as an accompaniment to singers or other instrumentalists. In the 1870s a bohemian crowd was drawn to the musical soirées of Nina de Villard, *alias* Nina de Callias. A talented pianist, she regularly held late-night open house for a circle of admirers who included politicians, poets – Verlaine, Mallarmé and Charles Cros – and artists such as Manet, Degas and Franc-Lamy. The latter's fresh and lively gouache in the shape of a fan captures a typical soirée at her bijou villa in the Batignolles, decorated in the latest *Japoniste* style (cat. 28). Nina is seen presiding at the piano, the composer Ernest Cabaner at her side, while the violinist framed in the doorway is thought to be Charles Cros. The all-male company is rendered respectable by the presence of the pianist's elderly mother, Mme de Villard, wearing a lavender dress. Two hostesses dominated the Paris musical scene around 1900, Madeleine Lemaire and Marguerite de Saint-Marceaux, both of whom could count on enticing the most brilliant professional performers to their salons. Between them they supplied the ingredients for the imperious Mme Verdurin in Marcel Proust's *À la recherche du temps perdu*.[33] It is the equivalent English upper crust society that we see represented in *Too Early* by James Tissot (cat. 10), a Frenchman who made a brilliant success of his career in London. Balls involved hiring musicians, and here the hostess goes through the preliminaries, perhaps setting the programme of music with the band comprising a trumpeter, fiddler, bass player and inevitable pianist. Through a clever use of space, the vast emptiness of the dance floor and the gaggle of early guests hanging around the entrance, Tissot conveys the awkwardness of the moment, one that all party-goers and party-givers recognise, whatever their station in society. A much more informal atmosphere typified the evenings at Misia and Thadée Natanson's apartment; in the 1890s they regularly entertained such friends as Mallarmé, Vuillard, Bonnard, Vallotton and Toulouse-Lautrec, typically inviting them back to dine 'sans cérémonie' after a Sunday afternoon Lamoureux concert.[34] Vuillard adeptly captured these musical moments in paintings such as *Misia at the Piano*, with the pianistic arabesques seemingly prolonged visually in the meanders of the gold-hued floral wallpaper (cat. 29). Misia regularly held guests in thrall to her spirited playing of Beethoven, Schubert or Grieg.

Artists too liked to make music or have music at their soirées. A shared love of music was the social glue that bound particular artistic circles together. This was true in the late 1860s of the Manet, Degas, Morisot and Stevens circle, whose typical form of entertainment comprised weekly musical soirées at one or other of their homes, with Mme Manet and Mme Paul Meurice playing Beethoven or Schumann duets. Manet's wife Suzanne, née Leenhoff, had first appeared in Manet's family home in the early 1850s as a piano teacher: coming to Paris from Holland as an independent professional, she was hired to give lessons to his younger brothers.

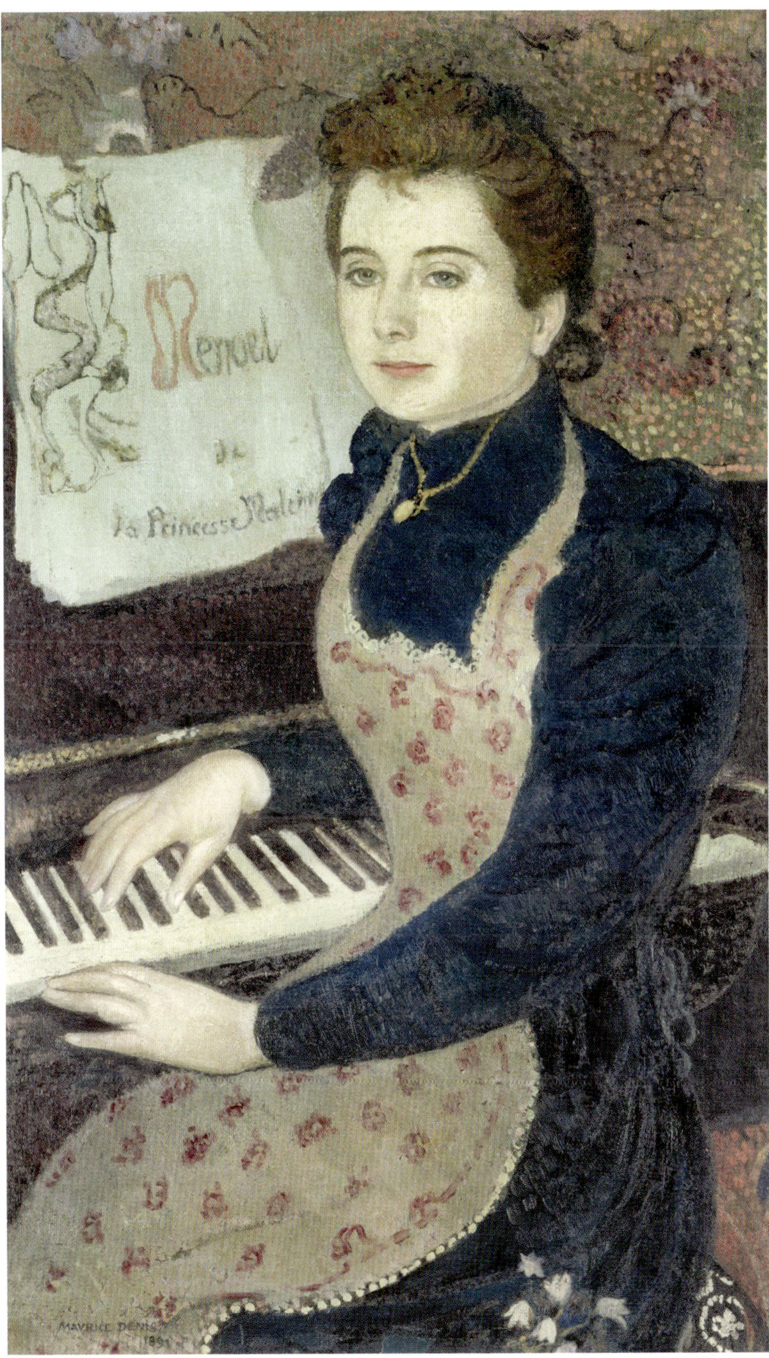

Fig. 21

Fig. 21. Maurice Denis
The Minuet from La Princess Maleine
or *Marthe at the Piano*, 1891
Oil on canvas, 95 × 60 cm
Musée d'Orsay, Paris,
RF 1999 3

Manet married Suzanne in 1863 in somewhat mysterious circumstances, eleven years after she gave birth to a boy now presumed to be his son. Manet remained touchy about some aspect of their relationship, for when Degas presented the couple with a dual musical portrait in which Suzanne, seen in profile, plays the grand piano while her husband lolls on a sofa listening (fig. 20), Manet took exception to what he considered her unflattering portrayal and cut off the offending segment of the canvas. It caused a temporary rift with Degas, who took the gift back. Manet's painting of Suzanne at the piano may have been painted in riposte; it featured the same piano in his mother's apartment (cat. 47). He eliminated himself as listener but made more of the grey and gilt panelled background that recalls the measured spatial treatment in Whistler's earlier *At the Piano*. He never exhibited it, and referred to it in an inventory drawn up in 1872 simply as *Young Woman at her Piano*.

Degas's initial attraction to music, which grew into an almost obsessive love of opera and dance, was nurtured through his family, his father being a *mélomane* who regularly invited musicians to his home. For Berthe Morisot, taught piano by Camille Stamaty and practising on an instrument chosen for her by Rossini, music was an alternative calling and she naturally engaged fully with her daughter's and niece's musical efforts. Pierre Bonnard, too, enjoyed a familial relationship with music through his sister Andrée, who married the composer Claude Terrasse in 1890. One of Bonnard's early masterpieces shows her playing a grand piano (cat. 50). He solves the problem of viewpoint in an inventive way, looking obliquely up at the pianist from below so that we see her hands on the keys, as though she were performing on a stage, breaking up the foreground with a decorative spray of chrysanthemums.[35] His portrait of his brother-in-law, executed some years later when the couple already had several children, includes the piano that was the tool of every musician's trade but shows Terrasse surrounded by music sheets, not playing (cat. 48).[36]

Most artists were not as privileged as Denis, who witnessed at first hand some of the early try-outs of compositions by Chausson and Claude Debussy. To hear professional performances, Gauguin and the Nabis attended the concerts of Colonne or Lamoureux. These affordable Sunday matinee concert series, established under Pasdeloup in the 1860s, brought classical music to a broad audience. In *The Lamoureux Concert*, within the small compass of a vertical composition Bonnard manages to evoke the immense interior space of the Cirque d'Été, brilliantly lit and thronging with people (cat. 15). He views the orchestra and conductor from above, from a vast distance. Evidently, the main performer is a female pianist dressed in white, and this detail may enable one to date the work. Could it be the German

virtuoso Sophie Menter, a pupil of Liszt, who performed at
two successive Lamoureux concerts in March 1893,
her outfits arousing as much commentary as her repertoire
of Tchaikovsky, Rubinstein and Schumann? We know
from reports in the press as well as from Misia's invitation
to Mallarmé that the concert attracted an elite audience.

CONCLUSION: THE SEARCH FOR ARTISTIC CONGRUENCE

In the early 1900s, the piano, whether heard in a public
concert or a domestic setting, was still the instrument
most likely to offer listeners their first taste of the musical
repertoire. For D. H. Lawrence, growing up in working-class
Nottinghamshire, memories of his mother were intrinsically
tied up with listening to her playing hymns on the upright,
with his ear against the piano case.[37] For Marcel Pagnol,
growing up in Marseilles, it was his chance encounter with a
girl from the *haute bourgeoisie* that initiated him to the thrill
of music, and he too pressed his ear against the piano's case,
letting its sonority transport his imagination.[38] Alain-Fournier,
in *Le Grand Meaulnes*, had his hero experience a similar
epiphany when he stumbled upon Yvonne playing to younger
children in the dining room of the enchanted domain.[39]
The piano was the vehicle for introducing these adolescents
to whole new vistas of pleasurable feeling, in part erotic
but, more importantly, aesthetic, their imaginations awakened
by the magic of music which, for Pagnol, seemed to make
time stand still.

Among such literary evocations one finds a wide
range of responses to piano playing, positive associations
with childhood, with dreamy imagination, with pleasurable
time-wasting, coupled with implicit class distinctions and
yearnings to climb the social scale. Other accounts vent
more negative feelings about the scourge of overhearing
fumbling and monotonous piano practice. Some of the most
scathing remarks come from musicians, Debussy complaining
to Chausson of the intolerable irritation of having a debutant
pianist as a neighbour[40] and Satie, whose pellucid piano
music brings such pleasure to millions, opining tersely (and
untranslatably), 'Le piano, comme l'argent, n'est agréable
qu'à celui qui en touche.' The same range of responses can
be found in the rich visual imagery inspired by the pianist at

this period, with artists of a musical bent often going beyond
the mere recording of a social reality to convey something of
the emotional and intensely personal feelings they associated
with the piano.

Perhaps, of all the examples explored here, it is Walter
Sickert in *Tipperary* who meets the challenge of painting the
modern pianist with greatest flair (cat. 25). After essaying a
different viewpoint involving the listening figure of a soldier,
Sickert refined his idea, put the piano and pianist centre
stage and settled on an oblique angle of vision. His painting
encapsulates the congruence between what is seen and
what is heard in the mind's ear, between a study of a specific
moment in time and a timeless study in reflections, the warm
veneer of the imposing grand offering a wealth of coloured
tints for his brush to explore. There is even an ironic clash
between opposing classes and musical registers, for what
seems at first the absorbed isolation of a young woman
at the piano is belied by her identity, Sickert's favourite model,
'Chicken', her jaunty hat and the populist music-hall tune
she is supposedly playing. The title, *Tipperary*, inevitably
brings to mind the painting's pressing historical context, the
first year of World War One, and offers a poignant adieu to
the heyday of the piano.

[1] See Michel Schulman, *Frédéric Bazille*, Paris, Éditions de l'Amateur, 1995, pp. 348–50.

[2] Monet's *Camille* (1866, Kunsthalle Bremen, Bremen) was a sensational success at the same Salon that rejected Bazille.

[3] An X-ray photograph of *Ruth and Boaz* (1870, Musée Fabre, Montpellier) reveals the composition of *Young Girl at the Piano* beneath the upper paint layer. The pianist is seated at an upright piano to the right of the composition, her ample skirt filling the centre of the space, while a male listener reclines on a sofa to the left. I am grateful to Kimberly Jones for advance information about this X-ray, published in the exhibition catalogue, *Frédéric Bazille and the Birth of Impressionism*, eds. Michel Hilaire and Paul Perrin, Montpellier, Paris, Washington, 2016, fig. 39, p. 75.

[4] A list of scores in one of his sketchbooks includes many Berlioz opera overtures transcribed for piano, as well as *Épisodes de la vie d'artiste* from the *Symphonie fantastique* arranged by Liszt. Cf. Schulman, *op. cit.*, p. 287. We know Bazille was also an ardent fan of the music of Schumann, Brahms and Wagner.

[5] It is an indication of the important role of the piano in this respect that Franz Liszt devoted much of his output as a composer to piano transcriptions of orchestral or operatic works, as did Camille Saint-Saëns.

[6] The list includes Alfred Stevens, *Absence* (1862, private collection), Edgar Degas, *Édouard Manet and Mme Manet* (fig. 20, p. 43), Édouard Manet, *Madame Manet at the Piano* (cat. 47), Paul Cézanne, *Overture to Tannhäuser* (fig. 16, p. 39), Alfred Vollon, *Interior Scene* (1870, private collection).

[7] For a fruitful and pioneering analysis of this topic, which also covers the earlier part of the century, see Charlotte Eyerman, *The Composition of Femininity: the Woman at the Piano from Daumier to Renoir*, doctoral thesis, University of Berkeley, 1997. The last chapter has been published in James Parakilas, *Piano Roles, A New History of the Piano*, New Haven and London, Yale University Press, 2001, pp. 176–83.

[8] The author's personal database of images of piano playing from the period 1860–1914 numbers well over 400.

[9] Statistics from *L'Annuaire des artistes de l'enseignement dramatique et musicale*, 1907.

[10] Walter Haacke, *Am Klavier, Werke europäischer Maler aus sechs Jahrhunderten*, Stuttgart, Die Blauen Bücher, 1968.

[11] William Bürger published a series of articles entitled 'Van der Meer de Delft' in the *Gazette des beaux-arts*, XXI, July–December 1866, p. 297 et seq.; consulted on bnf.gallica.fr.

[12] Letter from William Bürger to Édouard Manet, April/May 1867, Whistler archive, Glasgow University Library, available online: MS Whistler B212, system number 00433.

[13] For instance Kenneth Bendiner, 'Whistler's *At the Piano*', *Apollo*, CXXVIII, December 1988, pp. 399–401.

[14] Unpublished letter from Henri Fantin-Latour to his parents, 17 July 1859, Bibliothèque Municipale de Grenoble, R.8867, cahier 1, cited in Corrinne Chong, *The Musically Vague in the Art, Writings and Critical Reception of Henri Fantin-Latour*, doctoral thesis, University of Edinburgh, 2015, p. 29. The *Barcarolle d'Obéron* was one of 'six characteristic études' from Weber's opera *Oberon*, arranged for piano by Camille Stamaty.

[15] Catalogue no. 238. This work is appreciatively described in a review by Rodolphe Darzens (*La Pléiade*, May 1886) as a 'graceful study' and by Jean Ajalbert (*La Revue moderne*, 20 June 1886) in more detail: 'a woman, in a polka dot dress, is leafing through an album; next to her is her dog, with blue ribbons round its neck; a bit further on is a man sight-reading at the piano.' See ed. Ruth Berson, *The New Painting, Documents*, vol. 1, San Francisco, Fine Arts Museums of San Francisco, 1996, pp. 431, 439.

[16] From a letter from Frédéric Bazille to his parents, c. 23 December 1867, printed in Michel Schulman, *op. cit.*, p. 361.

[17] Set in 1831–2, George Eliot's *Middlemarch* was published in 1874. This reference is to the Oxford World's Classics edition, 1996, III, XXVIII, p. 258.

[18] Khnopff's *Listening to Schumann* (fig. 29, p. 58); Vallotton, *To Schumann*, woodcut, 1895; Redon, *Homage to Schumann*, c. 1905.

[19] See the extensive catalogue note by Michel Hoog in the exhibition catalogue, *Fantin-Latour*, Paris, Ottawa, San Francisco, 1983, pp. 304–8.

[20] Bazille, letter to his mother, early January 1867, Schulman, *op. cit.*, p. 353.

[21] J. T. in *Le Ménestrel*, 5 March 1893, p. 83.

[22] Félix Le Couppey, *De l'Enseignement du piano : conseils aux jeunes professeurs*, 2nd edition, Paris, L. Hachette, 1868; English translation, 1904.

[23] *Triste aveu* was the title of a hugely popular melody composed for the piano by Francis Thomé in 1878 and promptly transcribed for a variety of instruments. Several compositions appeared with the title *Tristesse*, including a piano nocturne by Alfred Jaëll published in Leipzig in 1857–1858.

[24] Félix Le Couppey, *op. cit.*, p. 19.

[25] When working on the portrait of *Mrs George Swinton*, 1896–7, Art Institute of Chicago, his sitter recalled: 'We wasted a lot of time playing the piano and singing, instead of getting on with the picture.' See Richard Ormond and Elaine Kilmurray, *John Singer Sargent: Portraits of the 1890s*, New Haven and London, Yale University Press, 2002, p. 114.

[26] *Jeunes filles au piano (esquisse)*, c. 1892, Guy-Patrice and Michel Dauberville, *Renoir, Catalogue raisonné, 1882–1894*, vol. 2, Paris, Bernheim Jeune, 2009, cat. 989.

[27] The version acquired for the Luxembourg by Henri Roujon, Director of Fine Arts, a purchase much encouraged behind the scenes by Mallarmé and Roger Marx, was not the best one in Renoir's own view, according to René Gimpel.

[28] See the exchange of letters between Bazille and his father following 14 December 1863, in Frédéric Bazille, *Correspondance*, ed. Guy Barral and Didier Vatuone, Montpellier, Les Presses du Languedoc, 1992, pp. 70–1.

[29] They were able to rent a piano for the 'exceptional' price of 15 francs a month instead of 25 thanks to the intervention of their landlady. Unpublished letter from Madeleine Bernard to her parents, July 1891, Pennsylvania State University.

[30] A letter from Clémence Sérusier to her son Paul, resident in Huelgoat, concerns the arrangements for the hire and positioning of a piano in the hotel where they planned to stay for the summer.

Unpublished letter, dated 17 June 1892, Getty Archives, no. 860131.

[31] Sérusier mentioned this and described the ease with which Gauguin picked up musical instruments in an interview with Charles Chassé, *Gauguin et son temps*, Paris, Bibliothèque des Arts, 1955, pp. 72–3.

[32] Letter to Theo van Gogh, Le Pouldu, 20 or 21 November 1889, in *Paul Gauguin: 45 Lettres à Vincent, Théo et Jo van Gogh*, ed. Douglas Cooper, The Hague and Lausanne, Bibliothèque des Arts, 1983, pp. 164–7. The term 'piano Chaudron' does not refer to a specific make, but rather to a rough and ready, honky-tonk variety of instrument.

[33] See the exhibition catalogue, *Femmes peintres et salons au temps de Proust de Madeleine Lemaire à Berthe Morisot*, Paris, Musée Marmottan, 2010. The *Journal de Marguerite de Saint-Marceaux, 1894–1927*, Paris, 2007, with preface by Myriam Chimènes, is an invaluable source for information about such social and musical gatherings. See also Chimènes, *Mécènes et musiciens*, Paris, Fayard, 2004.

[34] On 18 March 1893, Mallarmé received what may be the first of such invitations from Misia and Thadée Natanson, a month before they were married; see *Correspondance de Mallarmé*, ed. Henri Mondor and Lloyd James Austin, Paris, Gallimard, 1981, vol. 5, p. 65.

[35] The concert they held on 20 January 1891, for instance, featured contemporary piano music, much of it for two pianos, by such composers as Godard, Widor, Saint-Saëns, Chaminade and Mozkowski. See Philippe Cathé, *Claude Terrasse*, Paris, L'Hexaèdre, 2004, p. 39.

[36] For Bonnard and Terrasse's collaborations on musical publications see the author's second essay.

[37] D. H. Lawrence's poem *Piano*, 1918.

[38] Marcel Pagnol, *Le Temps des Secrets*, part 3 of *Souvenirs d'enfance*, Monte Carlo, Éditions Pastorelly, 1960, pp. 95–7.

[39] Alain-Fournier, *Le Grand Meaulnes*, Paris, Émile-Paul, 1913.

[40] Letter of 3 September 1893, in Claude Debussy, *Correspondance 1872–1918*, eds. François Lesure and Denis Herlin, Paris, Gallimard, 2005, p. 155.

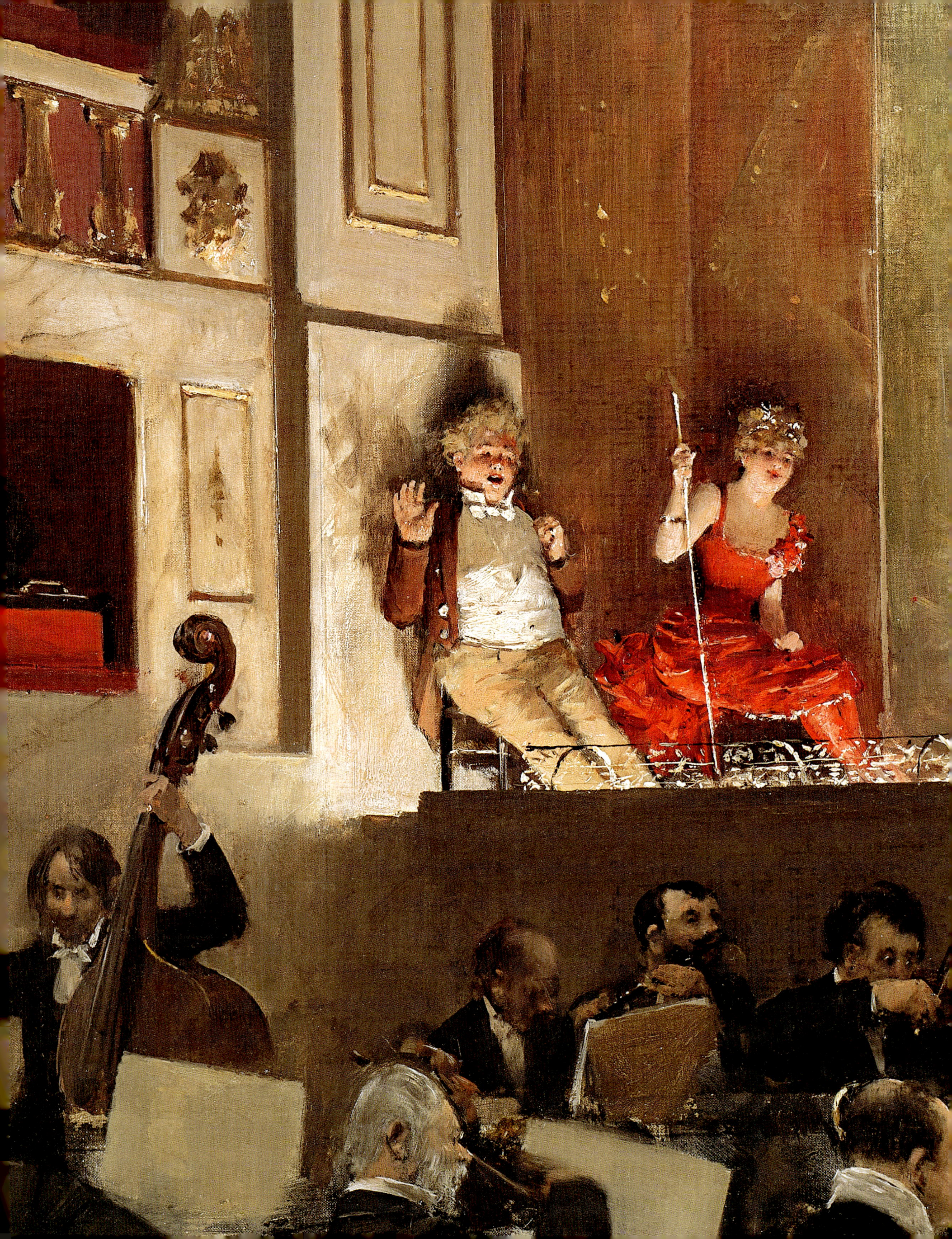

sounding bodies, listening subjects

Anne Leonard

In autumn 1874, the nineteen-year-old Ernest Chausson, still several years away from beginning composition lessons with Jules Massenet, met the artist Odilon Redon (fifteen years his senior) at the salon of Mme de Rayssac. Thus began a friendship that would last more than two decades. Although Redon was still relatively unknown – his first lithographic album, *Dans le rêve*, was not published until 1879 – he was a fervent musician, both violinist and pianist, and indeed Chausson's first known letter was written to Redon regarding a Schumann quintet: 'It is a lot of effort, but Schumann is worth it and we are all fanatical Schumannists.'[1] Chausson and Redon would play Schumann and also Beethoven trios over the first half of 1875. Another frequent visitor to Mme de Rayssac's salon was the artist Henri Fantin-Latour, a neighbour of hers on rue des Beaux-Arts – though he came only to listen, not to play. Chausson made note of a large Berlioz-inspired lithograph that Fantin-Latour presented to his hostess around Christmastime 1875, 'of a new kind and surprisingly original'.[2] This example of Fantin's work would also make a decisive impression on Redon, stoking his interest in lithography as a means of reproducing his charcoal drawings.

Some years later Mme de Rayssac's salon, by then relocated to rue Servandoni, became the site of another decisive introduction for Chausson: to his future wife, Jeanne Escudier, sister-in-law of the painter Henry Lerolle (1848–1929).[3] Through these ties of family and friendship, Chausson would find himself at the centre of a cultivated social circle where, once again, artists and musicians alike were welcome. A significant gathering place for the 'young French school' of composers – many of whom, like Chausson, had absorbed the lessons of César Franck – the Lerolle salon at 20 avenue Duquesne offered extraordinary musical moments.[4] Draft scores for the death of Mélisande (which was to become the germ of Claude Debussy's opera *Pelléas et Mélisande*) and the conclusion of Vincent d'Indy's *Fervaal* were played, practically with the ink still wet, on the Lerolle piano by the composers themselves. In an affectionate tribute from 1930, Maurice Denis recalled that Lerolle's piano 'became on certain days, under Cortot's fingers, a magical instrument where the soul of Beethoven and Chopin was present. And

Cat. 12
Jean Béraud
*Performance at the Théâtre
des variétés*, c. 1888
(detail, cat. 12, p. 80)

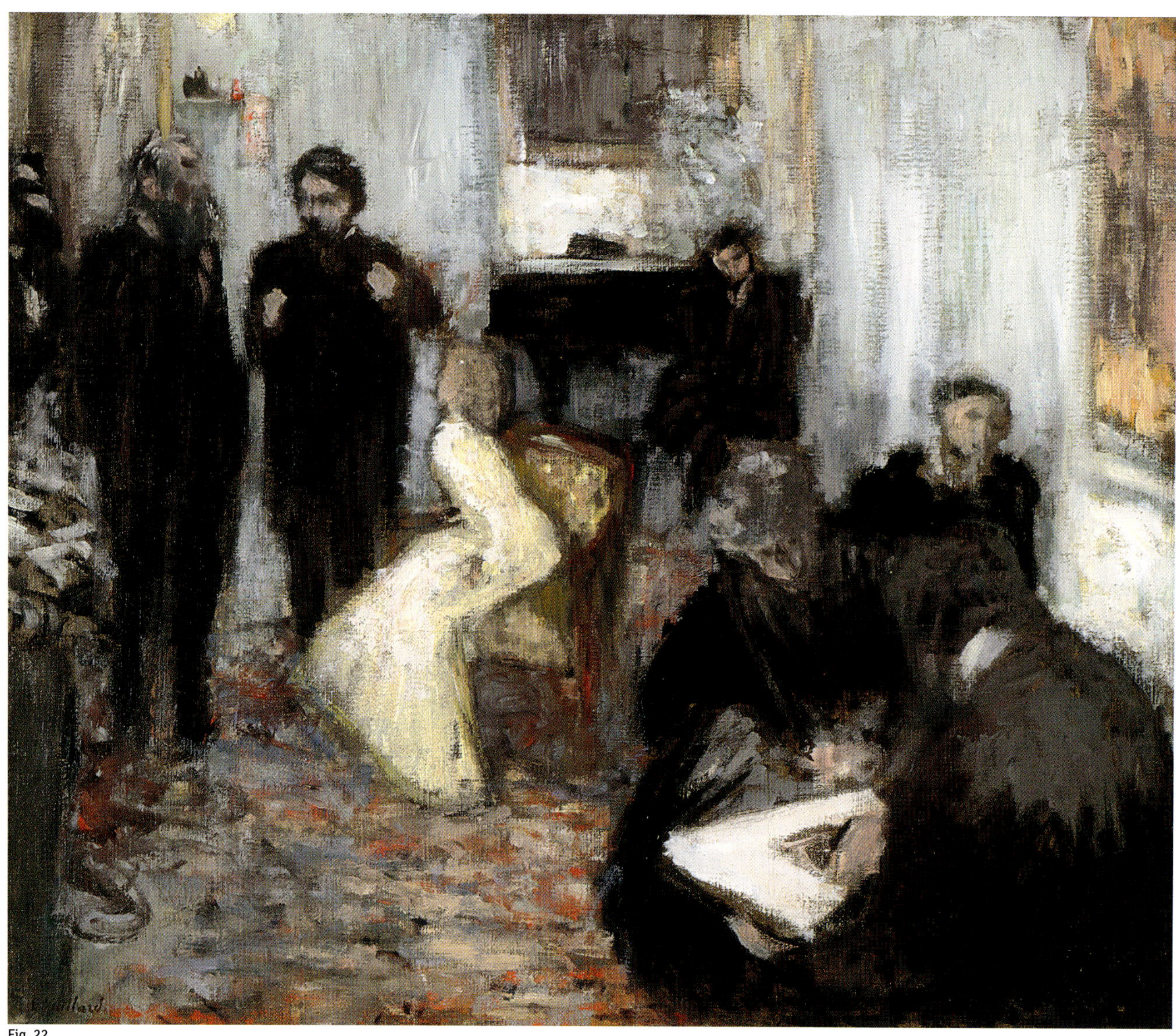

Fig. 22

there was also Ysaÿe's violin and the voice of Madame Croiza, and the admirable Selva. . . . But most of these music lovers also encountered each other in the exhibitions of Japanese art and Impressionist painting. Were they a hundred in all? They ended up getting to know each other. They formed an elite, and this elite led to the formation of a taste.'[5] A sense of this elite, high-culture taste springs from Édouard Vuillard's *Le Salon Lerolle* (fig. 22), which depicts three distinct clusters of activity: looking at a print portfolio, conversing and listening to music. While not all of the figures in the painting have been securely identified, the seated woman at centre is thought to be one of Lerolle's daughters, Yvonne or Christine, while the dark-haired, square-built man standing next to

her may be Denis, the leading theorist of the Nabi painters. The figure sitting next to the piano in the background is perhaps Ricardo Viñes, a frequent visitor chez Lerolle.[6]

Marguerite de Saint-Marceaux presided over another glittering salon of the period in her *hôtel particulier* at 100, boulevard Malesherbes. Her second husband, the sculptor René de Saint-Marceaux (1845–1915), did not really appreciate music, but such was Mme de Saint-Marceaux's force of personality that she was able to attract leading lights such as Debussy, Fauré and Ravel to her soirées. Her guests were likewise treated to an early hearing of *Pelléas et Mélisande*, but not from the hands of Debussy. In this case it was André Messager who brought the score, 'as if he

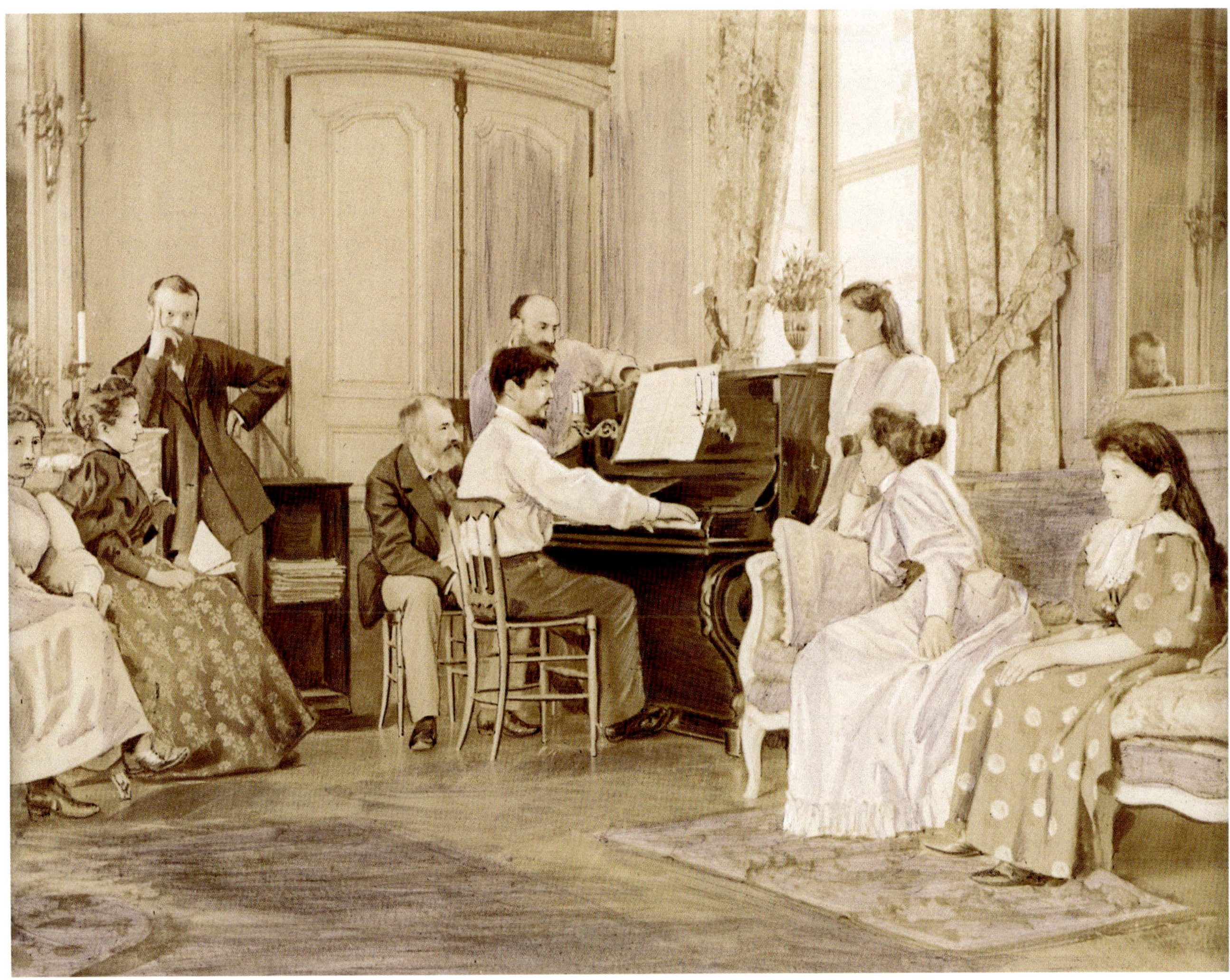

Fig. 23

Fig. 22. **Édouard Vuillard**
Le Salon Lerolle, c. 1900–3
Oil on canvas, 46 × 54 cm
Private collection, New York

Fig. 23. *Claude Debussy Playing
the Piano at Ernest Chausson's
Property at Luzancy*, 1893
Albumen photograph, 8.7 × 11.1 cm
Musée d'Orsay, Paris,
PHO 1985 5

had stolen it'.[7] (Debussy never set foot again in the Saint-Marceaux salon after 1894, when his broken engagement to Thérèse Roger caused irreparable scandal and rifts with friends of long standing.)[8] Although Mme de Saint-Marceaux was far less adventurous and up-to-date in her artistic tastes than in her musical ones, painters such as Jacques-Émile Blanche and Edmond Aman-Jean did frequent the salon.[9]

In short, the salons that structured bourgeois social life afforded encounters between musicians and painters on equal terms and provided the conditions for richly layered 'inter-art' relationships to emerge. If the Rayssac, Lerolle and Saint-Marceaux salons enabled social interactions that fostered a closer union between the work of artists and composers, they also benefited from a tendency that the writer and critic Camille Mauclair described as particular to the period: a more widespread familiarity with, and passion

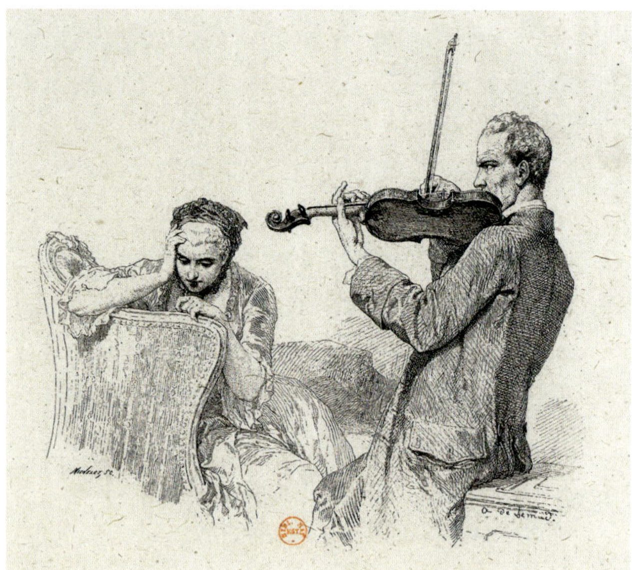

Fig. 24

for, all forms of art rather than just one. Mauclair noted that orchestral concerts, 'these great baths of diffuse sonorities', recalibrated aesthetic values across the full range of art; indeed he called music 'a synthesis of all forms of artistic creation'.[10] It was not only that artists and musicians could appreciate the same types of cultural production, but also that – in their activities of painting, writing, playing, viewing, listening, conversing – they felt themselves embarked on a common enterprise, underpinned by deep personal ties. This is not to say that such could not also produce confrontation. The warm friendship between Debussy and Chausson, for example, so well attested in a series of photographs from an 1893 visit to Chausson's country property at Luzancy, would break apart (fig. 23); and the generosity Fantin showed to Redon in teaching him the techniques of transfer lithography would be 'repaid' with an unkind assessment of Fantin's work in a collection of Redon's personal writings, *À soi-même*.[11]

Fig. 24. **Aimé de Lemud**
The Cremona Violin, n. d.
Ink with white gouache
Bibliothèque Nationale de France,
Département des Estampes
et de la Photographie, Paris,
Id : DC 290b

MASTERY

The relationships between individuals, as between the arts they practised, were not always perceived as equal or balanced. It might be said that these relations between artists and musicians mirror, or in some sense recapitulate, another set of relations among music performers, composers, conductors and listeners, which are similarly fraught with questions of relative power or hierarchy.

The first and most basic relationship here is the one between a musician and his or her instrument. This is based on a fundamental set of physical norms that are reinforced by the discipline of instruction, training and repeated practice. One learns how to sit at the piano, or how to hold a violin and bow, all in an effort to 'master' one's chosen instrument. However, contrary to the myth of Orpheus charming the animals with the music from his lyre, mastery is not always a one-way street. There can be a contest for power between player and instrument, as in the Romantic comparison offered by Franz Liszt when he said his relation to his piano was like an Arab rider's to his steed.[12] The musician's assertion of total identity with his instrument does not eliminate the possibility of over-mastery or betrayal by it, just as a rearing horse might throw even the most skilled rider.

This presumption of a unity or congruence between musician and instrument, or singer and voice, entails a corollary: the threat of non-congruence as a sign of trouble. In Ernest Theodor Amadeus Hoffmann's tales it forebodes something frighteningly unnatural, namely a voice or violin taking on a life of its own. In the orthodox version, a voice should perfectly correspond with the soul of the singer. It must be the image of its source. Otherwise, it has been kidnapped or taken possession of. In Hoffmann's tale 'Les maîtres-chanteurs' (German: 'Der Kampf der Sänger'), each master singer's songs fit exactly with his inner character – with the exception of Henri d'Ofterdingen's: 'Often he [Henri] combined his melancholic accents with harsh, angry sounds, which seemed to issue from a sickly nature and spread forth like venomous insects.'[13] In the tale of 'Le violon de Crémone' (German: 'Rat Krespel'), Hoffmann locates the soul of the gravely ill Antonia in the violin played by her father, Crespel. A drawing by Aimé de Lemud after this tale suggested to a contemporary critic that the sounds coming from the violin 'seem to be exhaled by a human chest' (fig. 24).[14]

In similar fashion, the listener must be construed as appropriately matched or 'tuned' to the music being played. The musician makes of his or her instrument a sounding body that, in turn, summons up a response in the listener. The blurring or mismatch of these roles can yield a disequilibrium – one evoked in certain paintings as if by the artist's design. The distinctive partitioning of Jean Béraud's painting *Performance at the Théâtre des variétés* (cat. 12) at first seems to keep each role in its own box, as it were: orchestra players in the pit, spectators in their side loges. But what about the couple on the stage? Seated like audience members, they are nonetheless located onstage and illuminated by the footlights, much like actors in the evening's entertainment. This ambiguity or disruption of expectations would be less acute if we could see the rest of the stage drama, which might explain the couple's particular role.

Quite another sort of disequilibrium emerges from the nearly contemporary *The Flageolet Player on the Cliff* (cat. 38) by Paul Gauguin. Here, a diminutive bombarde player stands on a bluff overlooking rocky cliffs and cascading waves – as if all nature, not just the Breton girl kneeling beside him, were his listener. In an instance of what one might call the 'Synthetist sublime', the mismatch of the instrument's high, reedy sound with the grand-scaled landscape and crashing water causes unease. This is an unusually powerful example of the synaesthetic dimension of Gauguin's painting. Colour, too, plays a large part in intensifying the experience of sight and sound, a phenomenon that brings the viewer/listener closer to the realm of the supernatural – to the point of being swallowed up.[15]

In an orchestral setting, the conductor's role likewise demands a proportional or balanced relation to the players. Yet this, too, can be ambiguous. Is the conductor the master, as the normative situation would have it, or over-mastered? Georges Lemmen, in his painting of a *Götterdämmerung* performance at the Théâtre de la Monnaie in Brussels (cat. 14), seems to dramatize the question with an emphasis on the conductor, a black silhouette whose gesture rhymes with that of the principal actor (Hagen?) on stage. Whereas the actor's upraised sword embodies an acted, factitious power, the conductor's raised hand (no baton is visible) compels the production of music that is, in a certain way, controlled by him. The appearance of spectators in the left foreground, meanwhile, reminds us of their rootedness – for just as long as the conductor continues his gesturing. This caged immobility, by the way, is one of the most salient features of an audience in a concert hall or opera house, as opposed to an open-air venue. Jules Janin in 1844 remarked on the distinction in seasonal terms (though with a focus on music made at home): 'For as long as winter lasts, the Parisian makes music in order to be applauded and admired; once summer comes, the Parisian makes music for himself and not for others. If you get some pleasure from hearing them sing or play their favourite instruments, at the right time, they let you applaud them; but you are completely in charge, if you do not like the music, you can always go for a walk in the garden.'[16] The power of an orchestral conductor like Jules

Pasdeloup to restrain an audience's comings and goings might seem minuscule, given how vastly outnumbered he was at the Sunday concerts he inaugurated in Paris in 1861. Yet Berlioz reported, among Pasdeloup's four to five thousand listeners, a silence that was 'religious and deep'.[17]

The implicit hegemony of the conductor over the orchestra, and by extension the audience, impressed Theodor Adorno in serious, even sinister terms. As suggested by the Lemmen *Götterdämmerung* example above, music by Richard Wagner tended to receive both the greatest credit and the greatest blame for sweeping audiences away. Adorno believed that Wagnerian audiences 'drift[ed] with the current', hapless and overpowered by a music that 'thunders . . . in endless repetitions to hammer its message home'.[18] Most worryingly, Wagner's operas were a 'commodity . . . purvey[ing] illusions'.[19] By means of his hidden orchestra pit, Wagner encouraged a perception of the musical product as self-producing, whereby the labour that went into making it is occulted. This dangerous manipulation of musical effort into disembodied sound Adorno called 'phantasmagoria'. According to him, its effect was to transform listeners into 'would-be buyers', sold on dreams of wish-fulfilment that were as illusory as any mirage.[20] While it is true that Adorno's vigorous critique was not written until the 1930s, the seed of it is already present in commentary from the 1890s. Martial de Villemoune, writing in *L'Art et la Vie* in 1894, proposed that music, of all the arts, was the one that best demonstrated Henri Bergson's notion: 'The aim of art is to lull the active or rather the resistant powers of our personality and thus bring us to a state of perfect docility.'[21] The basic idea goes at least as far back as Plato, who wrote in the *Republic* that music 'penetrates the inner soul, and takes possession of it in the most energetic fashion'.[22]

Like Adorno, Mauclair noted the power of the orchestra to create a visual illusion, though he expressed it in milder terms. Drawing on discourses of synaesthesia that were prevalent at the period he was writing, Mauclair lionised symphonic musicians as weavers of ornate tapestries of sound.[23] In the end, however, this metaphor made no claims for the instrumentalists as anything more than skilled manual labourers. Moreover, the listener's dependence on a visual correlate for music, which both Adorno and Mauclair allude to in their different ways, was not necessarily a sign of aesthetic sophistication or 'attunement' – often quite the opposite. Debussy, through his mouthpiece M. Croche, went so far as to caricature musical performers as circus acrobats, who thrilled audiences more by their physical antics than by their musical sensibilities. As he wrote, 'There is always a hope that something dangerous may happen: Mr. X may play the violin with Mr. Y on his shoulders; or Mr. Z may conclude his piece by grabbing the piano in his teeth.'[24] In keeping with my overall argument here, even these satirical examples are premised on disruptions to the normative power relationships that governed performance conditions.

BODIES AND SOULS

—

Yet there is plenty of evidence, especially at the individual level, for both playing and listening as more actively cerebral occupations. We might consider, in this connection, several portraits of string players in which the physical and intellectual components of performance receive varying degrees of emphasis. Playing appears as a physical encounter between individual and instrument, also entailing a mental struggle for mastery – and this meeting may look harmonious, or it may just as well not. In the case of Louis Hayet's *Cellist Practising* (cat. 33) the encounter produces a semi-comic effect, with the male cellist planted just as stiffly and solidly as the inanimate companion he grips by the neck (one suspects it is actually a double bass). The long (and incorrect) shadows cast by the two bodies make the man's stance seem all the more clumsy and little-nuanced: we have no more confidence in the power of the music to 'move' (*émouvoir*) than we do in the power of the musician to move (*se déplacer*). It is notable too that, in a painting where the instrument so dominates the space, the artist has chosen not to show its more beautiful side.

Compared with this, Vilhelm Hammershøi's *The Cello Player: Portrait of Henry Bramsen* (cat. 34) is a turnabout in every sense. Cellist and instrument face us, together exuding a harmony and mutual sympathy reinforced by the deep, rich colour tones. Although the viewer of this painting is now properly positioned as a listener, the musician appears oblivious to human presence, engaged in an exclusive communion with his instrument (note the sensitive depiction of the hands in particular). The posture and composition recall James McNeill Whistler's much earlier *Becquet* (fig. 25), with the difference that Whistler's cellist meets the gaze of the beholder challengingly, quasi-theatrically. In its way, the *Becquet* etching is far more radical than the later work by Hammershøi, owing to the near-total effacement of the instrument. All the emphasis is turned back to the player, especially his head, underscoring musical performance as an intellectual activity rather than a physical one. The source of the music is pinpointed to the mind, not the hands – and certainly not located in the brute body, which was all we could see of Hayet's player.

Edgar Degas's *The Cellist Pilet* (cat. 51) offers a striking alternative to the standard iconography. Pilet was a cellist

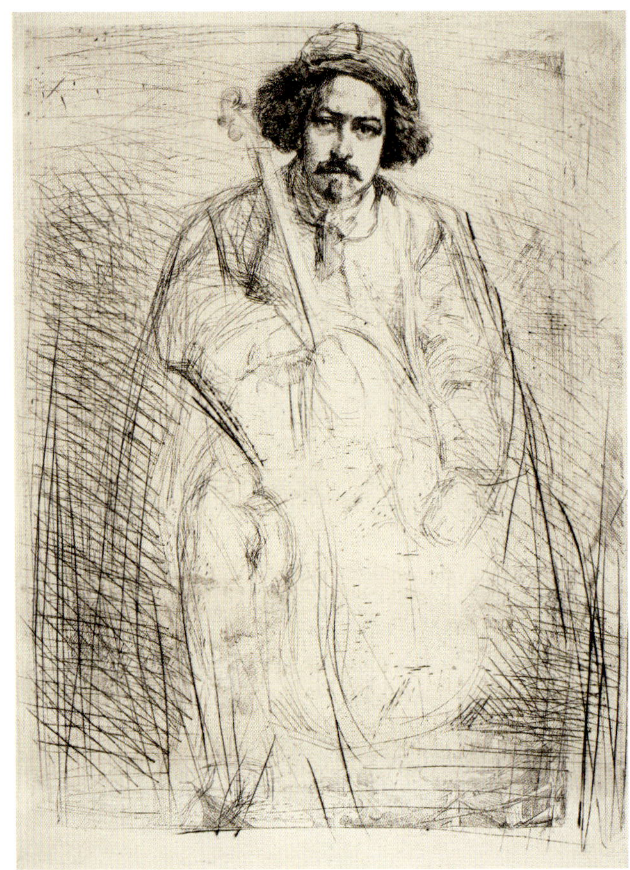

Fig. 25

in the orchestra of the Opéra who also makes a prominent appearance in Degas's painting of that title from 1872. In the portrait, Pilet is seated at a paper-strewn table, against which the cello leans at a nonchalant if not precarious angle. In a dense superposition of elements, the scroll of the cello crosses Pilet's seated form, while its neck intersects with the bow laid across the table. The cello case, meanwhile, opened towards the viewer, produces a 'doubling' that somehow makes Pilet's gaze away from it all the more pointed. Not only is this career cellist not playing, he is not looking! The gaze out the window is not blank; what it contains, or implies, positions Pilet (even in his 'off-hours') as a thinker rather than a mechanical producer of sound.

But what of the listener? Degas produced sensitive portraits of listeners, as well: not just Édouard Manet, in a casual pose, listening to his wife playing the piano (fig. 20, p. 43);[25] but also Degas's own father, Auguste de Gas, listening to Lorenzo Pagans playing the guitar (fig. 26). The framing of the elder De Gas's head within the music score behind him cannot be anodyne, given the associations of divine aureole it calls up. This listener, visually and aurally

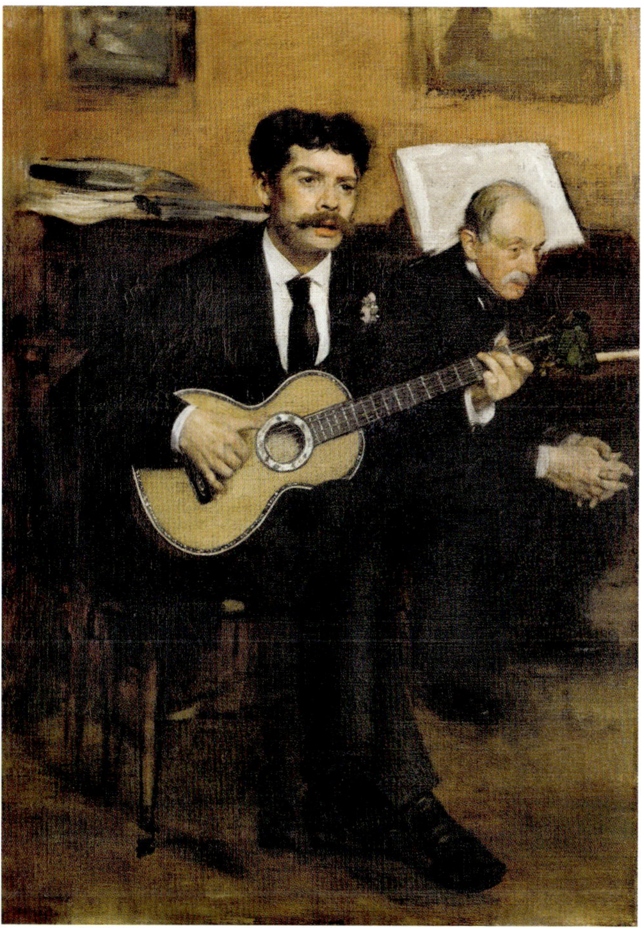

Fig. 26

surrounded by music, is ennobled (perhaps beatified) by the experience. Pagans, in making of his guitar a sounding body, has in turn made of De Gas an energised, 'live' listener, almost like sending a current through a wire. The activity is electrical and neuronal: circuits are crackling. This painting and others like it contradict the notion of passive listener as put forward by Adorno. In his pronouncements on the dangers and deceptions of Wagner's *Gesamtkunstwerk*, Adorno insisted

---

Fig. 25. James McNeill Whistler
Becquet (The Fiddler), 1859
Etching, 25.7 × 18.7 cm
The David and Alfred Smart
Museum of Art, The University
of Chicago, Chicago, Gift of
Brenda F. and Joseph V. Smith,
2004.149

Fig. 26. Edgar Degas
*Degas's Father Listening to
Lorenzo Pagans Playing the Guitar*,
between 1871 and 1872
Oil on canvas, 54.5 × 39.5 cm
Musée d'Orsay, Paris,
RF 3736

on the 'doziness' of the ear, which he called an 'archaic' organ compared to the eye: 'The eye is always the organ of effort, work, concentration; it apprehends something specific in an unambiguous way. The ear, in contrast, is unconcentrated and passive.'[26] Auguste de Gas does not look at anything in particular, suggesting that his experience of the music is something more interiorised – but no less powerful for that.

The sense of the listener's very engaged role emerges in personal recollections from the Romantic period and afterwards. George Sand felt a particular poignancy in this deep spiritual bond with the producer of the music. As she wrote to Liszt, 'My goodness, I feel your music too intensely not to have already heard its like with you somewhere, before we were born.'[27] Alphonse de Lamartine, for his part, characterised Liszt as a 'celestial spirit', 'angel' and 'metaphysical musician . . . he sings symphonies of the heavens more than melodies of the earth'.[28] The spiritualised, celestial quality of music that looms so large in these descriptions would shift, over the course of the nineteenth century, to a more scientistic, neuropsychological analysis of music's effects on the listener. The philosopher Paul Souriau (1852–1926), for example, likened aesthetic experience to the hypnotic state, though he noted that temporal arts such as music induce a more active contemplation, 'a rapid flow of ideas, images and emotions that does not give our mind a moment's respite'.[29] Souriau further asserted that when we arrive at pure musical contemplation, reality no longer exists for us. 'Where are we? In the immaterial and almost imaginary world of sounds. . . . It seems that we are out of our depth, that we are floating in empty space.'[30] But this model of suggestibility does not mean, for commentators of the period, that listening lacks effort or purpose.

On the contrary, Hippolyte Fierens-Gevaert (speaking of Wagner's works) believed that substantial intellectual effort, in proportion to the music's power over the nervous system, was required of the listener to obtain maximum emotional effect: 'It is not the person who listens with the most feeling who is always rewarded the most, but rather the person who has thought the most. As Wagner's music acts strongly on the senses, the listener finds himself under an almost paradoxical obligation to exert a great deal of intelligence in order to receive the maximum of nervous commotion.'[31] In these beliefs, commentators of the 1880s and 1890s were following precepts put forth much earlier by Arthur Schopenhauer that were repopularised during the vogue for Wagner.[32] In the words of art historian Paul Smith, Schopenhauer's belief was that 'music and musical art enable the listener or spectator to shed illusions of personal identity and achieve a selfless perspective . . . that musical art induces a dissipation of the egoistic self'.[33]

If the music listener were conceded to join the performer on a more cerebral plane, mutually absorbed in a spiritual communion, still neither one stood on the same intellectual pedestal as the composer. Such a figure, far removed from the pandering prestidigitations of the concert performer or the visual crutches of the common listener, was thought to inhabit a quasi-Olympian sphere of pure music. Nourished by the myth of Beethoven, who had been able to write his most sublime symphonies after losing his hearing, much contemporary discourse credited composers with superhuman faculties. Chief among these was 'interior listening', ascribed to writers of music who had no need of a piano to 'hear' what their works sounded like during the process of composition. As Carl Maria von Weber wrote, 'But how differently does he create whose *inner ear* is the sole judge of the things he has found and of what should be kept.'[34] This interior ear is central to the paradigmatic engraving of Beethoven by Aimé de Lemud, shown at the Salon of 1864 (fig. 27). Lemud sets up a sharp contrast between the composer slumped over his keyboard and the celestial orchestra beyond, which plays a music only heard in dream.[35]

Pierre Bonnard's *Portrait of the Composer Claude Terrasse with His Two Sons* (cat. 48) seems to endorse this view of composition as an activity of the mind rather than a manual, scribal art. At the same time, the inclusion of Terrasse's two children at the right side of the painting hints at a balance of obligations in the composer's life with the potential to compromise intense interior listening. Children, no doubt, were the inspiration and intended audience for the *Petit Solfège illustré*, a co-production of Terrasse and Bonnard. Yet children also interrupt, however charmingly, the meditative solitude that is a necessary condition of the composer's output. Liszt had alluded to much the same tension when he wrote to George Sand in 1837 that the artist, even in society (as Liszt very much was, at least before taking minor religious orders), must keep a quiet corner in his soul for his creative work: 'Divine, elusive forms appear before him, colours such as the most beautiful flowers in the brightness of spring never offered to his eyes; he hears the eternal harmony whose cadence reigns over worlds, and all the voices of creation come together for him in a marvellous concert.'[36] Achieving a state of mind in which such a 'marvellous concert' can be heard is a struggle that seems to register in Terrasse's equivocal expression.

Painters can be said to have had a special stake in these portraits, no matter how the balance of work versus outside pressures was accounted for, because of the relation to painters' self-image and the implicit claim for association. Although painters were creators, they could never overcome the fact that not just the tools but also the products of their art were obstinately material. Composers, on the other hand, used printed scores and physical instruments to

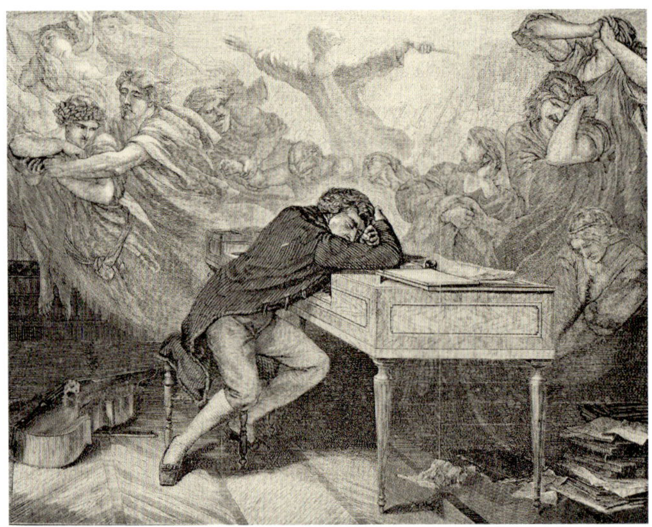

Fig. 27

produce something that, in the end, was as insubstantial and ephemeral as breath. Starting in the Romantic period, a fascination with music's immateriality had accounted for a major part of its prestige – and this conviction showed few signs of waning, even well into the twentieth century.

MAKING MUSIC IN PAINTING

Paradoxically, it was painters' disadvantageous position with regard to composers, allied with their acceptance of music as a paradigm for their own art, that spurred many of them to seek pictorial equivalents for musical experience. The very same 'baths' of sound that had drenched Wagnerian listeners – the very same intensity that had consumed listeners or subjected them to violent nervous attacks – did these not suggest some intriguing new directions for the pictorial art? What better way for painters to prove to doubters the supremacy of their own art than to record, in permanent

Fig. 27. **Aimé de Lemud**
Ludwig van Beethoven, 1864
Engraving, 22 × 17 cm
Bibliothèque Nationale de France,
Département Musique, Paris
Est. Beethoven 061

Fig. 28. **Léon Lhermitte**
The Quartet, 1881
Charcoal, 82 × 111.5 cm
Musée d'Orsay, Paris, on long term
loan at the Musée du Louvre,
Gift of Charles Hayem, 1898,
RF 2138 recto

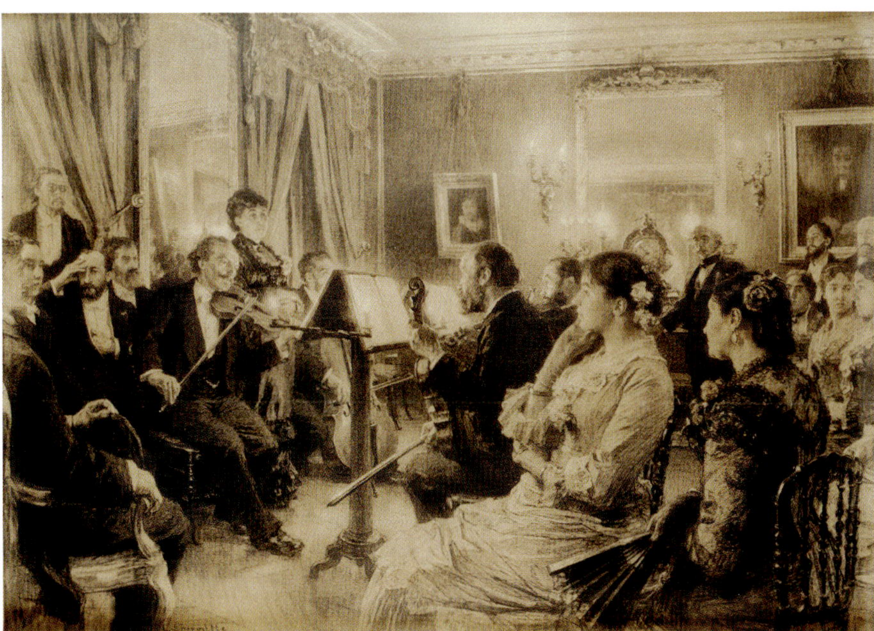

Fig. 28

material form, something of the experience of music?
(Not music itself; that was being taken care of by the sound
engineers, as Debussy lamented in 1913: 'In a time like ours,
when the genius of engineers has reached such undreamed
of proportions, one can hear famous pieces of music as easily
as one can buy a glass of beer. . . . Should we not fear this
domestication of sound, this magic preserved in a disc that
anyone can awaken at will?')[37] The impulse to capture music's
effects, besides being a worthy pictorial challenge, offered
a corrective to the asymmetric power relations alluded to
at the outset of this essay – giving artists the upper hand.

In Léon Lhermitte's *The Quartet* (fig. 28), for example,
the figures as well as the details of the bourgeois interior
are carefully and clearly delineated: music stands at
centre, chamber musicians gathered round with their
instruments, tall curtained windows and a crowd of listeners.
The play of light in the room is also a crucial feature,
somehow inseparable from the musical proceedings. It is
as if Lhermitte's masterful control of the light values and
reflections in the room is telling us something about what
that musical experience was *like* (both the kind of music
and how it was played). In the guise of the female listener in
profile in the foreground, we get a sense of that particular
occasion and what it was like to be there.

In *Portrait of the Violinist Irma Sèthe* by Théo van
Rysselberghe (cat. 57), the title figure is painted with great,
shining clarity against an interior wall. The unorthodox
spatial arrangements in the painting mean that the seated

listener, presumably Irma's sister (Maria?), is hidden except
for her lower half. Already, this monumental canvas gives
such primacy to the violinist that it seems heavily to favour
performing over listening. The hand in the listener's lap offers
some clues to a more complicated reading, however. One
interesting feature of this hand is that it is directly in the line
of the violinist's bowing arm. That is, if Irma fully extended
her right arm, her hand would be in the very same position, on
the canvas, as her sister's. This suggests a close connection
between the figures: not that one is eclipsing the other but
that each is in some way a part of the other.

Another interesting thing about this hand is the strange
reminiscence it offers of Fernand Khnopff's 1883 painting
Listening to Schumann (fig. 29).[38] That work places the listener
at centre, her right hand covering her face. Van Rysselberghe's
painting could be said to 'correct' the disproportionate
emphasis on the listener, restoring the performer's customary
limelight. But even though Khnopff's front-and-centre listener
also places a hand in her lap, it is not this hand that the Sèthe
sister's hand most resembles. The most eerie echo is with
the disembodied hand of the pianist in *Listening to Schumann*,
which seems almost to have been imported. This hand,
extended over the keys in the piano's high treble, is the sole
proof in Khnopff's canvas that music is being made; in Van
Rysselberghe's composition, the back-room sitter's hand is the
best indication that music is being listened to. Each painting
is a kind of limit case showing one activity's dependence
on the other. Just as the position of each central figure's head
and arms is maximally expressive of the given activity, so
the detached hand of each 'secondary' figure does the same
work of signification, but with minimal means.

Thus, despite their apparent mismatch in scale and
prominence, the two figures in each painting do balance or
complete each other. In so doing, they offer the beholder
access to a musical experience whose ephemerality should
have been fatal to its ever being remembered. In this sense,
they offer a remedy for the loss that Mauclair lamented in
Servitude et grandeur littéraires, a memoir of the years 1890
to 1900: 'When very old people talked to us about the playing
of Chopin or Liszt, about the mimicry of Frédérick-Lemaître,
about the voice of La Malibran, saying to us, "You should
have seen or heard them," we sensed that they must have
witnessed something extraordinary and inimitable, and our
feeling was reinforced by a thousand testimonials: and yet
this something is entirely destroyed, and we are reduced to
trusting them, we *know* that Liszt and Chopin, La Malibran
or Frédérick, were extraordinary enchanters, but we no longer
feel it.'[39] In these small gestures of musical remembrance
and commemoration, painters help us feel the power of the
experience while making a claim for the enduring power of
their own art.

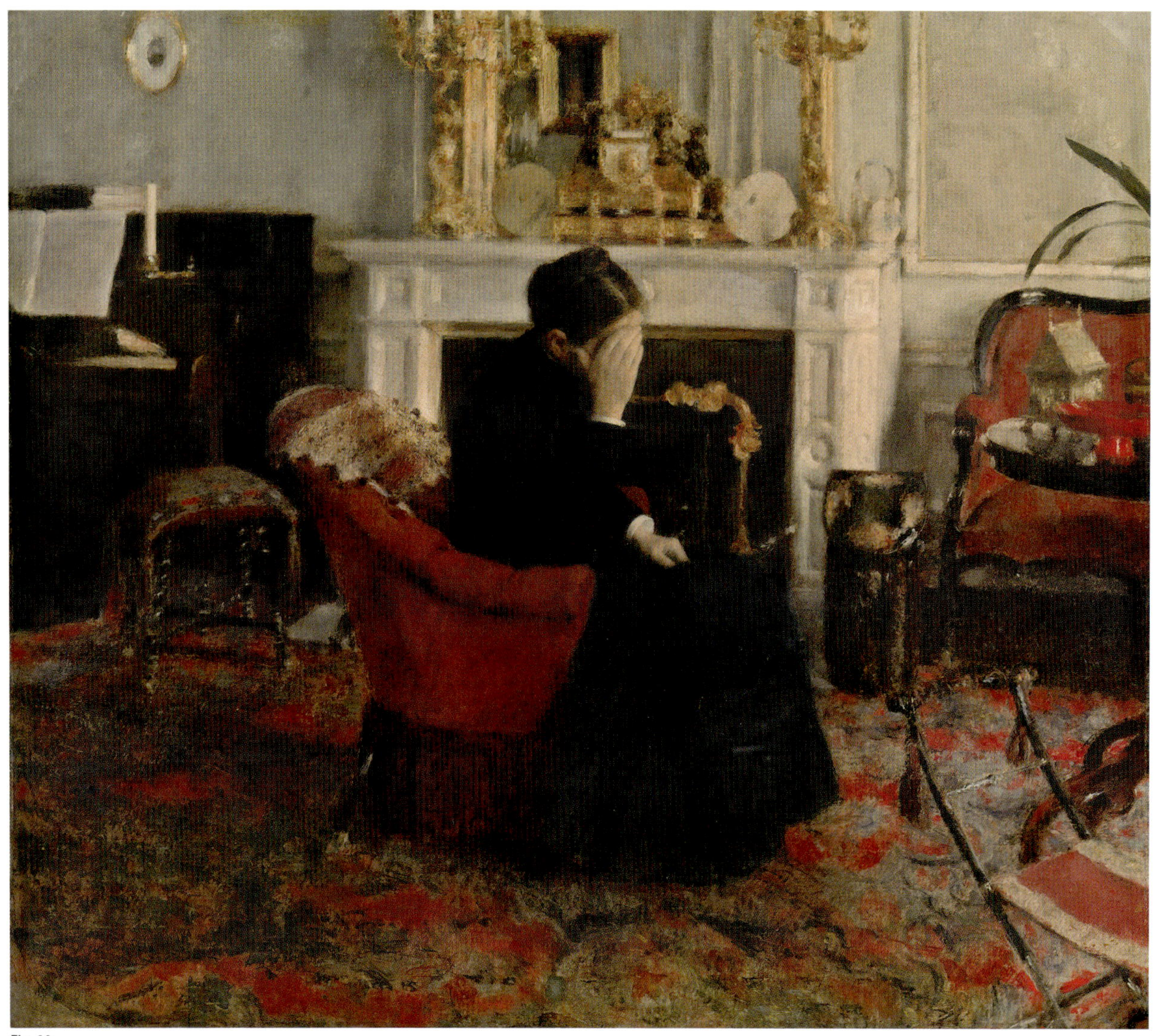

Fig. 29. **Fernand Khnopff**
Listening to Schumann, 1883
Oil on canvas, 101.5 × 116.5 cm
Musées Royaux des Beaux-Arts
de Belgique, Brussels,
6366

[1] Ernest Chausson, *Écrits inédits : Journaux intimes. Roman de jeunesse. Correspondance*, eds. Jean Gallois and Isabelle Bretaudeau, Monaco, Éditions du Rocher, 1999, p. 10.

[2] Ibid., p. 60. This is Fantin-Latour's *L'Anniversaire*, no. 7 in Germain Hédiard's catalogue raisonné.

[3] Maurice Denis, *Henry Lerolle et ses amis*, Paris, Imprimerie Duranton, 1930, p. 6.

[4] Ibid., p. 7.

[5] Ibid., pp. 8–9.

[6] Allison Morehead, 'A Certain *tour d'esprit*: Édouard Vuillard's *The Lerolle Salon*', in *Looking and Listening in Nineteenth-Century France*, exhibition catalogue, Chicago, Smart Museum of Art, University of Chicago, 2007, pp. 73–81.

[7] Sidonie-Gabrielle Colette, 'Un salon de musique en 1900', in *Maurice Ravel par quelques-uns de ses familiers*, Paris, Éditions du Tambourinaire, 1939, p. 118.

[8] Jean-Michel Nectoux, *Une famille d'artistes en 1900: Les Saint-Marceaux*, Paris, Réunion des Musées Nationaux, 1992, p. 55.

[9] Ibid., p. 5.

[10] Camille Mauclair, 'Le Symbolisme en France', *L'Art en silence*, Paris, 1901, p. 195; and *Servitude et grandeur littéraires*, Paris, Ollendorff, 1922, p. 217.

[11] English edition: *To Myself: Notes on Life, Art and Artists by Odilon Redon*, trans. Mira Jacob and L. Wasserman, New York, Braziller, 1968. For more on the relationship between Fantin and Redon, and their musical interests, see Anne Leonard, 'To Themselves: Music in the Art of Henri Fantin-Latour and Odilon Redon', *Imago Musicae* XXXVII–XXVIII, 2014–2015, pp. 127–49.

[12] 'My piano and I are like a sailor and his frigate, or like an Arab and his steed, even more perhaps, for my piano, thus far, it is me, it's my word, it's my life.' This letter, written to M. Adolphe Pictet from Chambéry in September 1837, appears in Franz Liszt, *Lettres d'un bachelier ès musique*, ed. Rémy Stricker, [Bègles], Le Castor Astral, 1991, p. 48.

[13] E. T. A. Hoffmann, 'Les maîtres-chanteurs', *Contes fantastiques d'Hoffmann*, trans. Xavier Marmier, Paris, Charpentier, 1843, p. 32.

[14] Ferdinand Des Robert, 'Aimé de Lemud', *L'Austrasie*, no. 5, July 1906.

[15] For more on this issue, see June Hargrove, 'Paul Gauguin: Sensing the Infinite', in *Sensational Religion: Sensory Cultures in Material Practice*, ed. Sally M. Promey, New Haven, Yale University Press, 2014, pp. 341–54; esp. p. 351, 'Colour became for Gauguin the musical medium that would catapult his art from mundane mimesis to the creative sublime.'

[16] Jules-Gabriel Janin, *L'Été à Paris*, Paris, Curmer, 1844, p. 241.

[17] Hector Berlioz, *Journal des débats*, 12 November 1861; quoted in Elisabeth Bernard, 'Jules Pasdeloup et les Concerts Populaires', *Revue de musicologie* 57, no. 2 (1971), p. 151.

[18] Theodor Adorno, *In Search of Wagner*, trans. Rodney Livingstone, London, NLB, 1981, p. 32.

[19] Ibid., p. 90.

[20] Ibid., p. 91.

[21] Martial de Villemoune, 'De l'imprécis en musique', *L'Art et la Vie* 2, 1894, p. 736. De Villemoune is quoting from an 1892 edition of Bergson's doctoral thesis, originally published in 1888; the passage can be found in Henri Bergson, *Essai sur les données immédiates de la conscience*, Paris, Presses Universitaires de France, 1991, p. 11.

[22] Plato, *Republic* III, 401d, quoted in Vladimir Jankélévitch, *La musique et l'ineffable*, Paris, Armand Colin, 1961, p. 7.

[23] Camille Mauclair, 'Eaux-fortes d'après l'orchestre', in *La religion de la musique* ([1909]; Paris, Fischbacher, 1928, p. 3.

[24] From Claude Debussy, *Monsieur Croche Antidilettante*; used as an epigraph to Sacheverell Sitwell, *Liszt*, trans. Françoise Vernan, Paris, Buchet-Chastel, 1961.

[25] This famously mutilated painting was a cause for dispute between the two painters. An account of the incident is given in Julie Manet, *Journal (1893-1899): sa jeunesse parmi les peintres impressionnistes et les hommes de lettres*, Paris, Klincksieck, 1979, p. 72.

[26] Adorno, *In Search of Wagner*, *op. cit.*, pp. 99–100.

[27] George Sand, *Correspondance*, ed. Georges Lubin, Paris, Garnier Frères, 1964, vol. 2, p. 871. This is letter 930 of the published correspondence, written in Nohant on 21 April 1835.

[28] Alphonse de Lamartine, *Cours familier de littérature*, tome 10, Paris, 1860, pp. 188–89.

[29] Paul Souriau, *La Suggestion dans l'art*, Paris, Félix Alcan, 1893, p. 6.

[30] Ibid., p. 70.

[31] Hippolyte Fierens-Gevaert, *La Tristesse contemporaine : essai sur les grands courants moraux et intellectuels du XIXᵉ siècle*, Paris, Félix Alcan, 1899, p. 131.

[32] Examples of this vulgarization include Théodule Ribot's *La philosophie de Schopenhauer*, published in 1874 and again in 1885, and Elme-Marie Caro's Schopenhauer lectures given at the Collège de France in winter 1878–1879. One of Caro's auditors was Georges Rodenbach, who reprised the ideas in his own lecture series upon his return to Belgium. See Francine-Claire Legrand, 'Fernand Khnopff – Perfect Symbolist', *Apollo*, n.s. 85 (April 1967), p. 284; and Pierre Maes, *Georges Rodenbach: 1855–1898*, Gembloux, Duculot, 1952, pp. 56, 58.

[33] Paul Smith, *Seurat and the Avant-Garde*, New Haven and London, 1997, p. 5. Smith elaborates later in the book that under Schopenhauer's theory, 'music shows the perceiver that what he or she construes as self is in fact only an illusion of Representation, and thus it induces a state of self-negation, in which the subject no longer seeks gratification in the illusory perceptual objects' (p. 93).

[34] Carl Maria von Weber, *La Vie d'un musicien et autres écrits*, trans. Lucienne Gérardin, ed. Gérard Condé, Paris, J.-C. Lattès, 1986, p. 29. Emphasis in original.

[35] This is the interpretation of Charles de Meixmoron de Dombasle in *Aimé de Lemud*, Nancy, Édition de la 'Revue publique illustrée', 1912, p. 14.

[36] Liszt, *Lettres, op. cit.*, pp. 31–32. This letter is dated Paris, 30 April 1837.

[37] Claude Debussy, 'Concerts Colonne', review for the Société Internationale de Musique, 15 May 1913; reprinted in *Debussy on Music*, trans. and ed. Richard Langham Smith, New York, Alfred A. Knopf, 1977, p. 288.

[38] Both Khnopff and Van Rysselberghe exhibited with Les XX, the Brussels-based avant-garde artists' group that programmed concerts of new music in tandem with its annual salons. Van Rysselberghe would certainly have known *Listening to Schumann*, which was shown at the Cercle Artistique in 1883 and at the Salon des XX in 1886.

[39] Mauclair, *Servitude et grandeur littéraires, op. cit.*, pp. 222–3.

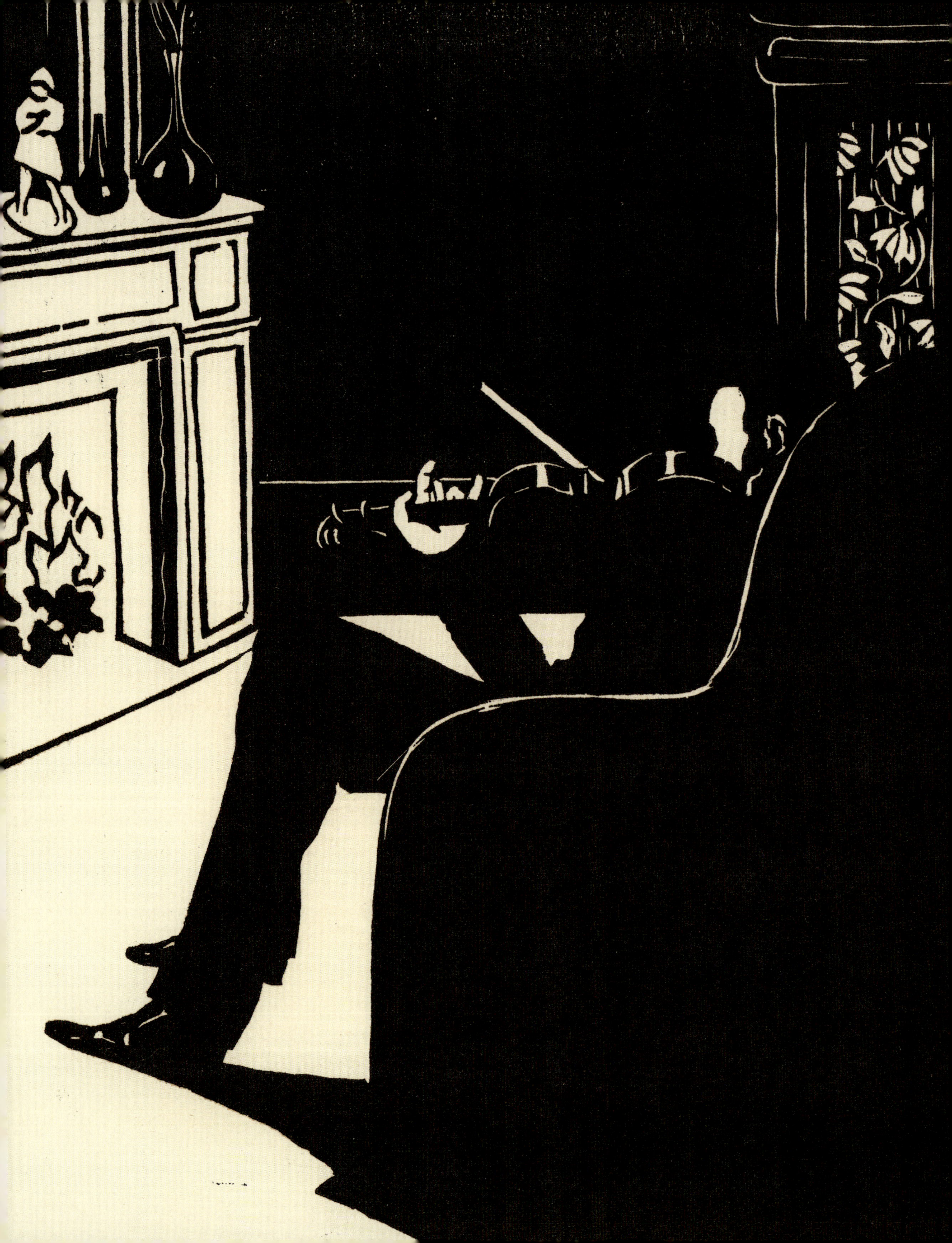

from steinway to steinlen: aspects of musical illustration

Belinda Thomson

The late nineteenth century was a lively period for printmaking in Paris. This can be attributed to various factors: the immense increase in the number of illustrated periodicals hungry for illustrations, the new and versatile technical means of producing images cheaply and attractively, particularly colour lithography and photomechanical reproduction, and finally the emergence of collectors eager to buy colour prints. Sheet music – hitherto a rather traditional and austere branch of publishing – was caught up in this broad movement, and music publishers started to appreciate the added value that artists could bring to song sheets and piano scores, resulting in what one writer has called a 'golden age of musical illustration'.[1]

The convergence between the domains of the visual and the aural, that is between the graphic arts and music, took diverse forms, ranging from the relatively new alliance represented by piano scores and popular song sheets to the perennial field of caricature. Sheet music and illustrated albums offered new artistic opportunities, while the design of posters to promote operas, concerts and café concerts guaranteed the artists' images wide dissemination (cat. 77). For certain artists like Jules Chéret (cat. 76 and 78), Théophile Alexandre Steinlen (cat. 49), Henri Rivière, Henri-Gabriel Ibels and George Auriol (cat. 85), musical illustration offered a steady stream of work. For others, like Maurice Denis (cat. 81) or Jacques Villon (cat. 86), it was a welcome opportunity to diversify their activities. To succeed in the commercial sphere meant negotiating contracts with some hard-headed businessmen and not all artists felt at home in the cut and thrust world of commercial publishing. Alongside the mass-produced illustrations, there were more discreet, non-commercial projects such as designing programmes for private concerts: Degas undertook one for friends in 1884,[2] and Denis for his sister-in-law in 1898.[3] Somewhere between these extremes stand the collaborative publishing ventures of Pierre Bonnard and Claude Terrasse.

HUMOUR AND MUSICAL INSTRUMENTS

The impact made upon society by certain musical instruments or certain styles of music – such as the bravura pianistic displays of Franz Liszt and the overpowering, ear-splitting

Cat. 70
Félix Vallotton
The Violin, Musical Instruments, III, 1896
(detail, cat. 70, p. 148)

volume of Richard Wagner's operas – provided ready opportunities for caricature in the earlier years of the century. A lively satirical tradition was established by Honoré Daumier and Gavarni in France, and John Leech and Charles Keene in Britain. Caricaturists had a tendency to fall back on tried and tested visual jokes. For example, that perennial scourge of urban living, noise pollution, which could render life intolerable for those forced to coexist or share a party wall with the inexpert piano player, inspired *Punch* cartoonist John Leech's cartoon of 1842 (fig. 30). The music that is the cause of the distress, *The Battle of Prague*, is even specified, its title alone enough to conjure an idea of thumping and repetitive militaristic rhythms.[4] The image was recycled two decades later, virtually unchanged, by George du Maurier.[5] New-fangled consumer goods often give rise to humour and, in 1867, the mass rush to procure the latest technological marvel, Steinway pianos, following the firm's triumphant success at the Paris Exposition Universelle, was lampooned by the French cartoonist Cham (fig. 31). We see jostling men besieging the Steinway representative, not wielding cheque books but holding out eager fingers towards the keyboard, implying a desire to play the instrument themselves rather than simply to buy one to impress their female companions. The awkwardness of moving pianos was another stock joke. One finds various examples of the fun cartoonists had at the expense of the tricky manoeuvring of the instrument up stairs, complicated in the case of Henri Detouche's 1884 image by the head-on confrontation, on a typical Parisian winding stair, with a descending coffin.[6] And then the slightly sleazy seductiveness associated with the music lesson or piano duet, which went back at least to the seventeenth century, was a theme musical illustrators, as well as caricaturists, continuously exploited. In 1903 we see it in both Georges Redon's sheet music cover for *Intimate Waltz* (cat. 87), and Henri Meunier's image for *Le Rire* (cat. 90), whose witty caption recycled a pun from decades earlier on the syllables associated with *solfège*.

The line between caricature and illustration is not always clear, and where the instrument itself, particularly the various woodwind and brass instruments, required extreme, distorting effort to play, artists often resorted to humour. Louis Anquetin's promotional image for the trombonist Marguerite Dufay (cat. 75) emphasises her powerful biceps, producing an exuberant image to match the sound she produced. In 1893 Charles Maurin and Henri de Toulouse-Lautrec were closely allied in their experimental printmaking activities, trying out new spatter and sugar-resistant techniques, and in one instance similar musical subjects: the oboist in Maurin's *Orchestra Pit* (cat. 64) and the bassoonist Désiré Dihau in Lautrec's print are both given somewhat demonic characteristics (cat. 67). In Lautrec's

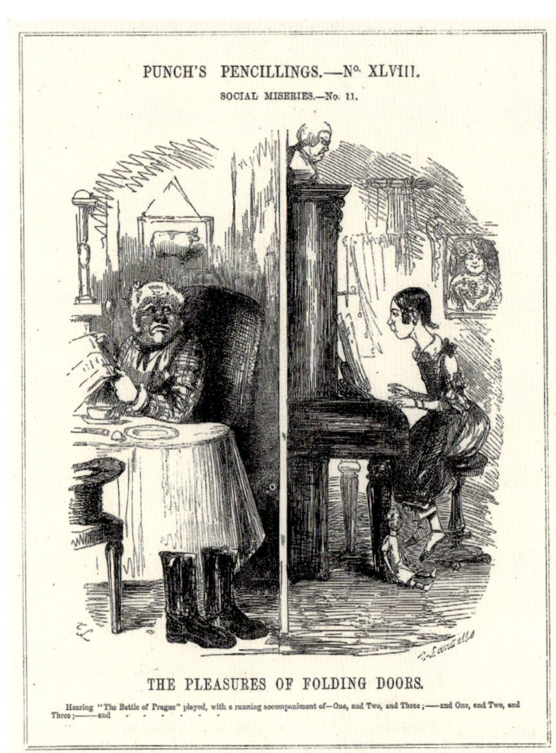

Fig. 30

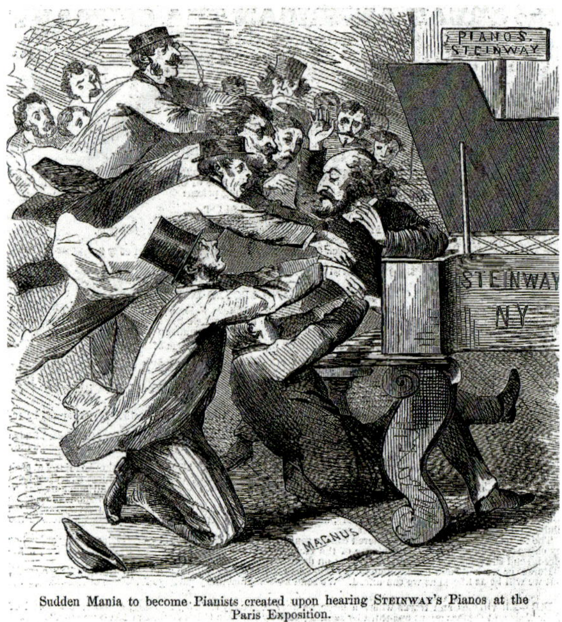

Fig. 31

Fig. 30. **John Leech and E. Landelles**
The Pleasures of Folding Doors,
from *Punch's Pencillings,* no. XLVIII,
Social Miseries no. 11, 1842
Private collection

Fig. 31. **Cham**
'Sudden Mania to become Pianists
created upon hearing Steinway's
Pianos at the Paris Exposition',
Harpers Weekly, 10 August 1867

poster for Jane Avril, the obstructive head of the double bass, that so often obtruded itself between audience members and performers on stage, contributes its distinctive form to the resulting design (cat. 74). In the case of Louis Legrand's *Teutonophony* (cat. 66), it is not so much humour as national stereotype that is invoked, for not only the title but the provincial setting and characterisation of the musician, soon to be rewarded by a foaming *stein* of beer proffered by his daughter, add up to a clichéd view of the typical player of the euphonium. Indeed, peripatetic brass bands originating from Alsace were a feature of the musical life of the time. Félix Vallotton made a memorable series of six woodcuts dedicated to different instrumentalists (cat. 68–73). Although he apparently used contemporary musicians as his models, for instance Eugène Ysaÿe for the violinist and Raoul Pugno for the pianist, he adapted his settings to the assumed class status of the typical player of each instrument. Thus his flautist plays in an exquisite interior to an elegant white cat and his guitarist plays in a winter garden, whereas his cellist keeps time in an unadorned interior and his cornet player – the instrument of the working class man, not of the bourgeois – exerts himself in a modest room by the light of a candle. As Jules Renard put it, Vallotton had a 'troubling way of being simple'.[7]

ARTISTS AND MUSICAL PUBLISHERS

Vallotton was at the forefront of the revival of the black-and-white woodcut technique in the 1890s, but it was Jules Chéret's experiments with colour lithography in the 1860s that really kick-started the boom in printmaking. Chéret produced his signature posters, printed with three or more coloured inks, in a lively neo-rococo style that evoked Giambattista Tiepolo. His poster for the Ambassadeurs *café-concert* uses lettering and bright prismatic colours, as well as the device of an array of playing cards to convey detailed information about the performers, whilst fanciful figures wielding tambourine, cymbals and cello circle around the central lyre (cat. 76). Such was Chéret's commercial success that he founded his own print company, Chaix, an effective way of cutting out the middleman. His typically light-hearted tone inspired many followers, including Bonnard.

As well as for posters there is no doubt that a huge demand existed for sheet music at this period, and there were many minor music publishers operating cheek by jowl with the artists on the lower slopes of Montmartre. The ability to read music was far more widespread than it is today, hence the number of journals offering sheet music as a bonus for their subscribers. This was not just a ploy of music journals like *Le Ménéstrel*; subscribers of such daily newspapers as *Le Figaro* and *L'Intransigeant* were also offered free gifts of new music to cut out and keep. No art work was involved here, but certain publishers cottoned on to the advantage of enhancing their scores with attractive cover illustrations. One such was the 'publisher-philanthropist-librettist-dramatist' Georges Hartmann (1843–1900).[8] He made a fortune from publishing piano transcriptions of the popular operas of the day. Among the composers he promoted were Georges Bizet, César Franck, Édouard Lalo, Camille Saint-Saëns and Jules Massenet. As well as writing opera libretti himself, Hartmann commissioned opera posters and scores in the 1870s and 1880s from such artists as Célestin Nanteuil and Georges Clairin. In 1874, still only thirty-one, he commissioned Auguste Renoir to paint a life-size portrait of his wife, the opera singer Louise Grémont (cat. 26). How Renoir and Hartmann met is not known, although it may have been through their mutual friendship with the music critic Edmond Maître. (Certainly Renoir enjoyed music, attending Pasdeloup concerts with Bazille in the 1860s and in the 1870s moving in musical and theatrical circles in the rue Saint Georges; indeed his painting *Leaving the Conservatory* (1876, Barnes Foundation) was acquired by the composer Chabrier.) Renoir's portrait, set in their well-appointed apartment – probably 19, boulevard de la Madeleine, which was Hartmann's address in 1875 – hints at the couple's professional involvement with music. Behind the model, sumptuously dressed in black, he features an enormous ebony grand piano piled with musical scores, a strong black horizontal to offset her verticality. Madame Hartmann is not otherwise connected with the instrument, but a younger woman, her accompanist perhaps, barely glimpsed in the upper left corner of the composition, is apparently playing it. When Hartmann's business failed in 1890, he sold it to his major rival, Henri Heugel, publisher of *Le Ménéstrel*, France's principal music journal. It was presumably this deal that allowed Hartmann to re-emerge as representative of the German music publishers, Schott, and as the major financial backer of Claude Debussy in the 1890s, but at his death in 1900, when the picture came to the Luxembourg, his affairs were in some disarray.

Despite the high profile of such artists as Toulouse-Lautrec and Bonnard, we know surprisingly little about the circumstances in which they undertook musical commissions. Occasionally from the artists' correspondence we gain an insight into the realities of working for such big name publishers, but it is rare to marry those up with pertinent information on the musicians' side. Clearly, in the musical sphere, as in that of avant-garde theatre, social networks existed and facilitated cross-disciplinary creative undertakings. Steinlen, one of the most prolific musical illustrators, produced nearly three hundred and fifty musical designs, including one hundred and fifty for popular scores, for such publishers as Ondet, Enoch and Heugel, and singers such as Aristide Bruant, Maurice Boukay, Paul Delmet and Marcel Legay. In 1889 Steinlen was commissioned by *La Semaine artistique et musicale* to illustrate a series of piano music supplements featuring fashionable composers like Cécile Chaminade, Francis Thomé (cat. 49) and Henri Maréchal, which presumably made him some serious money. However, the rewards were scant for artists who only occasionally picked up such work. Henri-Gabriel Ibels, for instance, was often hard up, despite producing many song sheet cover designs popularising cabaret songs. These followed a set pattern, a simple folded sheet of paper printed on the cover with an image relating to the content of the song, the words and music appearing on the opened double page, the back page given over to advertisements. These so-called 'petits formats' enabled the amateur musician to follow the melody line for one franc, or to try out the piano accompaniment as well for an outlay of three.[9] Armand Seguin was paid just fifteen francs for a song sheet cover in 1897, complaining that *Le Journal* and *Le Courrier français* were bad payers. 'It's not all about doing the drawings, but about placing them,' he observed, concluding that in his circumstances such work was too precarious and a distraction.[10]

It is within this economic and artistic context that we should understand the ambitions and immensely creative musico-artistic relationship Bonnard had with his sister Andrée and brother-in-law Claude Terrasse, a composer who trained at the École Niedermeyer. The couple were married in September 1890, a year after Terrasse had secured a teaching job in Arcachon. As dowry, Andrée brought two grand pianos to their new home, the Villa Bach. Although Bonnard's collaboration with Terrasse is well known (notably for the *Almanach illustré du Père Ubu* projects in the later 1890s), recently published sketches, studies and sketchbook pages reveal how consistently he engaged with musical illustration between 1891 and 1895.[11] The Terrasse marriage was a happy one from all appearances, but initially the love match did not meet with parental acceptance, presumably due to the social gulf between the families.[12] The Bonnards were *rentiers* and Bonnard *père*, from the Dauphiné, was a *chef de bureau* in the Ministère de la Guerre; Terrasse's father, living apart from his wife, was a self-made man from L'Arbresle (Rhône) working in the textile industry. Reading between the lines of correspondence, just as Bonnard's reputation as a poster designer and independent painter was beginning to take off in Paris, enabling him to drop his hated law studies, he clearly felt a responsibility to help the Terrasses get established in Arcachon, prolonging his stays there to that end.[13] At the Villa Bach, Bonnard willingly immersed himself in the 'waves of music' the couple produced, whilst ensuring that the muse of Painting was avenged by the 'waves of green, blue and yellow' flowing from his paint box.[14]

If Bonnard's portrait of his sister at the piano probably relates to one of their ambitious weekly in-house concerts (cat. 50), the immediate prompt for its decorative Japoniste design and tender colour scheme may have been Steinlen. It seems likely that Andrée owned the score Steinlen designed for Francis Thomé's *Scherzo* (cat. 49), since Thomé, originally from Mauritius, had been her own piano teacher in Paris. Nor can it be coincidental that it was two further piano works by Thomé, *Mandoline, sérénade espagnole* and *Espièglerie*, published with uninspiring covers by H. Lemoine in 1883 and 1885 respectively, that prompted Bonnard to devise his own ingenious and inventive covers, although neither was eventually published (fig. 32). He was clearly working on these projected piano scores at the same moment, probably in Arcachon in 1891.[15] Both feature a young woman: the mandolin player could be Andrée, while the girl with the mischievous cat looks like his cousin Berthe Schaedelin.

Andrée features in Bonnard's inventive design for Terrasse's *Suite for Piano* (cat. 83) with its variations on the treble clef, which sadly seems not to have been taken up by the Brussels branch of the German music publisher A. Cranz, despite complex negotiations. The correspondence implies that, were publication to have gone ahead, it would have been at the musician's and artist's own financial risk.[16] One piano score design of Bonnard's that did get into print in 1891 was a promotional spin-off from his successful poster for the France-Champagne brand, intriguing evidence of the popularity of salon waltzes at this date (cat. 82). Published by P. Schott, the illustration, leaving a rectangular reserve for the wording, develops the theme used in the poster: a giddy girl surrounded by effervescent bubbles and moustachioed male admirers. In spring 1891 Bonnard and Terrasse also began work on their *Petit Solfège illustré* (cat. 80). Bonnard evidently puzzled over how best to approach the challenge, citing ancient missals and Japanese prints. Among his sources it would appear that he also referred to Maurice Boutet de Monvel and his *Traditional Songs for Small Children* (cat. 79).[17] But he substituted for the clear-cut, English-influenced manner of de Monvel his own more quirky and playful draughtsmanship. The *solfège* project proceeded quickly at first, with Terrasse dreaming of large print runs and of pitching the publication to schools.[18] However, after several false starts, it was not until 1893, having received late page proofs from the Grenoble printer Allier, that they persuaded Quantin to publish it and only by economising on production costs: the cover was no longer to be 'in coloured grain leather' but in 'grey cloth'. At this juncture it was Andrée, with her brother, who was making design decisions, which Terrasse confidently left in their hands.[19] The resulting album and its many preparatory studies have become collectors' items today. Delightful for young and old though they are, one would be interested

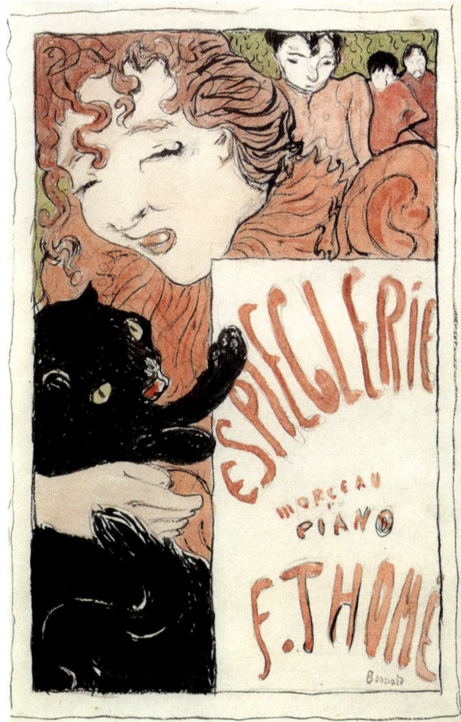

Fig. 32

to know whether the technical information Bonnard had to convey – closely following Terrasse's guidelines – was elucidated or obscured by the inspired illustrations.

Petites Scènes familières, an album of piano music by Terrasse based on songs by Franc-Nohain, was begun in 1893, but did not finally reach published form until 1895, with the music publisher Froment (cat. 84). A more straightforward undertaking from the artist's point of view, its black and white drawings are responsive both to the playful content of the musical pieces and to life in the growing Terrasse family in Arcachon and at the Bonnard family home at Le Grand Lemps.

The ups and downs of Bonnard's experience with musical publishing throw into sharp relief the fact that at this era of enticing opportunities, success was by no means a given. It was rare to find the disinterested approach of a publisher like Edmond Bailly, who commissioned original lithography from Maurice Denis to accompany Debussy's *La Damoiselle élue* (a score that can be glimpsed in the

photograph by Van de Velde, cat. 55), achieving a harmonious congruence between musician and artist: most music publishers were hard-nosed operators. While there is much to enjoy among the illustrative prints that conformed to the commercial demands of the day, there were also a number of inspired potential designs that slipped through the net and, were it not for the fame of the artists concerned, would have been lost to posterity.

[1] Michel Desproges, in *Chansons sensuelles, le petit format illustré et la chanson à texte au tournant du siècle*, Paris, Les Éditions Fortin, 2004.

[2] In 1884 Degas tried out a number of designs involving a prominent double bass for the programme for a 'Soirée artistique' to be performed by former pupils of the Lycée de Nantes, of which one was sold at Christie's, New York, 13 November 2015, lot 1066. The transfer lithograph is reproduced in Jill DeVonyar and Richard Kendall, *Degas & Music*, Glens Falls, NY, The Hyde Collection, 2009, p. 110.

[3] Denis, *Programme pour l'audition des élèves de Mme Parrot-Lecomte*, December 1898, in Pierre Cailler, *Catalogue raisonné de l'œuvre gravé et lithographié de Maurice Denis*, Geneva, Cailler, 1968, no. 102.

[4] The *Battle of Prague* was composed in 1788 by Czech composer Frantisek Kotzwara.

[5] George du Maurier's caricature, 'The Philosopher's Revenge', *Punch*, March 1866, essentially repeats and develops the same storyline.

[6] Henri Detouche, *Une rencontre* from *Le Courrier français*, 21 December 1884. The same joke formed the basis of the excruciating Laurel and Hardy film *The Music Box*, 1932 and the 1962 popular song, *Right, said Fred*.

[7] Comment made by Jules Renard in a letter of 24 November 1894, cited in Gilbert Guisan and Doris Jakubec, *Vallotton, Lettres et documents*, vol. 1, Lausanne, Bibliothèque des Arts, 1973, p. 117.

[8] As described by Howard Goodall in the exhibition catalogue *Diaghilev*, London, Victoria and Albert Museum, 2010–2011, p. 169.

[9] See article by Michel Desproges, *op. cit.*

[10] Letter of 11 February 1898 from Armand Seguin to Roderic O'Conor, in eds. Denys Sutton and Catherine Puget,

Une vie de bohème, Lettres du peintre Armand Seguin à Roderic O'Conor, 1895–1903, Pont-Aven, Musée de Pont-Aven, 1989, p. 69.

[11] For an informative discussion of these projects, see the essay by Helen Giambruni in the exhibition catalogue *Pierre Bonnard, The Graphic Work*, New York, The Metropolitan Museum of Art, 1989, pp. 39ff. See also Gilles Genty and Pierrette Vernon, *Bonnard inédits*, Paris, Éditions Cercle d'art, 2003.

[12] I owe these biographical details to Philippe Cathé, *Claude Terrasse (1867–1923)*, doctoral thesis, Université Paris IV – Sorbonne, 2001. See also Cathé's synoptic monograph, *Claude Terrasse*, Paris, L'Hexaèdre, 2004.

[13] Letter from Bonnard dated 13 April 1891, quoted by Guy Cogeval and Antoine Salomon, *Vuillard. Le Regard innombrable. Catalogue critique des peintures et pastels*, vol. 1, Milan, Skira, Paris, Wildenstein, 2003, pp. 457–8.

[14] From a letter to his sister Andrée anticipating a coming stay in Arcachon, cited in Genty and Vernon, *op. cit*, p. 62.

[15] One study for *Espièglerie* has a drawing for *Mandoline* on the verso. Exhibited in *Les peintres graveurs, 1890–1900*, Galerie Berès, Paris, 2002, no. 31. The date given there of c. 1895 is surely too late.

[16] See the letter from Cranz to Terrasse reprinted in Genty and Vernon, *op. cit*, p. 222.

[17] See his previously cited letter of 13 April to Vuillard. The connection to Boutet de Monvel has been made by several previous authors.

[18] See Cathé, *op. cit*, pp. 71ff.

[19] Letters on the topic were exchanged in October 1893 between Andrée and Claude Terrasse, cited in Cathé, *Claude Terrasse*, p. 72.

Fig. 32. **Pierre Bonnard**
Espièglerie, c. 1891
Watercolour and ink, 28.5 × 18.7 cm
Private collection

catalogue
of the works

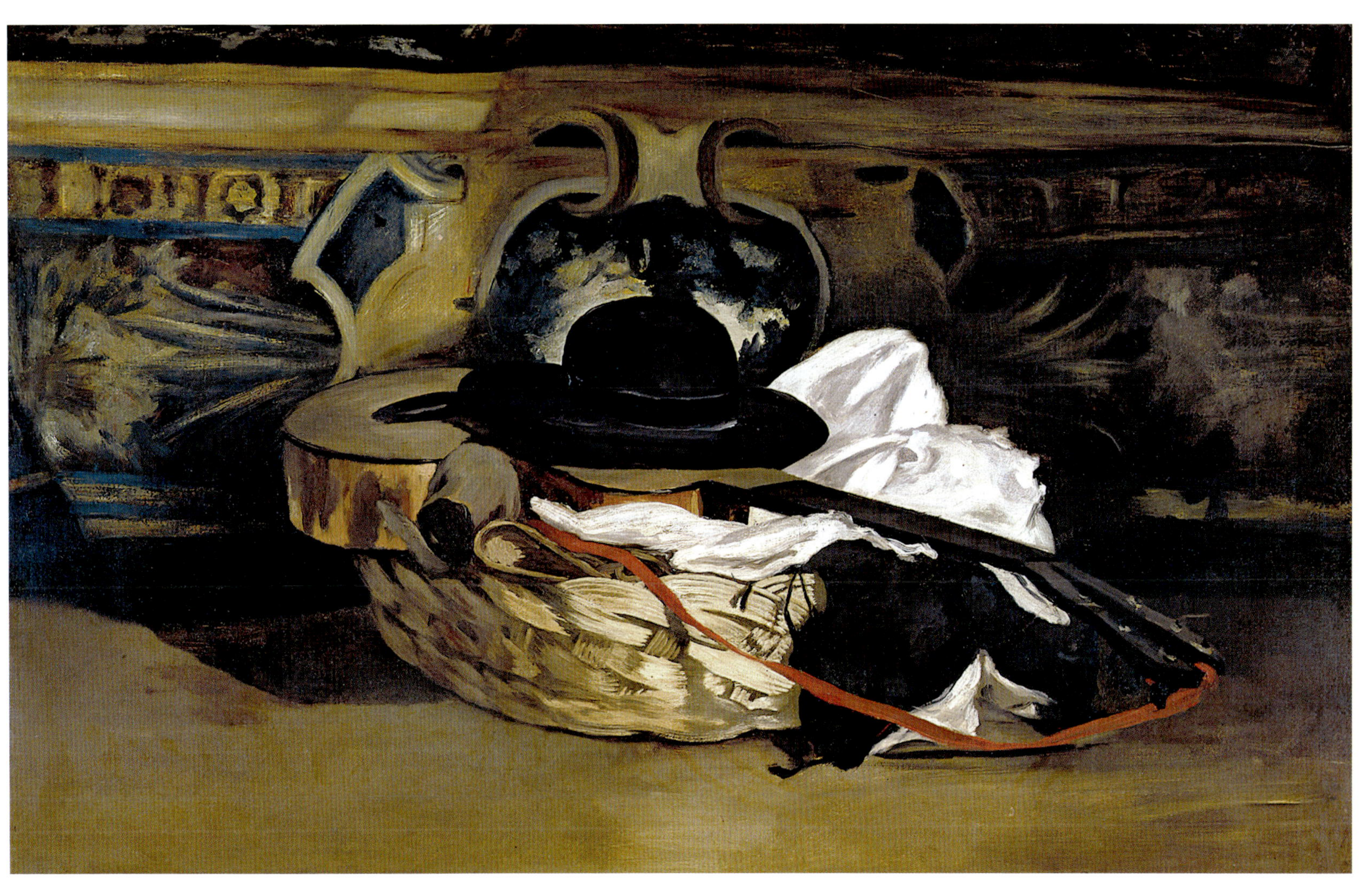

—

Cat. 1
Édouard Manet (1832–1883)
Still Life – Hat and Guitar, 1862
Oil on canvas, 77 × 120 cm
Fondation Calvet, Ville d'Avignon,
Gift of Joseph Rignault, 1947,
22.273

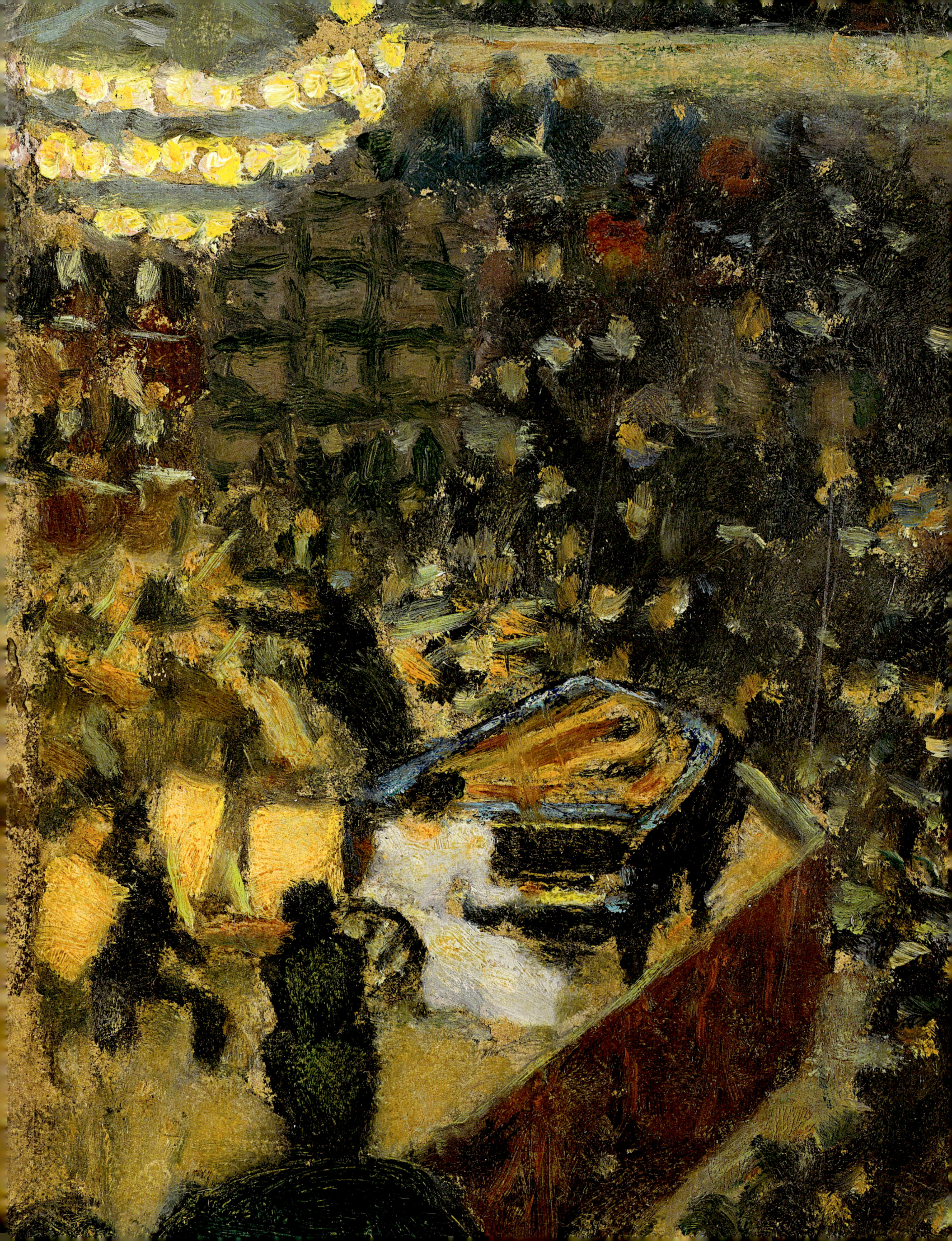

musical = divertissements

usic featured prominently in public life in the years from 1860 to 1910,
especially in the parks and major streets of Europe's big cities. Eva Gonzalès
was inspired by Édouard Manet's *The Fife Player* in her *The Little Soldier*
(*The Bugler*, cat. 2), which shows how young children were introduced to music
by brass bands, just like the one in the Jardin du Luxembourg painted by
Gabriel Boutet (cat. 3). Artists also depicted the phenomenon of musicians playing
in the courtyards of buildings that were a feature of Haussmann's Paris, as in
Albert Bartholomé's *Musicians*, also known as *Musicians in a Courtyard* (cat. 4).
Saltimbanques, the street acrobats whose performances sometimes had a tragic
dimension, as in Gustave Doré (cat. 6), and travelling circuses fascinated artists
like Lucien Simon (cat. 7), who went to fairs to see the shows (here we inevitably
think of *La Parade* by Georges Seurat).

The late nineteenth century also witnessed the explosion of cafés-concerts,
cabarets and music halls, notably in Paris (Café des Ambassadeurs, Divan Japonais,
Alcazar, Folies-Bergère) and London (where The Old Bedford was a favourite haunt
of Walter Richard Sickert's). In such places one could listen to popular tunes or
opera songs, or watch sketches or dances like the *chahut* in Jean Béraud's *Valmy
and Léa* (cat. 8), performed at the Café des Ambassadeurs.

Haussmann's Paris boasted new theatres complete with orchestra pits, which
were depicted by Béraud (cat. 12), and the period witnessed the construction of new
buildings dedicated to classical music to complement the leading theatres, most of
which dated from the seventeenth and eighteenth centuries. In Brussels, La Monnaie
was rebuilt in 1855. Georges Lemmen captured a performance of Wagner's opera
The Twilight of the Gods there (cat. 14). In Paris the Théâtre de la Ville and Théâtre du
Châtelet were inaugurated in 1862. The Musikverein opened in Vienna in 1870, the
Royal Albert Hall in London in 1871 and the Opéra de Paris in 1875. Garnier's building
hosted the great ballet companies, as portrayed by Edgar Degas. The period also
saw the flourishing of big independent orchestras such as the Orchestre Lamoureux,
represented here by Pierre Bonnard (cat. 15), and it was a golden age, not only
for popular dance halls, but also for the kind of society dances shown in *Too Early*
by James Tissot (cat. 10).

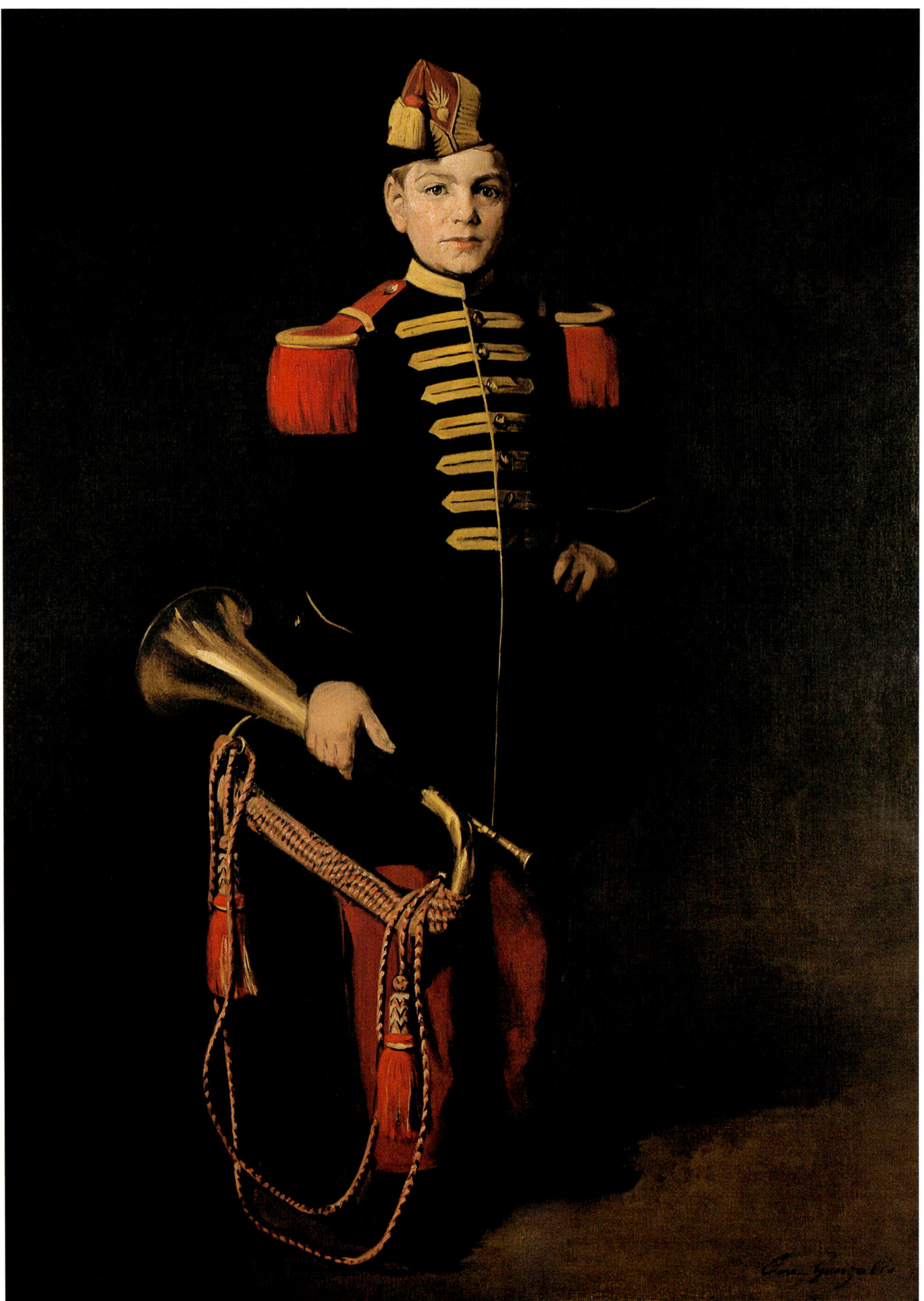

Cat. 2
Eva Gonzalès (1849–1883)
The Little Soldier or
The Bugler, 1870
Oil on canvas, 133 × 109 cm
Collection Musée de Gajac,
Villeneuve-sur-Lot,
D874.1.1

Cat. 3
Gabriel Boutet (1848–1900)
*The Republican Guard Band in
the Luxembourg Gardens*, 1887
Oil on wood, 90 × 71 cm
Musées d'Art et d'Histoire,
La Rochelle, Gift of the
Société des Amis des Arts
de La Rochelle,
MAH 1899.1.4

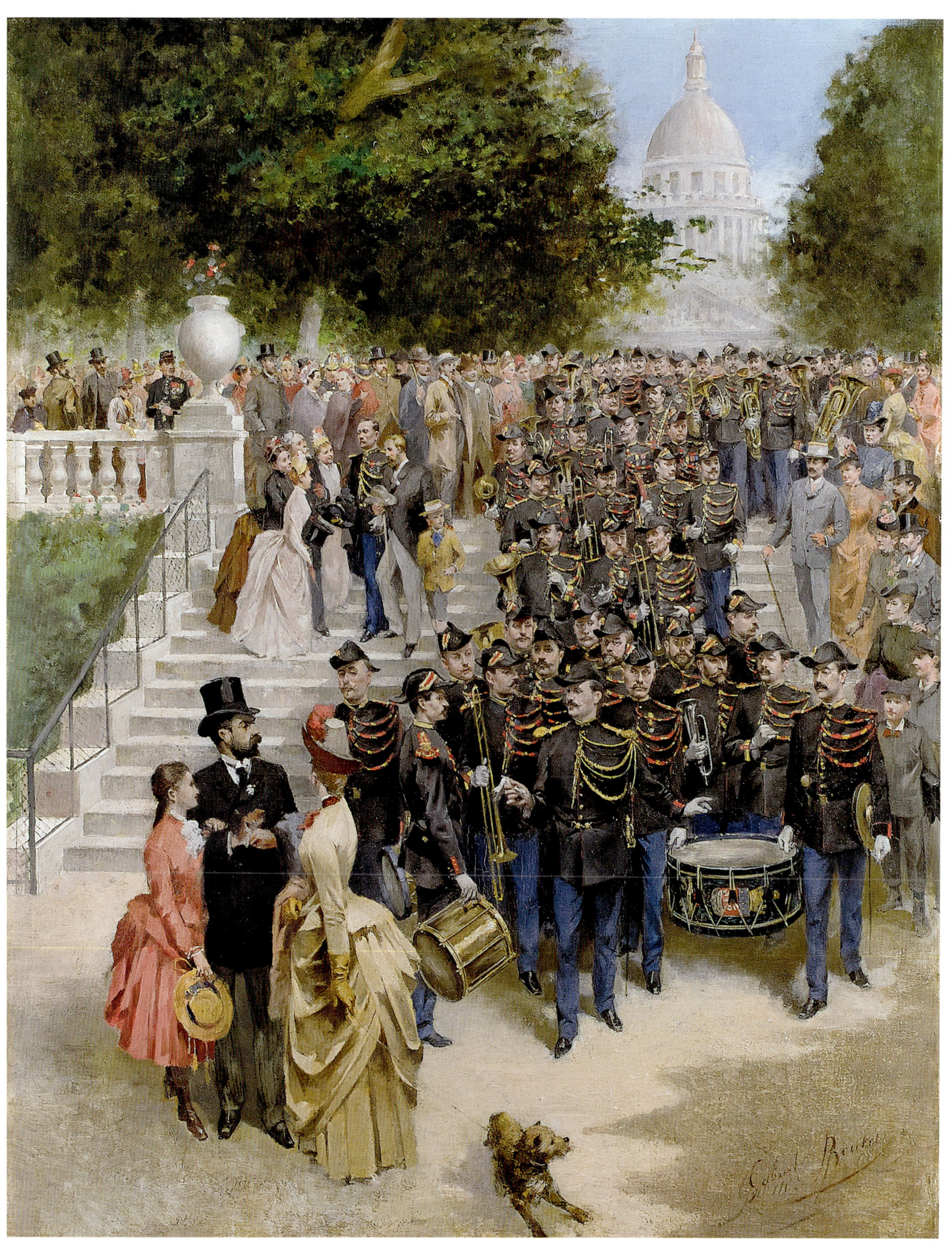

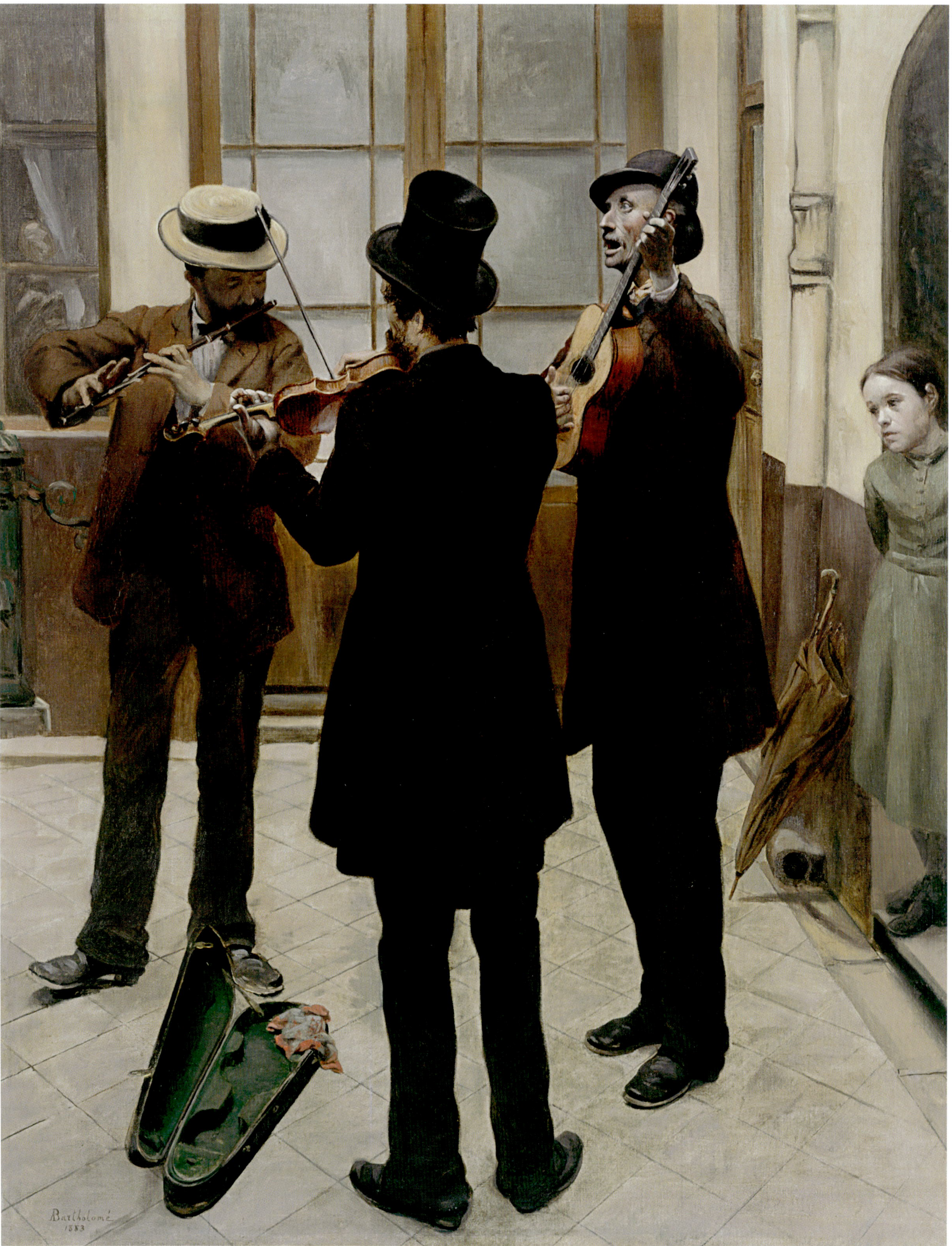

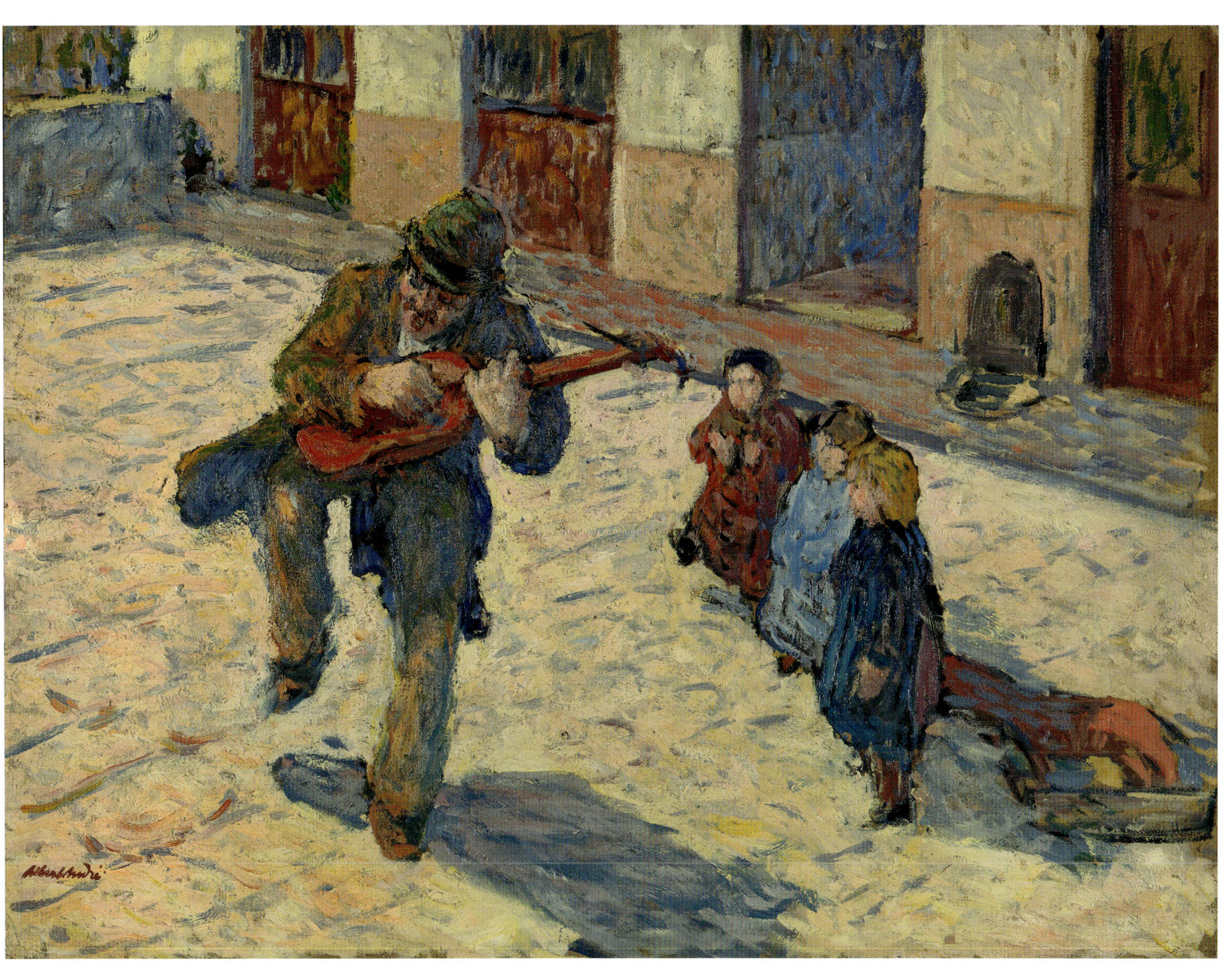

Cat. 4
Albert Bartholomé (1848–1928)
The Musicians, also known as
Musicians in a Courtyard, 1883
Oil on canvas, 78 × 64 cm
Petit Palais, Musée des Beaux-
Arts de la Ville de Paris,
PDUT1460

Cat. 5
Albert André (1869–1954)
Street Musician, 1893
Oil on board, 58.5 × 78.5 cm
Musée d'Orsay, Paris, on long term
loan at the Musée d'Art et d'Histoire
de Saint-Denis, Gift of Mme Jacqueline
George-Besson, 1991,
RF 1975-79

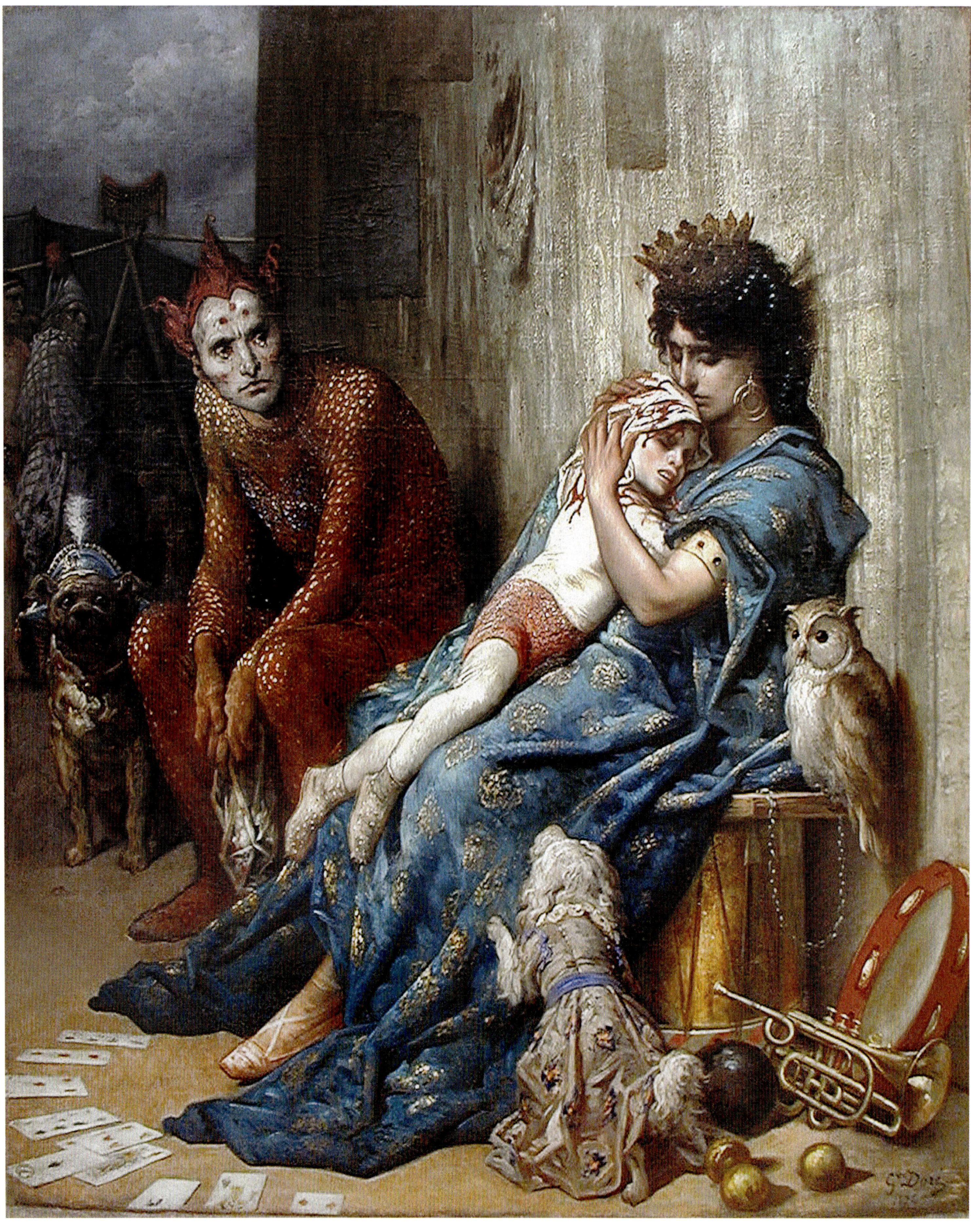

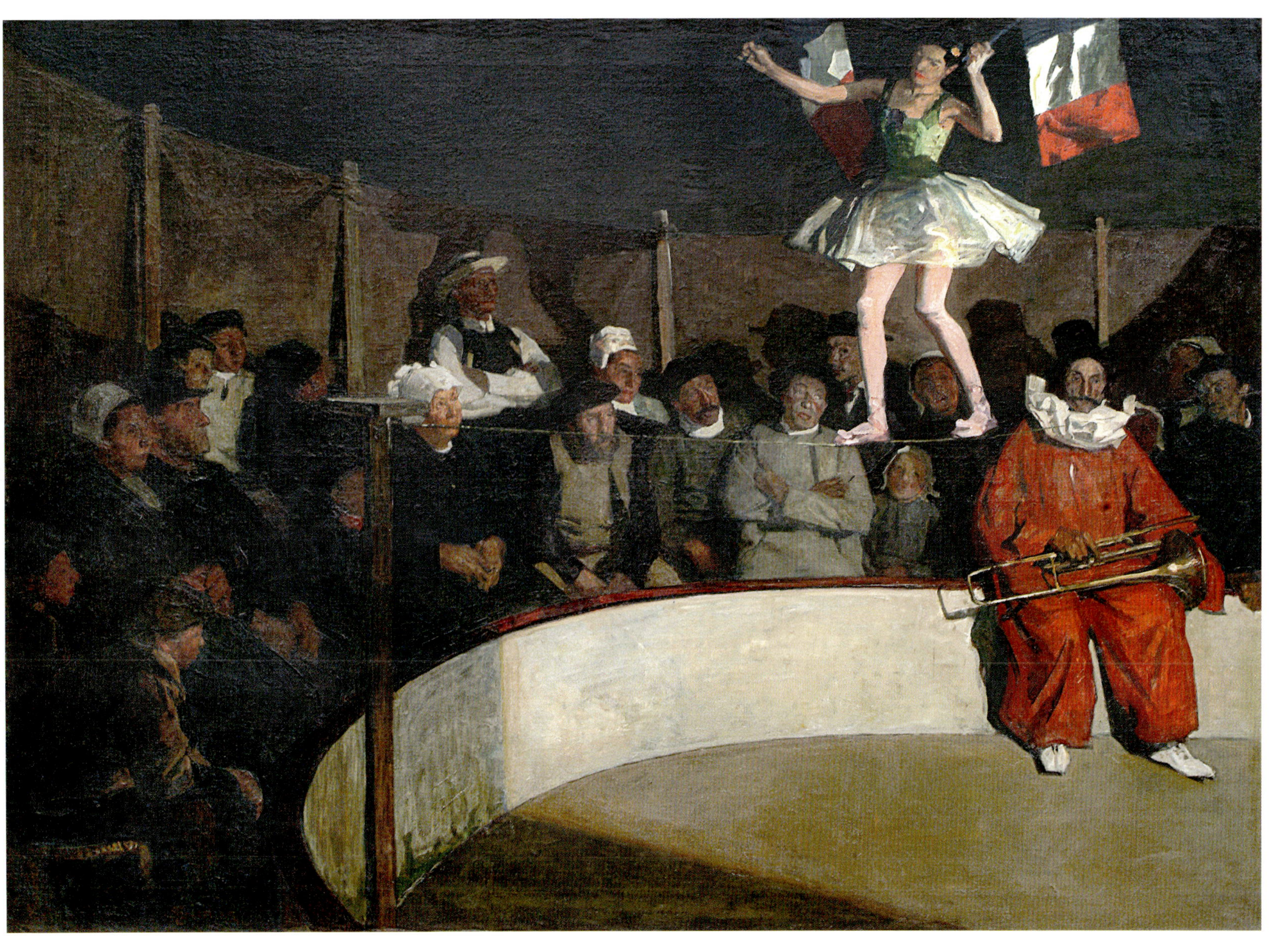

Cat. 6
Gustave Doré (1832–1883)
The Circus Family, also known
as *The Injured Child*, 1874
Oil on canvas, 224 × 184 cm
Musée d'Art Roger-Quilliot,
Ville de Clermont-Ferrand,
2714

Cat. 7
Lucien Simon (1861–1945)
Travelling Circus in Brittany, 1898
Oil on canvas, 167 × 236 cm
Musée des Beaux-Arts de la
Boverie, Ville de Liège,
AM 339/177

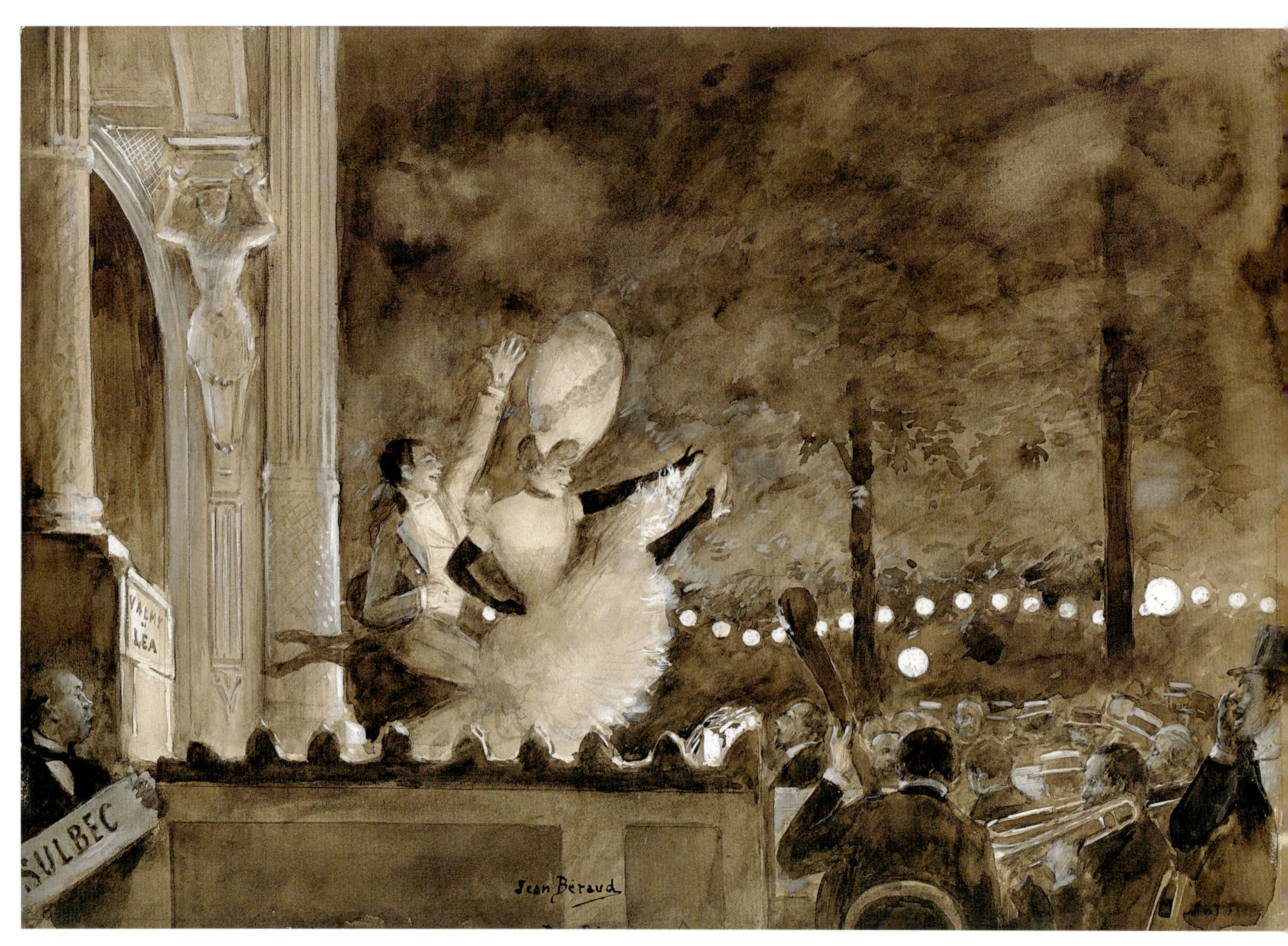

Cat. 8
Jean Béraud (1848–1935)
Valmy and Léa, c. 1885–95
Brush and brown wash,
heightened with white gouache
over graphite, 36 × 51.7 cm
The Cleveland Museum
of Art, Bequest of Muriel Butkin,
2008.407

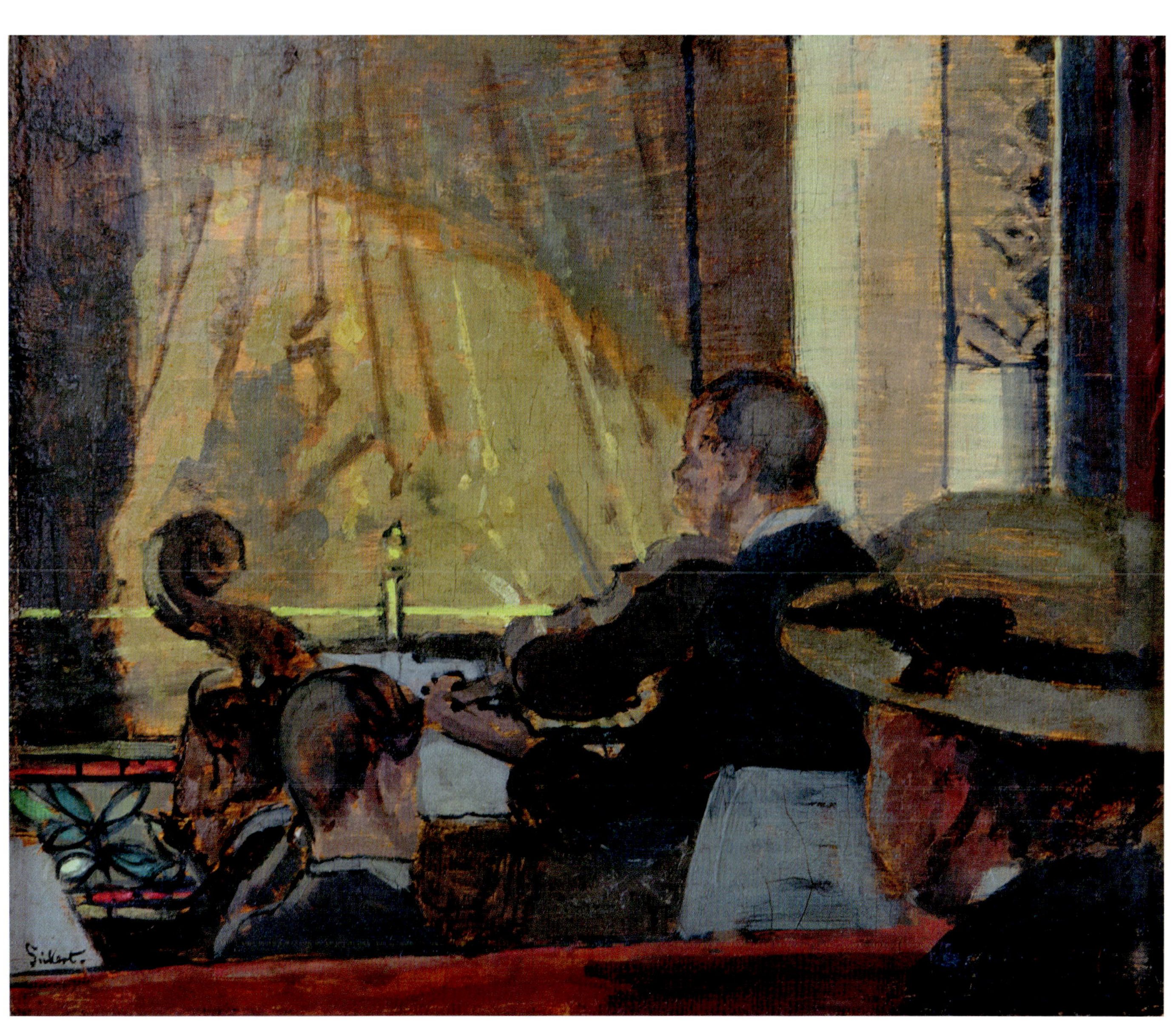

Cat. 9
Walter Richard Sickert
(1860–1942)
Music-Hall, c. 1889
Oil on panel, 19.8 × 24.1 cm
Bemberg Foundation, Toulouse,
2210

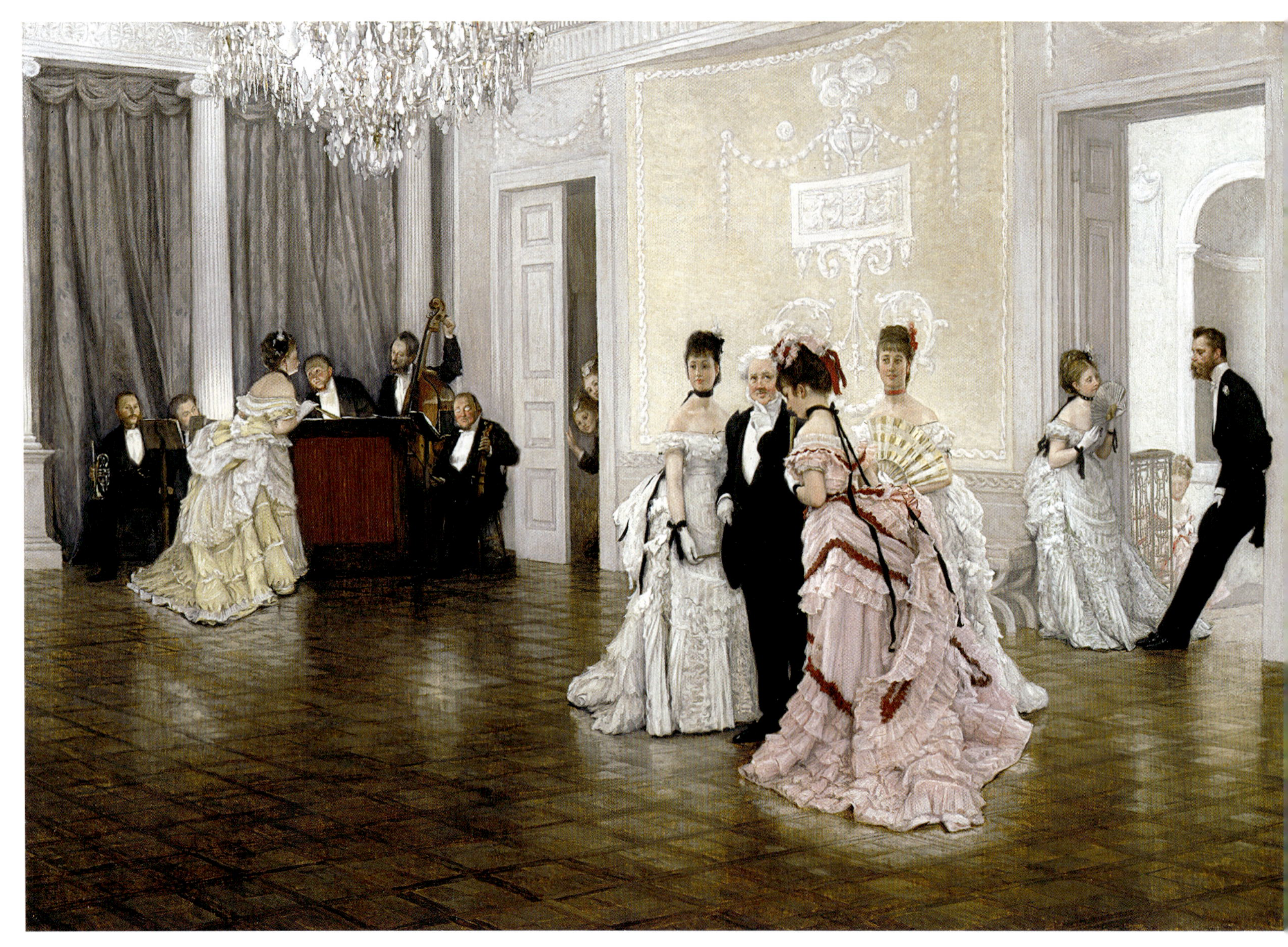

Cat. 10
James Tissot (1836–1902)
Too Early, 1873
Oil on canvas, 71 × 102 cm
Guildhall Art Gallery,
City of London,
737

Cat. 11
Edgar Degas (1834–1917)
Dancer, 1891
Oil on panel, 22 × 15.8 cm
Hamburger Kunsthalle, Hamburg,
Bequeathed by Erdwin and
Antonie Amsinck, 1921,
HK-2418

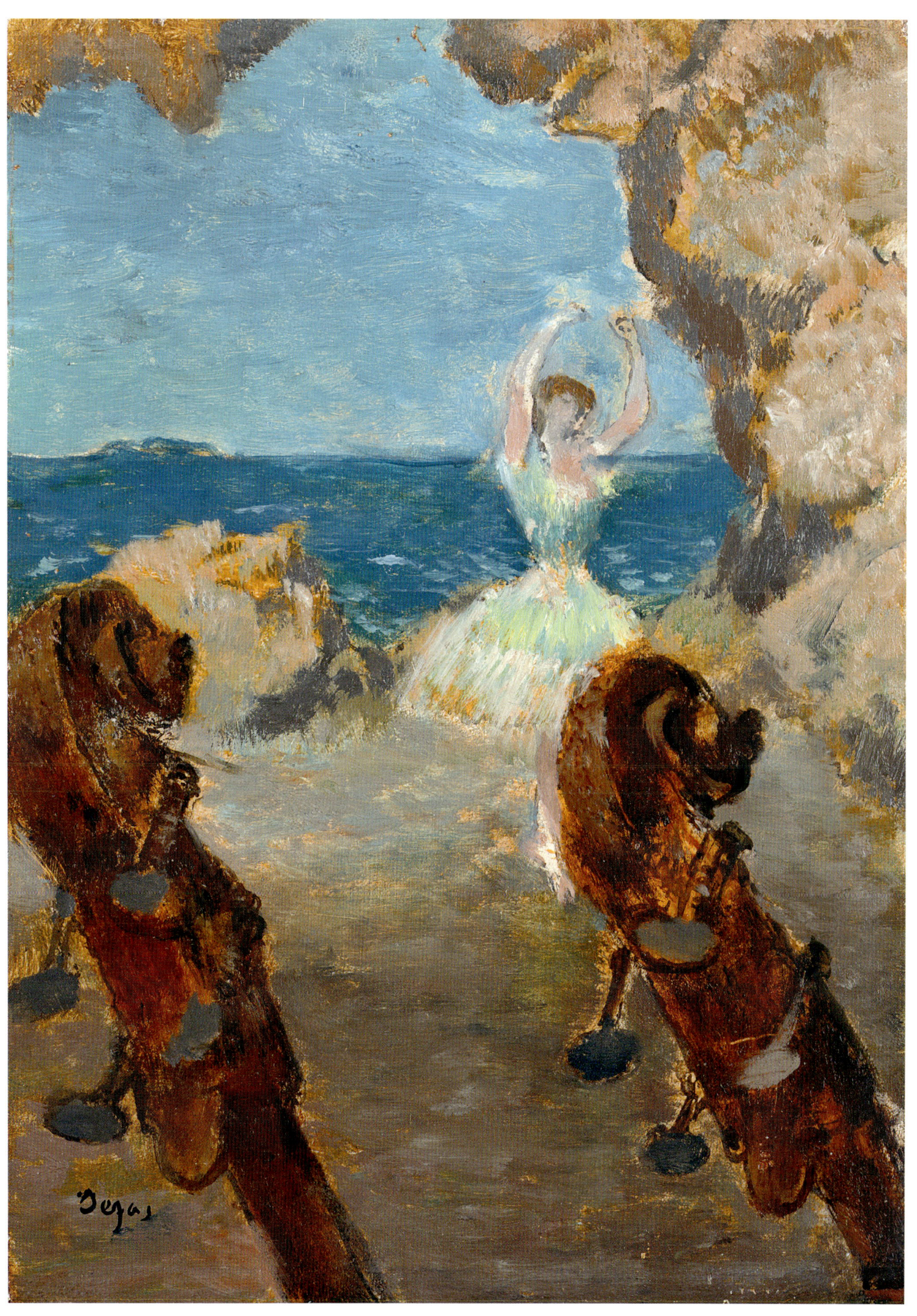

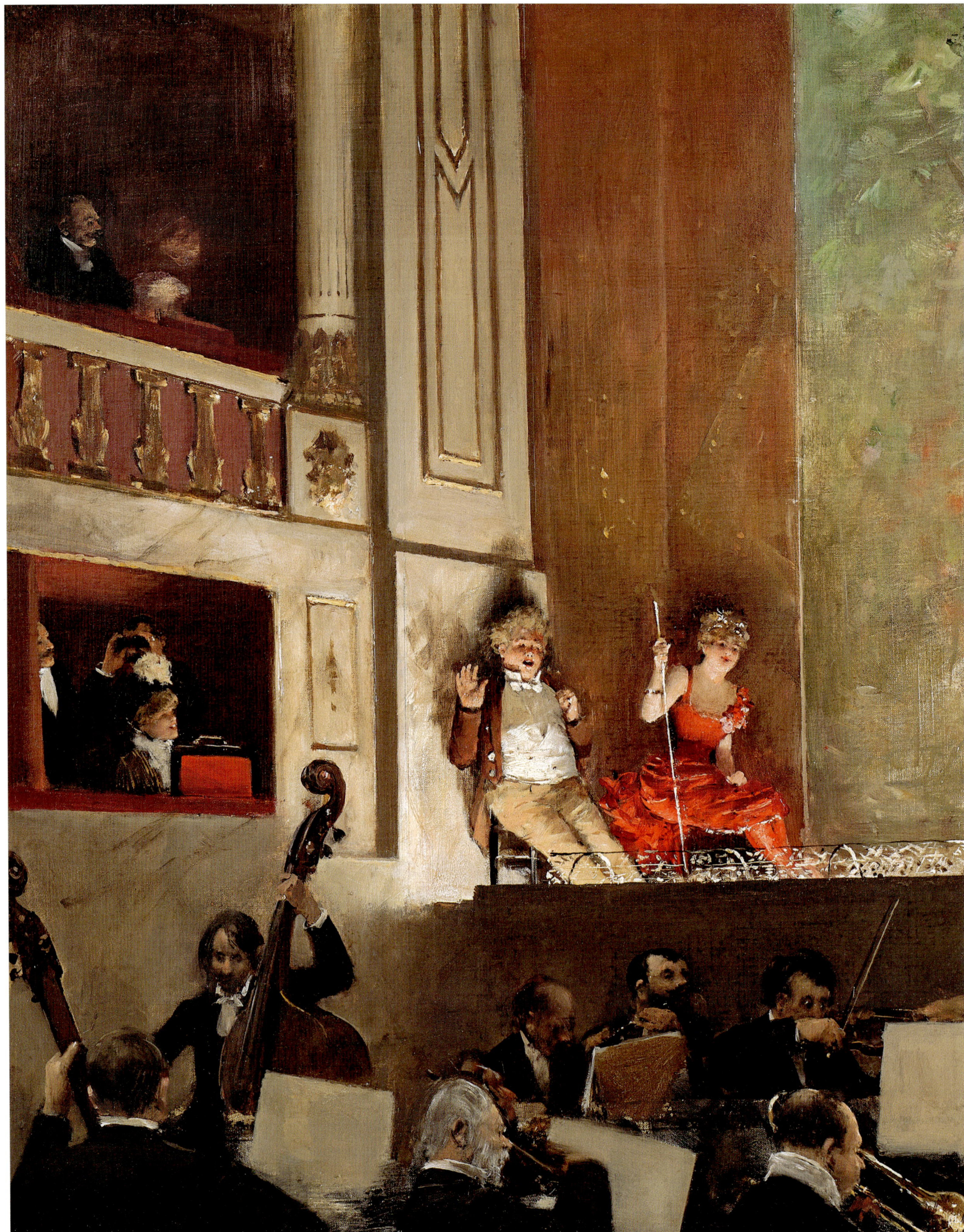

Cat. 12
Jean Béraud
*Performance at the Théâtre
des variétés*, c. 1888
Oil on canvas, 46.5 × 38.5 cm
Les Arts Décoratifs, 19th Century
Department, Paris,
32411

Cat. 13
Jean Béraud
Leaving the Theatre, c. 1900
Gouache, graphite and
watercolour, 56.5 × 72 cm
Musée d'Orsay, Paris,
RF 39111

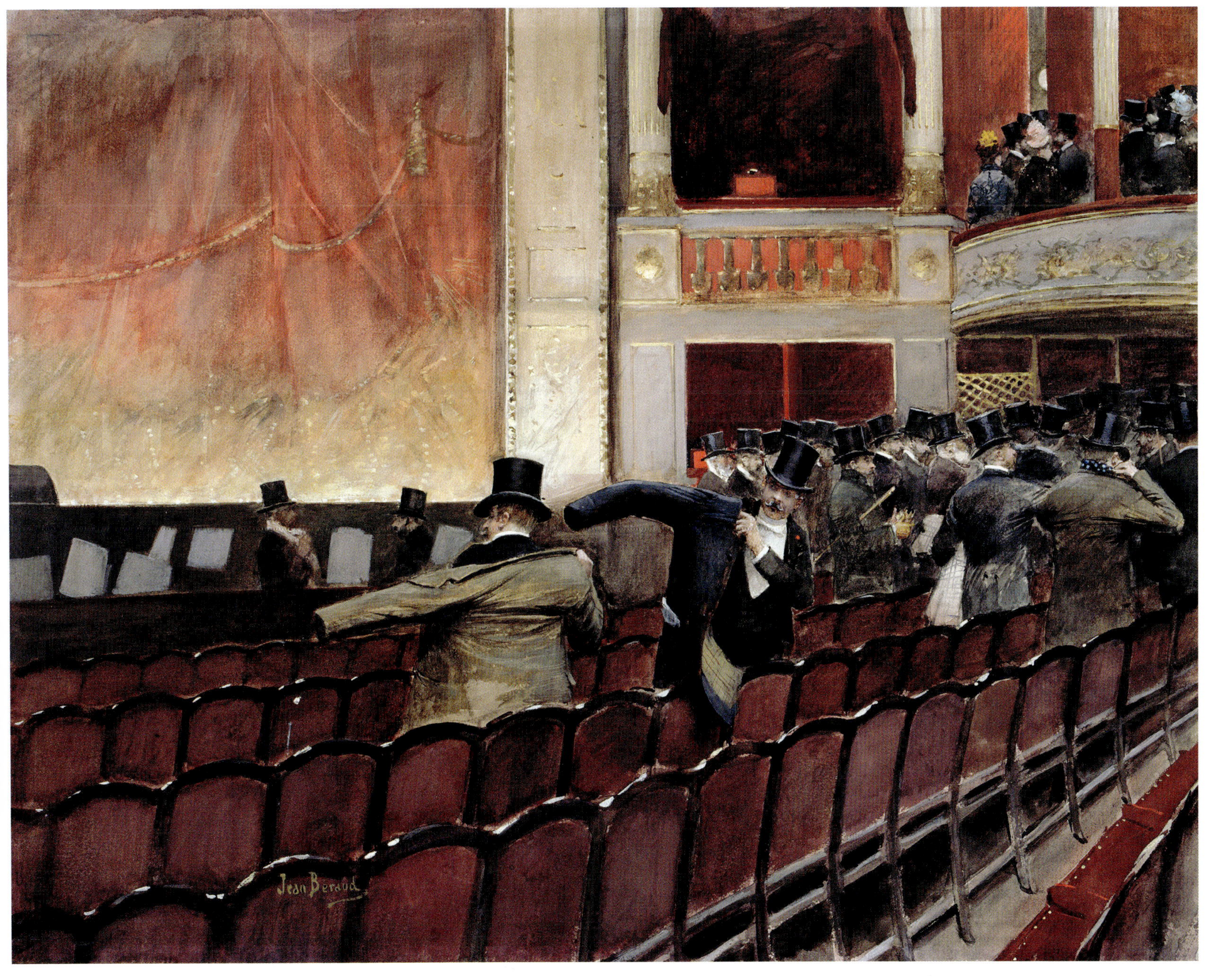

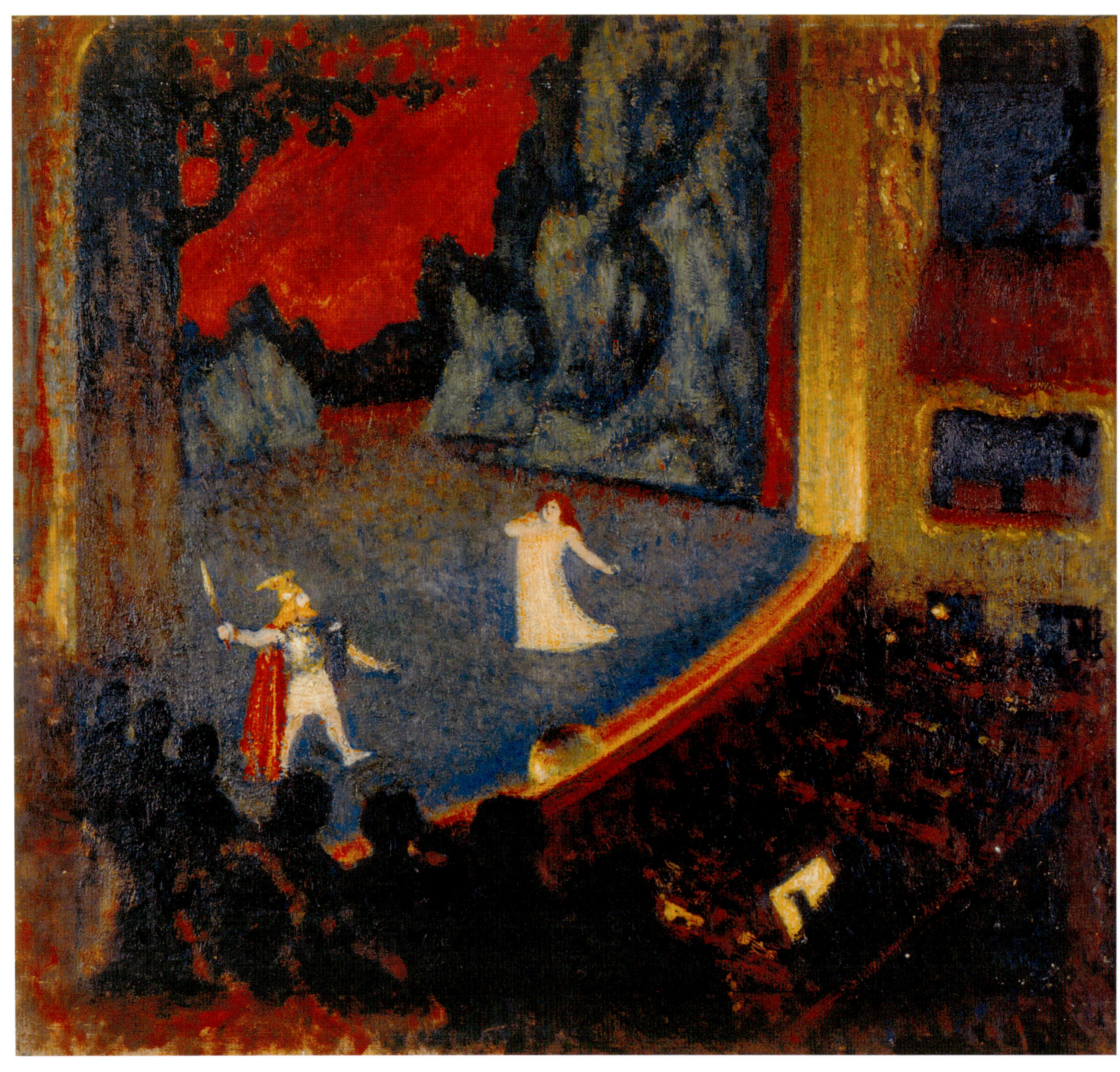

Cat. 14
Georges Lemmen (1865–1916)
Performance of the Opera
'The Twilight of the Gods' at
La Monnaie, c. 1903
Oil on wood, 60 × 65 cm
Mu.ZEE, Ostende,
SM002444

Cat. 15
Pierre Bonnard (1867–1947)
The Lamoureux Concert, c. 1895
Oil on panel, 35.2 × 18.8 cm
Bemberg Foundation, Toulouse,
2024

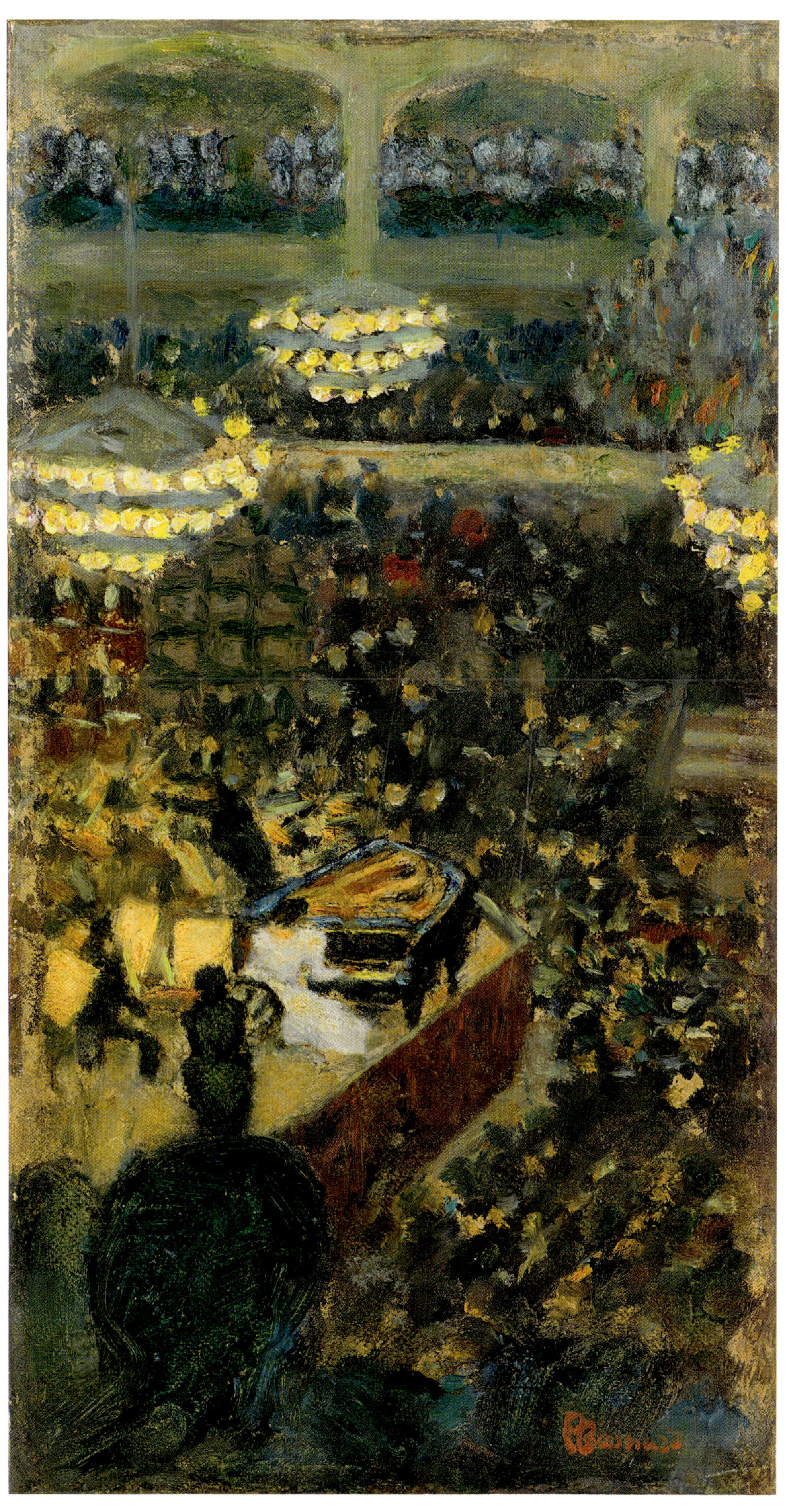

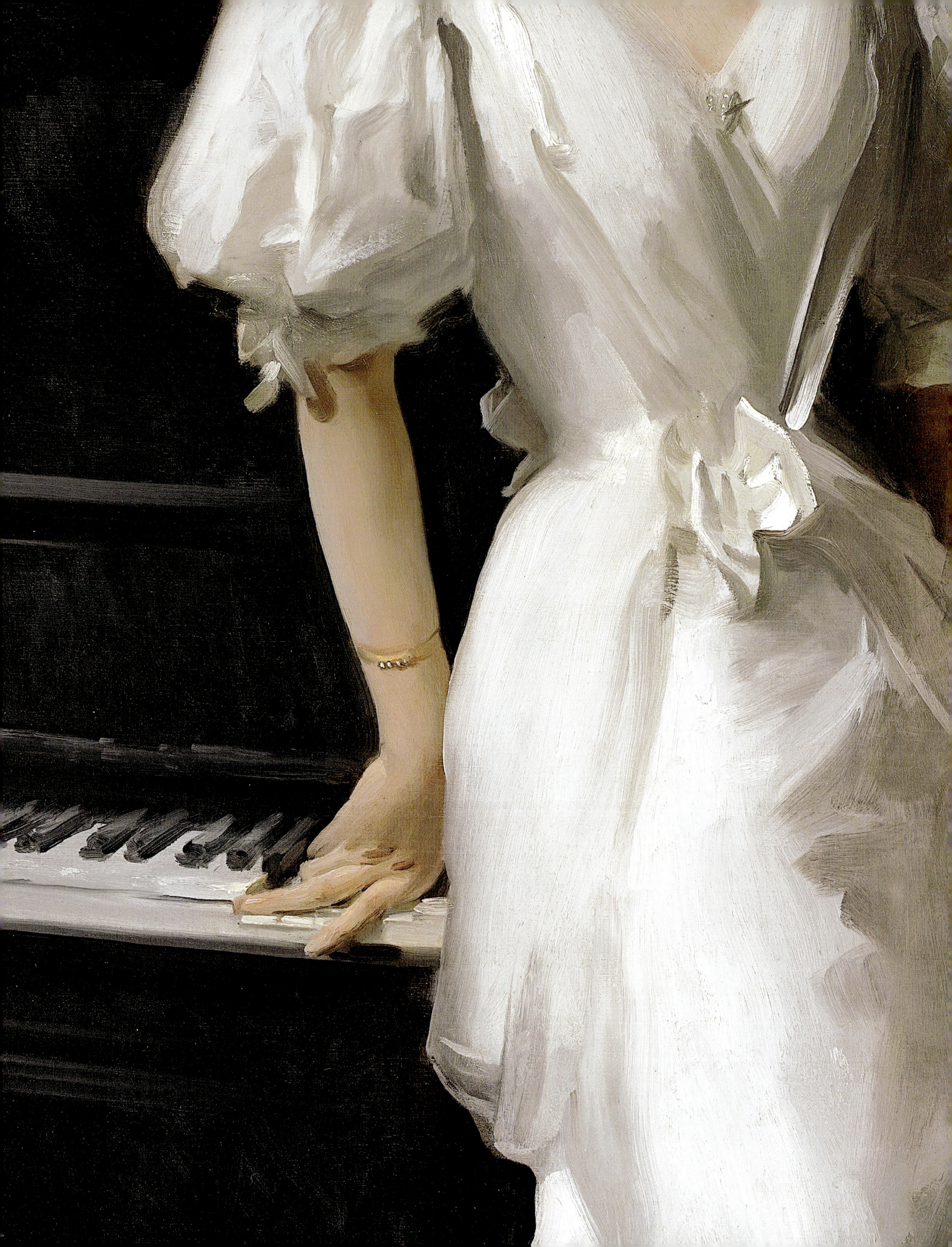

music at home

During this period musical instruments became more affordable, and it was the done thing for the rising, music-loving bourgeoisie to have them at home. Pianos were particularly popular.

Paintings of music lessons, in particular, evoked this private practice, showing a great diversity of instruments, be it the banjo (Mary Cassatt, cat. 17), the violin (Berthe Morisot, cat. 19) or the piano (Gustave Caillebotte, cat. 20). Those learning were usually children, of course, but women too were very much involved in this domestic music making and are often shown playing or standing by the piano. Musical ability was part of the accomplishments of the complete hostess, who was expected to be able to entertain her guests, like Renoir's Madame Hartmann (cat. 26), the wife of an important music publisher who frequented artistic circles. Some of these women were indeed more than just amateur musicians, having given up fine careers when they married. Madame Hartmann, for all that she has the look of a comfortable bourgeoise, is understood to have been the professional opera singer Louise Marie Rose Grémond. Alfred Stevens's *Violinist* (cat. 32), likewise, has the look of a professional musician given the way she is presented and the artificial lighting, although it is probable that the artist had one of his favourite models pose for the painting. The cello appears to have been exclusively masculine (*Cellist Practising* by Louis Hayet, cat. 33 – although this is more probably a double bass – and *The Cello Player* by Vilhelm Hammershøi, cat. 34), and its evocation tends to be more introspective.

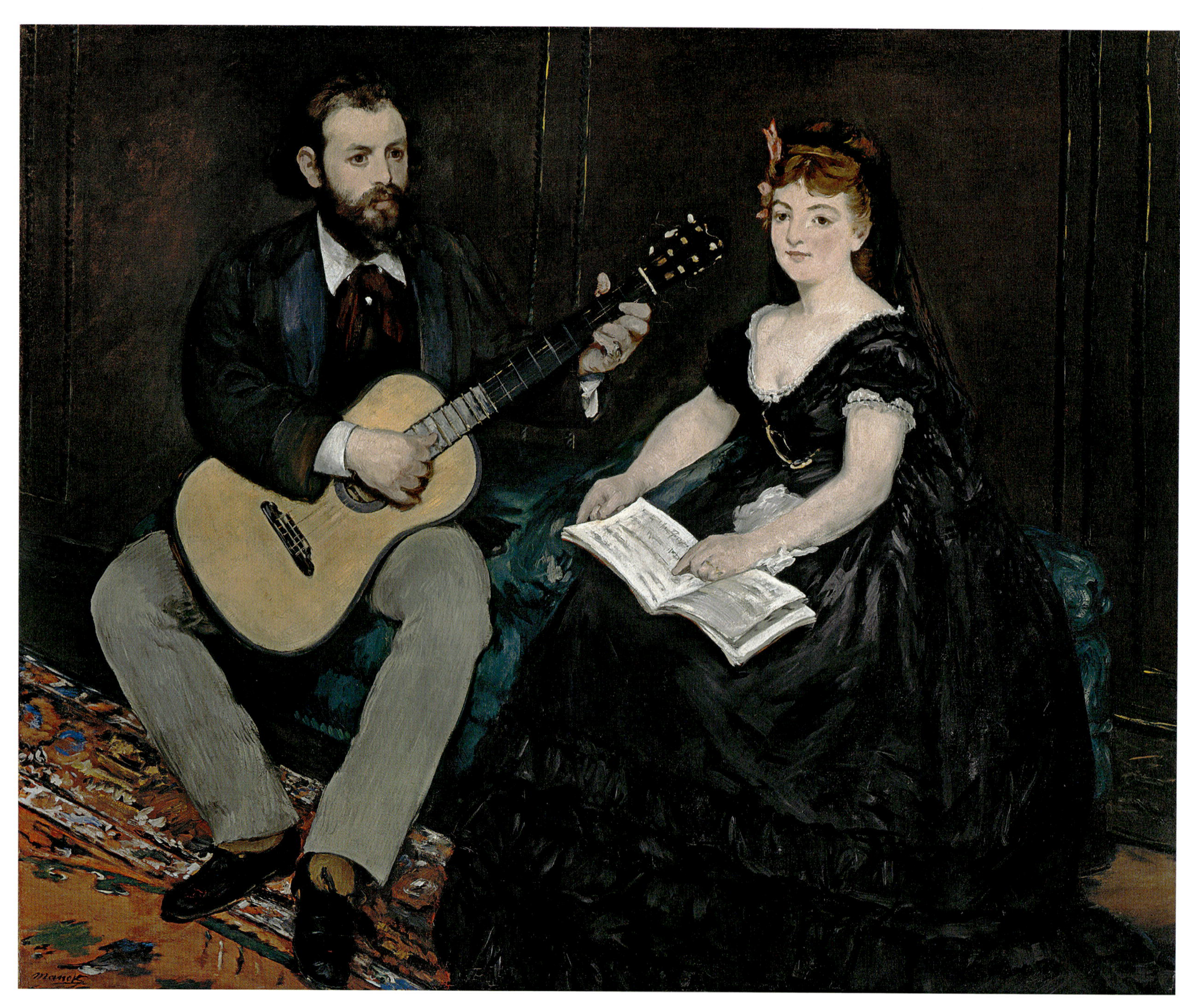

Cat. 16
Édouard Manet
Music Lesson, 1870
Oil on canvas, 141 × 173.1 cm
Museum of Fine Arts, Boston,
Anonymous Centennial gift in
memory of Charles Deering,
69.1123

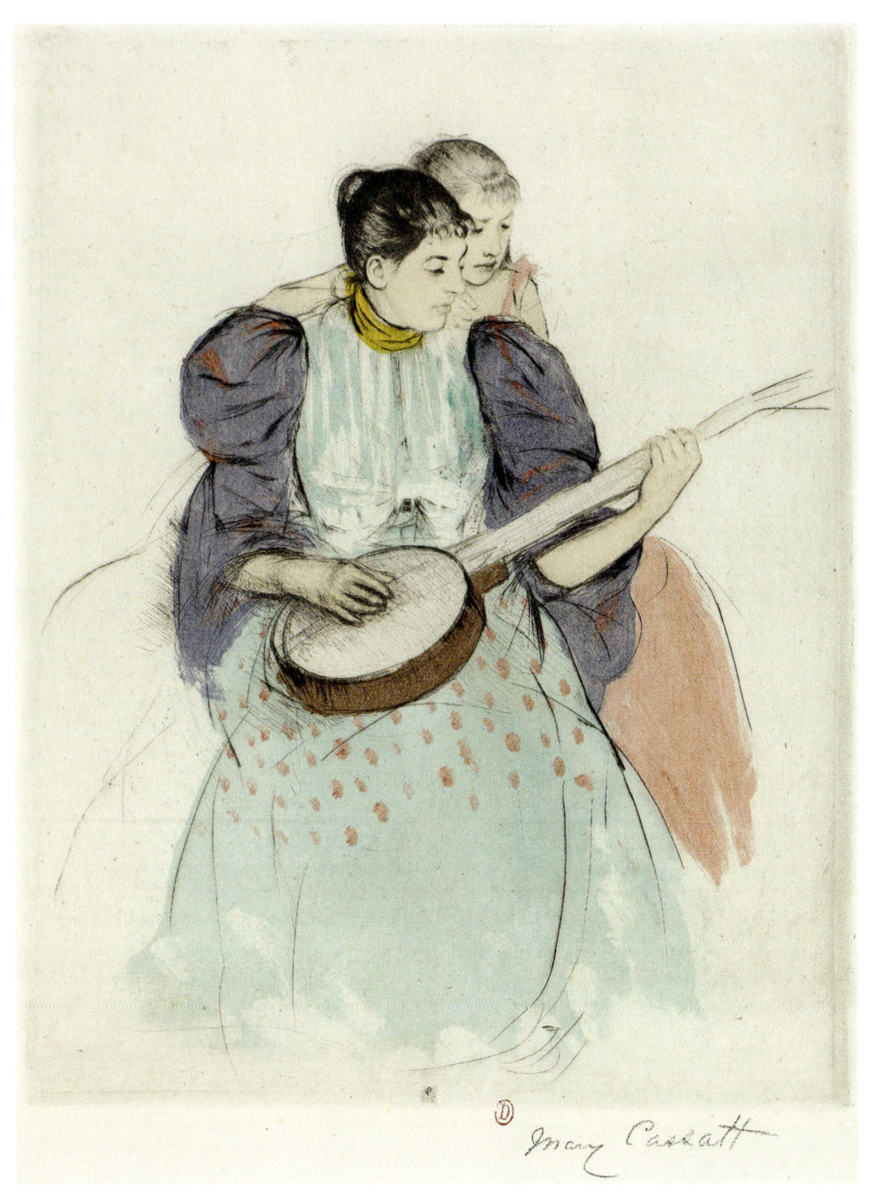

Cat. 17
Mary Cassatt (1844–1926)
The Banjo Lesson, 1893
Drypoint and aquatint with
monotype inking on light green
paper, 29.8 × 23.4 cm
Institut National d'Histoire de
l'Art, Bibliothèque, Jacques
Doucet Collection, Paris,
EM CASSATT 9b

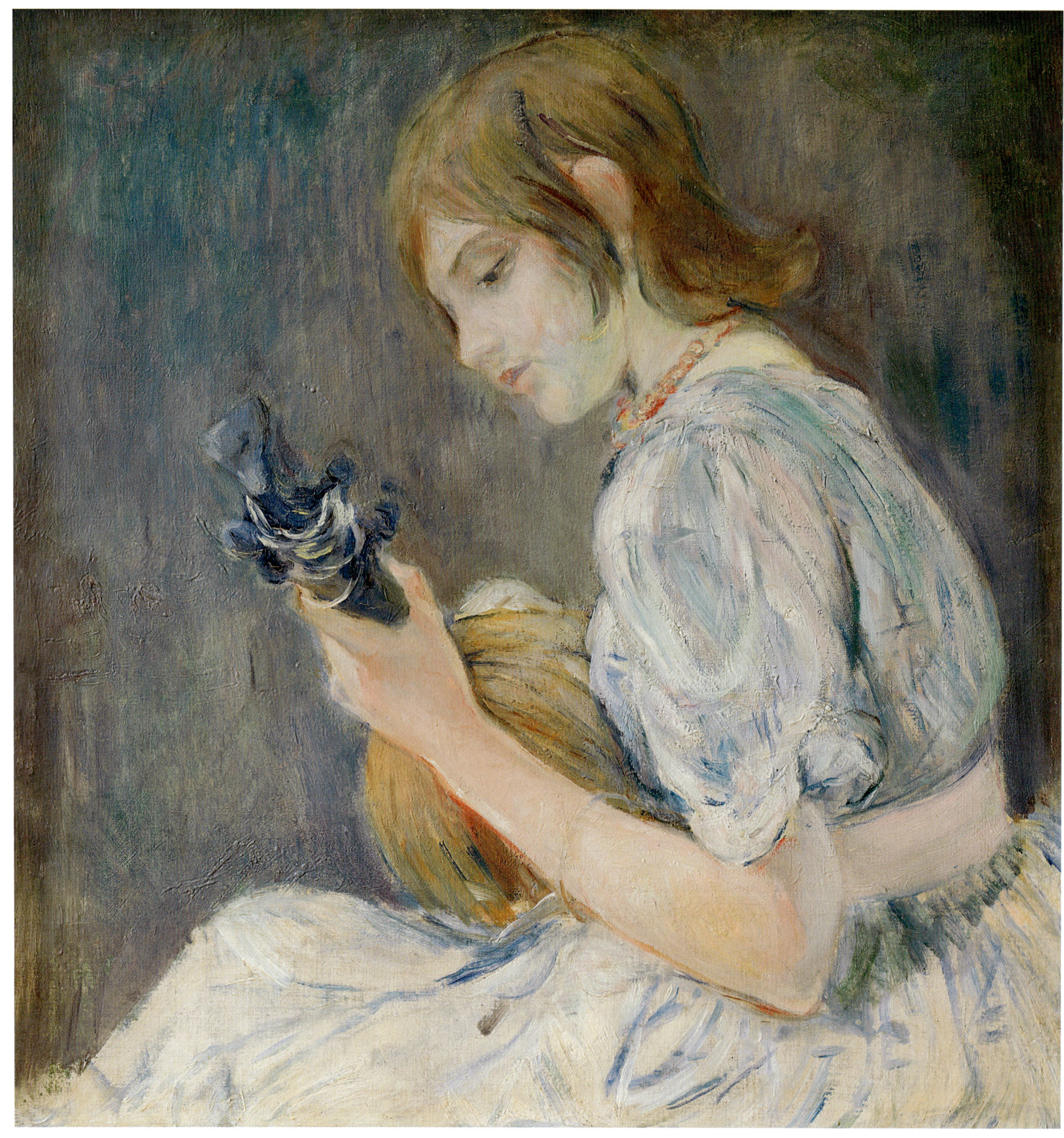

Cat. 18
Berthe Morisot (1841–1895)
The Mandolin, 1889
Oil on canvas, 55 × 57 cm
Private collection

Cat. 19
Berthe Morisot
Julie Manet Playing the Violin,
1893
Oil on canvas, 65 × 54 cm
Private collection

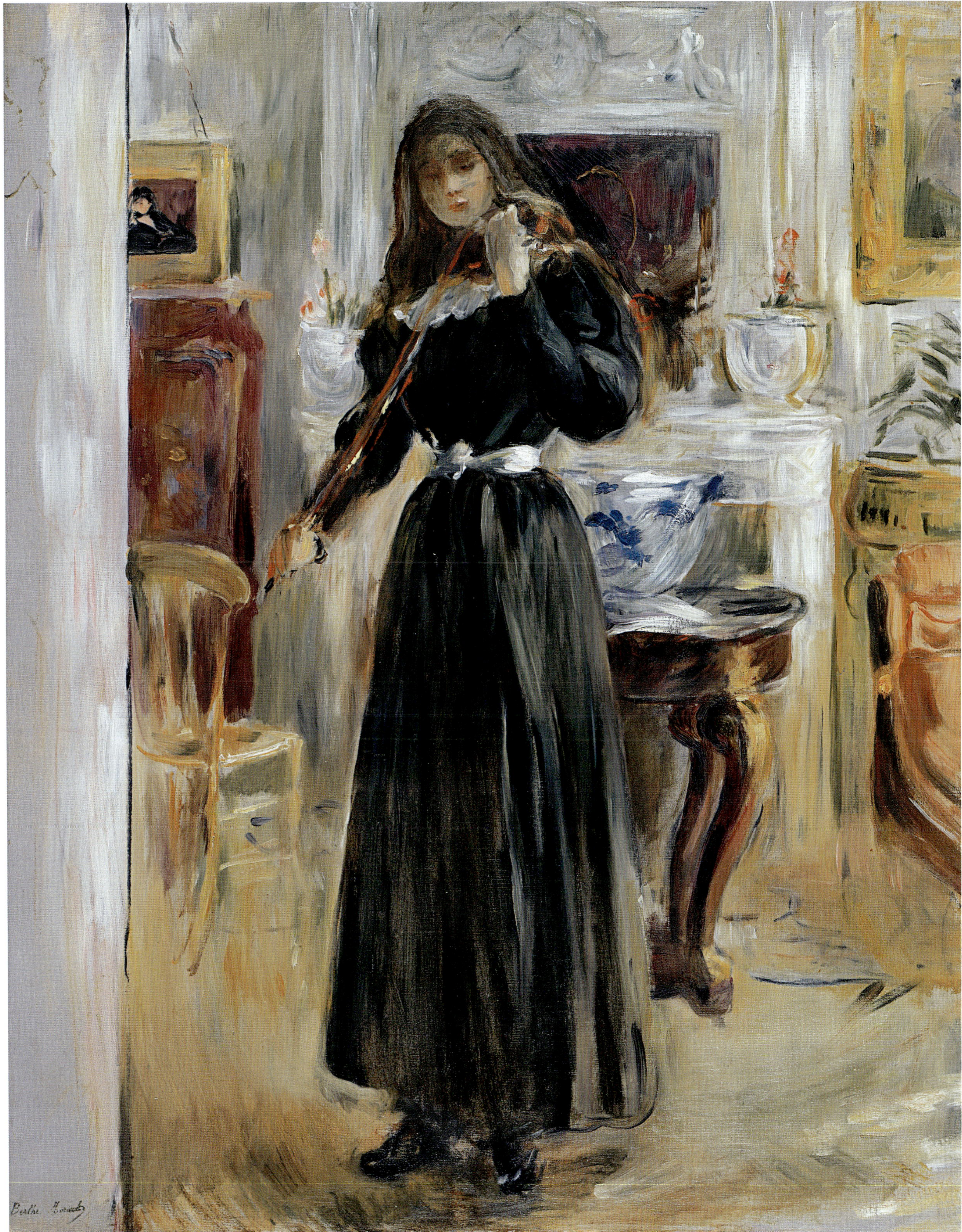

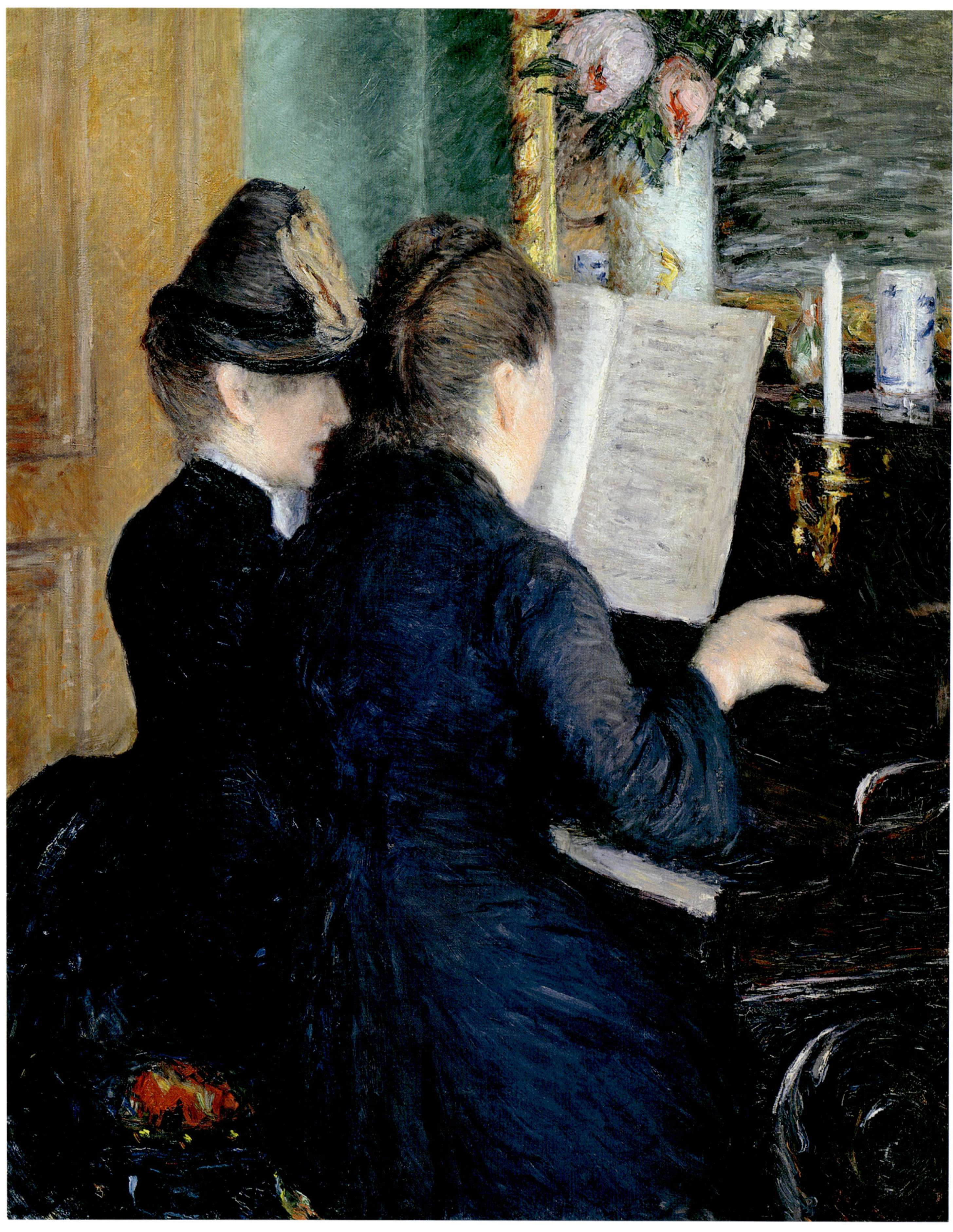

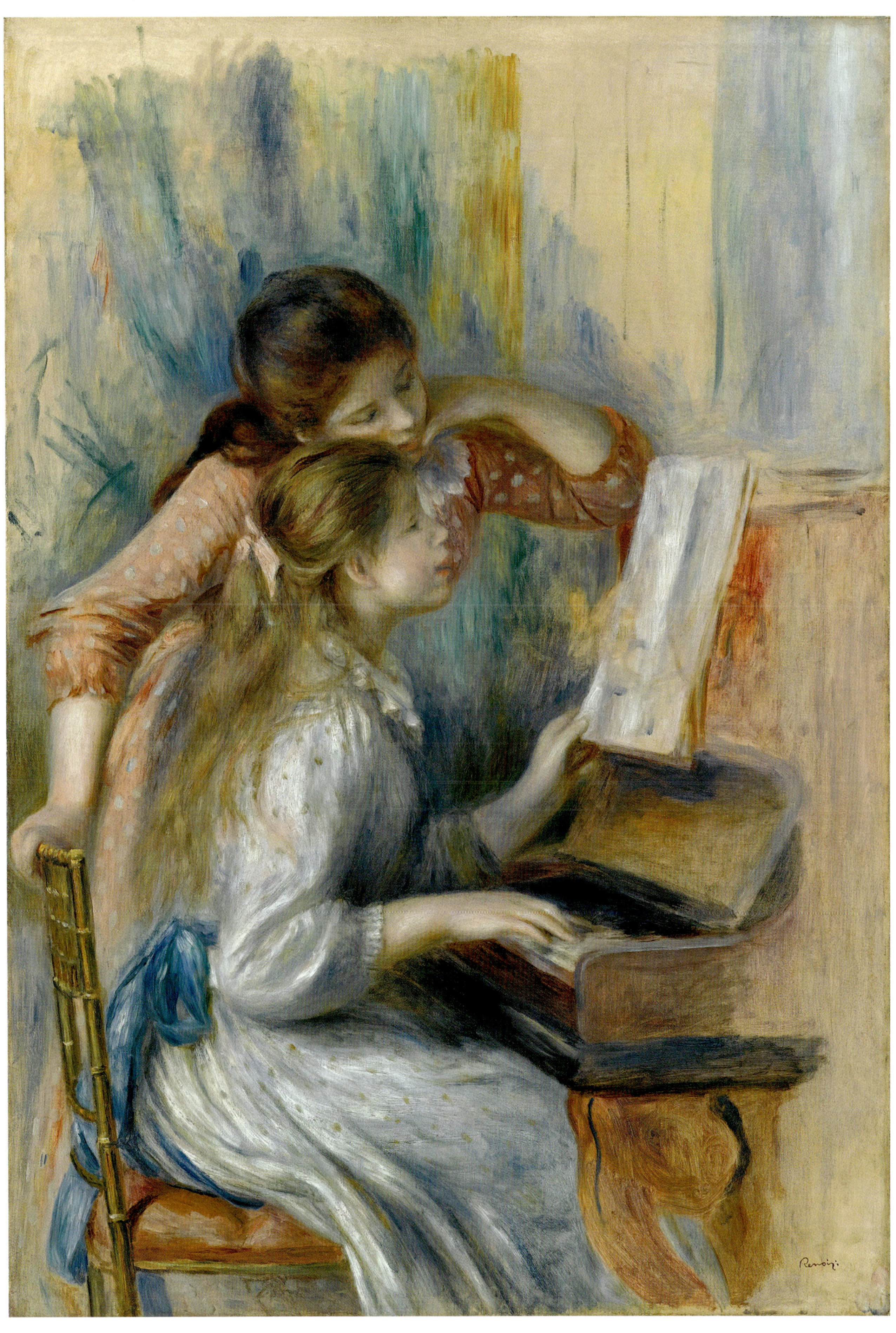

Cat. 20
Gustave Caillebotte
(1848–1894)
The Piano Lesson, 1881
Oil on canvas, 81 × 65 cm
Musée Marmottan Monet, Paris,
Bequest of Michel Monet, 1966,
5028

Cat. 21
Auguste Renoir (1841–1919)
Young Girls at the Piano, c. 1892
Oil on canvas, 116 × 81 cm
Musée de l'Orangerie, Paris,
Jean Walter and
Paul Guillaume Collection,
RF 1960-16

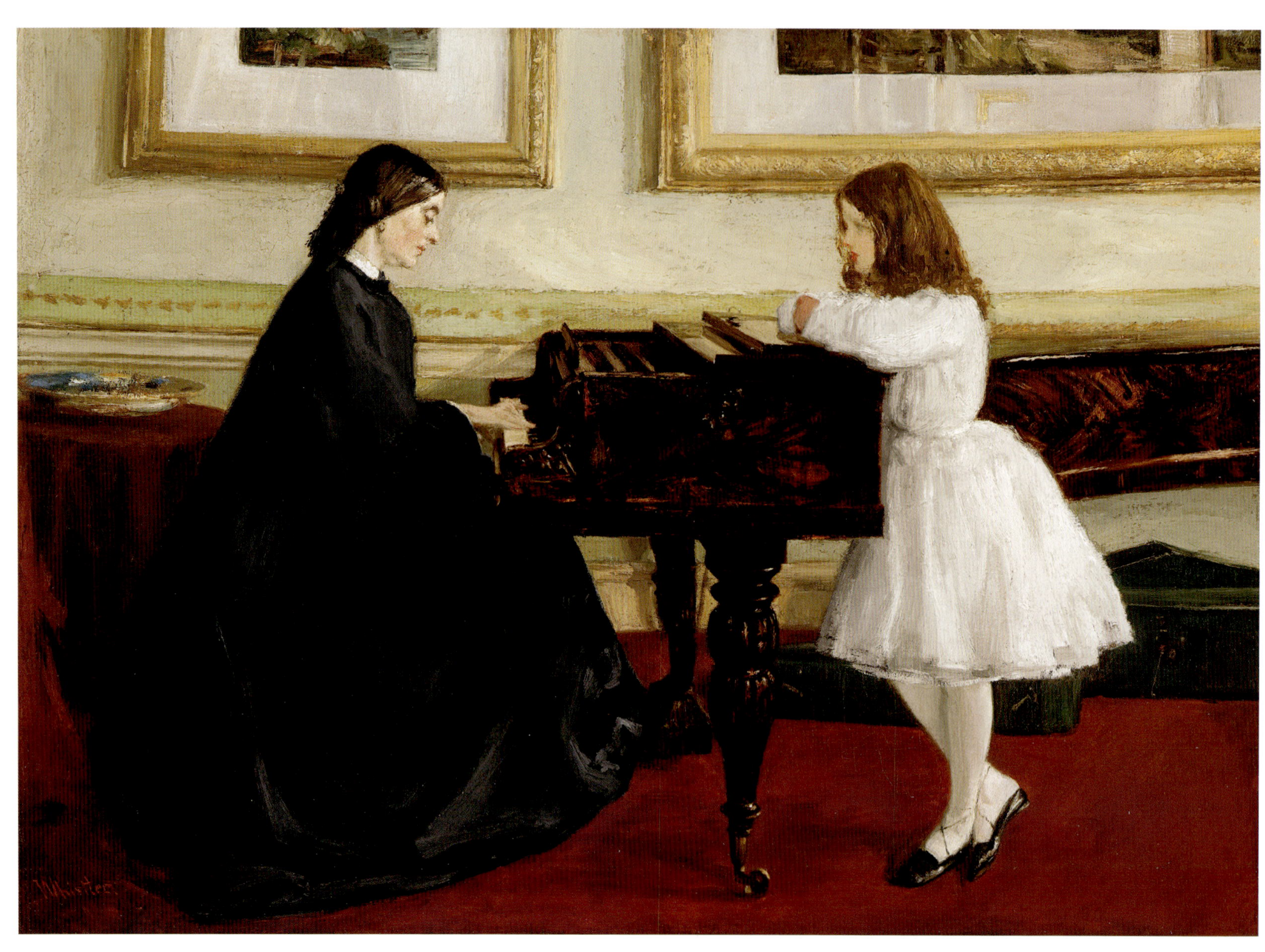

Cat. 22
**James McNeill Whistler
(1834–1903)**
At the piano, 1858–9
Oil on canvas, 67 × 91.6 cm
Taft Museum of Art, Cincinnati,
Bequest of Louise Taft Semple,
1962.7

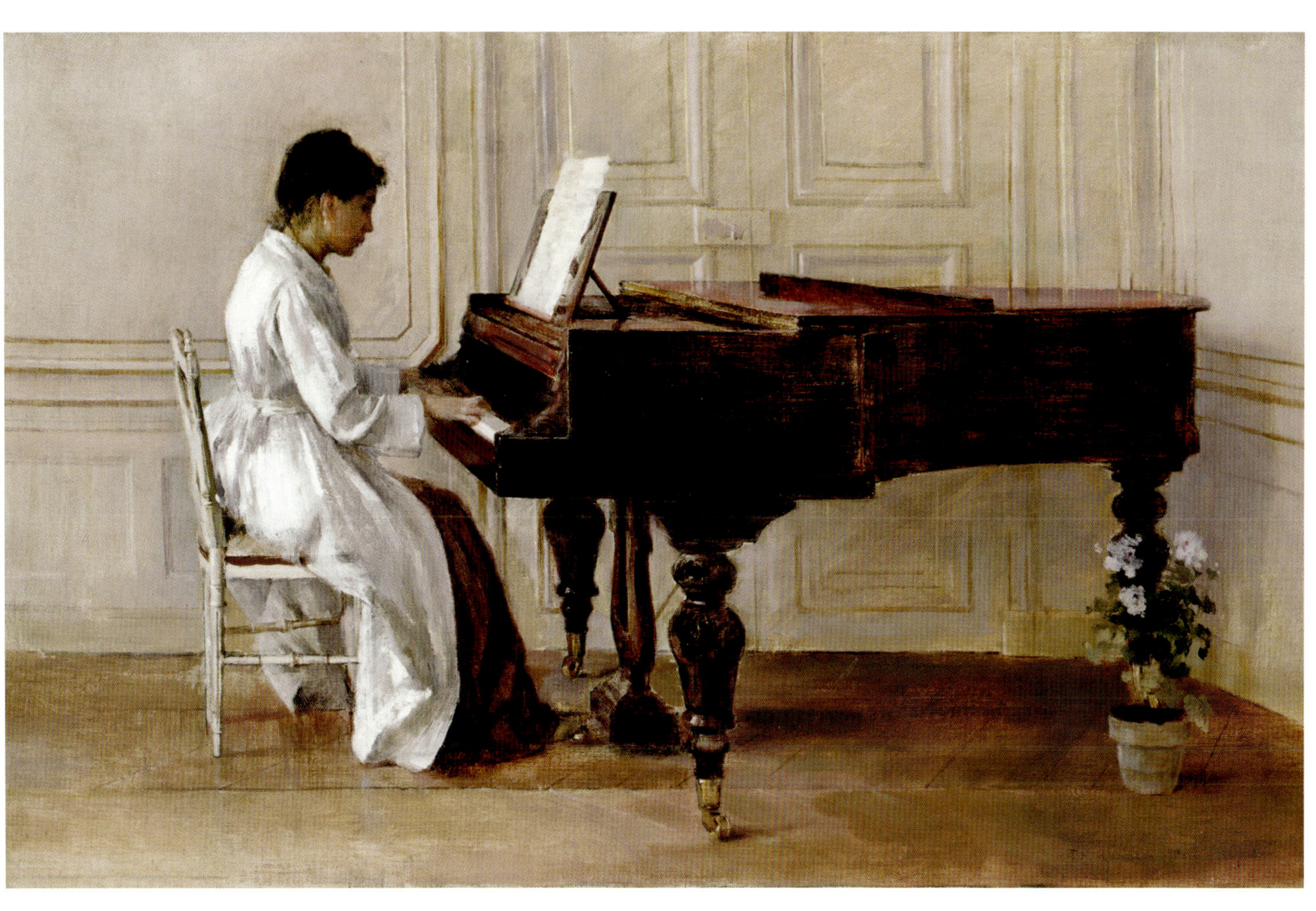

Cat. 23
Theodore Robinson (1852–1896)
At the Piano, 1887
Oil on canvas, 41.8 × 64.2 cm
Smithsonian American Art
Museum, Washington,
Gift of John Gellatly,
1929.6.90

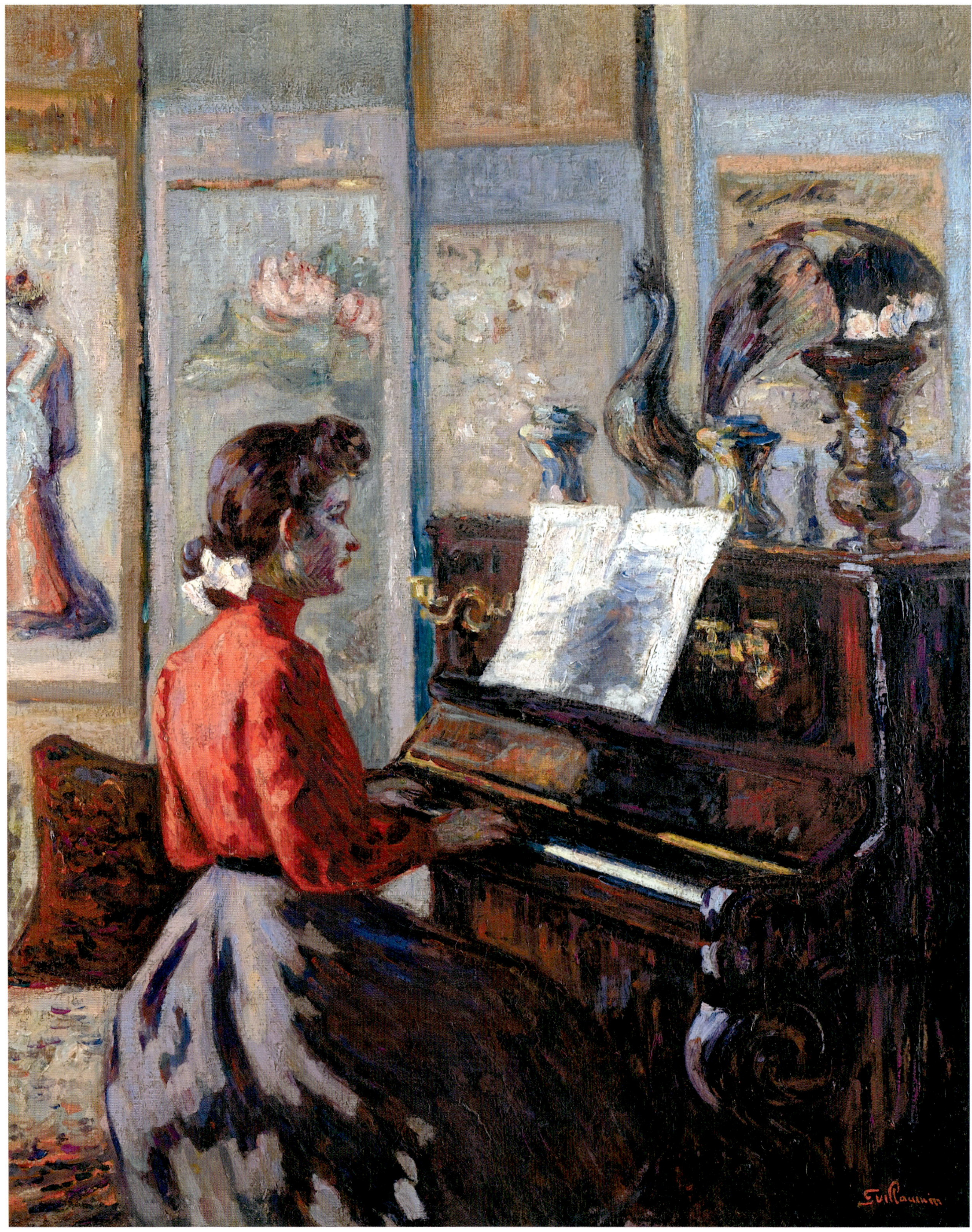

Guillaumin

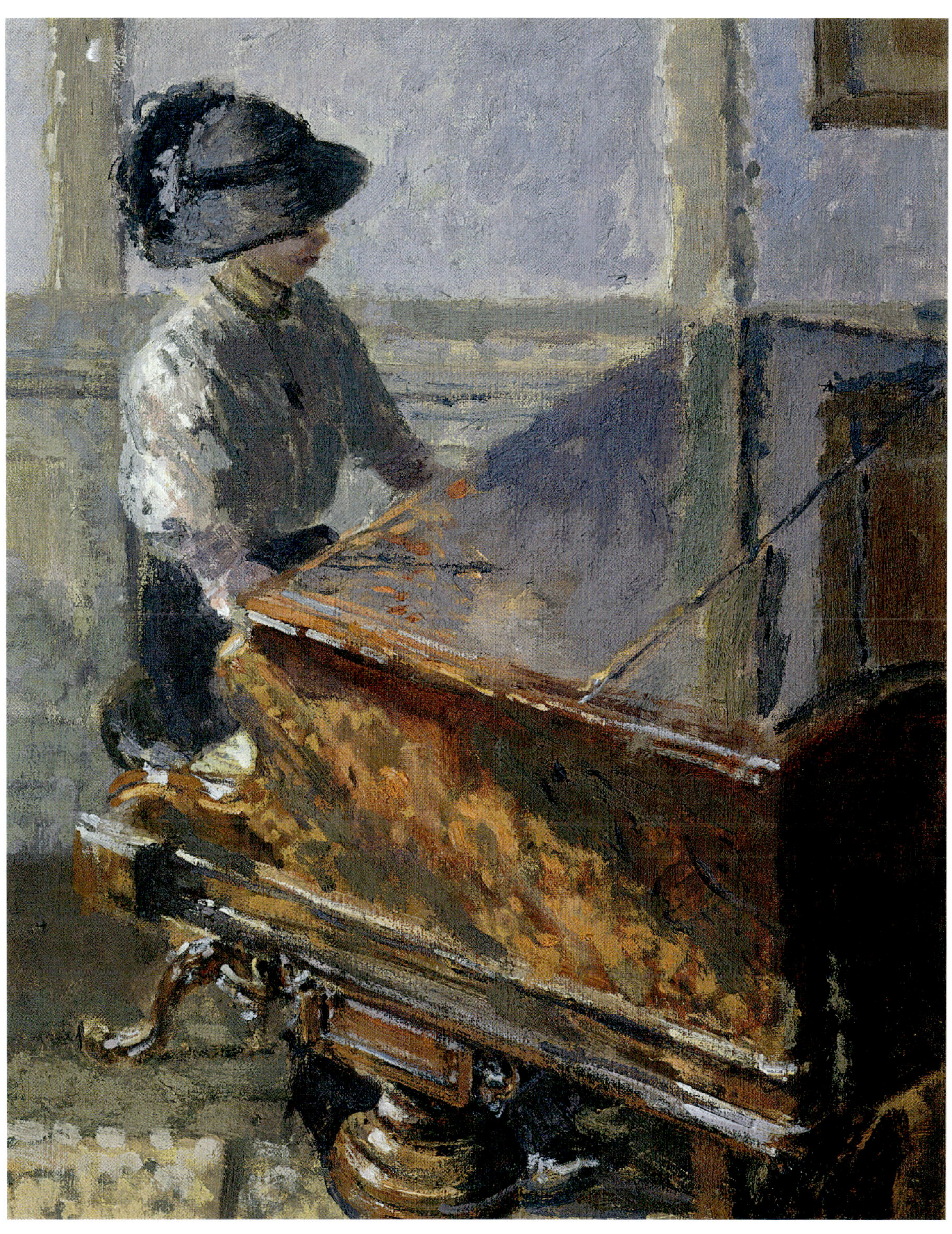

Cat. 24
Armand Guillaumin (1841–1927)
Piano Practice, c. 1889
Oil on canvas, 73.1 × 60.2 cm
Private collection

Cat. 25
Walter Richard Sickert
Tipperary, 1914
Oil on canvas, 50.8 × 40.6 cm
Tate, London, Bequeathed by
Lady Henry Cavendish Bentinck, 1940,
N05092

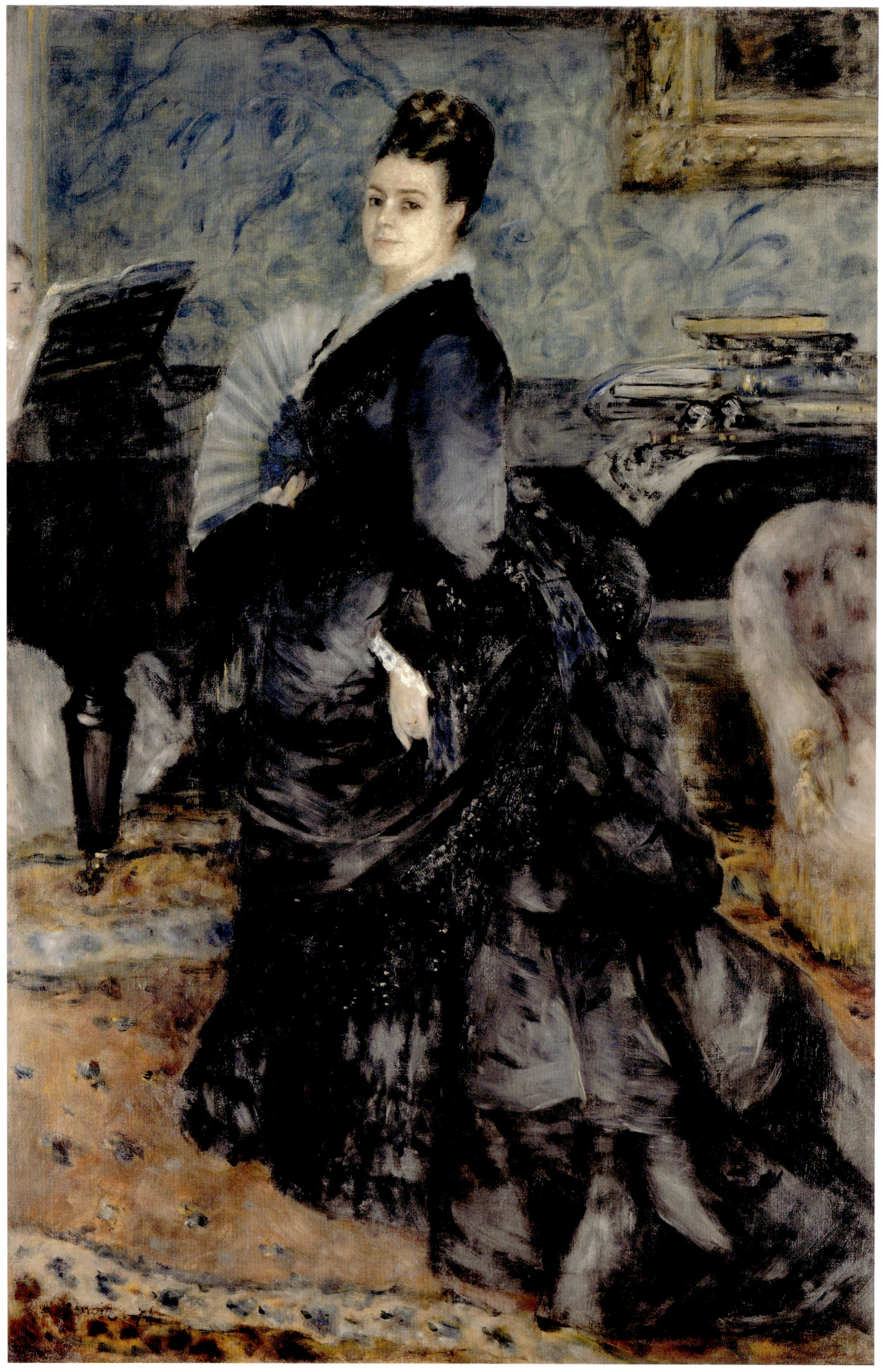

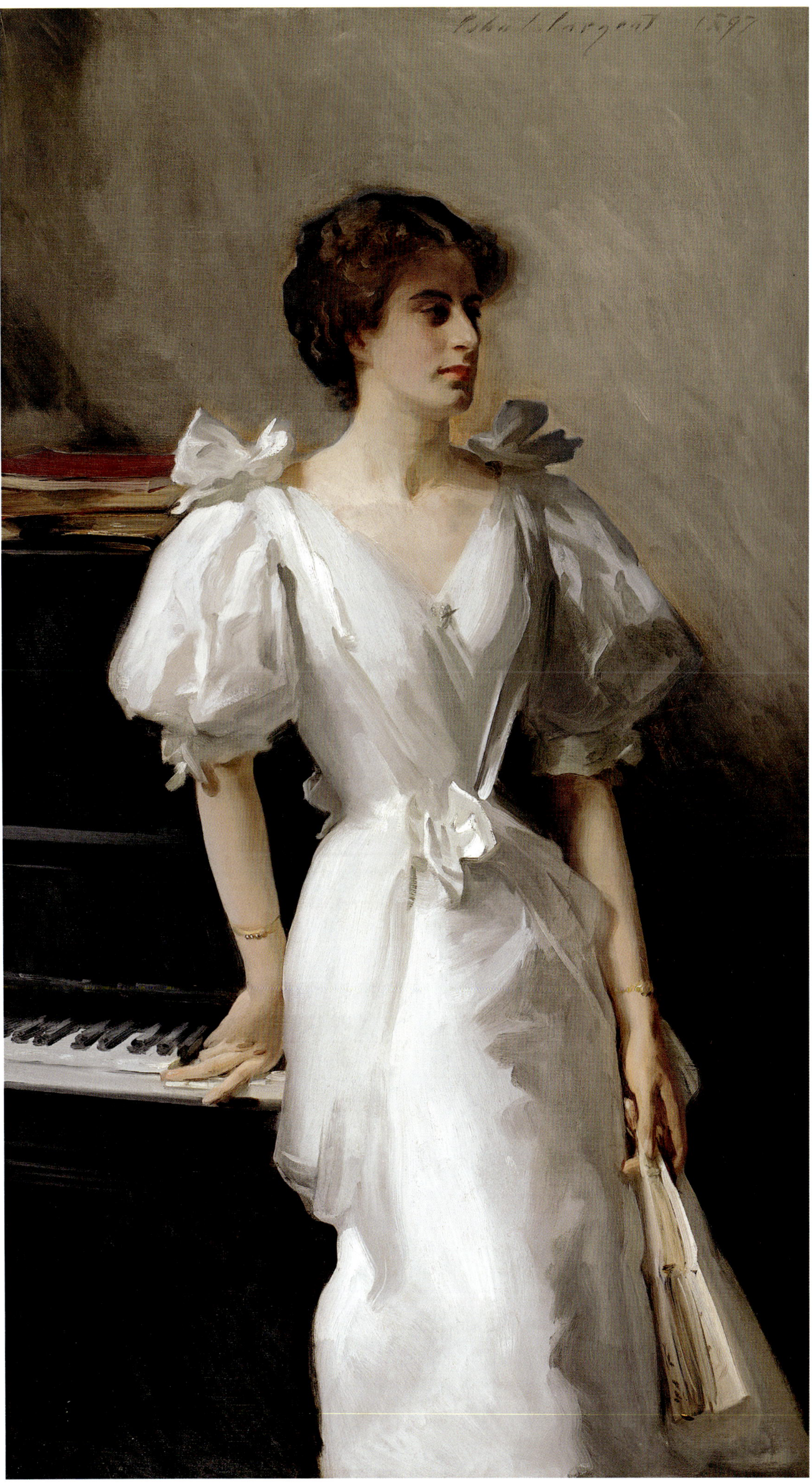

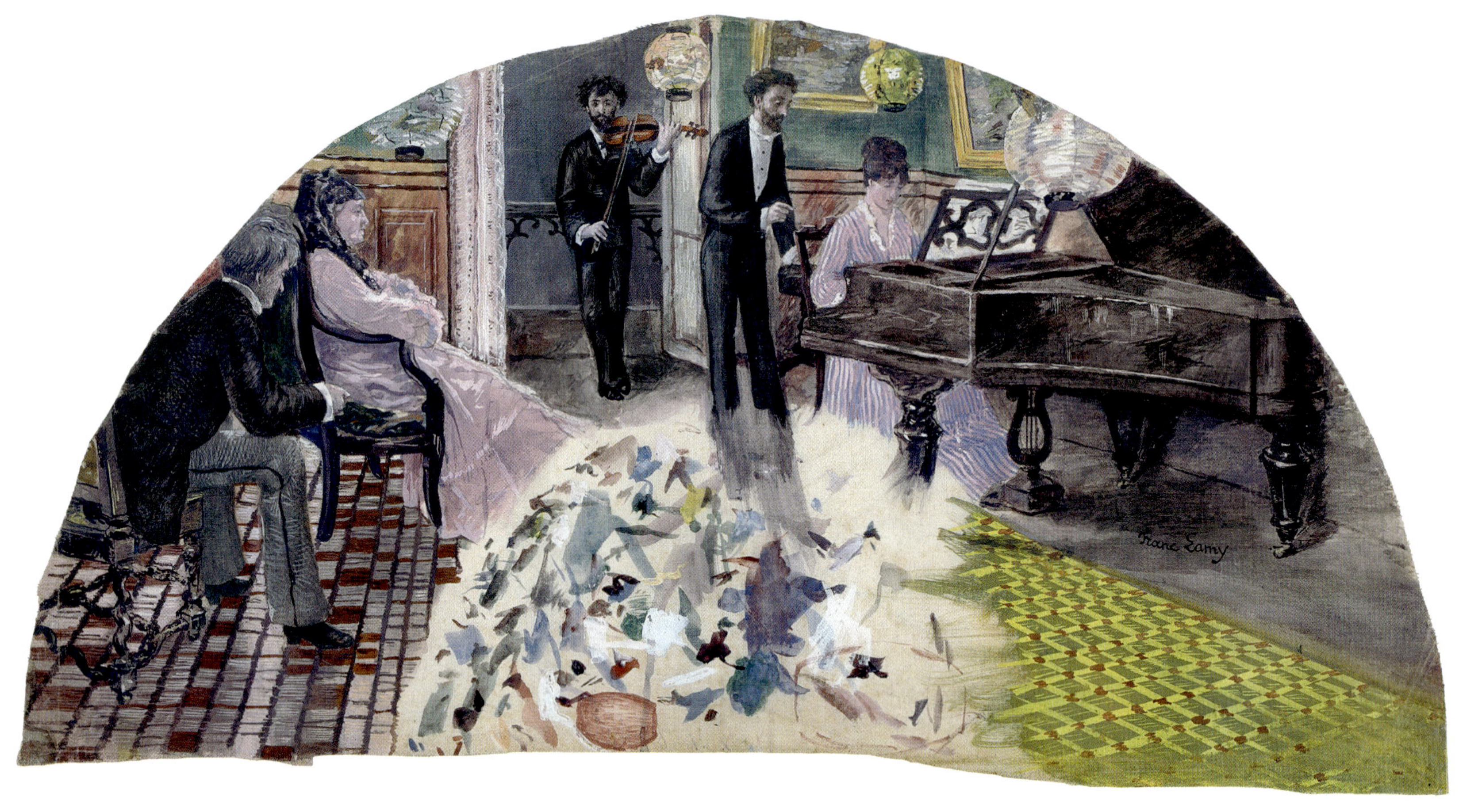

Cat. 28
Pierre Franc-Lamy (1855–1919)
*Design for a Fan: The Salon of
Nina de Callias*, c. 1875–7
Gouache on canvas, 30 × 60 cm
Musée d'Orsay, Paris,
RF 41910

Cat. 29
Édouard Vuillard (1868–1940)
Misia at the Piano,
1895 or early 1896
Oil on cardboard, 26 × 25 cm
The Metropolitan Museum of Art,
New York, Robert Lehman
Collection,
1975.1.224

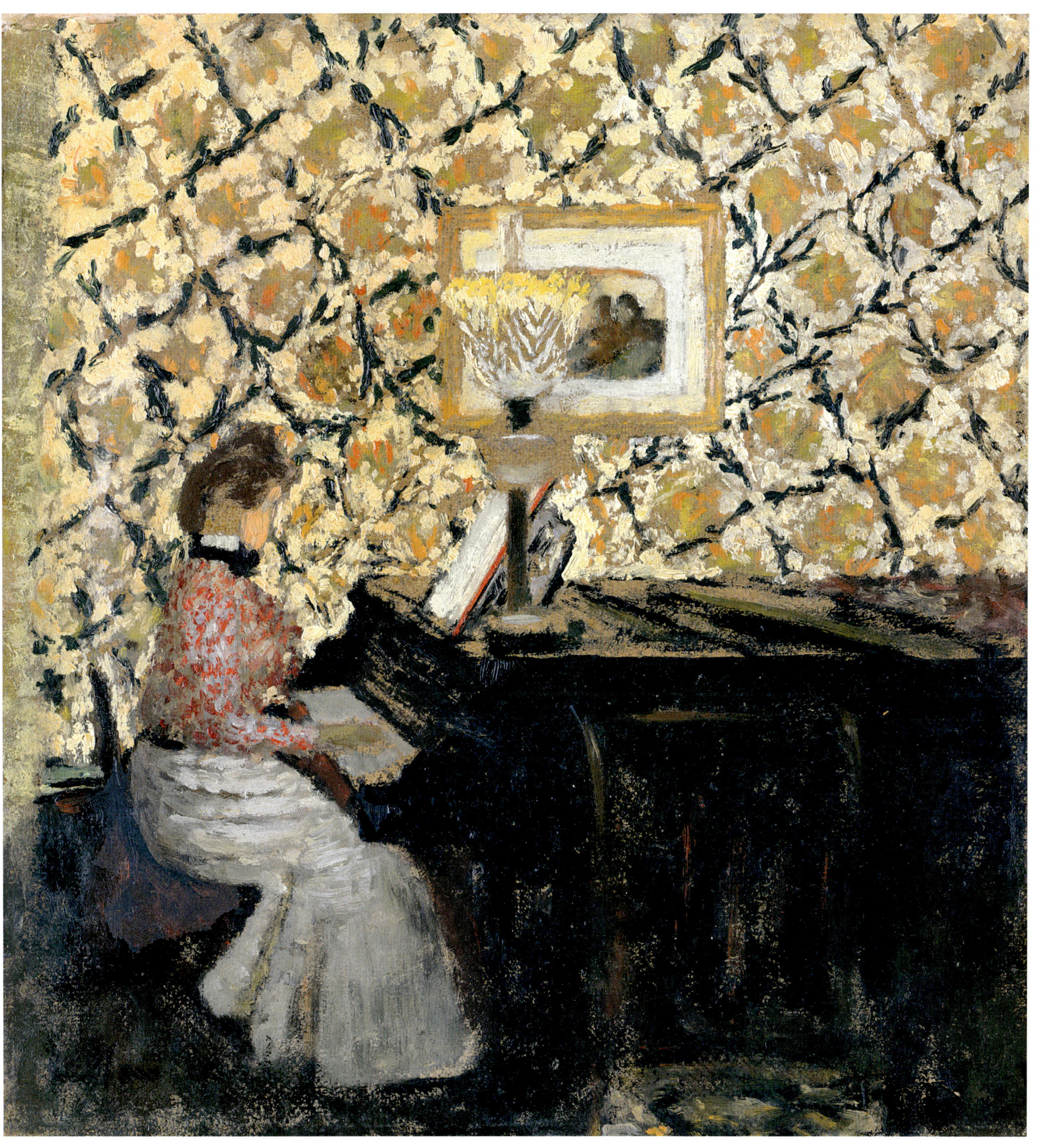

Cat. 30
René Prinet (1861–1946)
The Kreutzer Sonata, 1901
Oil on canvas, 116.8 × 104.1 cm
Dobra Collection

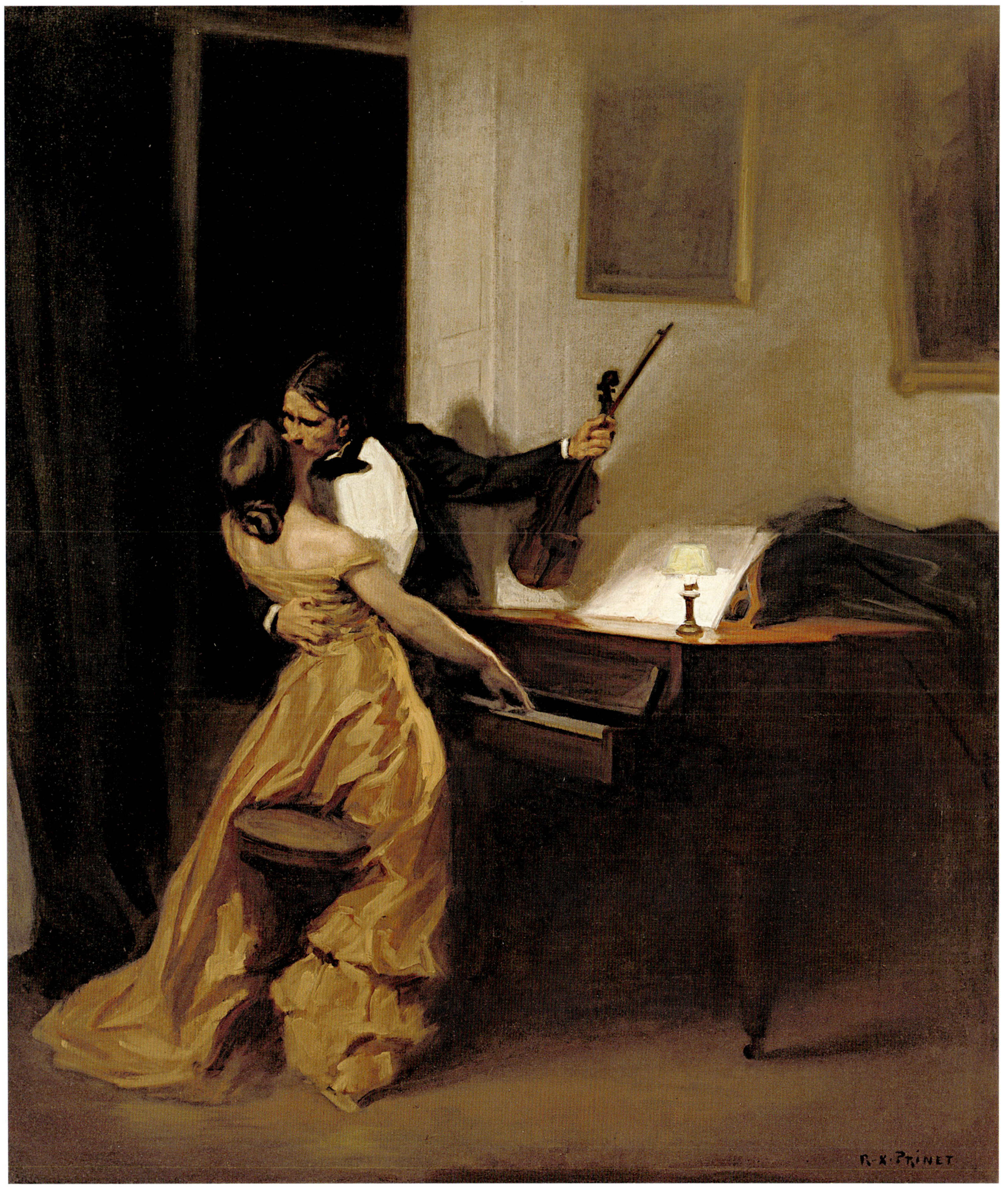

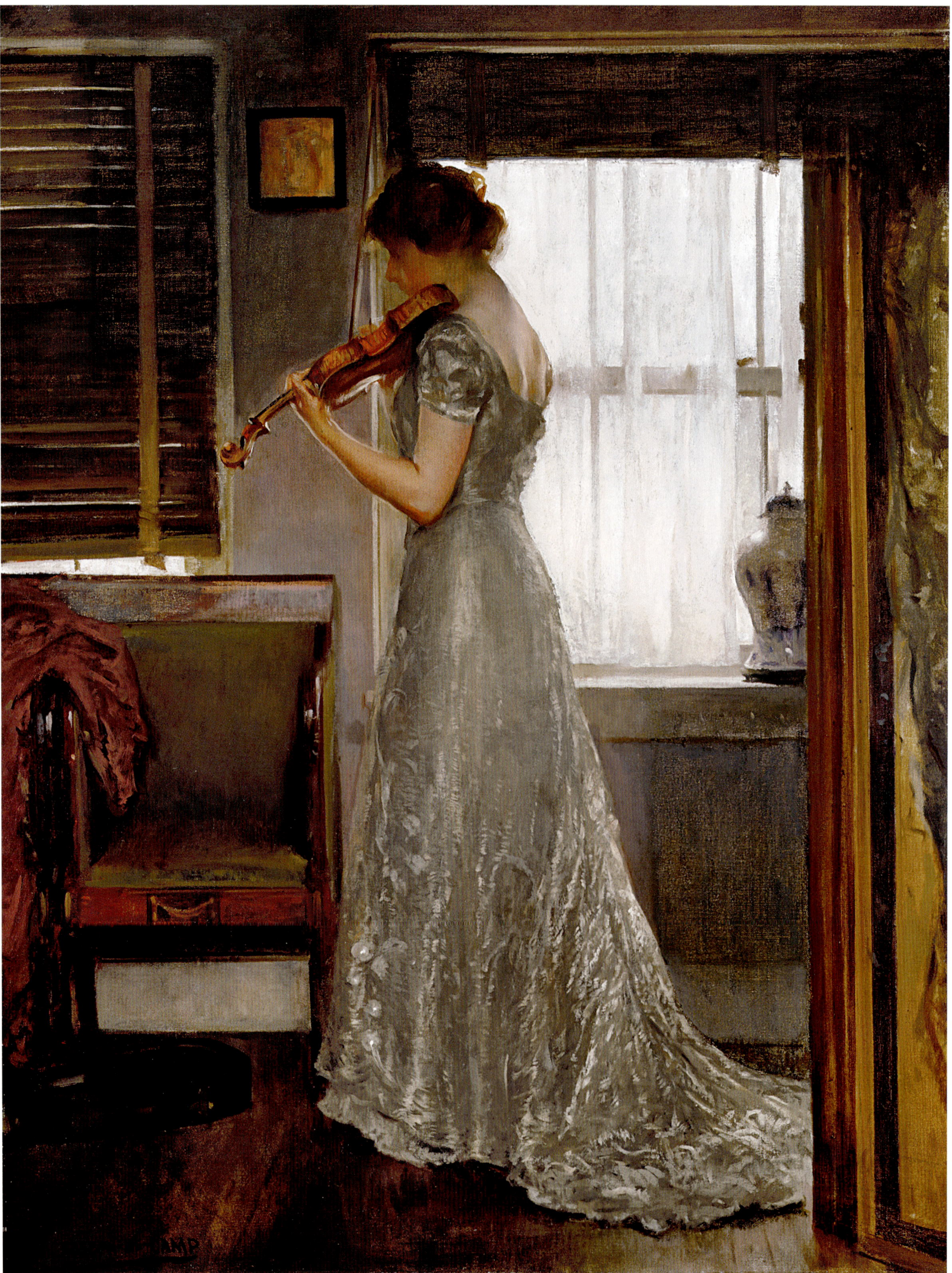

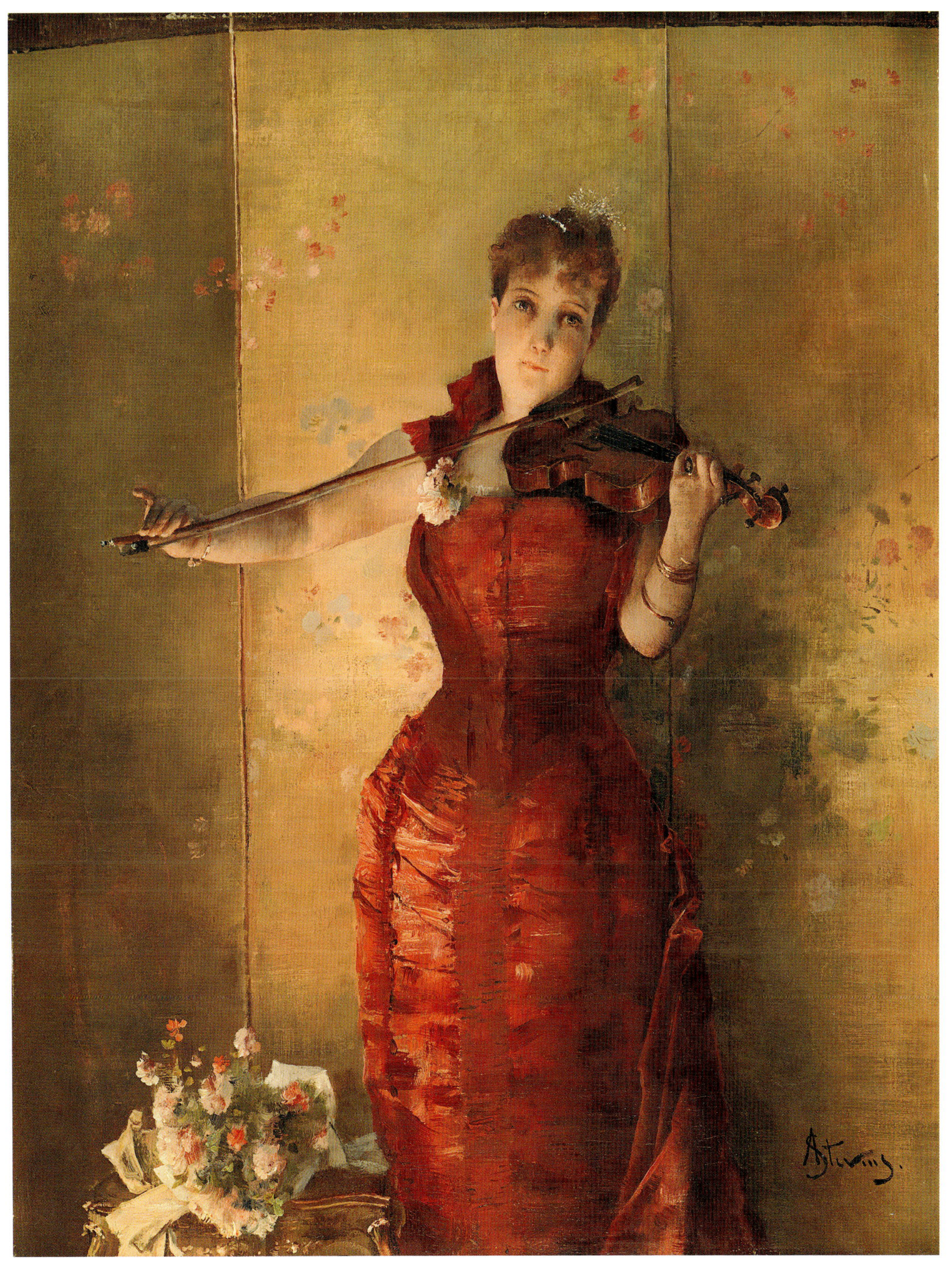

Cat. 31
Joseph DeCamp (1858–1923)
The Violinist, c. 1902
Oil on canvas, 92.7 × 71.8 cm
Terra Foundation for
American Art, Chicago,
Daniel J. Terra Collection,
1999.43

Cat. 32
Alfred Stevens (1823–1906)
The Violinist, c. 1875
Oil on canvas, 67.5 × 53 cm
Musées Royaux des Beaux-Arts
de Belgique, Brussels,
6832

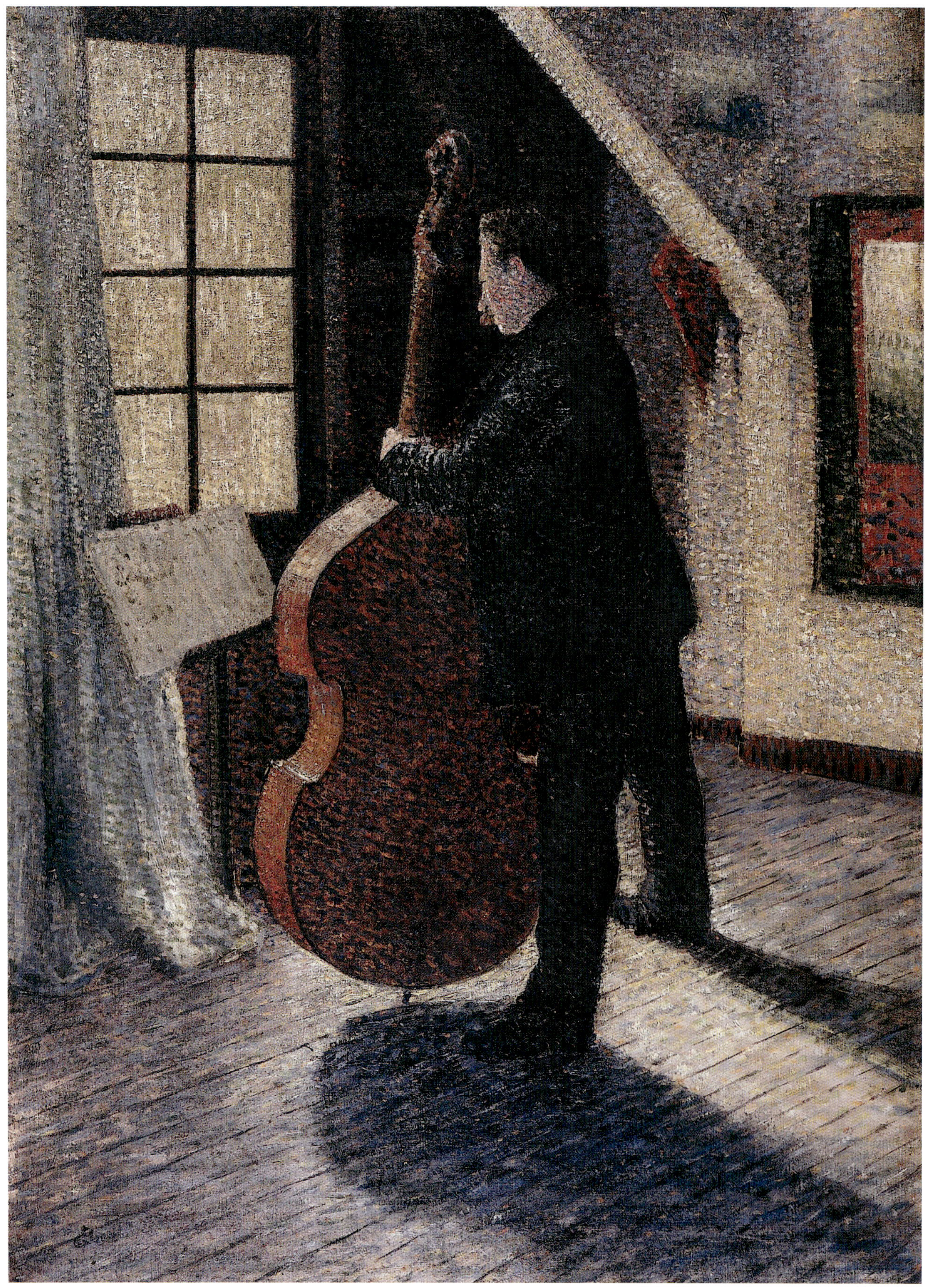

Cat. 33
Louis Hayet
(1864–1940)
Cellist Practising, 1889
Oil on canvas, 82 × 61 cm
Collection of the Conseil
départemental du Val-d'Oise,
Cergy-Pontoise

Cat. 34
Vilhelm Hammershøi
(1864–1916)
*The Cello Player: Portrait
of Henry Bramsen*, 1893
Oil on canvas, 142 × 105.5 cm
Brandts Museum of Art &
Visual Culture, Odense,
FKM/1259

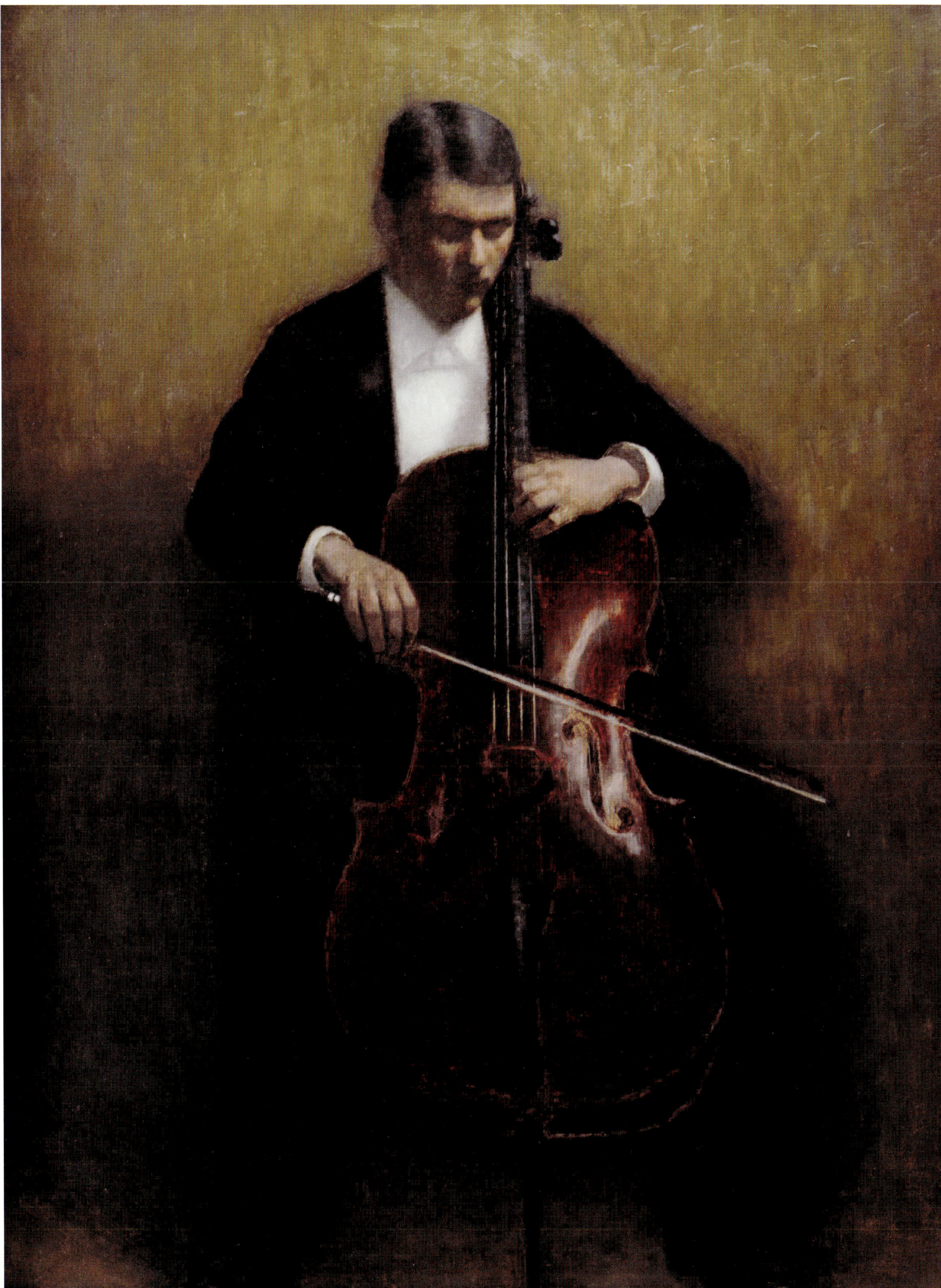

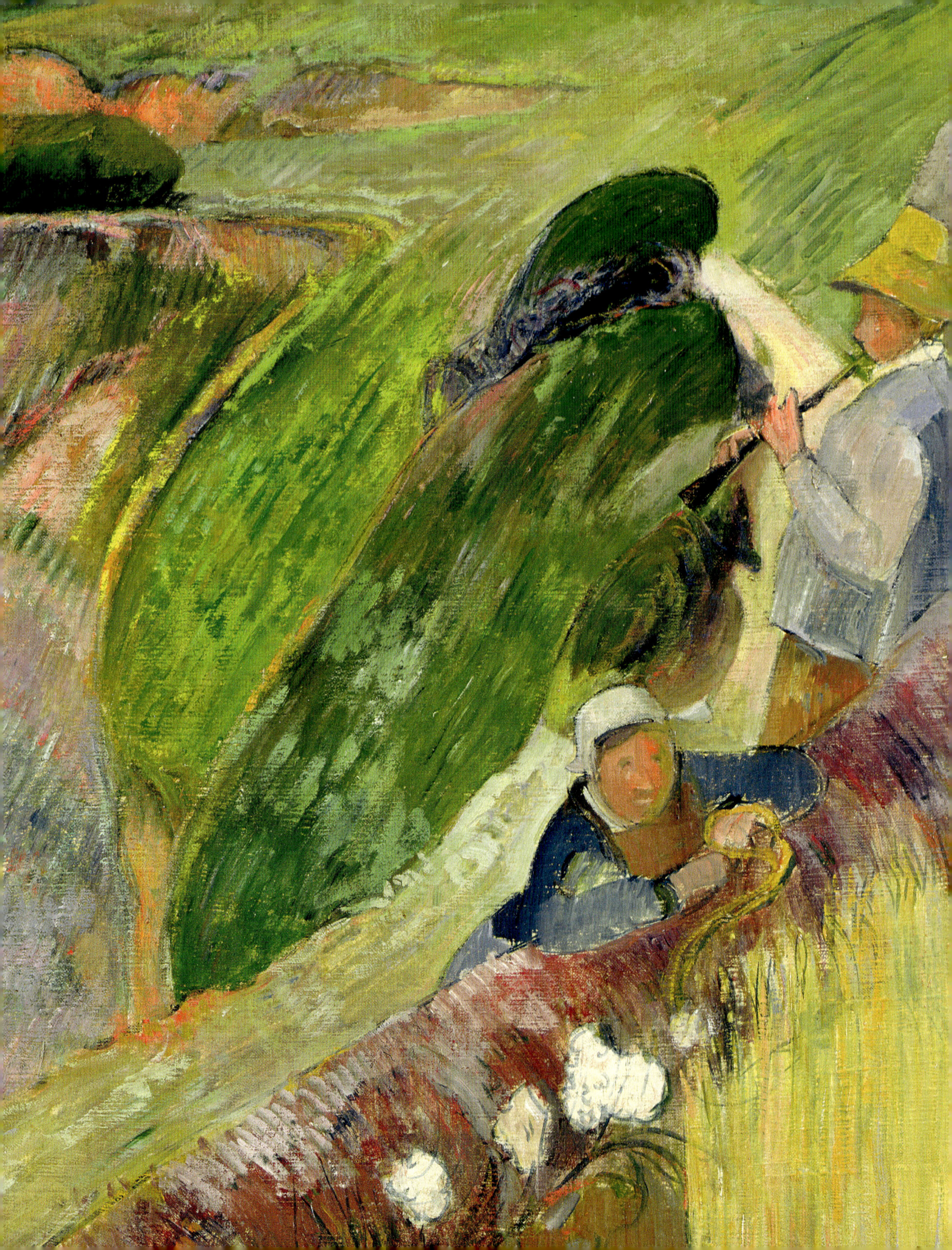

musical escapism

many painters in the late nineteenth century were drawn to pastoral, bucolic, exotic or even primitive ideals of life, and the depiction of music very much reflected this trend.

Indeed this era was characterised by yearnings for utopia in which music played a key role, as one sees in Berthe Morisot's young girl with flageolet (cat. 35). Hence we find music, often taking the concrete form of a flageolet or some other wind instrument, coming to represent not only a folkloric element, as is the case with Gauguin's bombardon (cat. 38) – hitherto wrongly identified as a flageolet – but also a kind of return to the roots, including, by association, the roots of painting.

Far from contradicting the spirit of modernity driving painting and reflected in its depictions of musical scenes, these more Arcadian images can be taken as evoking certain longstanding inspirations of painting that were drawn on and revisited by the artistic movements of the day. In this respect, Hispanism affected music (Chabrier, Bizet, etc.) as much as it did painting, and notably certain musical themes painted by Auguste Renoir (cat. 45), Théo van Rysselberghe (cat. 41 and 42) and Émile Bernard (cat. 46), among others. The Spanish guitarist, a figure popularised by Édouard Manet, became the cliché of this Iberian trope.

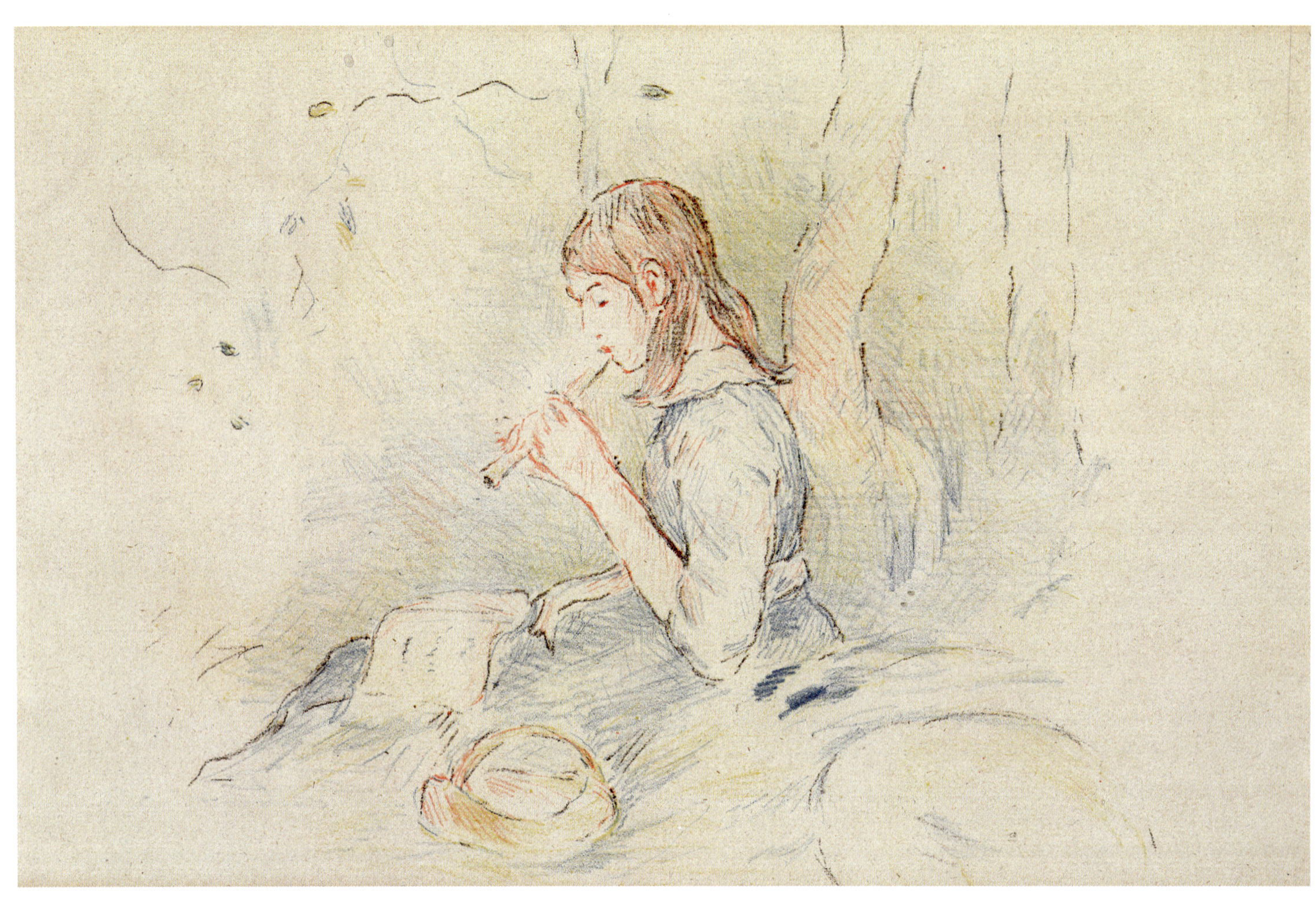

Cat. 35
Berthe Morisot
The Flageolet, 1890
Coloured crayons, 16 × 26 cm
Musée Marmottan Monet, Paris,
Bequest of the Denis and Annie
Rouart Foundation, 1993,
6044

Cat. 36
Henri Manguin (1874–1949)
Claude with Recorder, 1908
Oil on canvas, 116 × 89 cm
Private collection

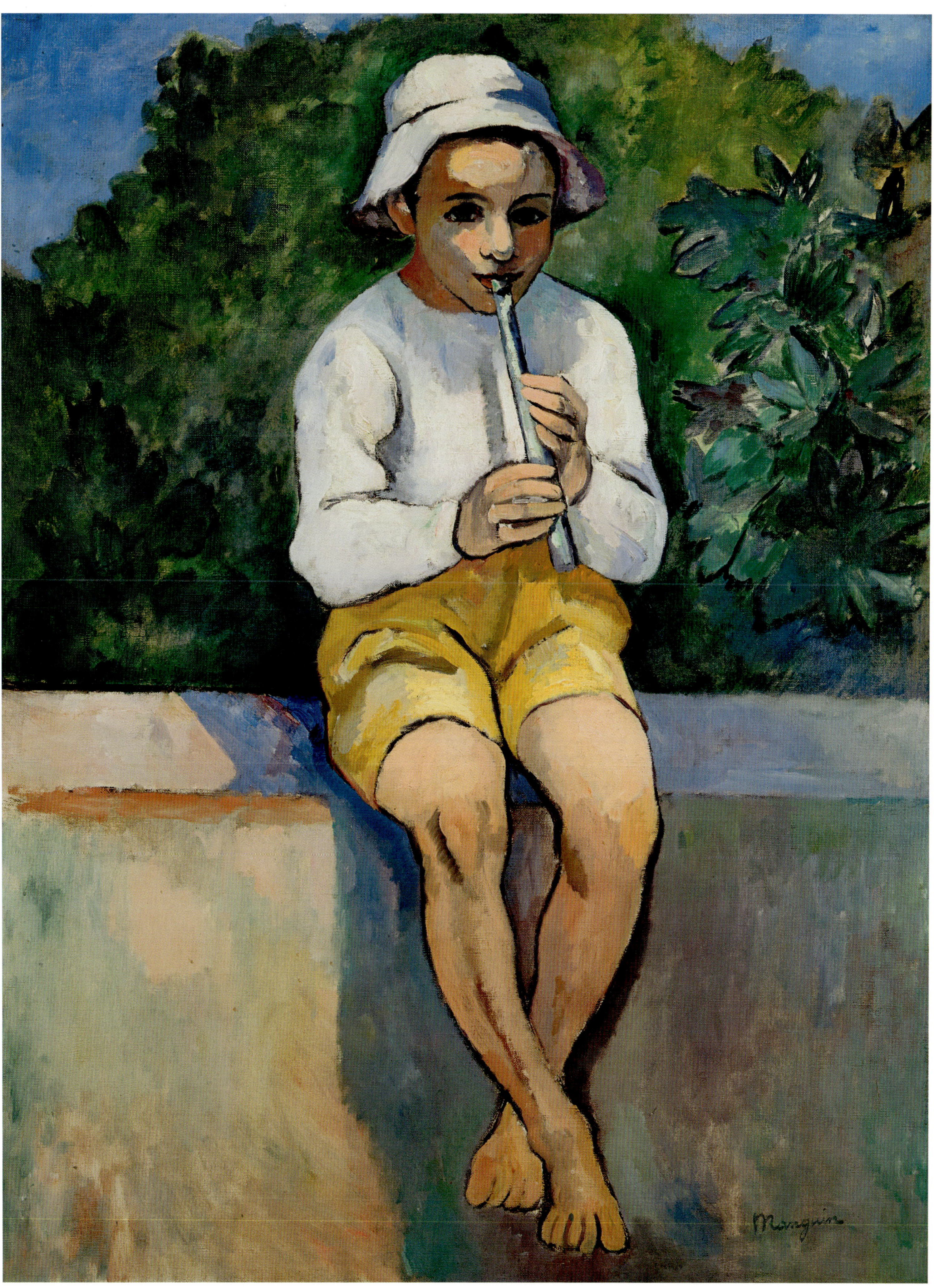

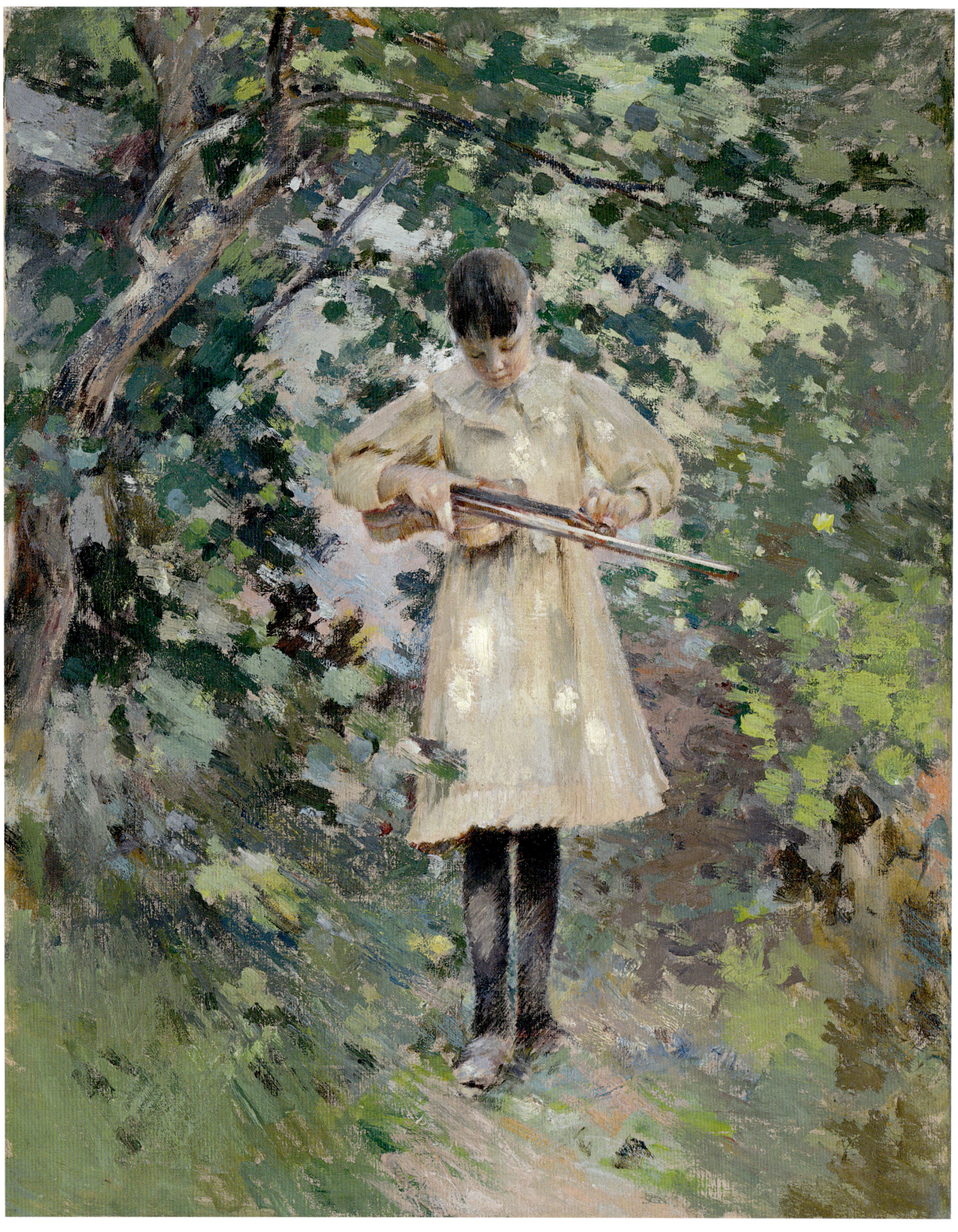

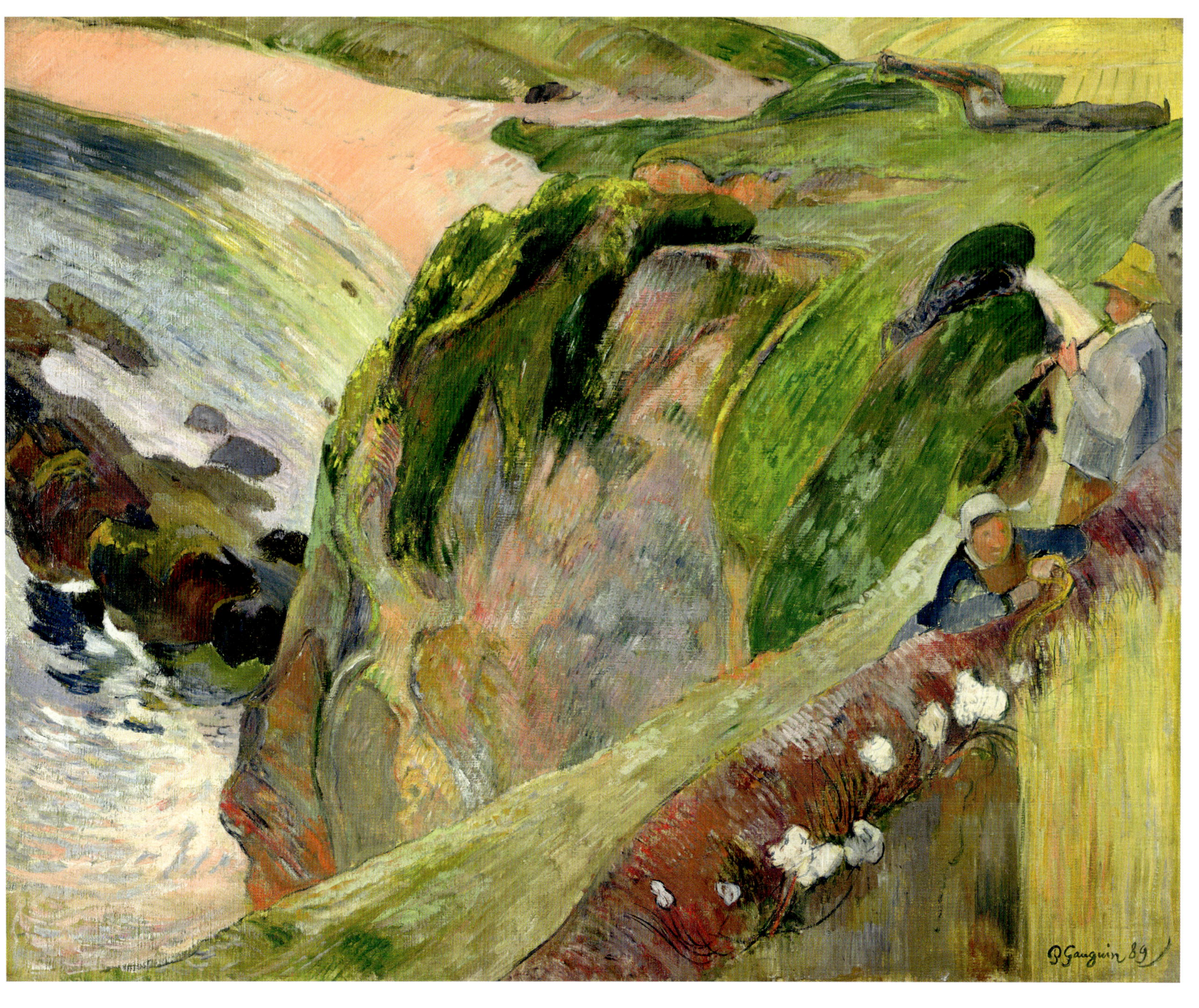

Cat. 37
Theodore Robinson
*The Young Violinist
(Margaret Perry)*, c. 1889
Oil on canvas, 81.8 × 66.4 cm
The Baltimore Museum of Art,
The Cone Collection,
formed by Dr. Claribel Cone and
Miss Etta Cone of Baltimore,
BMA 1950.290

Cat. 38
Paul Gauguin (1848–1903)
*The Flageolet Player
on the Cliff*, 1889
Oil on canvas, 70.96 × 91.28 cm
Indianapolis Museum of Art,
Samuel Josefowitz Collection of the
School of Pont-Aven, through the
generosity of Lilly Endowment Inc.,
the Josefowitz Family,
Mr. and Mrs. James M. Cornelius,
Mr. and Mrs. Leonard J. Betley,
Lori and Dan Efroymson, and other
Friends of the Museum,
IMA 1998.168

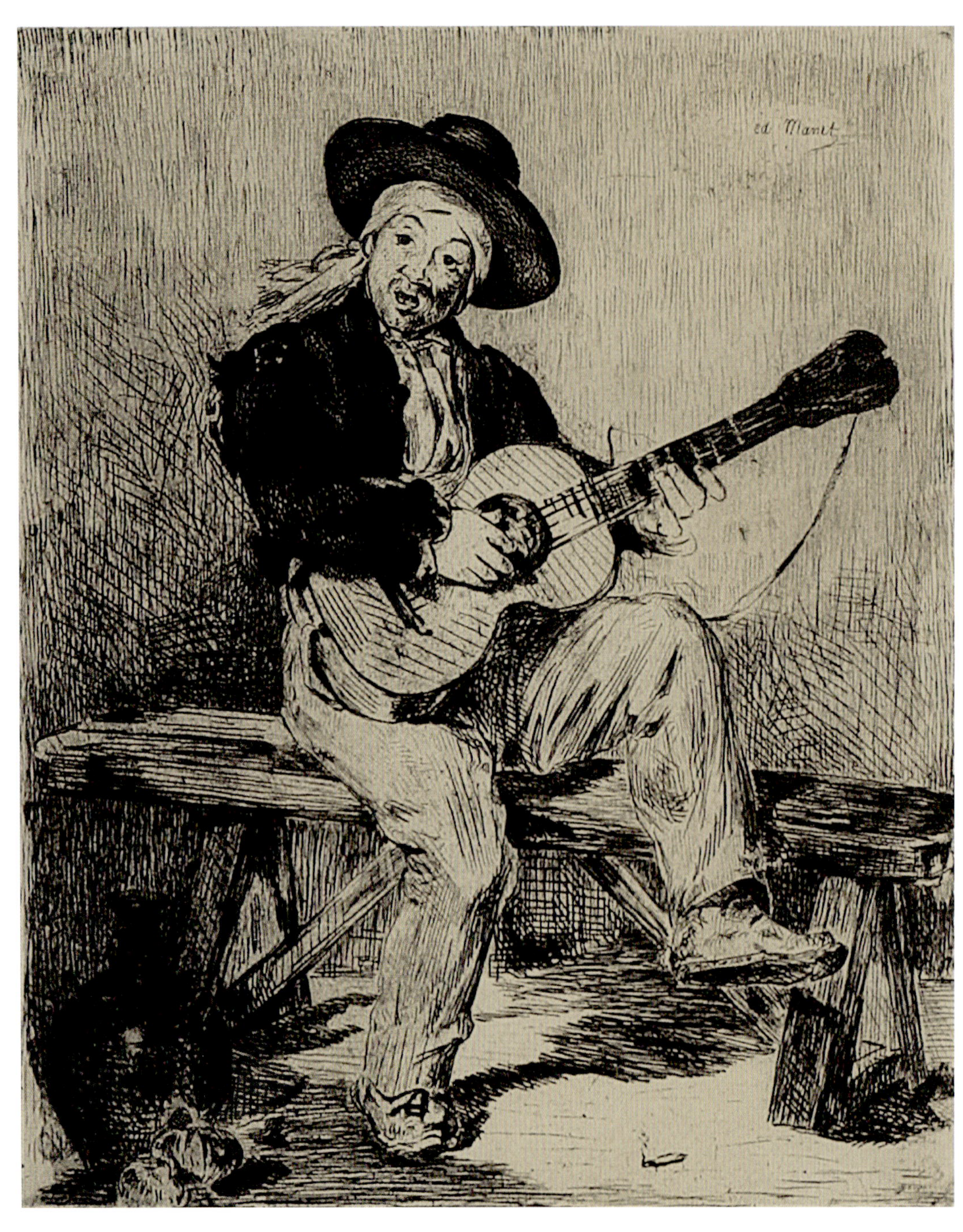

Cat. 39
Édouard Manet
The Spanish Singer
or *Guitarrero*, 1861
Etching, 29.7 × 24.3 cm
Institut National d'Histoire de
l'Art, Bibliothèque, Collection
Jacques Doucet, Paris,
EM MANET 17

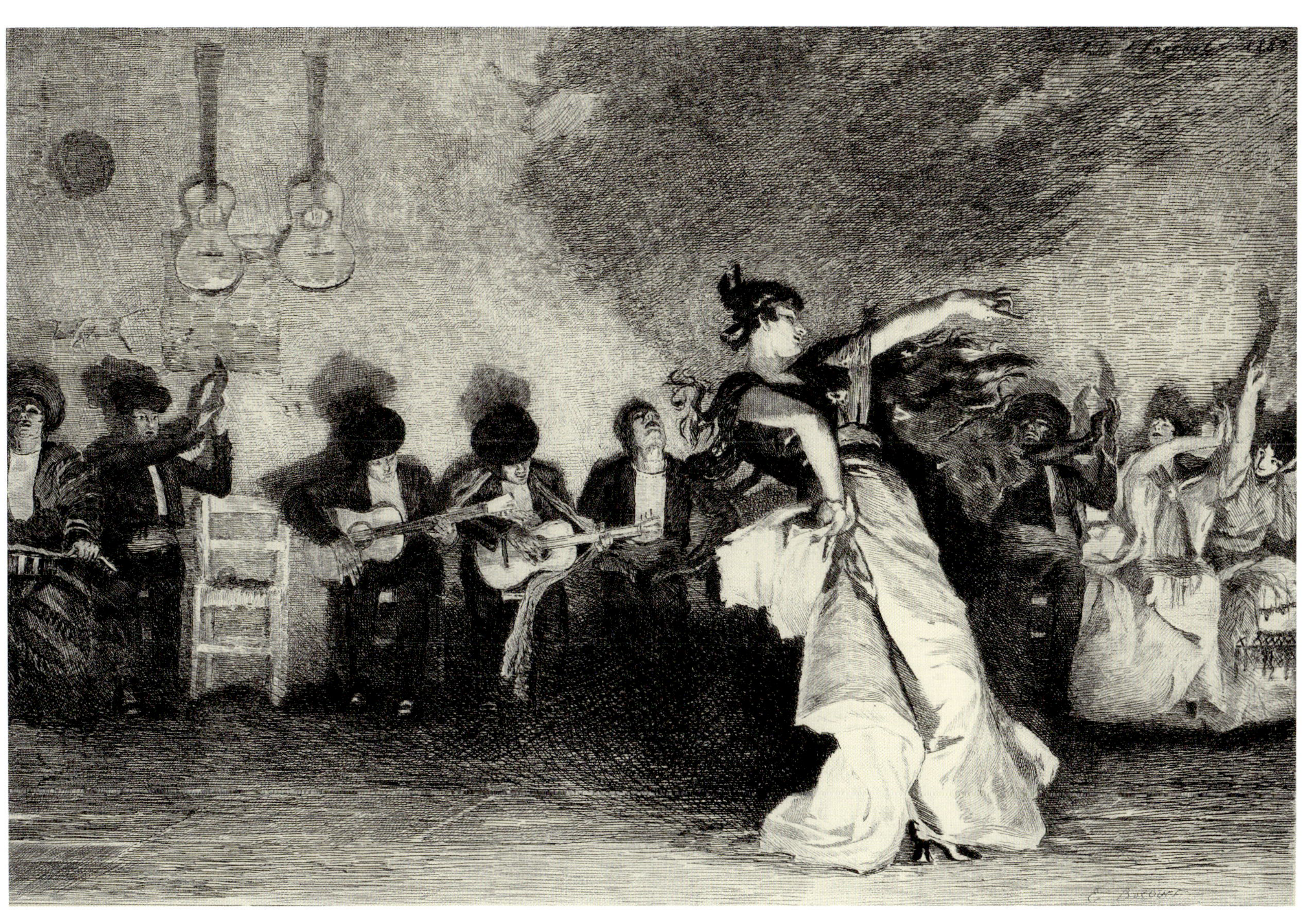

Cat. 40
Étienne Bocourt (1821–19..?)
after John Singer Sargent
El Jaleo – Gypsy Dance, 1882
Etching, 27.2 × 37 cm
First published in the journal
L'Art, 30 (1882) facing page 138
Musée Franco-Américain
du Château de Blérancourt,
Blérancourt,
SansAG 2005.29

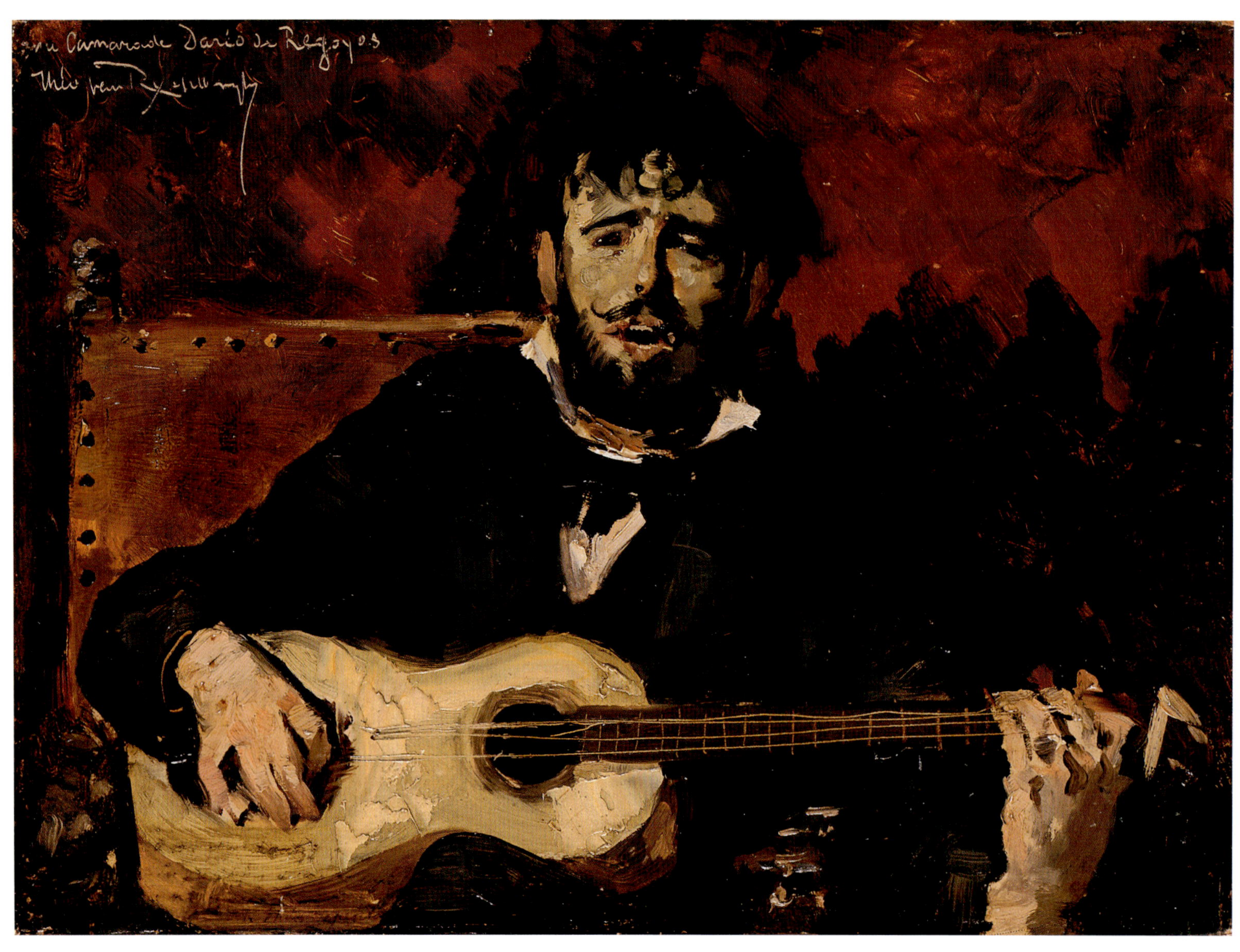

Cat. 41
Théo van Rysselberghe
(1862–1926)
Darío de Regoyos playing
the Guitar, c. 1882
Oil on panel, 26.5 × 36 cm
Private collection

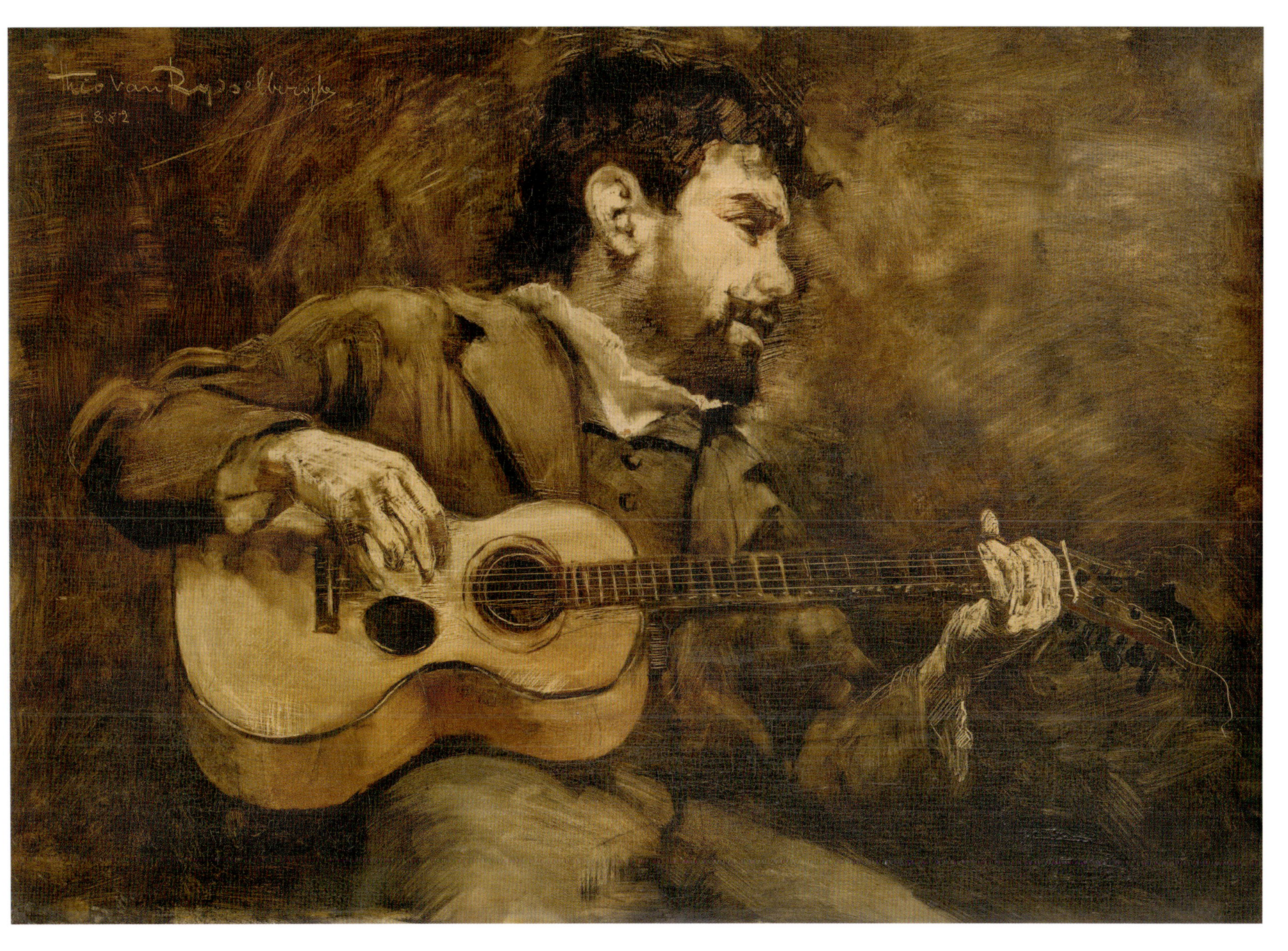

Cat. 42
Théo van Rysselberghe
*Guitar Player – Portrait of
the Spanish Painter,
Darío de Regoyos*, 1882
Oil on wood, 30 × 42.5 cm
Musées Royaux des Beaux-Arts
de Belgique, Brussels,
3728

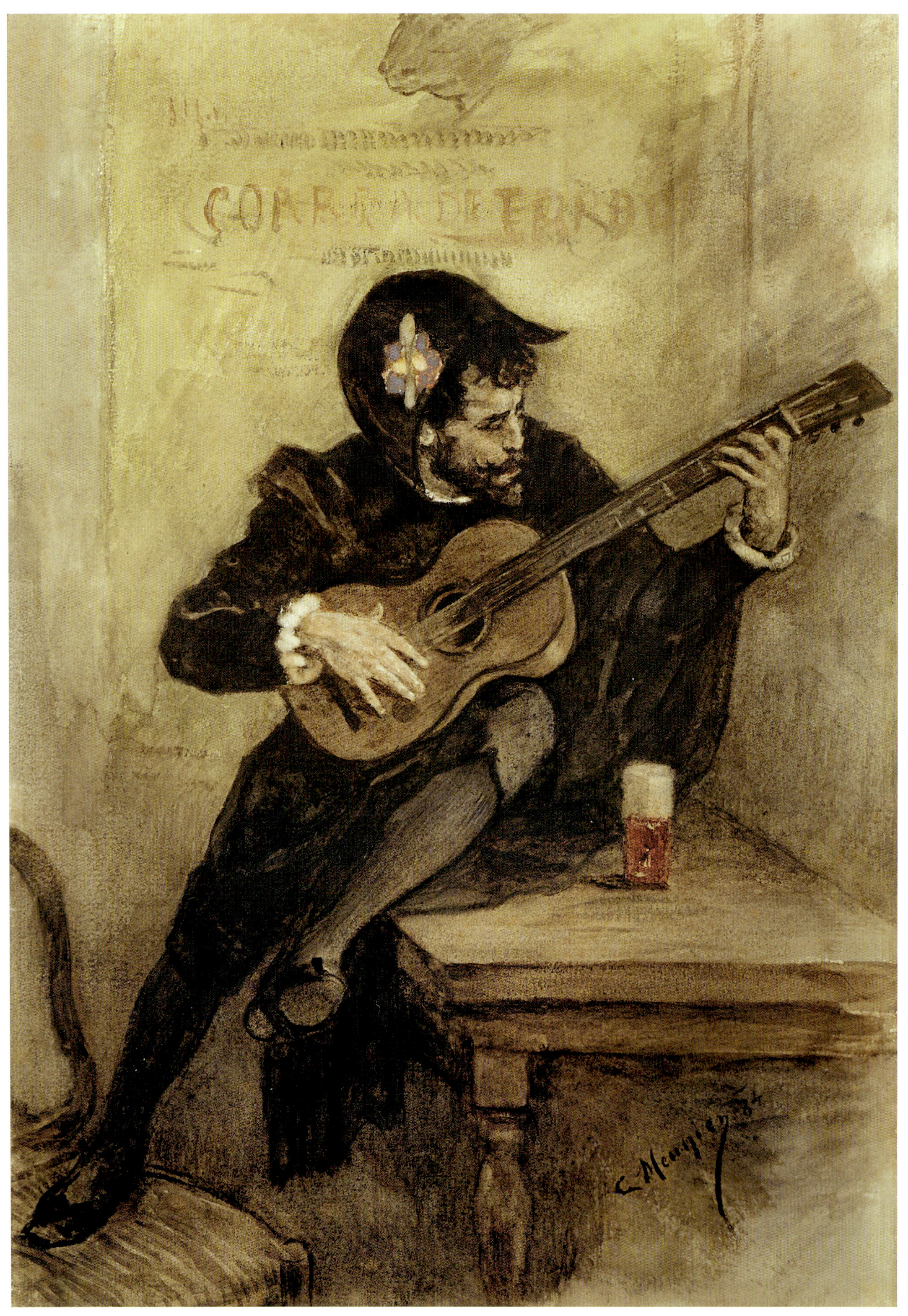

Cat. 43
Constantin Meunier
(1831–1905)
Portrait of Darío de Regoyos, 1884
Watercolour on paper, 44 × 32 cm
Collection Juan San Nicolás,
Madrid

Cat. 44
James Ensor (1860–1949)
Portrait of Darío de Regoyos, 1884
Oil on canvas, 68 × 56.7 cm
Belfius Art Collection, Brussels,
1136

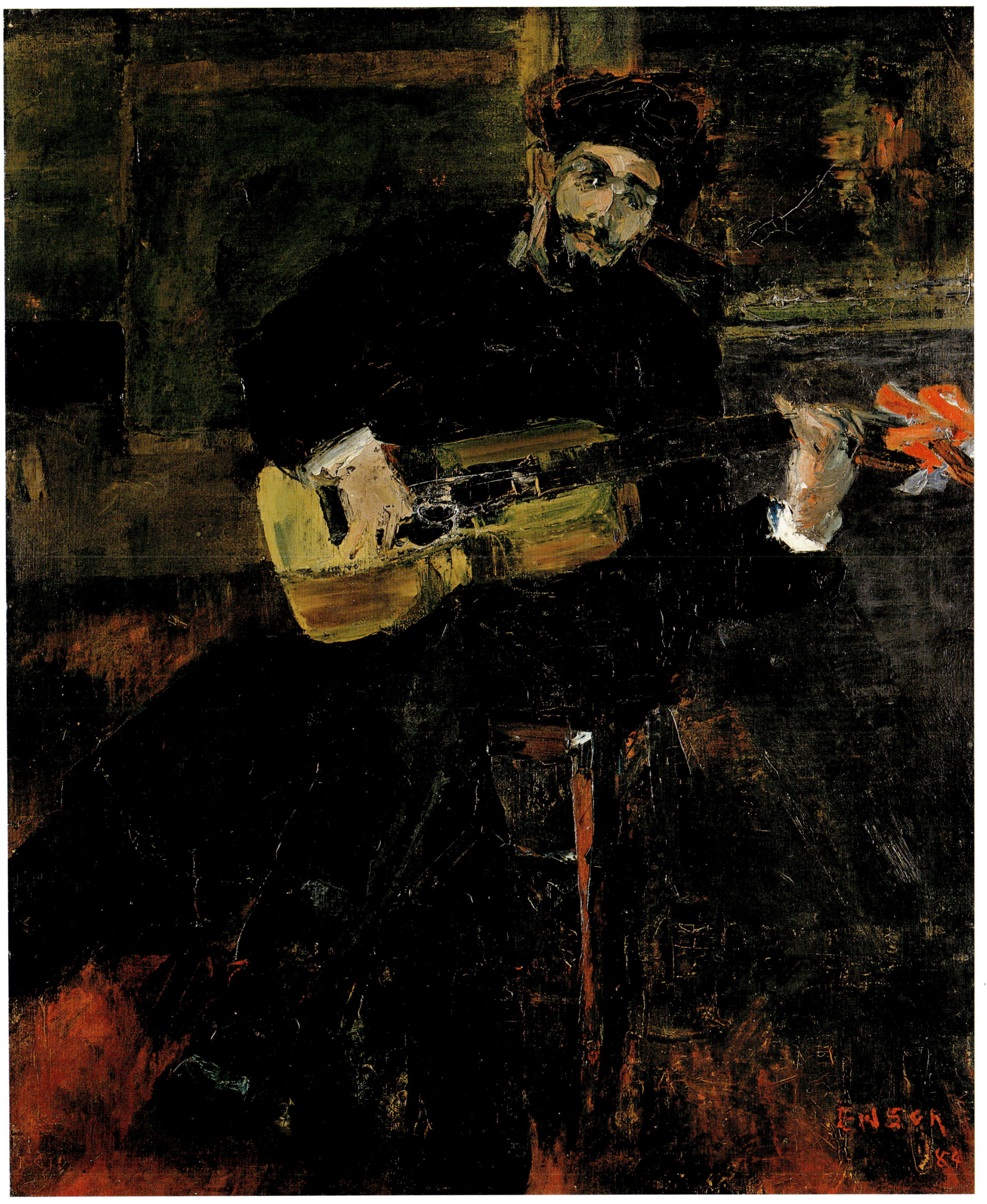

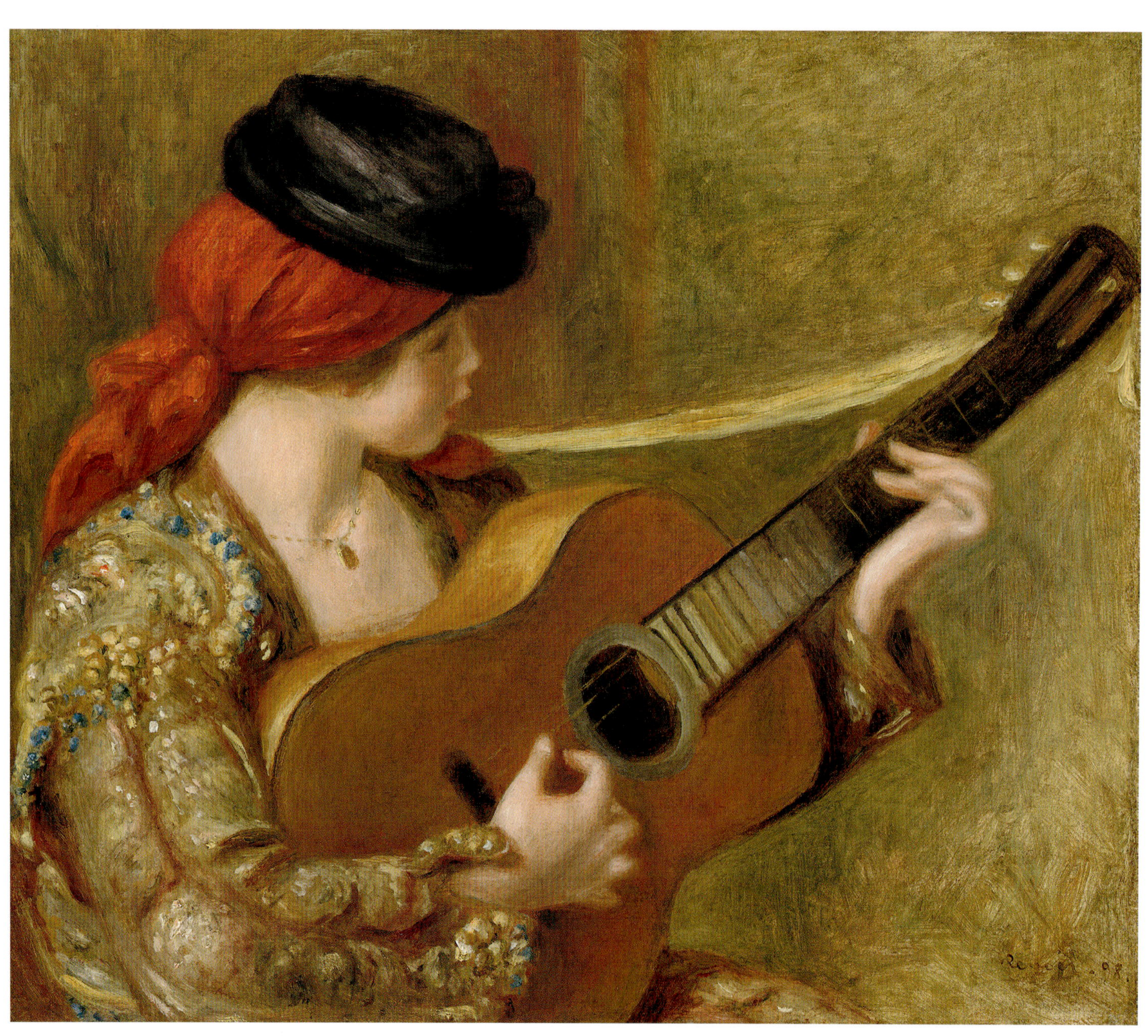

Cat. 45
Auguste Renoir
*Young Spanish Woman
with a Guitar*, 1898
Oil on canvas, 55.6 × 65.2 cm
National Gallery of Art, Ailsa Mellon
Bruce Collection, Washington,
1970.17.76

Cat. 46
Émile Bernard (1868–1941)
Spanish Beggars, 1897
Oil on canvas, 182 × 120 cm
Private collection

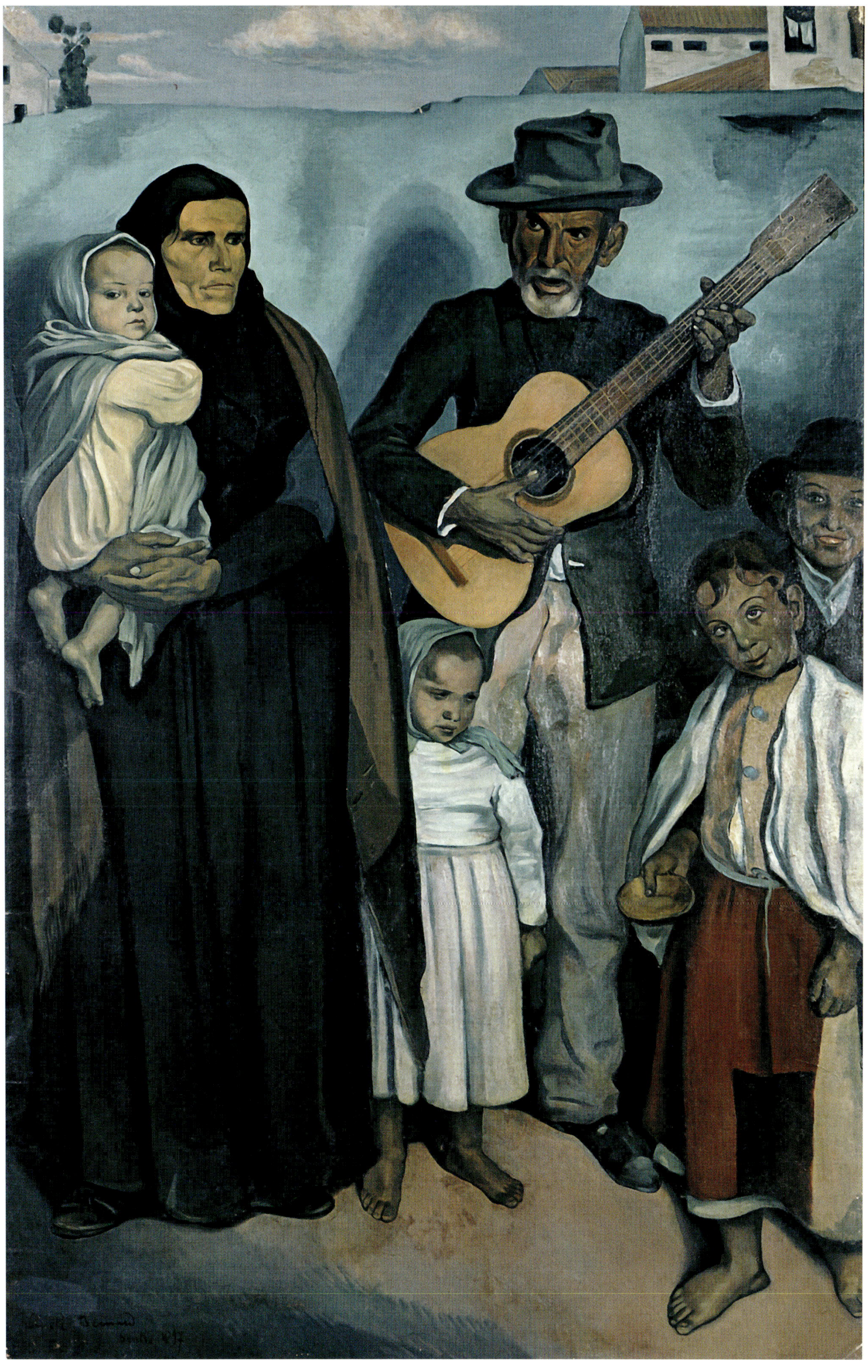

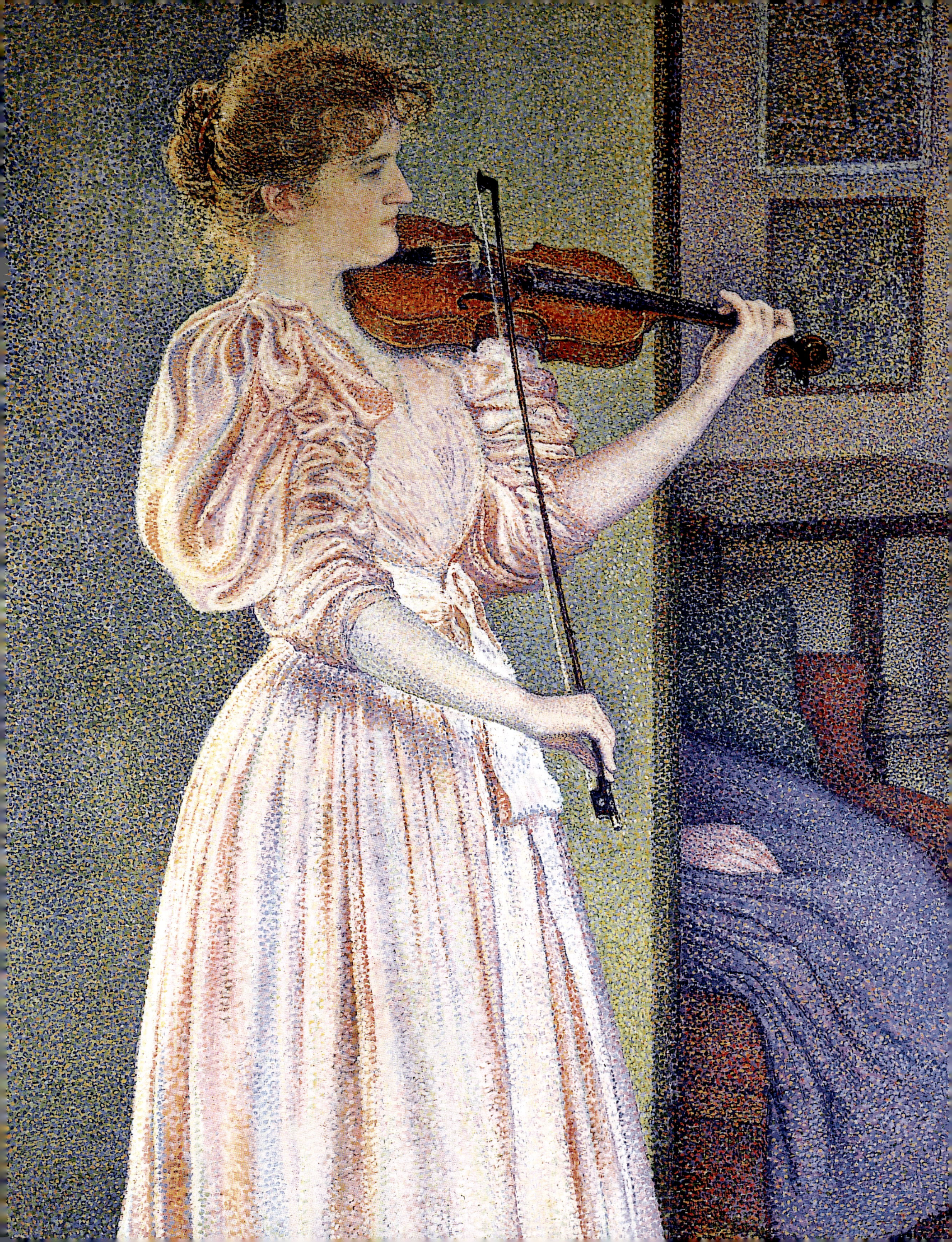

convergences

he representation of instruments reflected artists' attempts at this period to bring the visual arts and music closer together. The piano in the studio was a common theme. One frequently comes across pictures in which painters, poets, writers and musicians are shown gathering around the instrument, as in Henri Fantin-Latour's *Around the Piano* (cat. 60).

Artists' circles and societies also issued regular invitations to musicians, such as the violinist Achille Lerminiaux painted by Fernand Khnopff (cat. 54) and the Sèthe sisters (cat. 55, 56 and 57, fig. 34, p. 131) painted by Théo van Rysselberghe, who played in Brussels at the salons of Les XX and, later, La Libre Esthétique.

Friendships and family connections between painters and musicians were frequent. Manet's wife, Suzanne Leenhoff, was a piano teacher, while Claude Terrasse, the husband of Bonnard's sister Andrée, was a composer. Their closeness is reflected in his portraits of the couple (cat. 48 and 50) and Bonnard also illustrated many of his brother-in-law's scores and methods, including his *Petit Solfège illustré* (cat. 80).

Edgar Degas was friends with the bassoonist Désiré Dihau, who introduced him to the cellist Pilet (cat. 51) and his pianist sister, Marie (cat. 52). The same Dihau siblings were later painted by Henri de Toulouse-Lautrec (cat. 53 and 67), indicating the real affinities linking painters and musicians at the time.

Finally, there were painters who themselves played an instrument. Eva Gonzalès, for example, was represented at the piano by Alfred Stevens (cat. 59), just as, somewhat later, Lucie Cousturier, a pupil of Henri-Edmond Cross and Paul Signac, was shown playing the piano by their mutual friend Maximilien Luce (cat. 58).

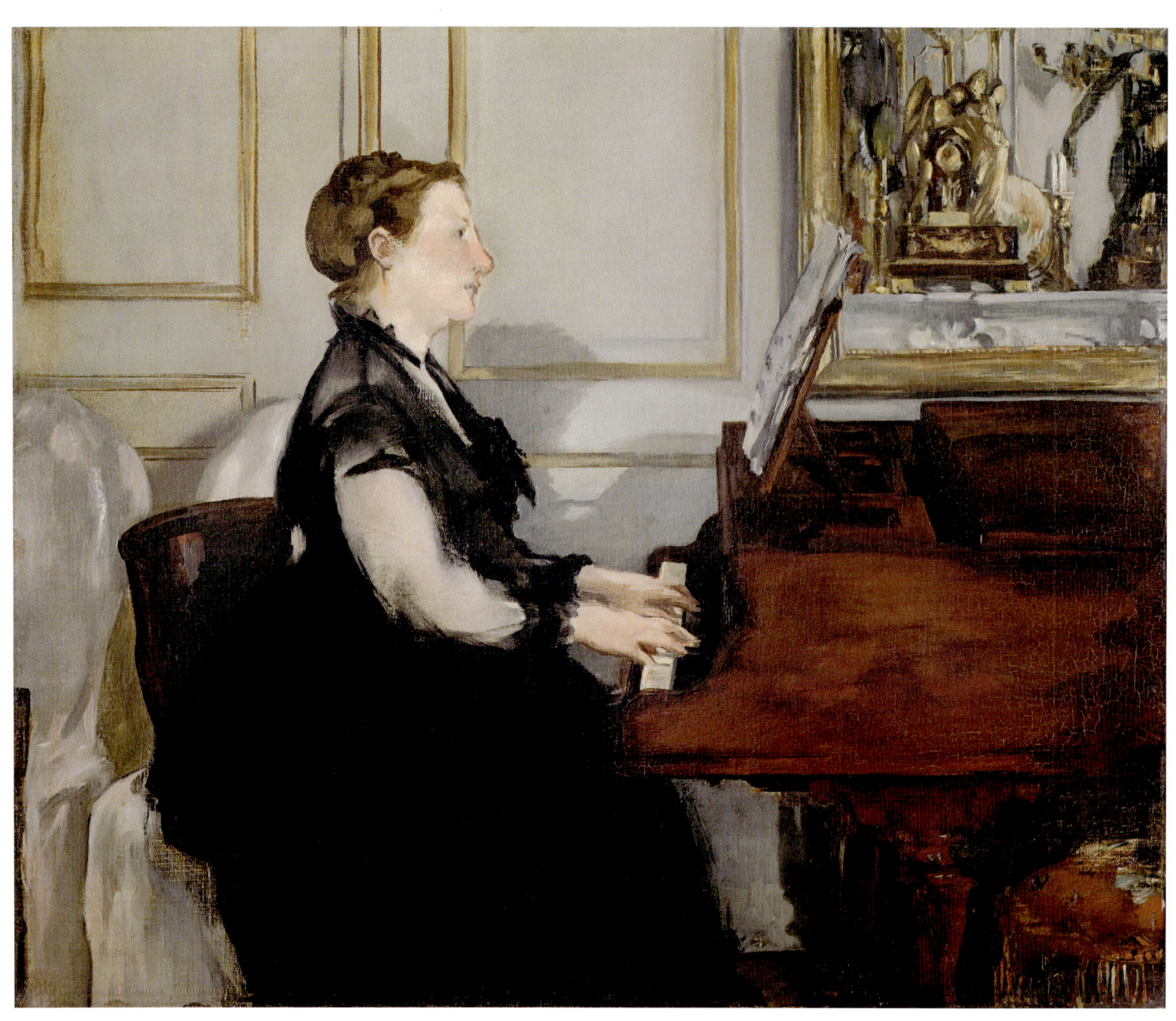

Cat. 47
Édouard Manet
Madame Manet at the Piano, 1868
Oil on canvas, 38 × 46.5 cm
Musée d'Orsay, Paris, Bequest of
Comte Isaac de Camondo, 1911,
RF 1994

Cat. 48
Pierre Bonnard
*Portrait of the Composer Claude
Terrasse with His Two Sons*, 1902–3
Oil on canvas, 95 × 77.5 cm
Musée d'Orsay, Paris,
RF 1980-2

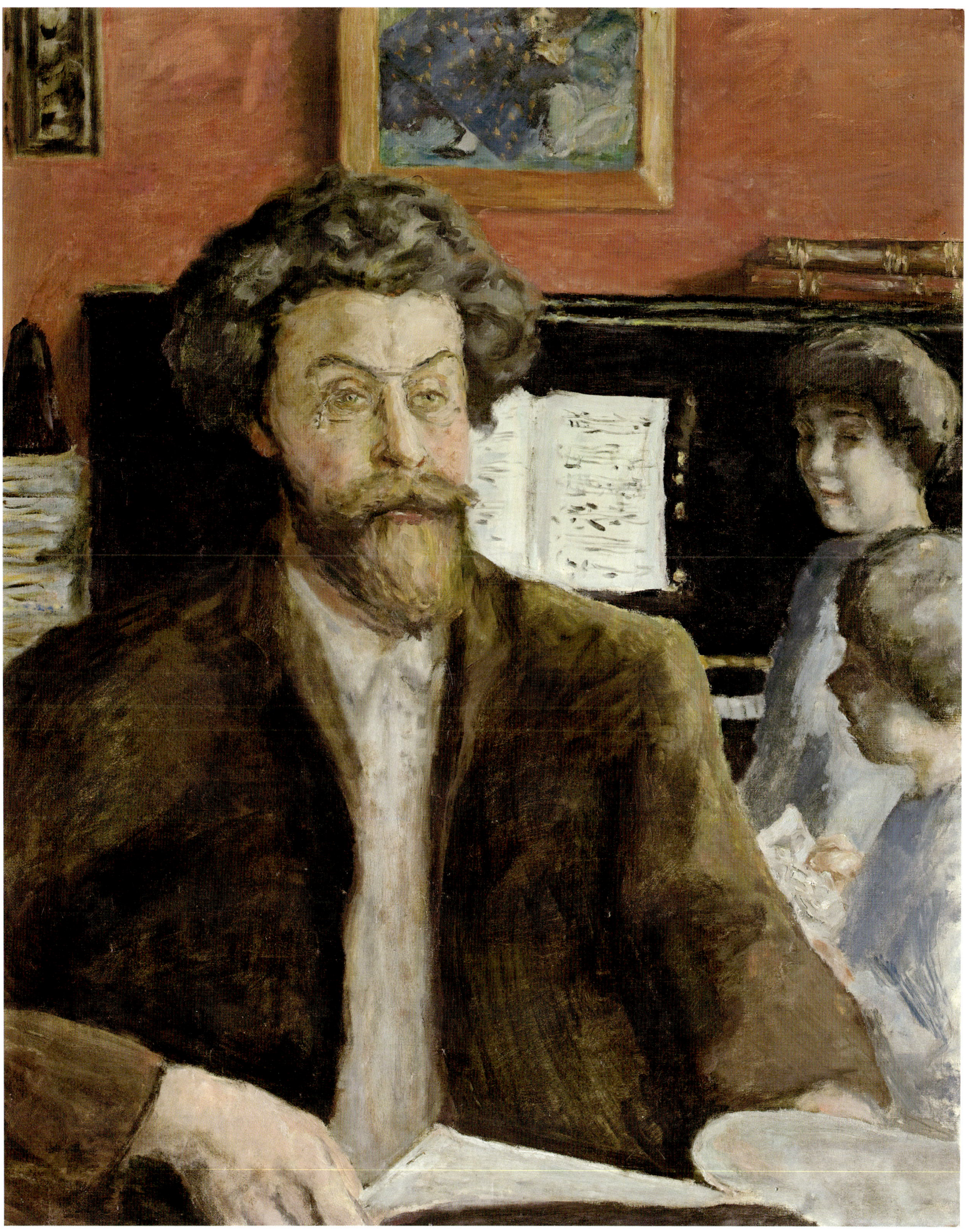

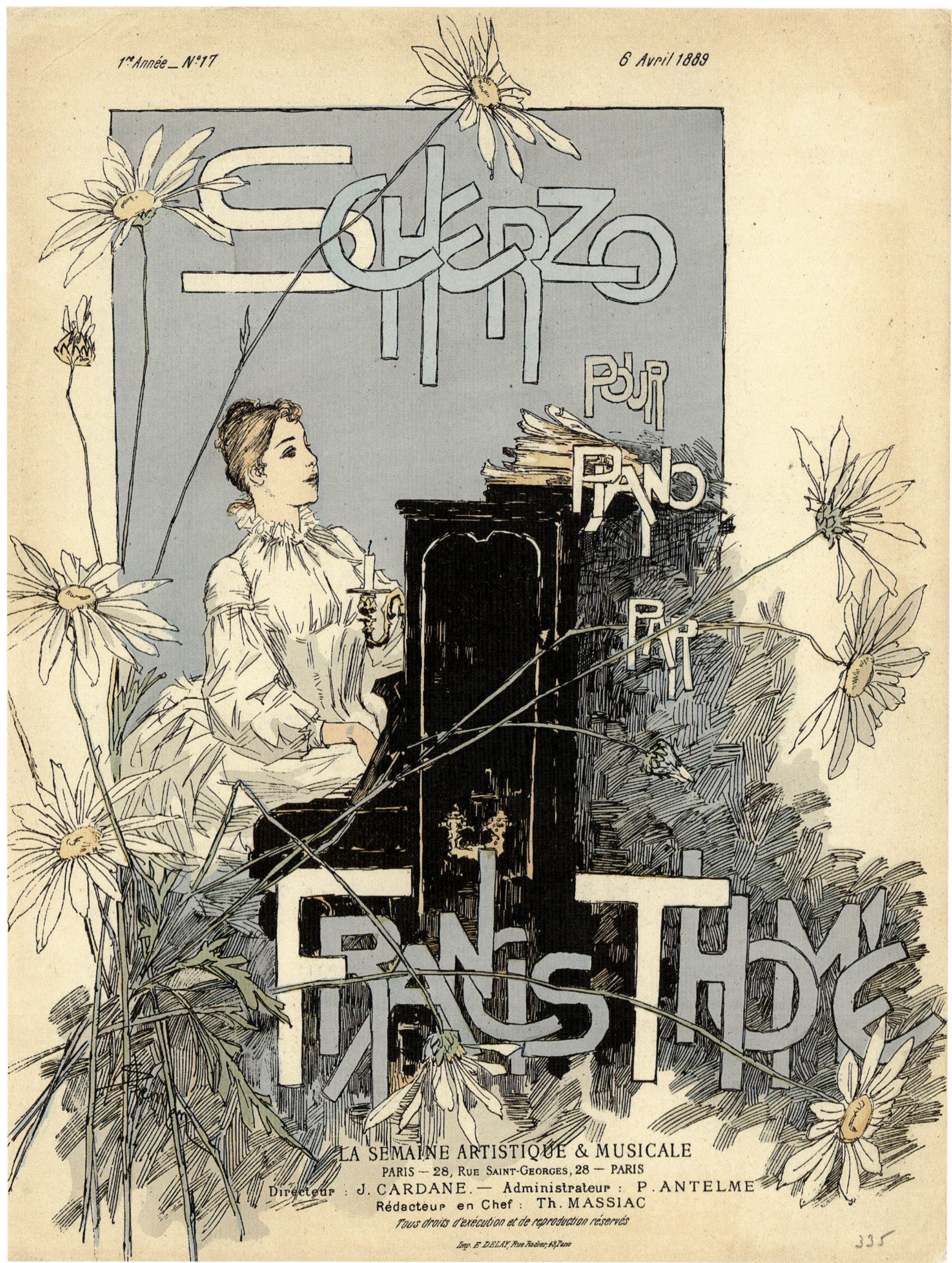

Cat. 49
Théophile Alexandre Steinlen (1859–1923)
Scherzo pour piano by Francis Thomé, sheet music offered as an unpublished supplement for the subscribers of *La Semaine artistique & musicale*, no. 17, 6 April 1889
Transfer lithograph in black, stenciled with watercolour, and letterpress printing in black on wove paper, 35 × 27 cm
Van Gogh Museum, Amsterdam, p2538S2010

Cat. 50
Pierre Bonnard
Young Woman at the Piano, 1891
Oil on canvas, 37.5 × 32 cm
Private collection

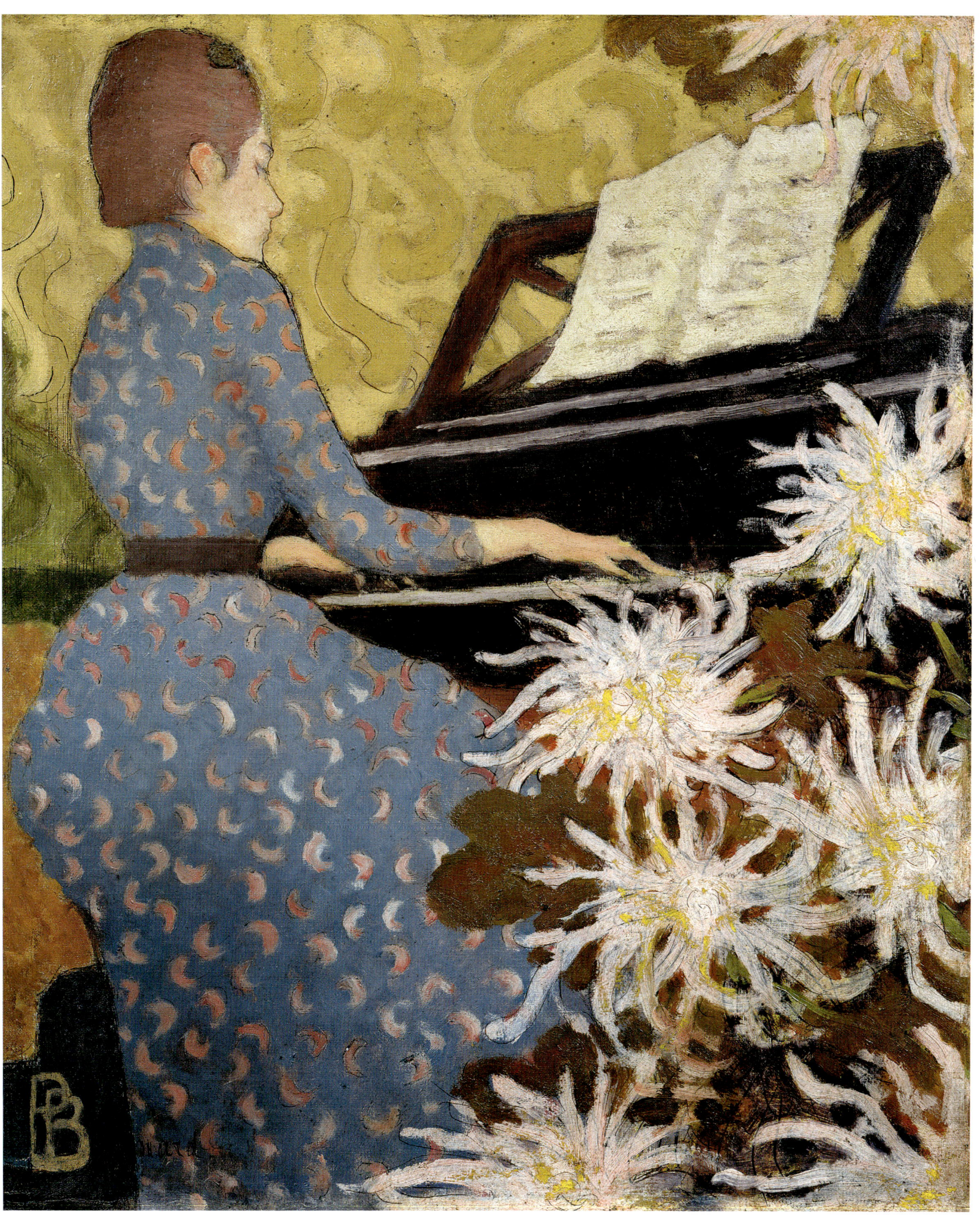

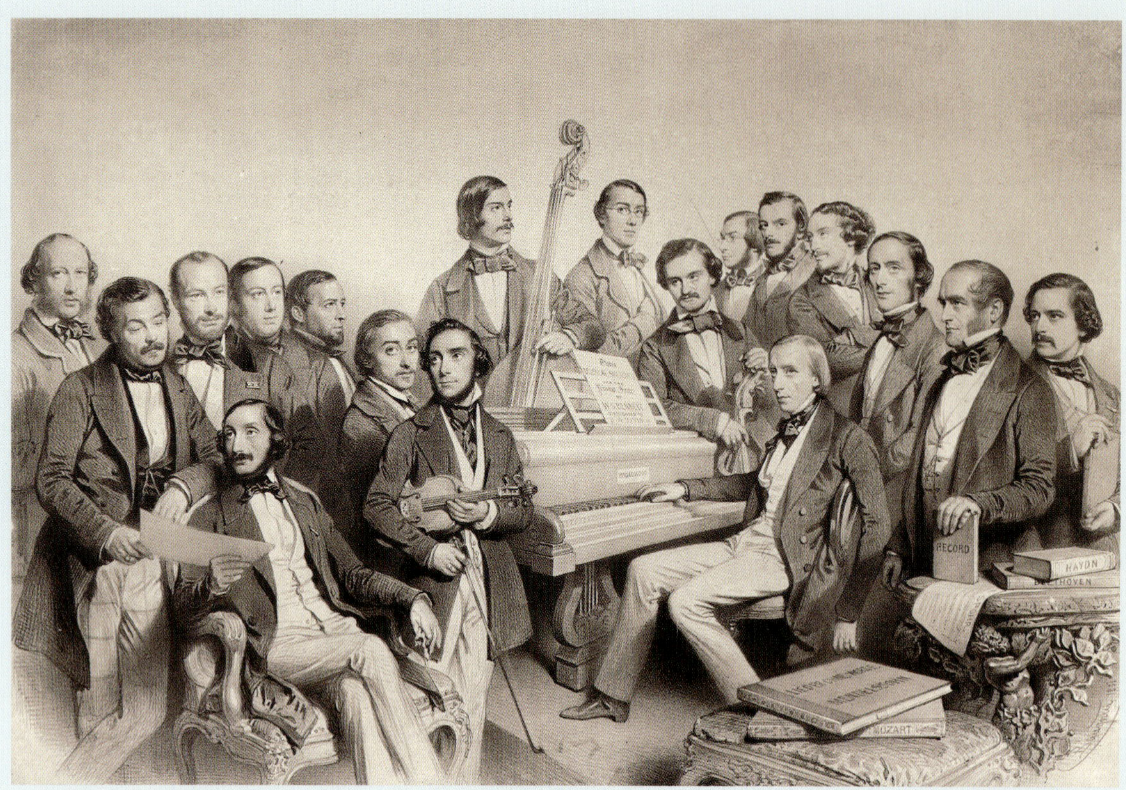

Fig. 33
Charles Baugniet
The Musical Union, 1851
Lithograph, 40.8 x 60 cm
Royal Academy of Music, London,
2003.1508

Degas's painting of *The Cellist Pilet* (cat. 51) dates from his period of most intense involvement with professional musicians. Through his friendship with the Dihaus, the bassoonist Désiré and his sister Marie, singer and pianist, Degas began to meet and mix socially with various members of the Opéra orchestra, among them Pilet. His meticulously composed painting goes beyond mere facial resemblance to show the cellist at work, seated at his desk in the act of composing, his cello and its case by his side. Pilet had joined the Opéra orchestra as cellist in 1852. Prominently hung on the wall behind him is a black and white image of a group of musicians gathered around a piano. Frances Palmer, formerly of the Royal Academy of Music, recently identified this as a lithograph by Charles Baugniet recording the 1851 Musical Union concert series held in St James's Hall, London. The Union's founder, John Ella, had hired this distinguished group of international musicians, including Pilet himself. (Pilet appears in profile between fellow cellist Carlo Alfredo Piatti and the German violinist Joseph Menter, standing directly behind the pianist seated at a Broadwood grand, Charles Hallé, who went on to create the famous orchestra of that name in Manchester.) By including the print, Degas tacitly acknowledged that, for Pilet, this London season, coinciding with the Great Exhibition of 1851, was a memorable personal milestone. It contains the seed of the portrait of Dihau surrounded by his musician colleagues that Degas would paint later, *Musicians of the Orchestra* (c. 1870, Musée d'Orsay, Paris), which may owe something to Baugniet's print too, although it is decidedly more ingenious and dynamic in composition.

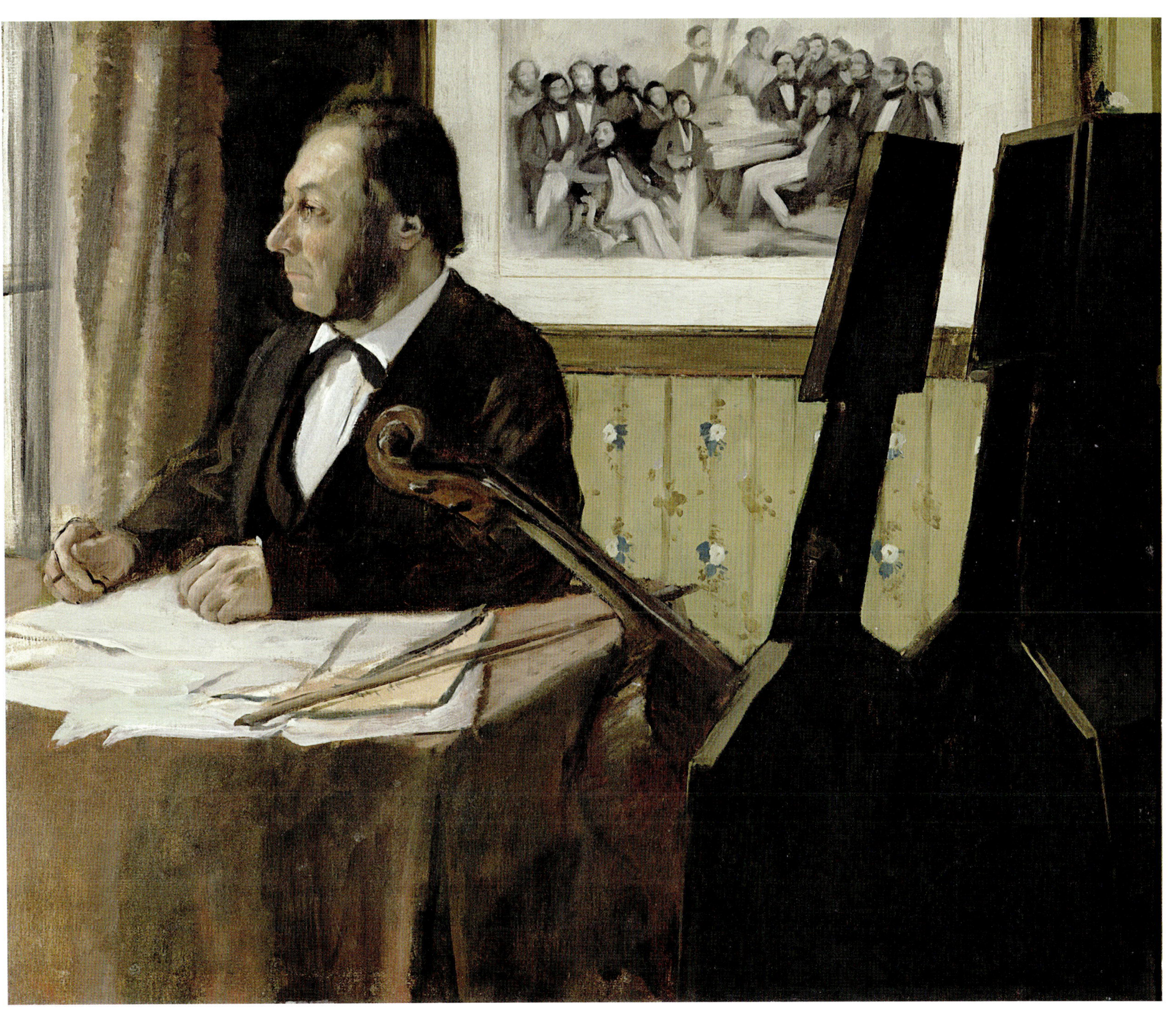

Cat. 51
Edgar Degas
The Cellist Pilet, between
1868 and 1869
Oil on canvas, 50.5 × 61 cm
Musée d'Orsay, Paris, Gift
of Charles Comiot, 1926,
RF 2582

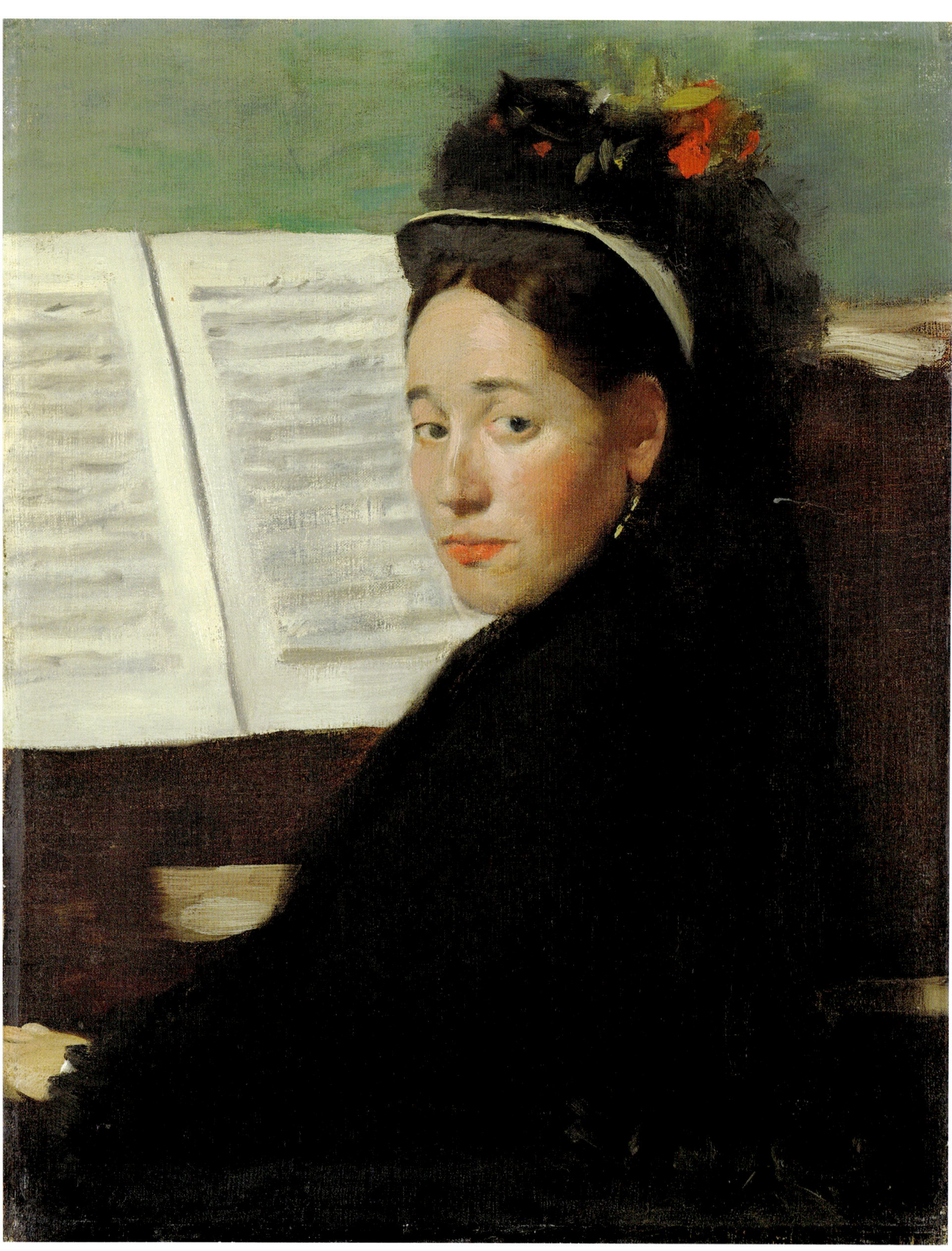

Cat. 52
Edgar Degas
Mademoiselle Dihau at the Piano,
between 1869 and 1872
Oil on canvas, 45 × 32.5 cm
Musée d'Orsay, Paris,
RF 2416

Cat. 53
Henri de Toulouse-Lautrec
(1864–1901)
Mademoiselle Dihau
at the Piano, 1890
Oil on board, 68 × 48.5 cm
Musée Toulouse-Lautrec, Albi,
MTL 132

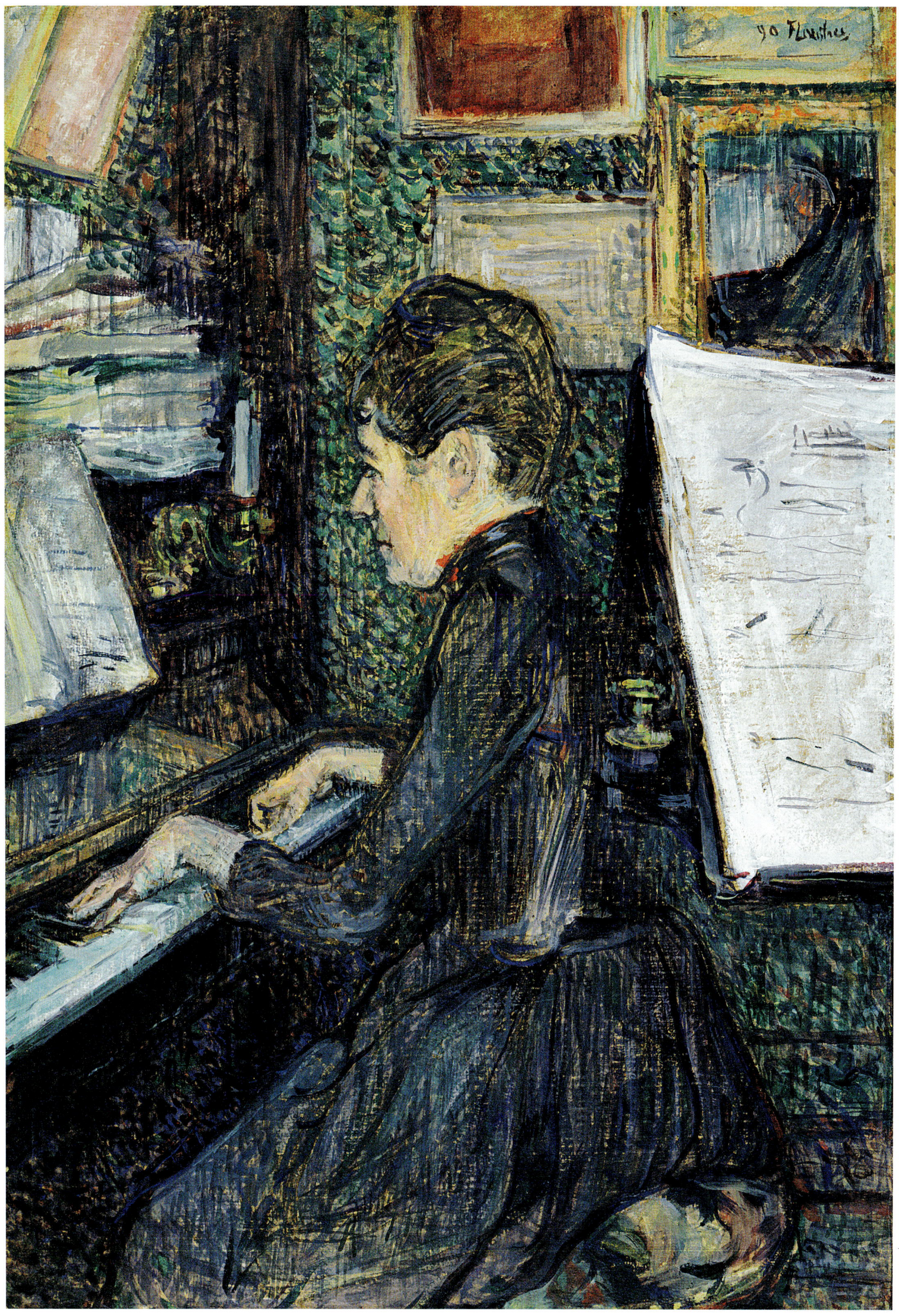
yo Flerties

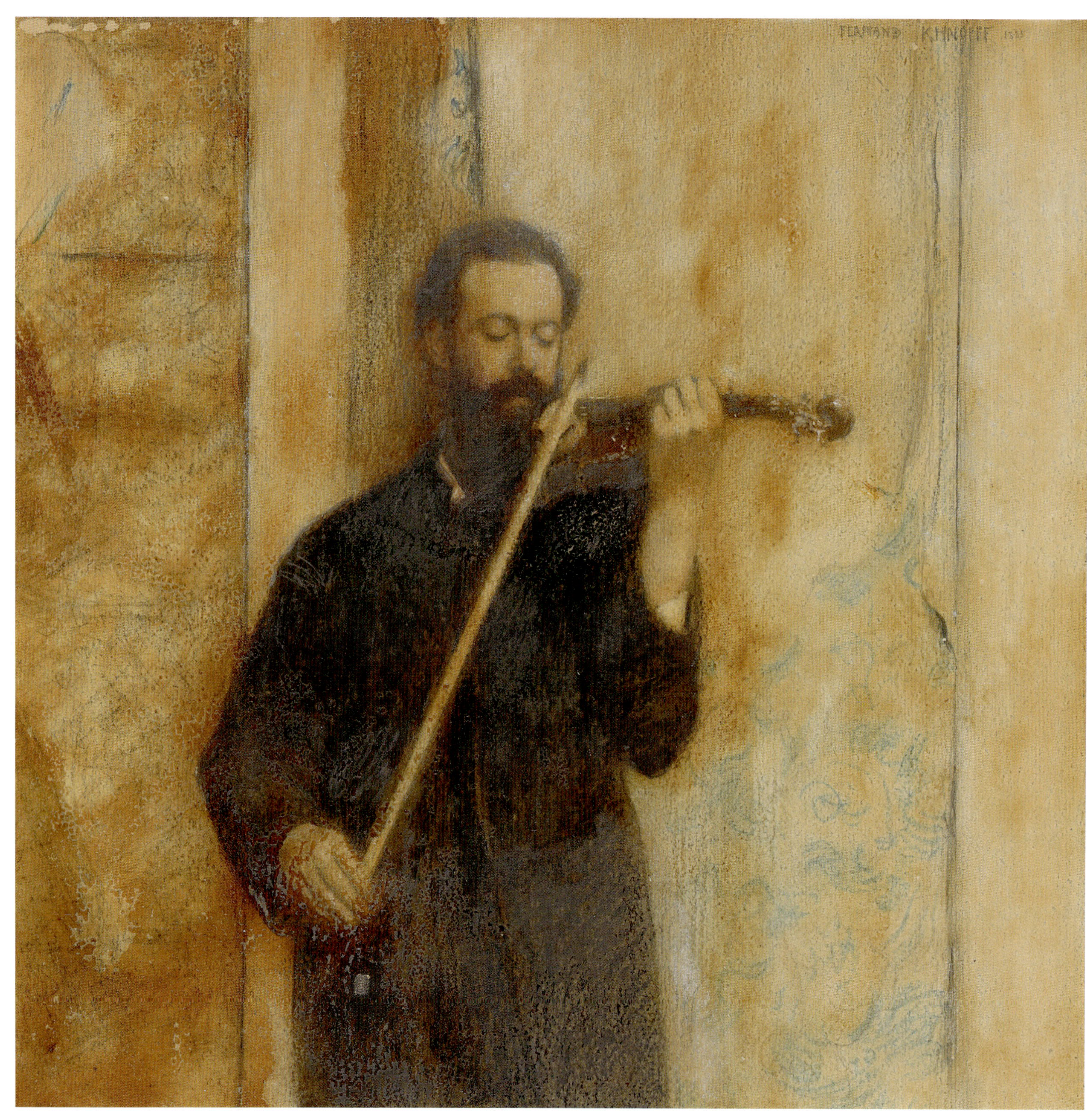

Cat. 54
Fernand Khnopff (1858–1921)
*Portrait of the Violinist
Achille Lerminiaux*, 1885
Pencil, color pencil, chalk,
on cardboard, 16.6 × 16.6 cm
Van Gogh Museum, Amsterdam,
d911 M/1989

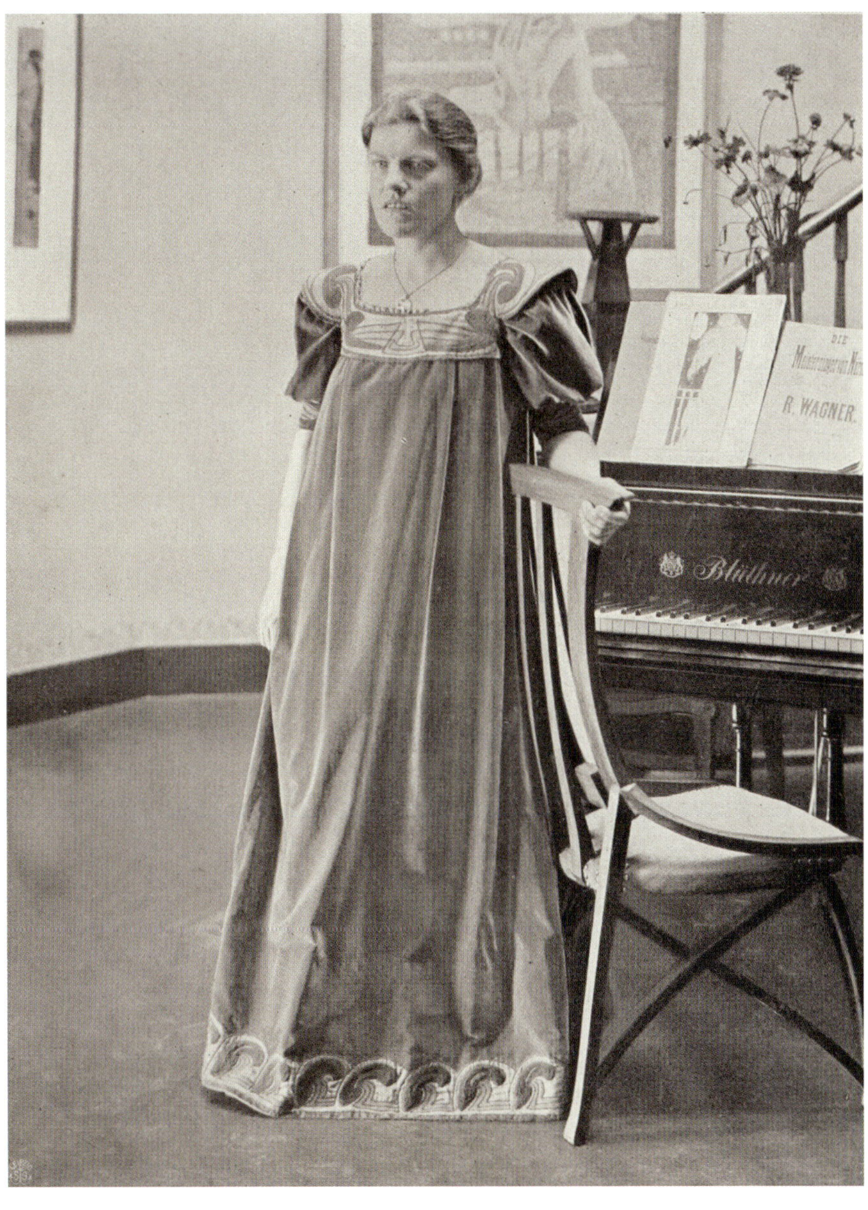

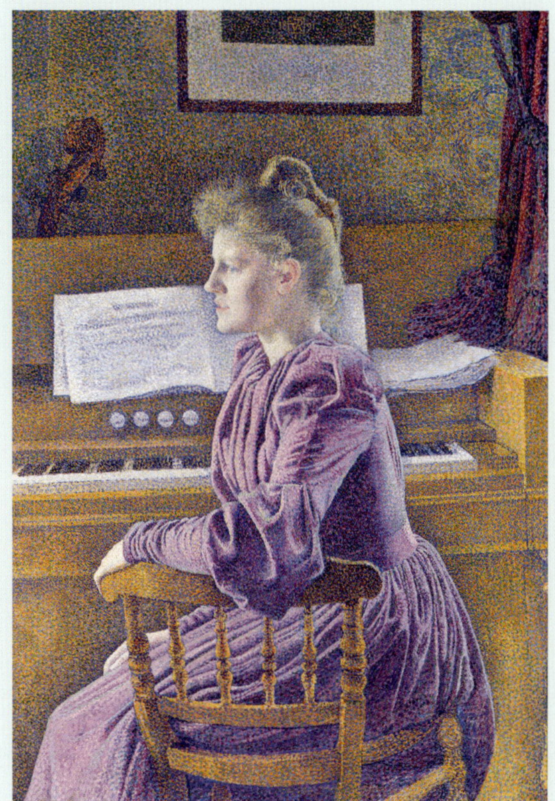

Fig. 34
Théo van Rysselberghe
*Portrait of Maria Sèthe Seated
at the Harmonium*, 1891
Oil on canvas, 118 x 84.5 cm
Koninklijk Museum voor
Schone Kunsten, Antwerp,
2690

Cat. 55
Henry van de Velde (1863–1957) and
Maria van de Velde Sèthe (1867–1943)
*Album moderner, nach
Künstlerentwürfen ausgeführter
Damenkleider (Album of Modern
Women's Clothing Executed According
to Artistic Designs)*, Düsseldorf,
Verlag von Friedr. Wolfrum,
Krefeld, J.B. Klein'sche
Buchdruckerei, M. Buscher, 1900
Bibliothèque Royale
de Belgique, Brussels,
FS10 01039/0882/001-011, Taf 4

The linkage between women and pianos was frequently made in fashion plates. In 1900, Henry Van de Velde, a Belgian Neo-Impressionist painter-turned-architect, designed a collection of women's clothes for his wife Maria, née Sèthe, an accomplished keyboard player, who poses wearing them in the album *Damenkleider*. The setting is their house, *Bloemenwerf*, in Uccle, Van de Velde's first constructed building, its simple lines and accoutrements displaying the couple's advanced tastes. On the music stand of Maria's Blüthner piano we see Maurice Denis's 1892 lithographic cover design for the piano score of *La Damoiselle élue* by Claude Debussy, next to music by Wagner; on the wall, a Japanese print and Théo van Rysselberghe's divisionist *Portrait of Maria Sèthe Seated at the Harmonium* (fig. 34), the second of his trio of portraits of the musical Sèthe sisters.

The tea gown featured is a velvet smock trimmed with Art Nouveau embroidery worked by Maria herself. Its flowing, somewhat medieval lines denote the emancipated role of the new woman in society. Maria van de Velde's introductory text to the album promotes the advanced ideas behind the clothes whilst rejecting the Paris fashion trade for its superficiality and caprice.

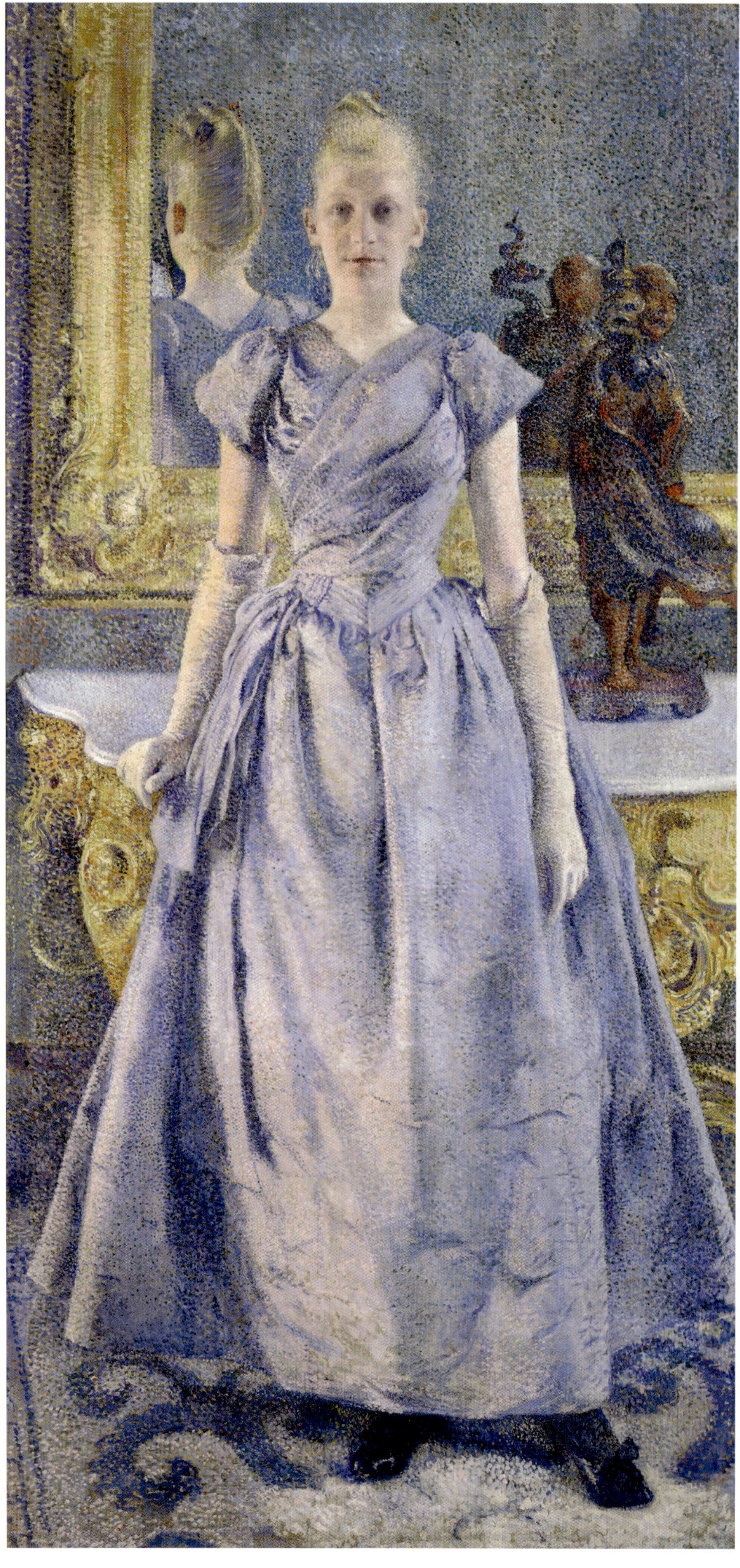

Cat. 56
Théo van Rysselberghe
Portrait of Alice Sèthe, 1888
Oil on canvas, 195 × 98 cm
Musée Départemental
Maurice-Denis,
Saint-Germain-en-Laye,
PMD 978.13.1

Cat. 57
Théo van Rysselberghe
*Portrait of the Violinist
Irma Sèthe*, 1894
Oil on canvas, 197.5 × 114.5 cm
Association des Amis
du Petit Palais, Geneva,
12277

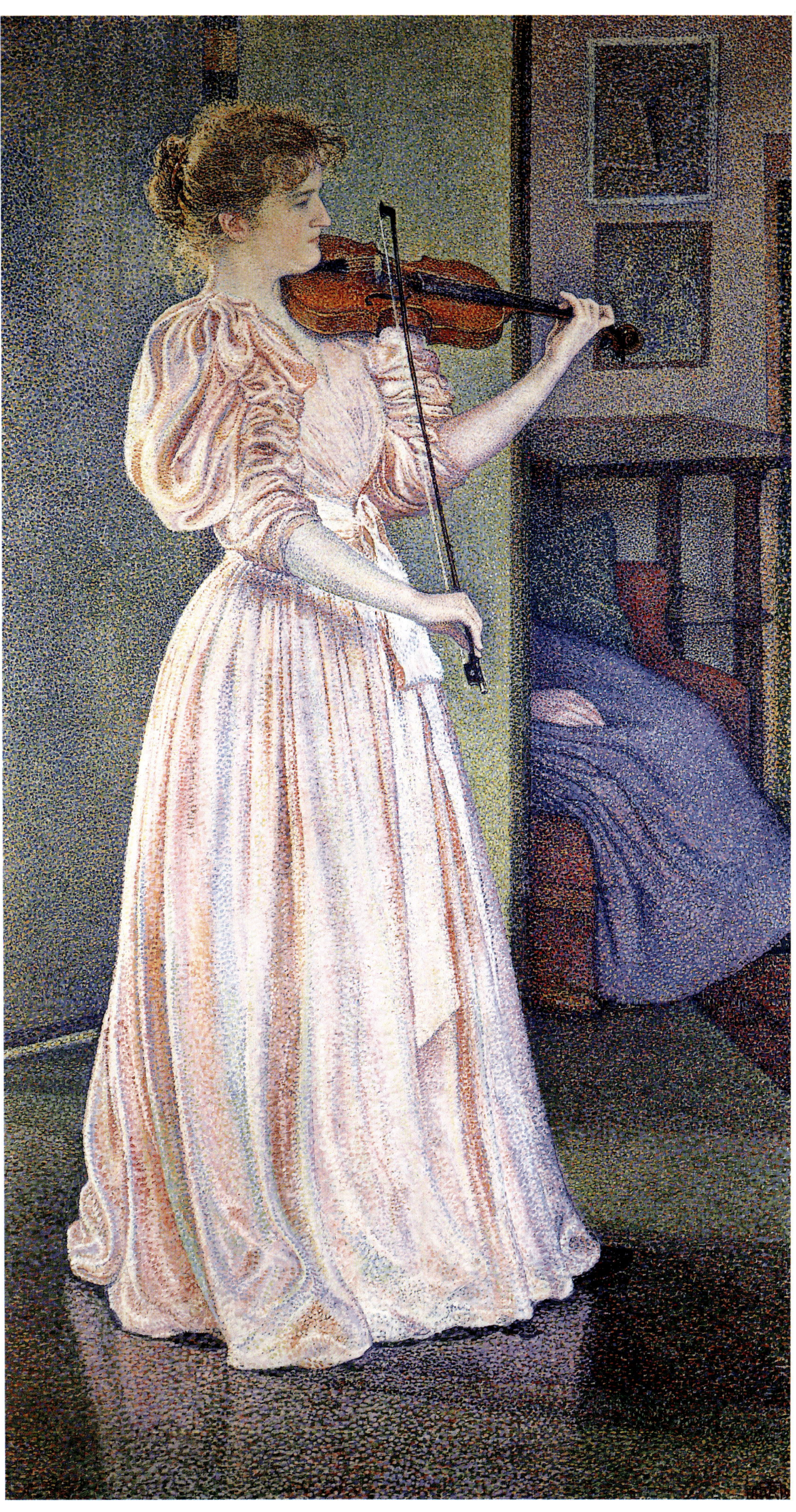

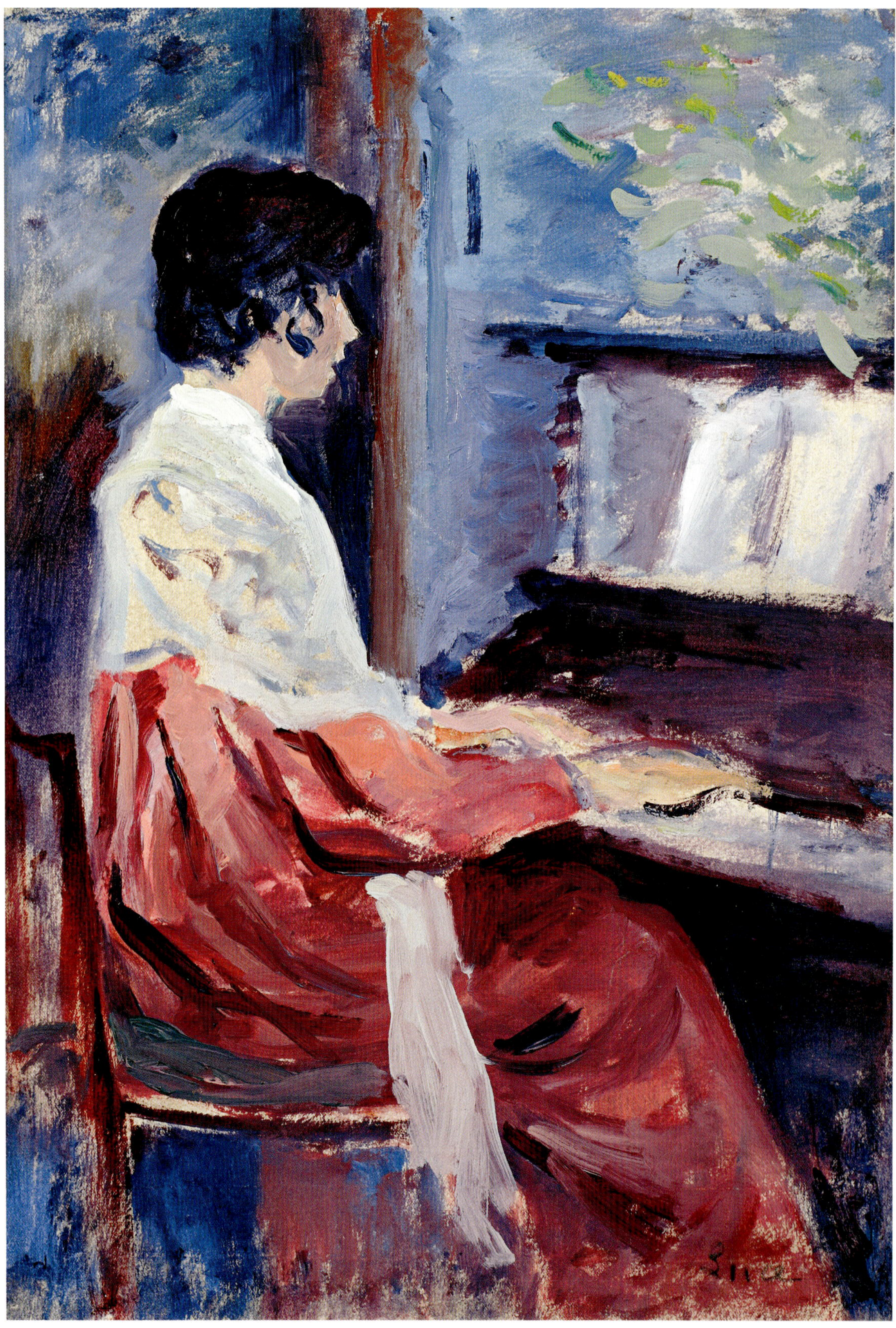

Cat. 58
Maximilien Luce (1858–1941)
Lucie Cousturier at the Piano,
c. 1905
Oil on board, 41.5 × 29.5 cm
Private collection

Cat. 59
Alfred Stevens
Eva Gonzalès at the Piano, 1879
Oil on panel, 54.9 × 45.4 cm
The John & Mable Ringling
Museum of Art, Sarasota,
Bequest of John Ringling, 1936,
SN438

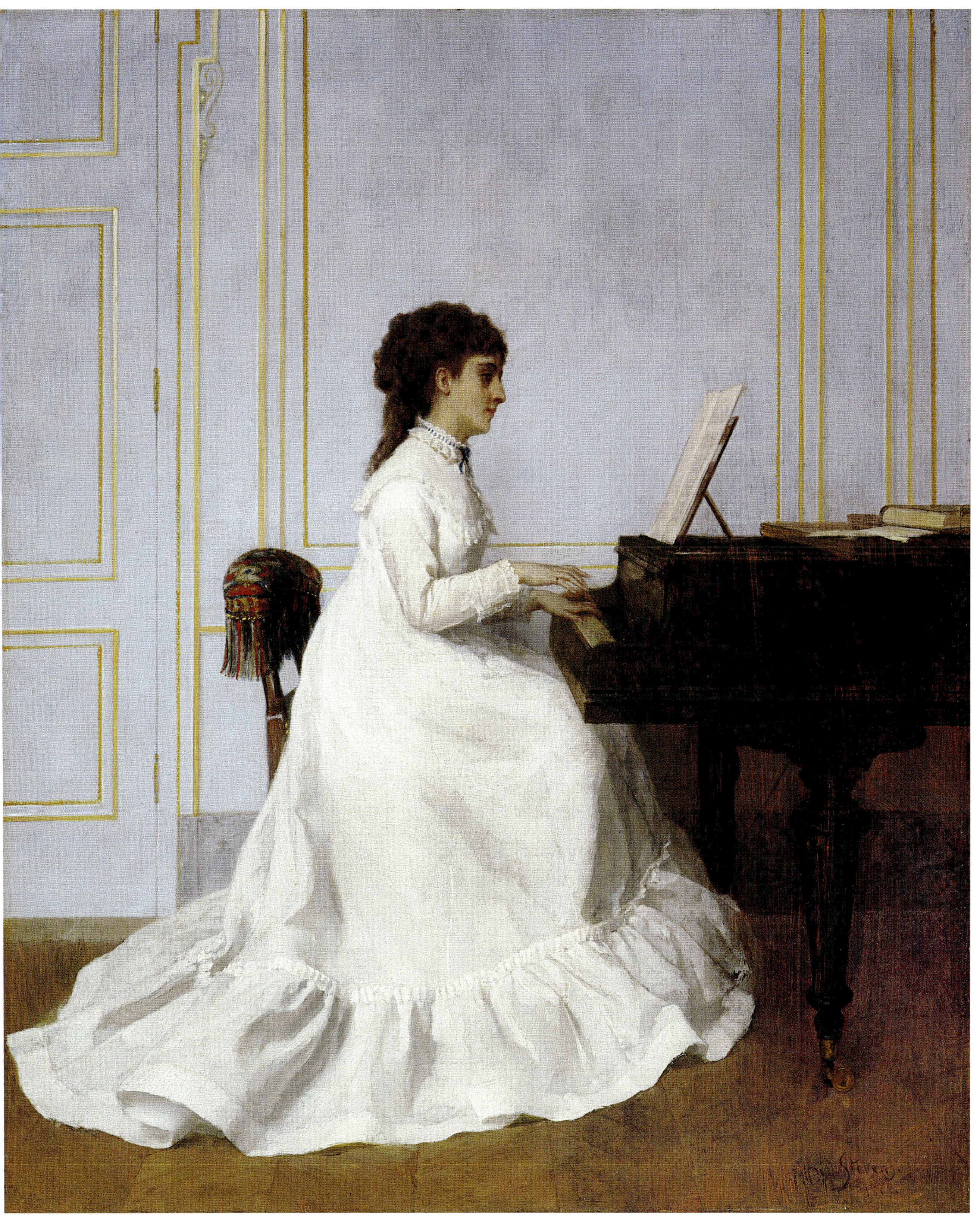

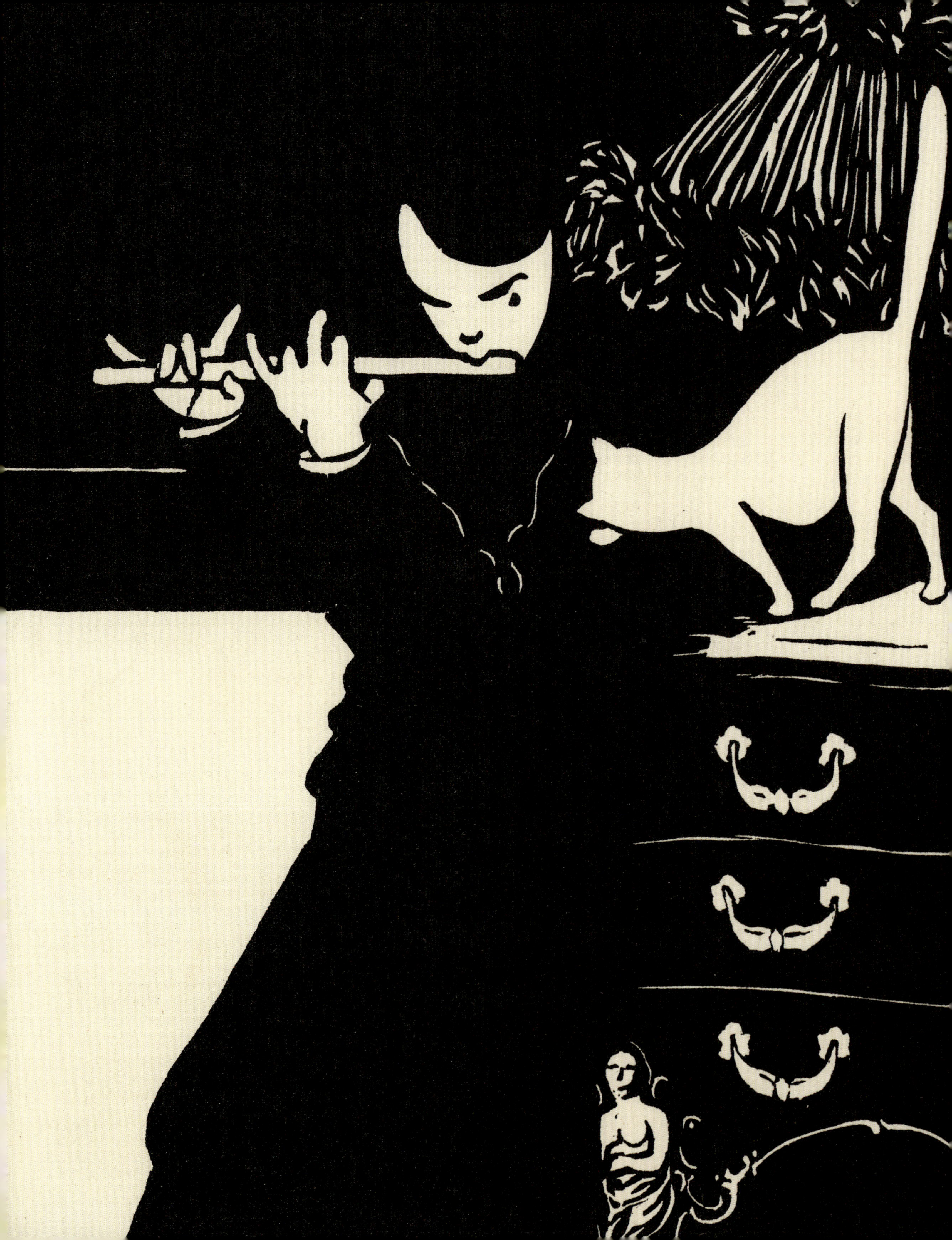

graphic arts

In this golden age of printmaking and illustration, there was also a rapprochement between artists and musicians through the various graphic media, drawing, etchings, lithographs, press illustrations, posters and illustrations for scores. A host of common projects bear witness to painters' efforts to enhance and give support to the music they loved. The posters of Henri de Toulouse-Lautrec (cat. 74) and Louis Anquetin (cat. 75) reflect this willingness to promote the musical activities of the time, and especially the artists who performed at the cafés-concerts. Following in the tradition of the musical albums for children by Maurice Boutet de Monvel (cat. 79), Maurice Denis (cat. 81) and Pierre Bonnard (cat. 80, 82–84) illustrated scores and methods for learning music for both young and old. Whether they took the form of caricature or straightforward portrait, press illustrations were another means to pay homage to composers or musicians – or to make fun of them, as Georges Meunier does in *Le Rire* (cat. 90).

In sum, drawings, lithographs and engravings are testimony to the interest artists had in musical instruments, a good example being Félix Vallotton's not unhumorous series on the subject (cat. 68–73).

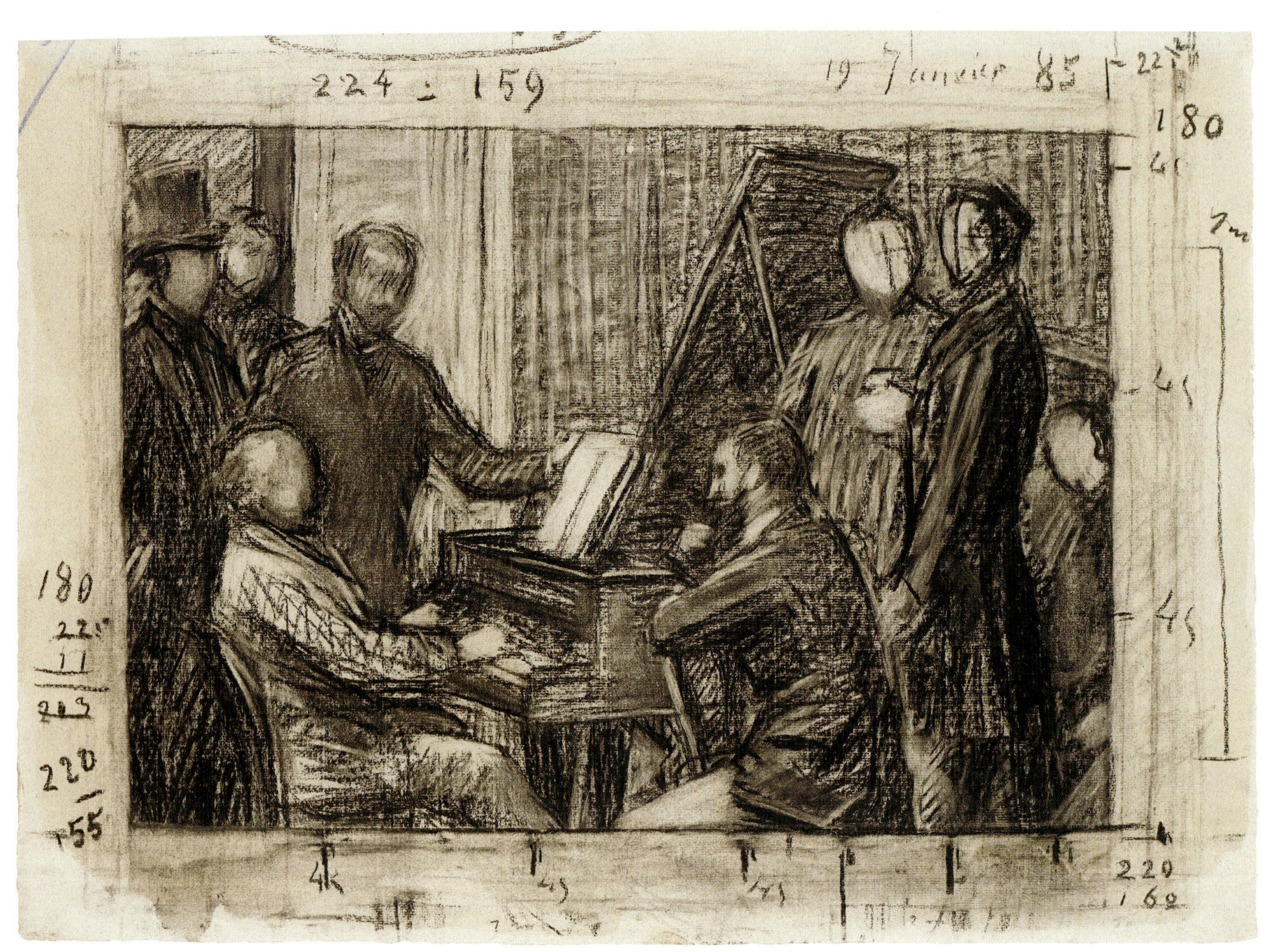

Cat. 60
Henri Fantin-Latour (1836–1904)
Preparatory drawing for
Around the Piano, 1885
Charcoal on grey paper,
43.7 × 62.6 cm
Musée d'Orsay, Paris,
RF 23522 recto

Cat. 61
Berthe Morisot
The Violin, 1894
Sanguine and black chalk,
39 × 28 cm
Musée Marmottan Monet, Paris,
Bequest of the Denis and Annie
Rouart Foundation, 1993,
6065

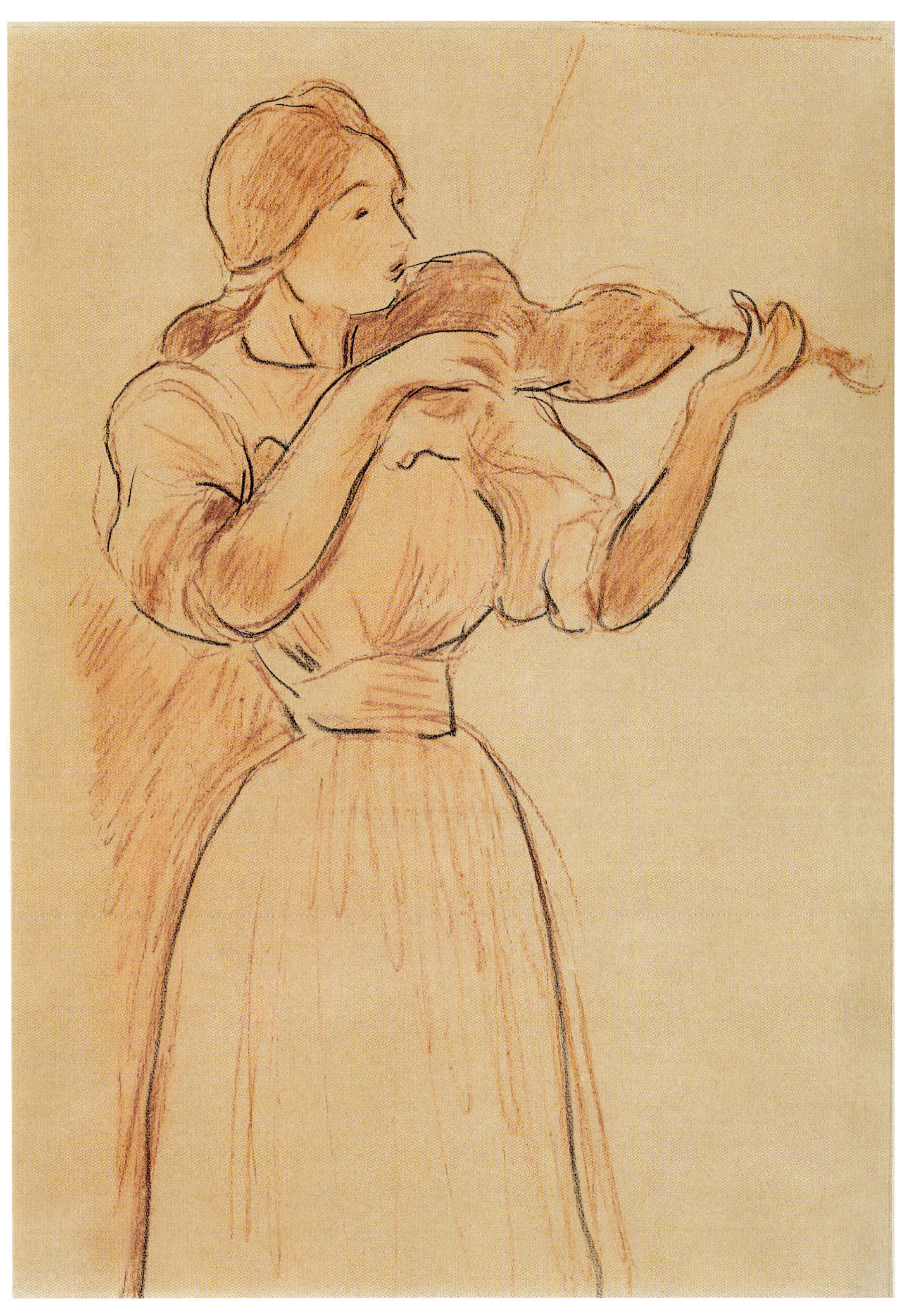

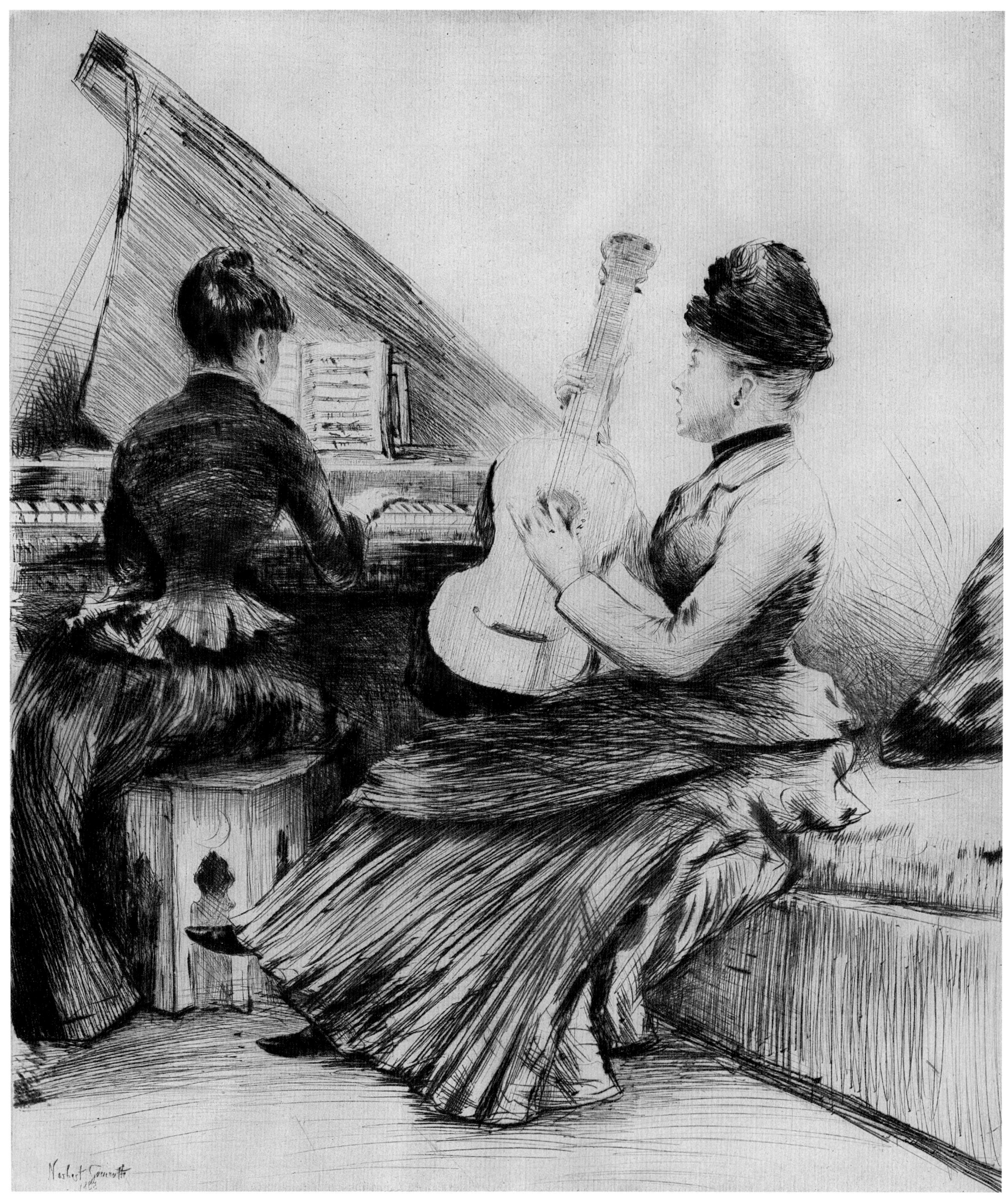

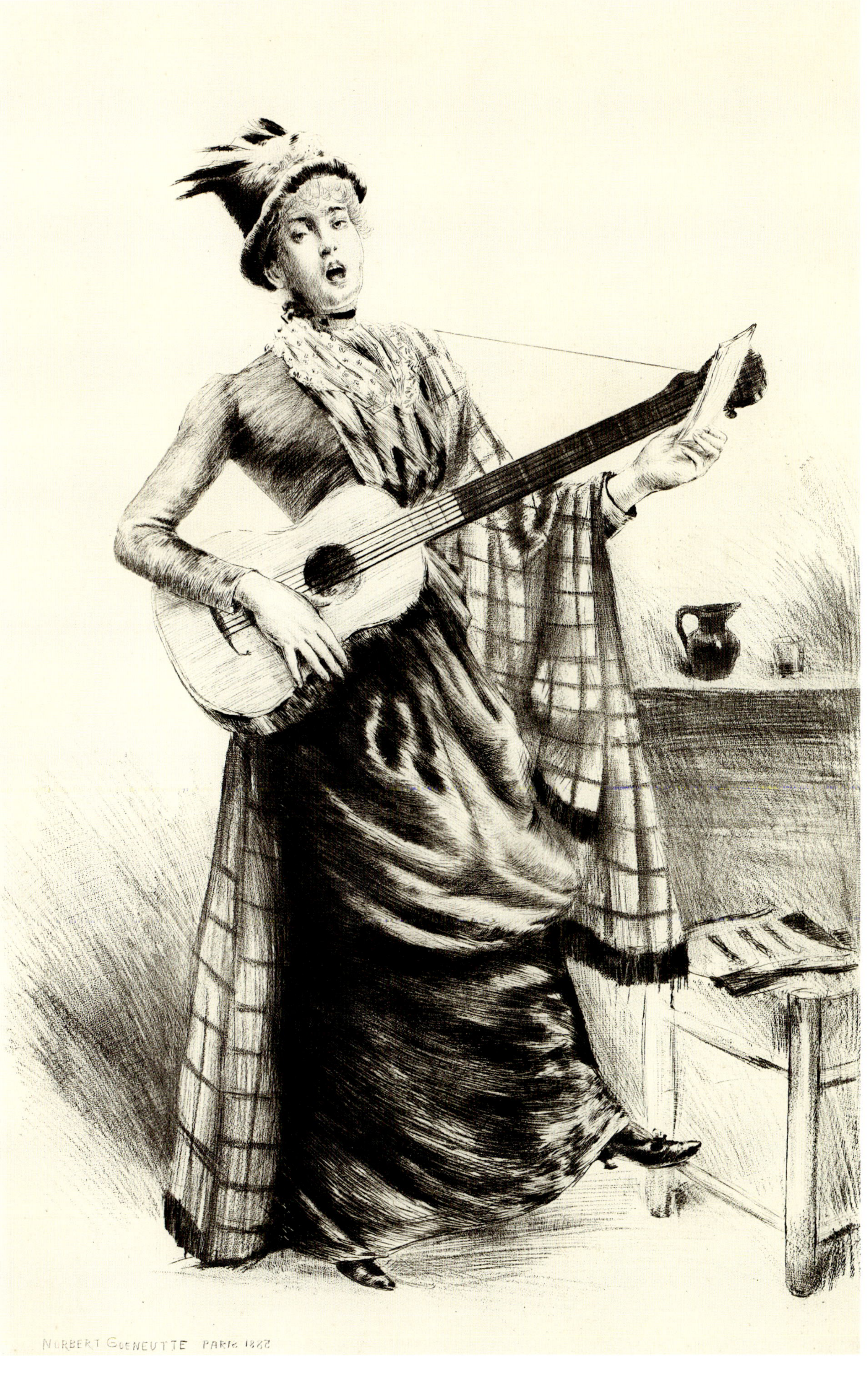

Cat. 62
Norbert Goeneutte (1854–1894)
Duet, Chamber Music, 1885
Drypoint in black on laid paper,
54 × 41.5 cm
Van Gogh Museum (Vincent van
Gogh Foundation), Amsterdam,
p220V1966

Cat. 63
Norbert Goeneutte
Woman with a Guitar or
The Grasshopper, 1885
Drypoint, 55.5 × 37 cm
Private collection

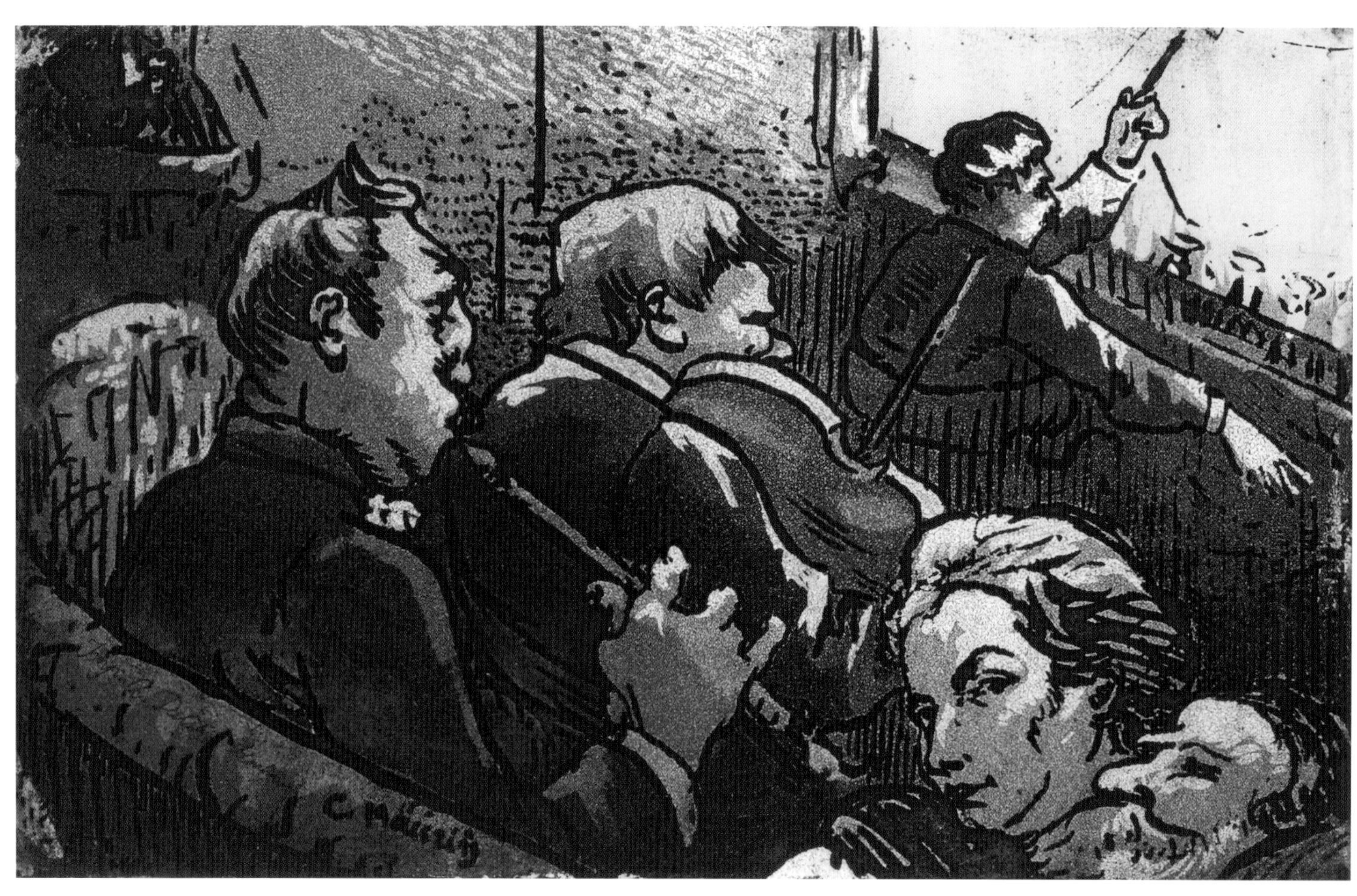

Cat. 64
Charles Maurin (1856–1914)
The Orchestra Pit, 1893
Etching and aquatint,
13.9 × 21.9 cm
Private collection

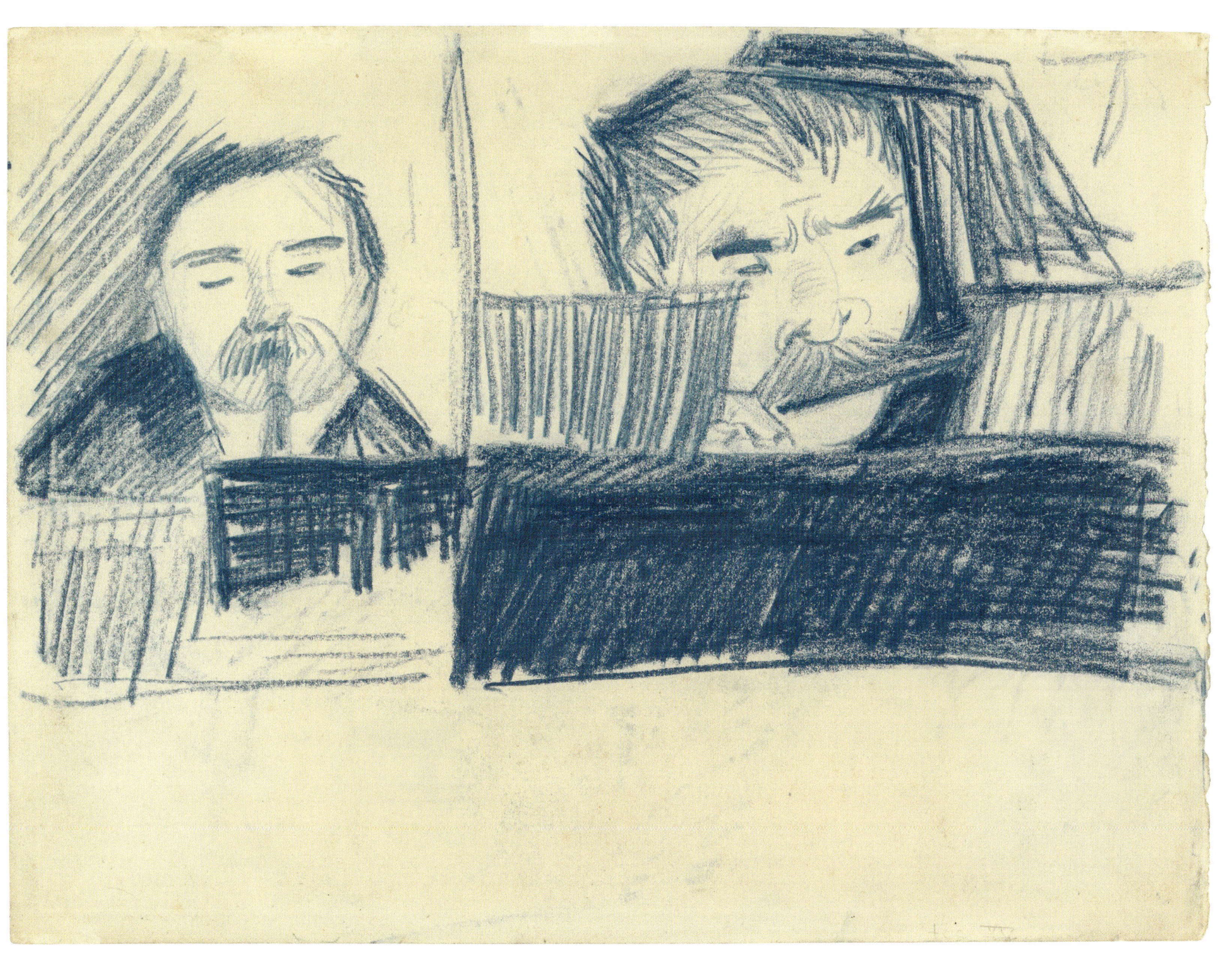

Cat. 65
Vincent van Gogh (1853–1890)
*Clarinetist and Piccolo
Player*, 1887
Blue chalk on wove paper,
25.7 × 34.9 cm
Van Gogh Museum (Vincent van
Gogh Foundation), Amsterdam,
d0019V1962r

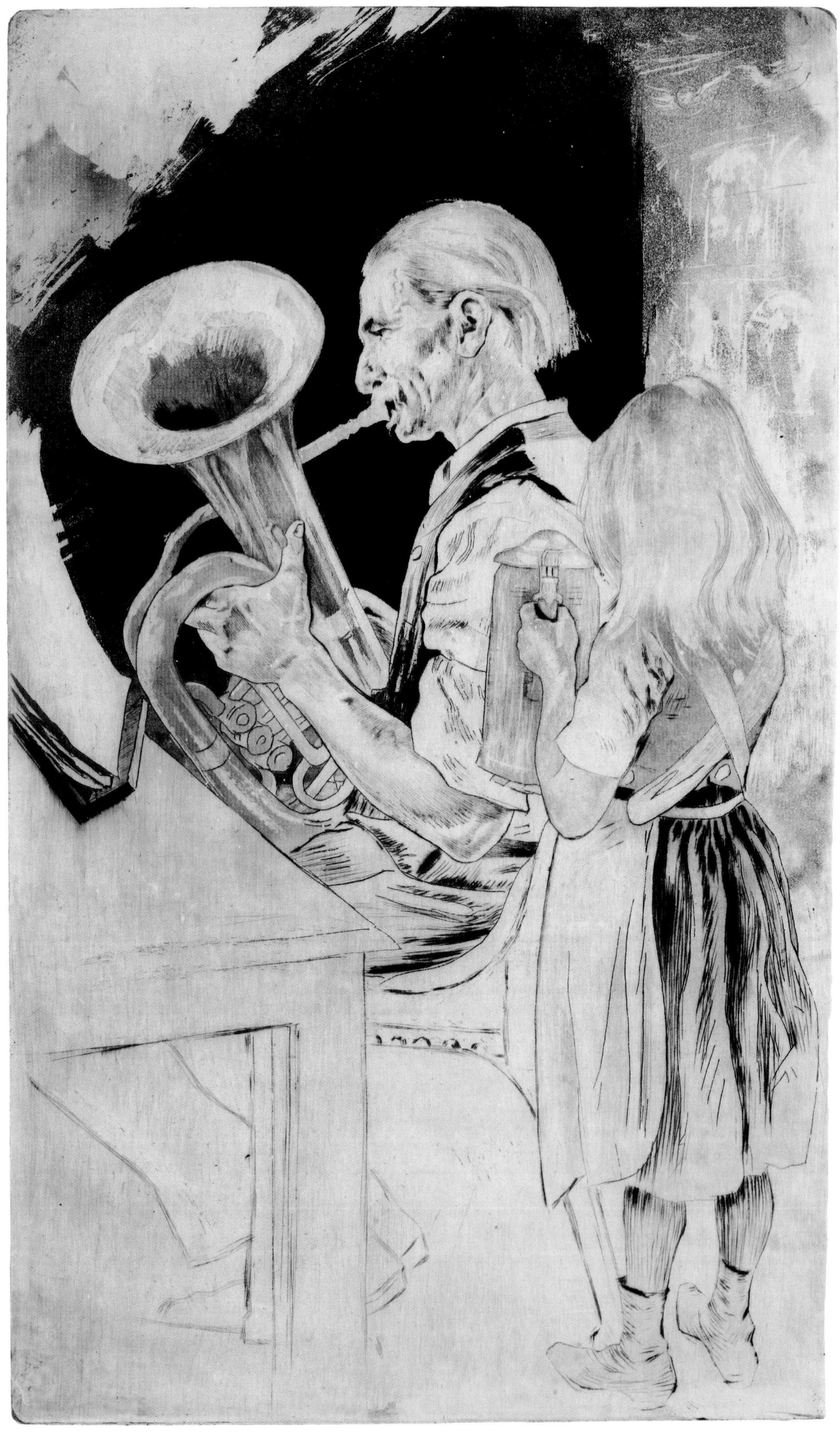

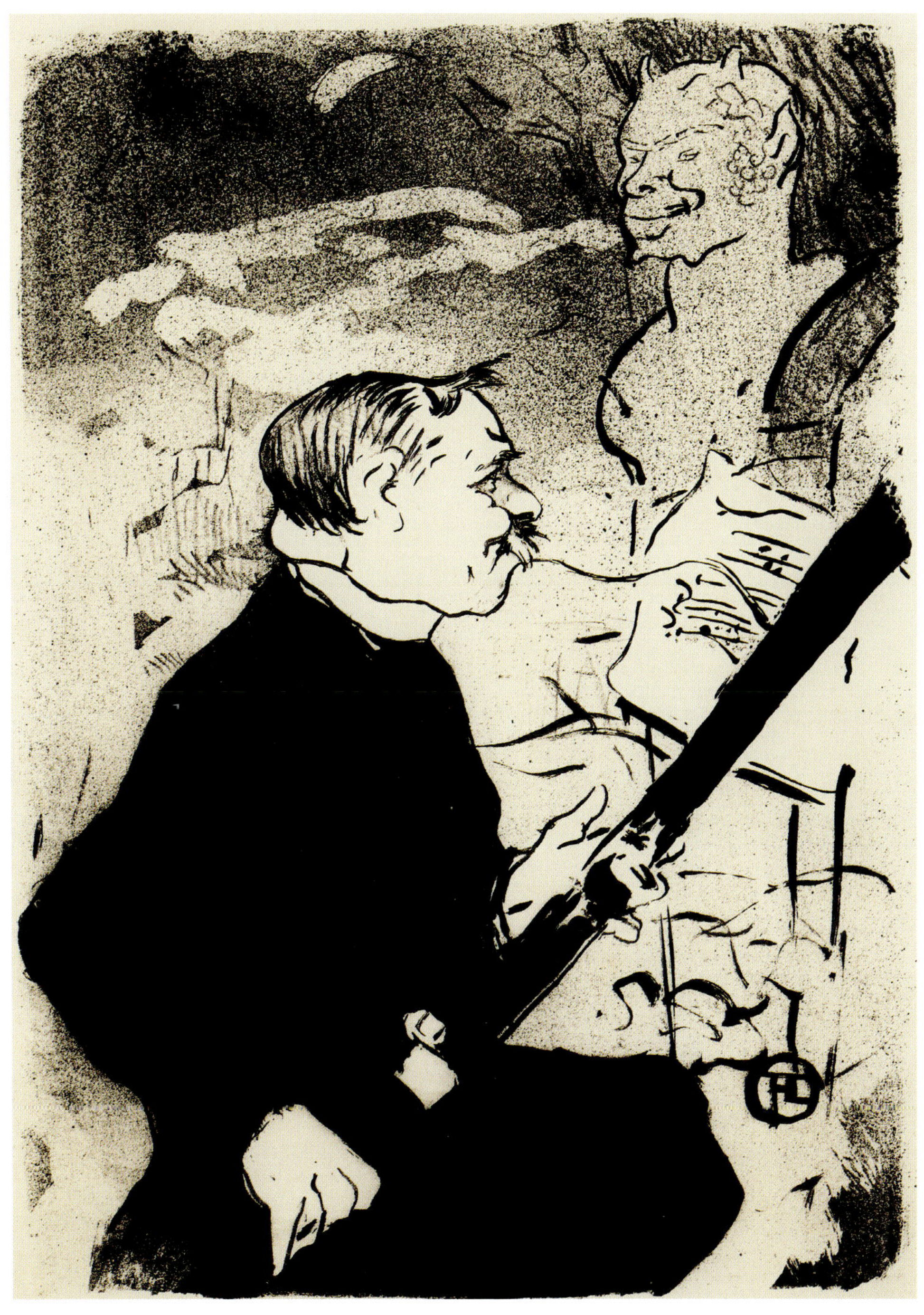

<table>
<tr><td>

Cat. 66
Louis Legrand (1863–1951)
*Teutonophony–Souvenir of
Huningue*, 1892
Etching and drypoint,
44 × 26.5 cm
Private collection

</td><td>

Cat. 67
Henri de Toulouse-Lautrec
For You!..., from the series
Les Vieilles Histoires published
by G. Ondet, poems by
Jean Goudezki set to music
by Désiré Dihau, 1893
Lithograph on Japan paper,
27.5 × 19.7 cm
Private collection

</td></tr>
</table>

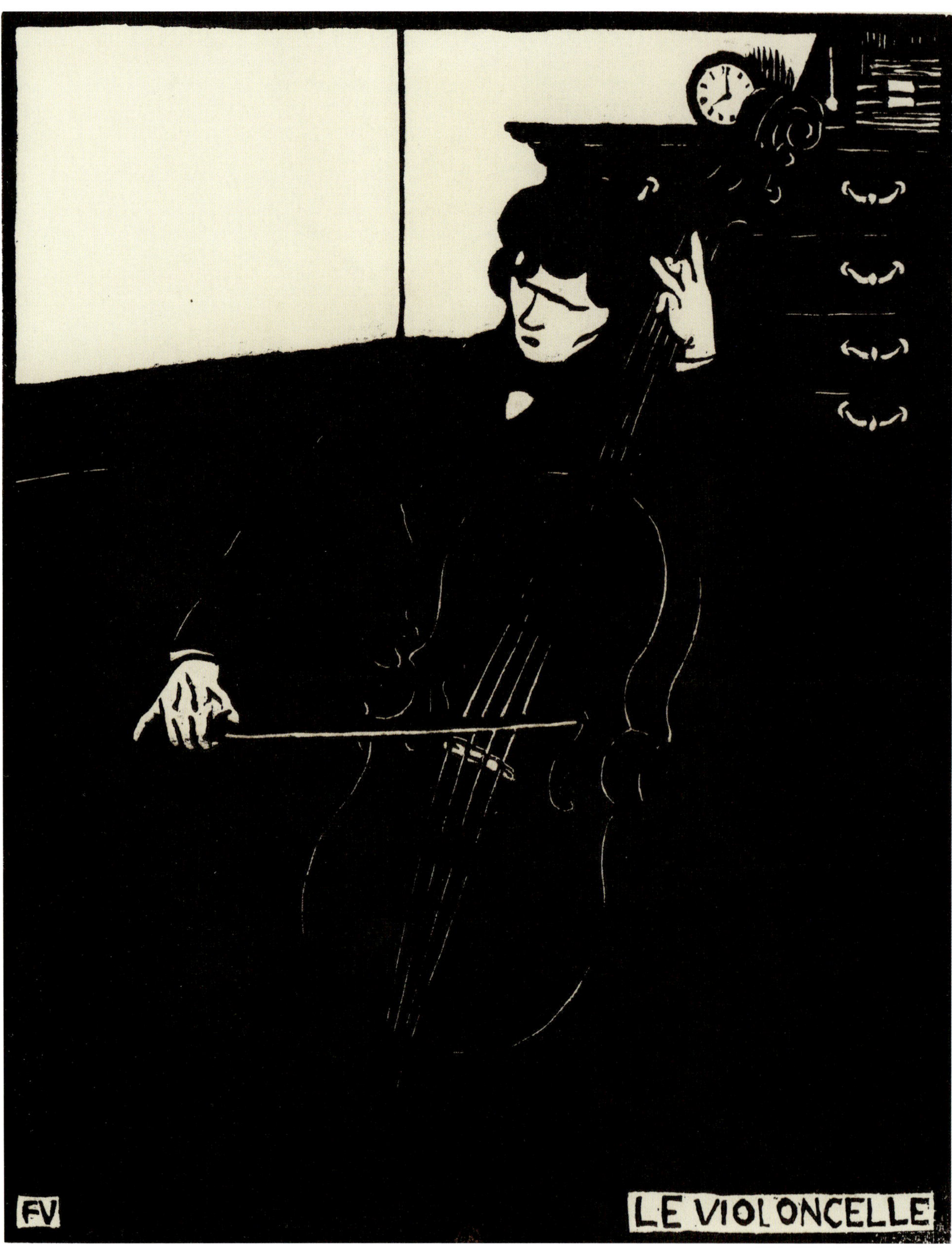

Cat. 68
Félix Vallotton
(1865–1925)
The Cello, Musical Instruments, I, 1896
Woodcut, 22.3 × 17.8 cm
Bibliothèque Nationale de France, Département des Estampes et de la Photographie, Paris,
DC-292 (C, 2 bis),
FOL 143 IFN-6951718

Cat. 69
Félix Vallotton
The Flute, Musical Instruments, II, 1896
Woodcut, 22.4 × 18 cm
Bibliothèque Nationale de France, Département des Estampes et de la Photographie, Paris,
DC-292 (C, 2 bis),
FOL 144 IFN-6951719

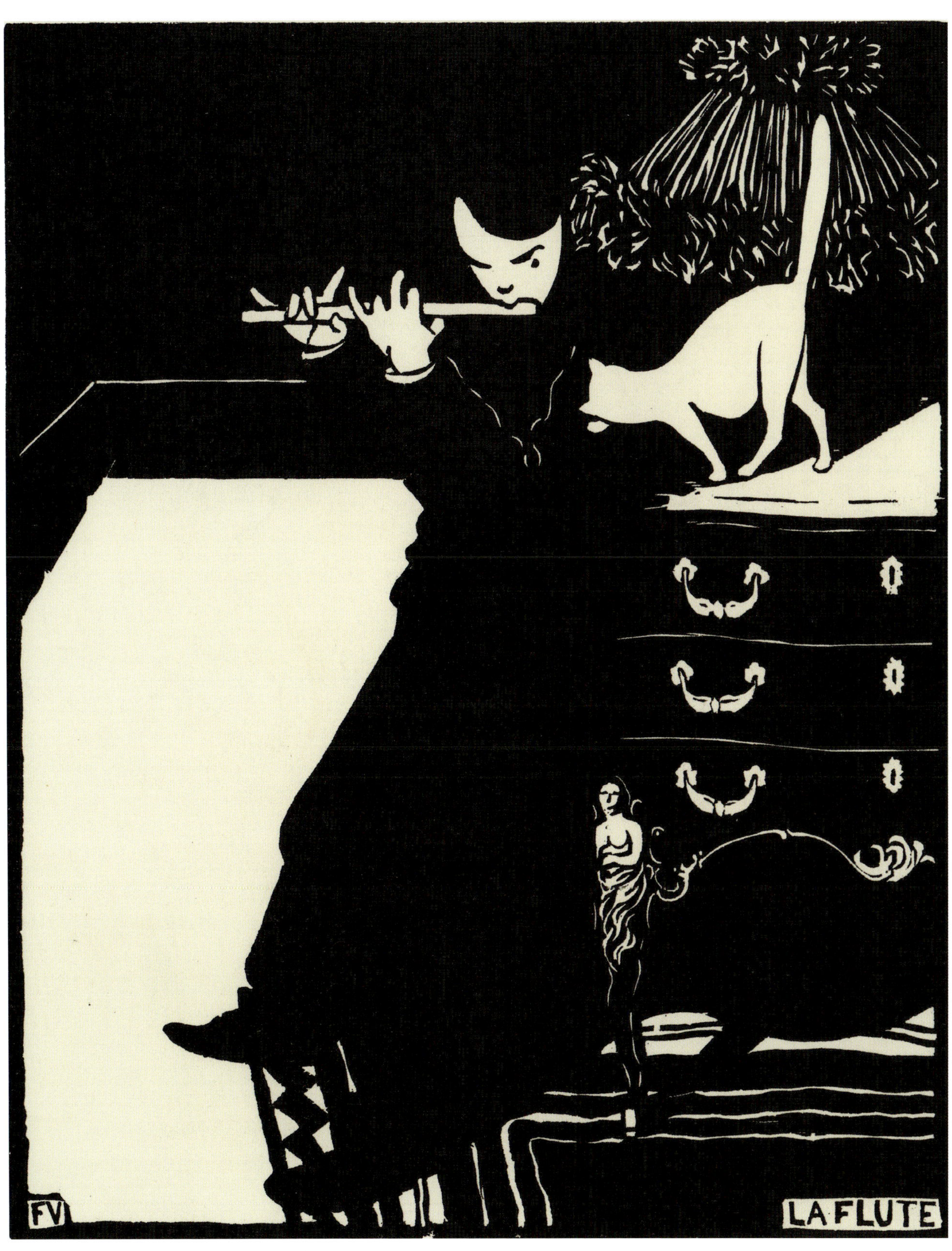
FV
LA FLUTE

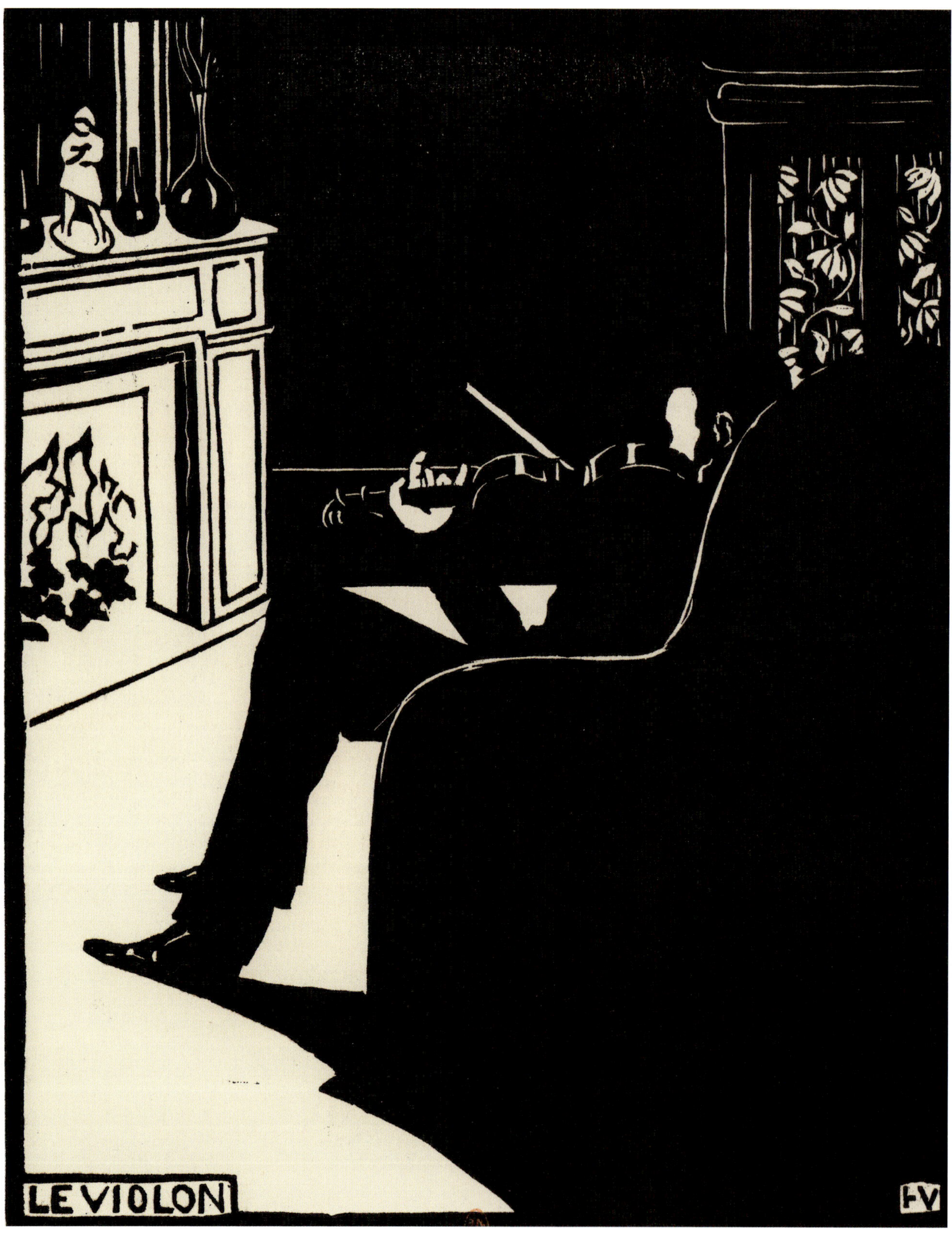
LE VIOLON

Cat. 70
Félix Vallotton
The Violin, Musical Instruments, III, 1896
Woodcut, 22.4 × 18 cm
Bibliothèque Nationale de France, Département des Estampes et de la Photographie, Paris,
DC-292 (C, 2 bis),
FOL 145 IFN-6951720

Cat. 71
Félix Vallotton
The Piano, Musical Instruments, IV, 1896
Woodcut, 22.4 × 18 cm
Bibliothèque Nationale de France, Département des Estampes et de la Photographie, Paris,
DC-292 (C, 2 bis),
FOL 146 IFN-6951721

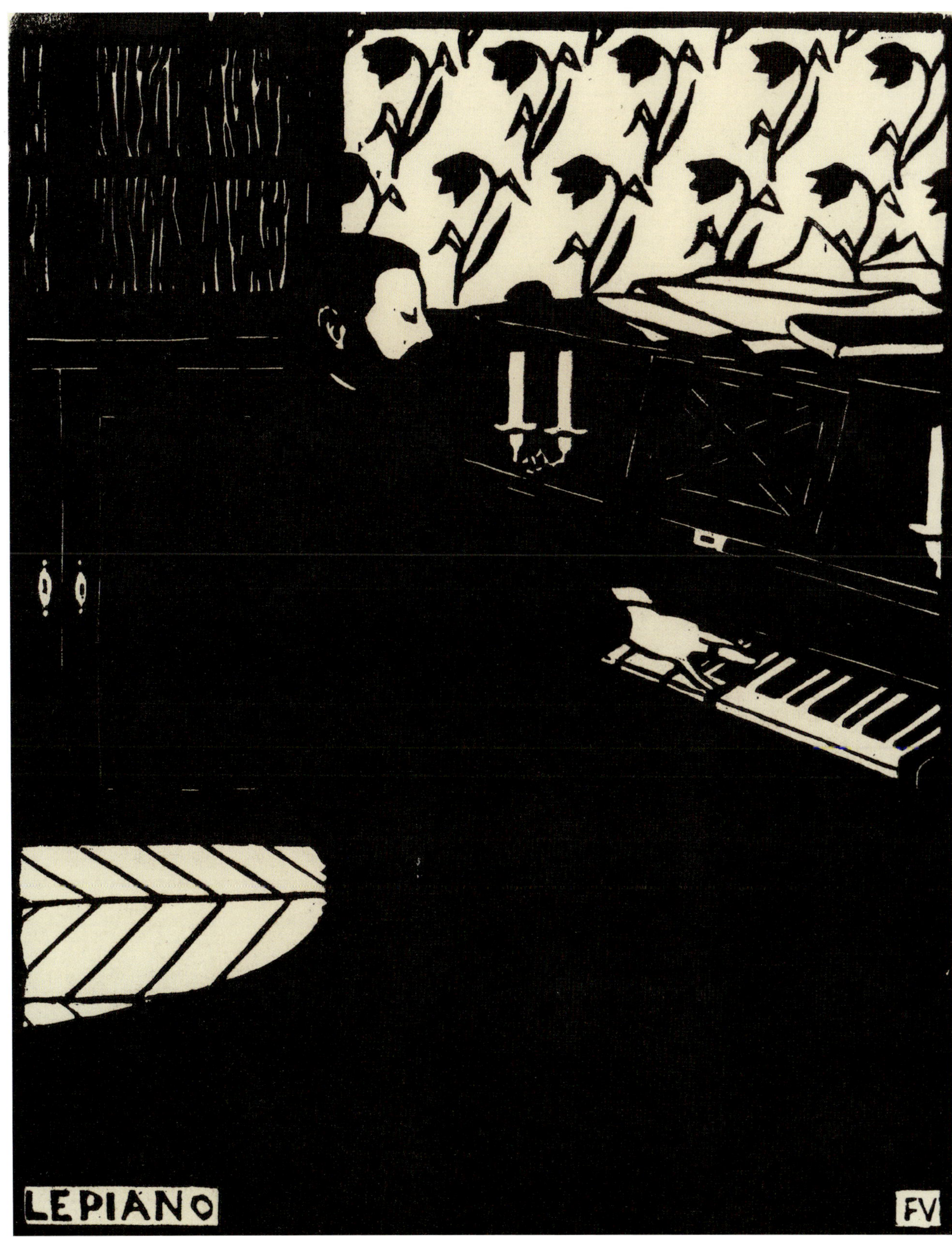

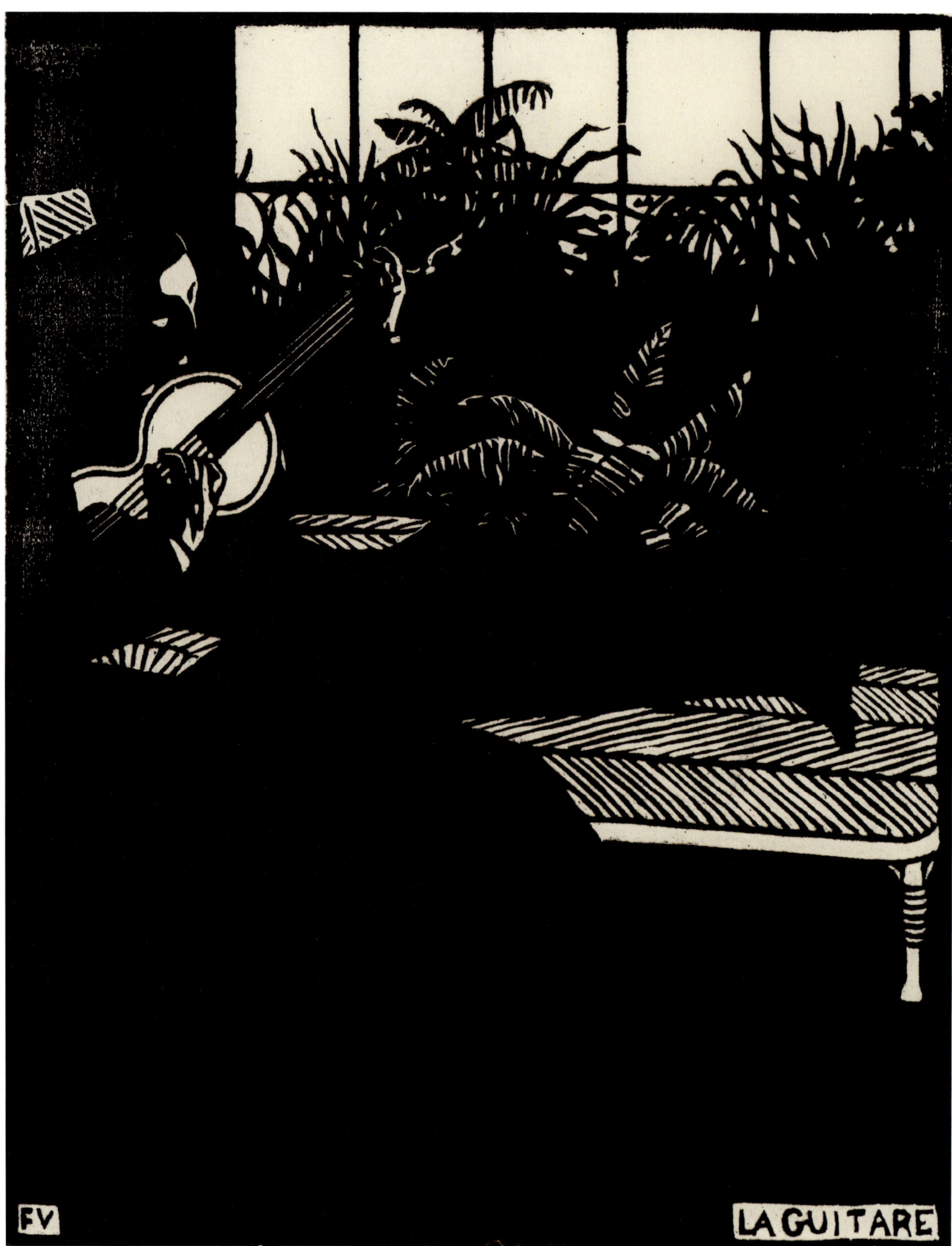

Cat. 72
Félix Vallotton
The Guitar, Musical Instruments, V, 1896
Woodcut, 22.5 × 18 cm
Bibliothèque Nationale de France, Département des Estampes et de la Photographie, Paris,
DC-292 (C, 2 bis),
FOL 147 IFN-6951722

Cat. 73
Félix Vallotton
The Cornet, Musical Instruments, VI, 1896
Woodcut, 22.5 × 17.7 cm
Bibliothèque Nationale de France, Département des Estampes et de la Photographie, Paris,
DC-292 (C, 2 bis),
FOL 148 IFN-6951723

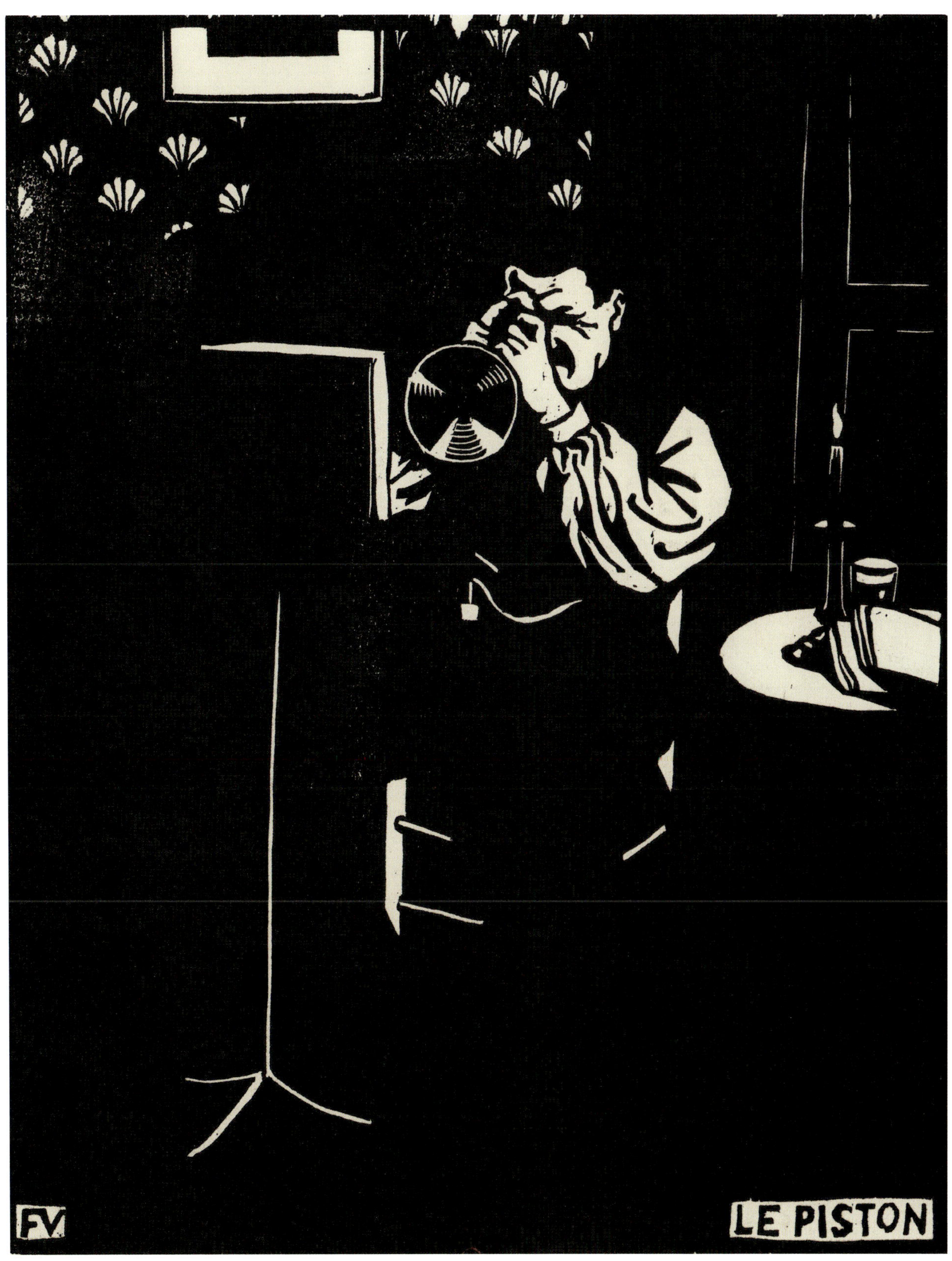

LE PISTON

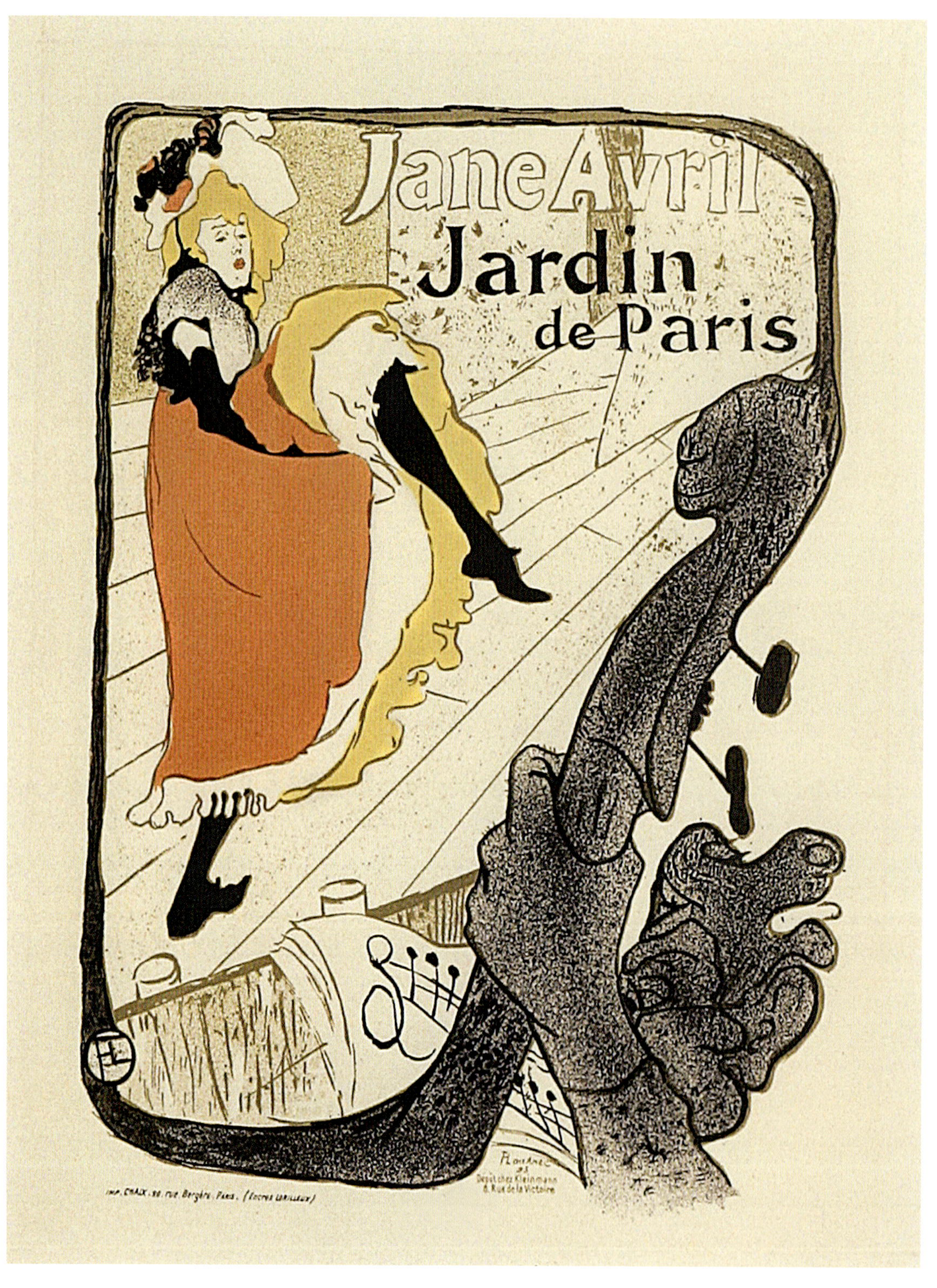

Jane Avril
Jardin
de Paris

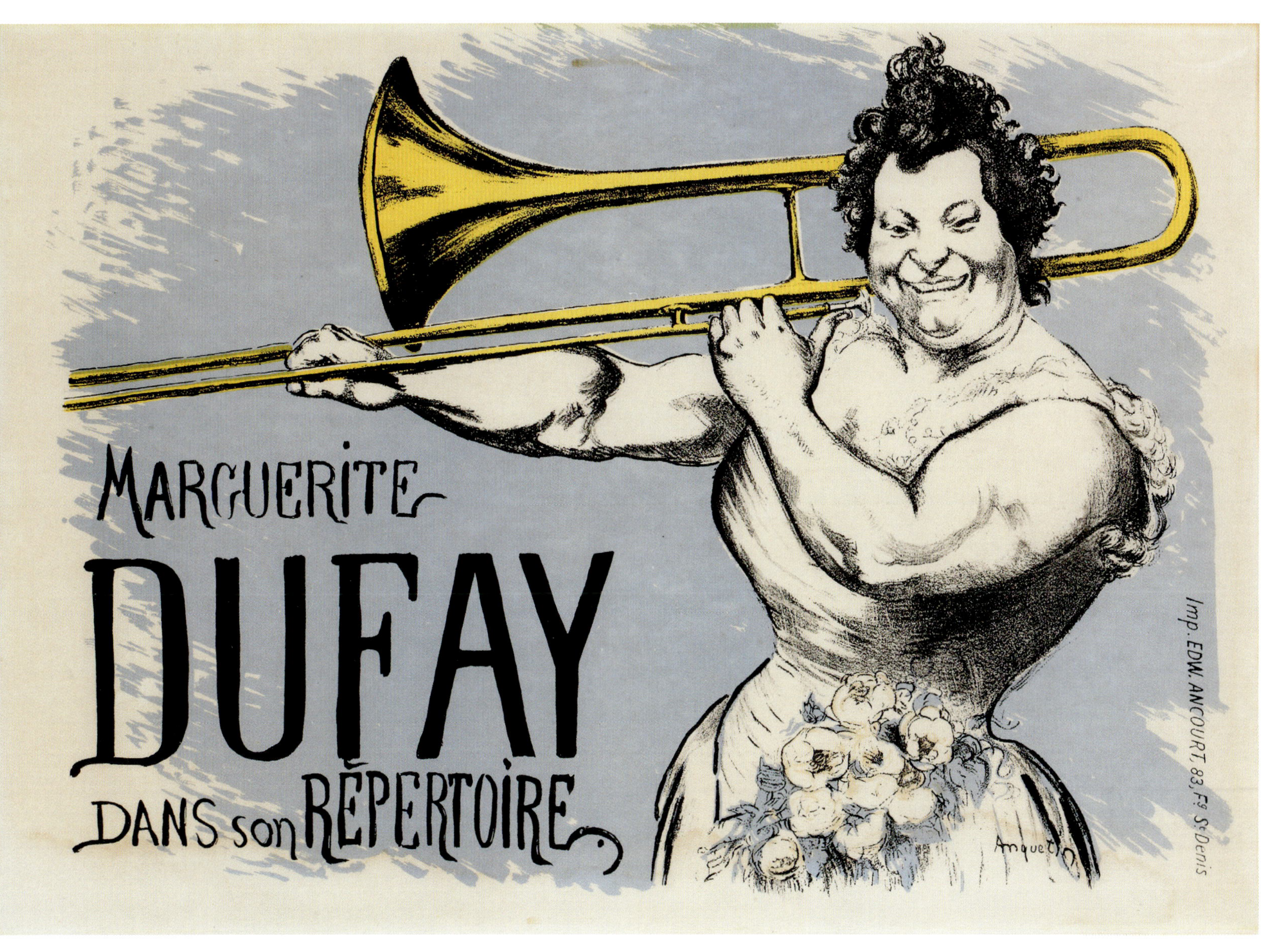

Cat. 74
Henri de Toulouse-Lautrec
Jane Avril, 1893
Four colour lithograph,
18.7 × 13.2 cm
Institut National d'Histoire
de l'Art, Bibliothèque,
Collection Jacques Doucet, Paris,
EM TOULOUSE-LAUTREC 134

Cat. 75
Louis Anquetin (1861–1932)
Marguerite Dufay, 1894,
published in the album
Les Maîtres de l'Affiche,
vol. IV, plate 150, 1899
Colour lithograph,
46.5 × 65.5 cm
Private collection

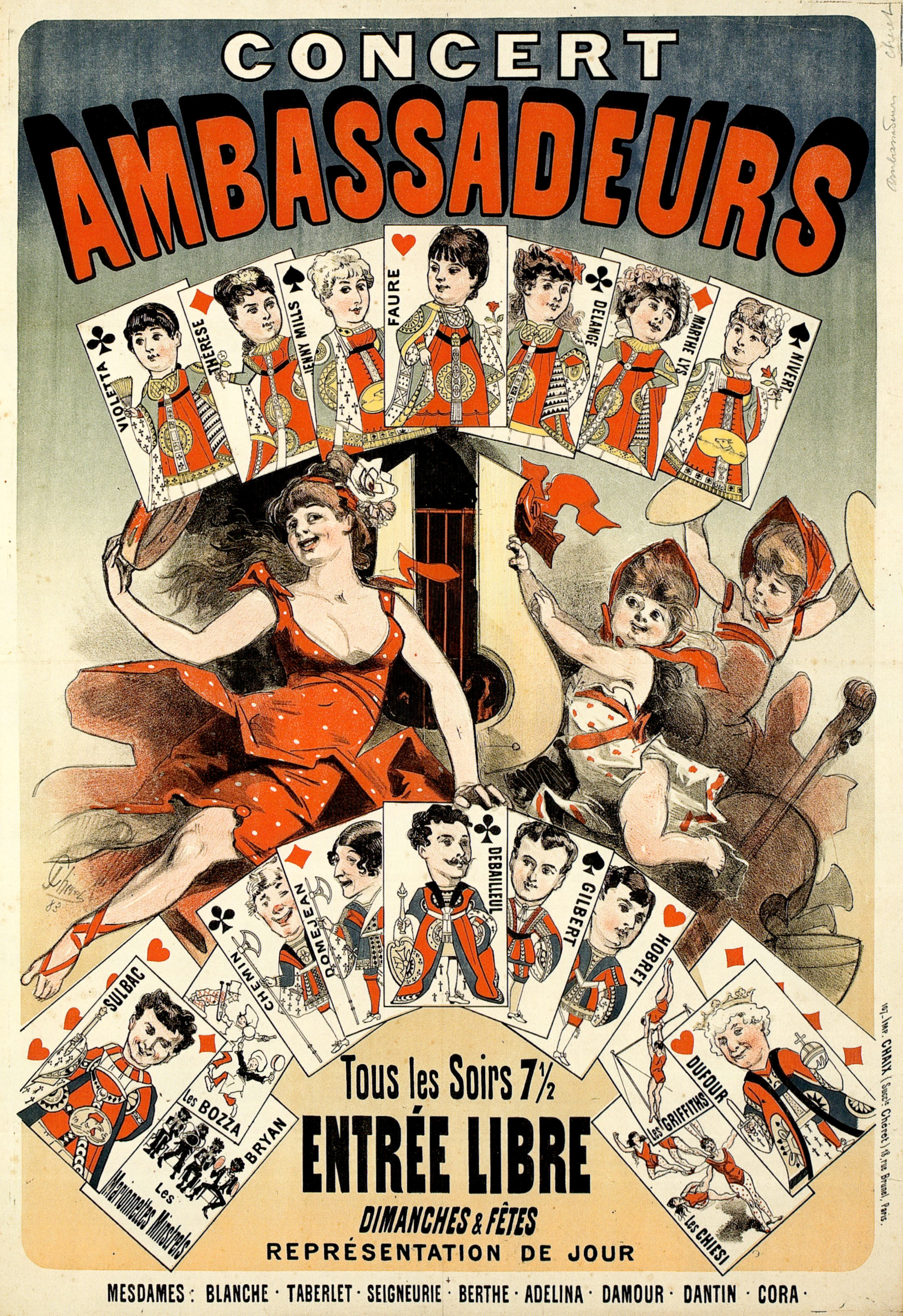

CONCERT
AMBASSADEURS
VIOLETTA
THÉRÈSE
JENNY MILLS
FAURE
DELANGE
MARTHE LYS
NIVERT
DOMÉJEAN
CHEMIN
DEBAILLEUL
GILBERT
HOBBET
SULBAC
Les BOZZA
BRYAN
Les Harmonicles Musicals
DUFOUR
Les GRIFFITHS
Les CHIESI
Tous les Soirs 7½
ENTRÉE LIBRE
DIMANCHES & FÊTES
REPRÉSENTATION DE JOUR
MESDAMES : BLANCHE · TABERLET · SEIGNEURIE · BERTHE · ADELINA · DAMOUR · DANTIN · CORA ·
Imp. CHAIX (Succ. Chéret) 18, rue Brunel, Paris.

Cat. 76
Jules Chéret
(1836–1932)
Ambassadeurs Concert Every Night 7.30 Free Entry, 1883
Colour lithograph, 124 × 87.5 cm
Les Arts Décoratifs, Paris,
RI 2004.20.106

Cat. 77
Henri Meunier (1873–1922)
Poster for the *Ysaÿe Concerts*, Salle du Cirque Royal, Brussels, Katto, music publisher, published in the album *Les Maîtres de l'Affiche*, vol. 1, plate 40, 1896
Colour lithograph, 39.5 × 29 cm
Private collection

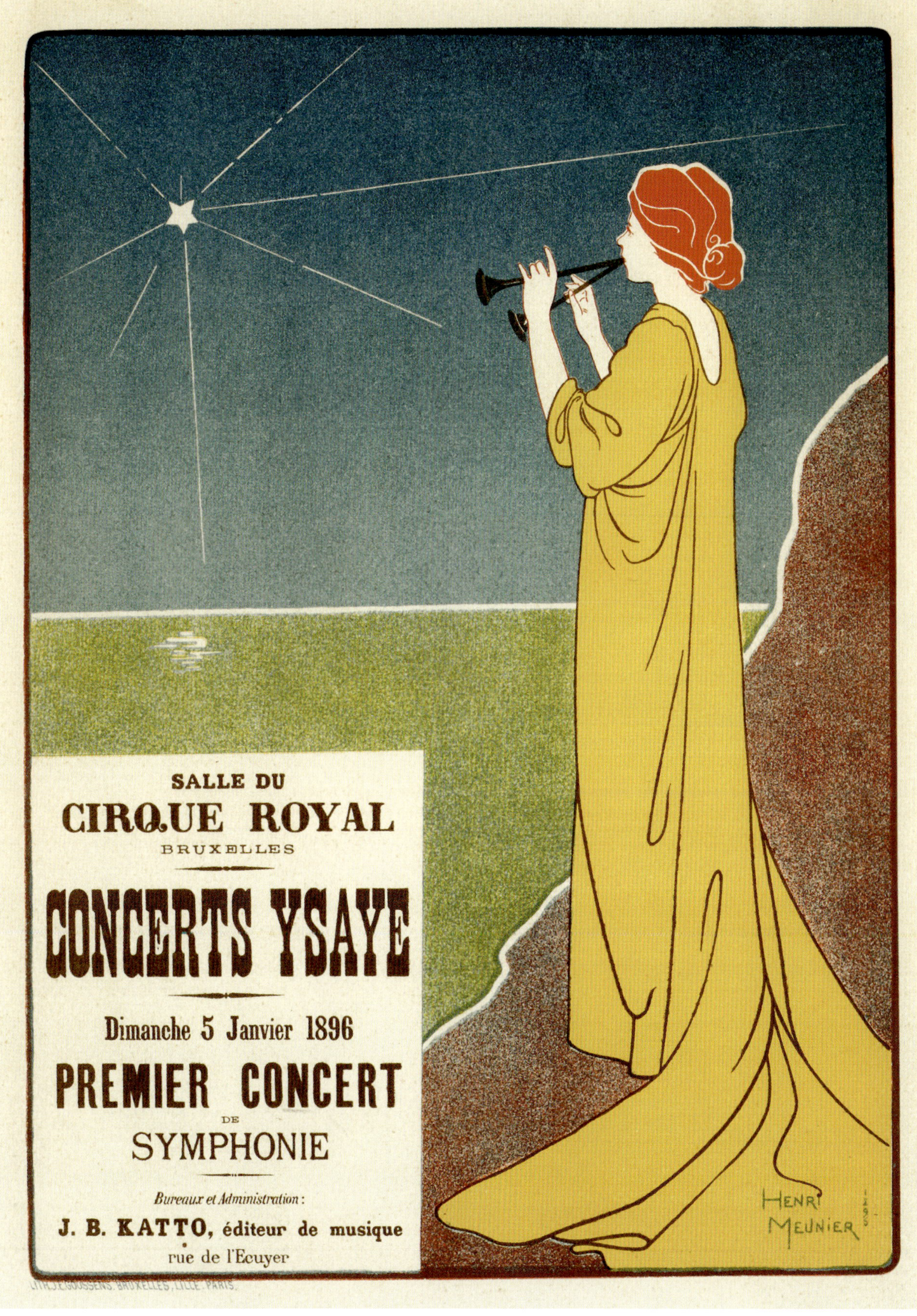

SALLE DU
CIRQUE ROYAL
BRUXELLES
CONCERTS YSAYE
Dimanche 5 Janvier 1896
PREMIER CONCERT
DE
SYMPHONIE
Bureaux et Administration :
J. B. KATTO, éditeur de musique
rue de l'Ecuyer

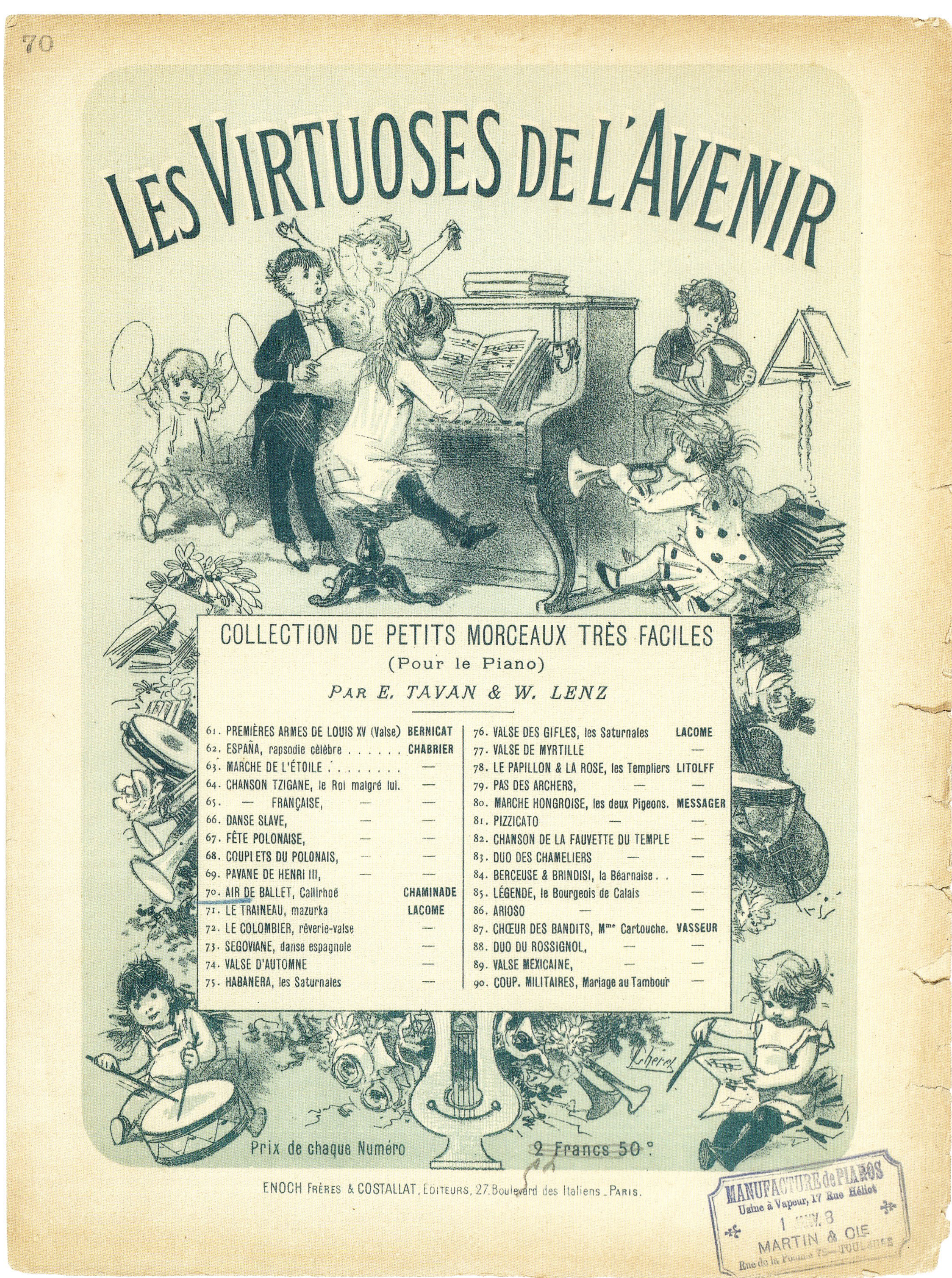

LES VIRTUOSES DE L'AVENIR
COLLECTION DE PETITS MORCEAUX TRÈS FACILES
(Pour le Piano)
PAR E. TAVAN & W. LENZ
61. PREMIÈRES ARMES DE LOUIS XV (Valse) BERNICAT
62. ESPAÑA, rapsodie célèbre . . . . . . CHABRIER
63. MARCHE DE L'ÉTOILE . . . . —
64. CHANSON TZIGANE, le Roi malgré lui. —
65. — FRANÇAISE, —
66. DANSE SLAVE, —
67. FÊTE POLONAISE, —
68. COUPLETS DU POLONAIS, —
69. PAVANE DE HENRI III, —
70. AIR DE BALLET, Callirhoë CHAMINADE
71. LE TRAINEAU, mazurka LACOME
72. LE COLOMBIER, rêverie-valse —
73. SEGOVIANE, danse espagnole —
74. VALSE D'AUTOMNE —
75. HABANERA, les Saturnales —
76. VALSE DES GIFLES, les Saturnales LACOME
77. VALSE DE MYRTILLE —
78. LE PAPILLON & LA ROSE, les Templiers LITOLFF
79. PAS DES ARCHERS, —
80. MARCHE HONGROISE, les deux Pigeons. MESSAGER
81. PIZZICATO —
82. CHANSON DE LA FAUVETTE DU TEMPLE —
83. DUO DES CHAMELIERS —
84. BERCEUSE & BRINDISI, la Béarnaise . . —
85. LÉGENDE, le Bourgeois de Calais —
86. ARIOSO —
87. CHŒUR DES BANDITS, Mme Cartouche. VASSEUR
88. DUO DU ROSSIGNOL, —
89. VALSE MEXICAINE, —
90. COUP. MILITAIRES, Mariage au Tambour —
Prix de chaque Numéro 2 Francs 50 c
ENOCH Frères & COSTALLAT, Éditeurs, 27, Boulevard des Italiens — Paris.

Cat. 78
Jules Chéret
The Virtuosi of the Future.
Collection of Short Easy Pieces
for the Piano, 1881
Colour lithograph, 35 × 27 cm
Les Arts Décoratifs, Paris,
RI 2011.1.101

Cat. 79
Maurice Boutet de Monvel
(1850–1913)
Traditional Songs for
Small Children, music by
Charles Widor, *La Mist en Laire*,
double page, 1883
Printed book, 23 × 27.5 cm
Private collection

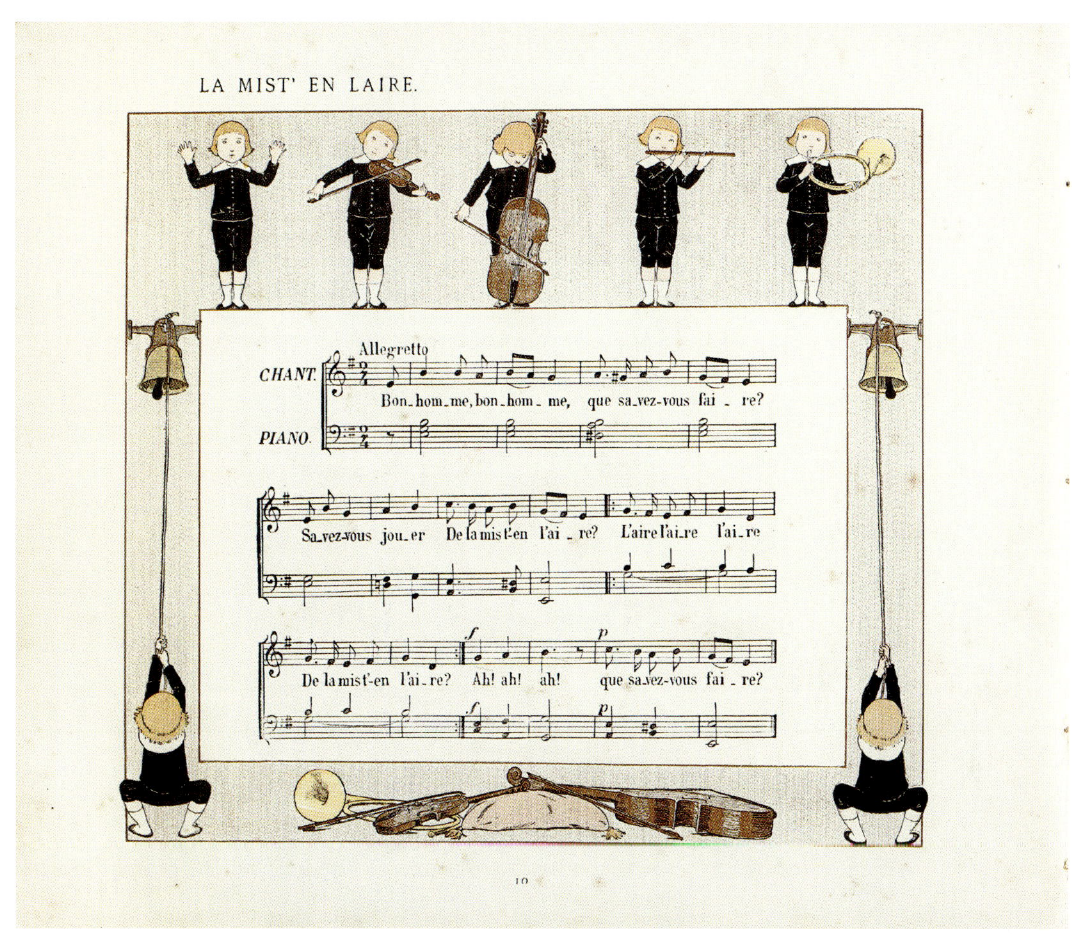

LA MIST' EN LAIRE.
Allegretto
CHANT.
Bon_hom_me, bon_hom_me, que sa_vez-vous fai _ re?
PIANO.
Sa_vez-vous jou_er De la mist'en l'ai_re? L'aire l'ai_re l'ai_re
De la mist'en l'ai_re? Ah! ah! ah! que sa_vez-vous fai _ re?
10

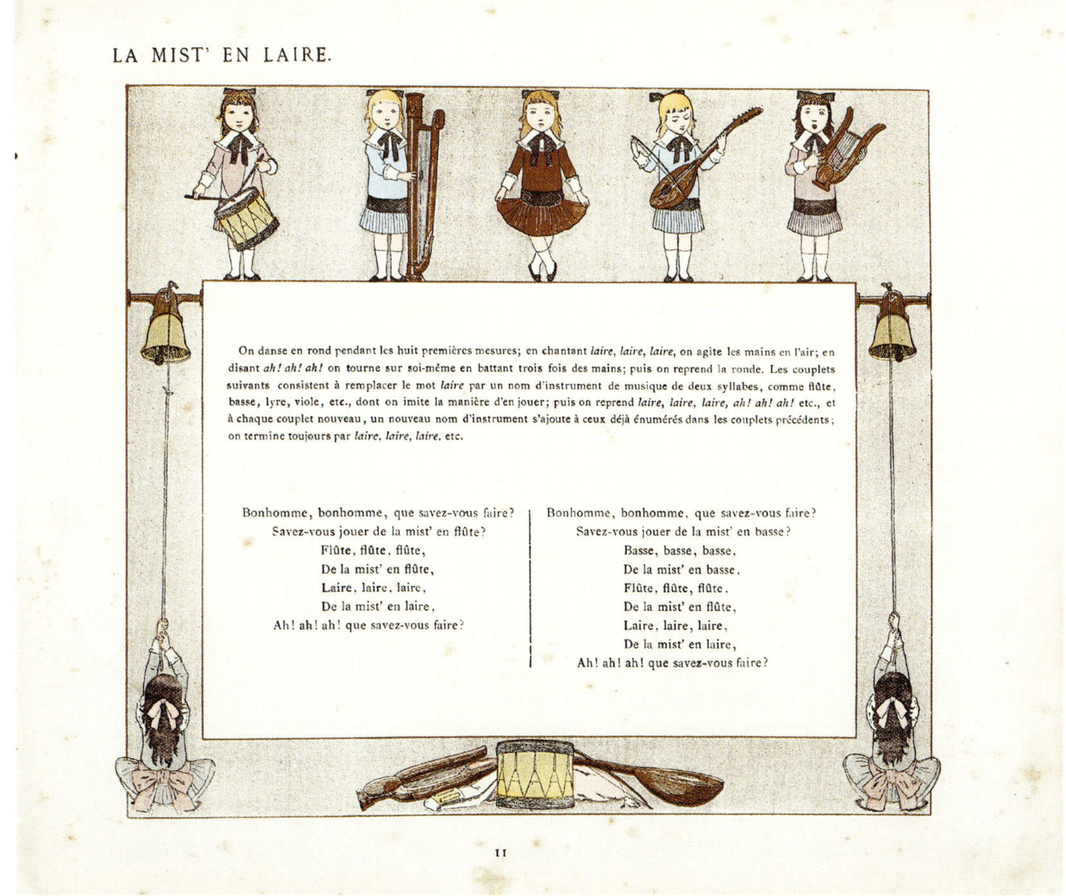

LA MIST' EN LAIRE.

On danse en rond pendant les huit premières mesures; en chantant laire, laire, laire, on agite les mains en l'air; en
disant ah! ah! ah! on tourne sur soi-même en battant trois fois des mains; puis on reprend la ronde. Les couplets
suivants consistent à remplacer le mot laire par un nom d'instrument de musique de deux syllabes, comme flûte,
basse, lyre, viole, etc., dont on imite la manière d'en jouer; puis on reprend laire, laire, laire, ah! ah! ah! etc., et
à chaque couplet nouveau, un nouveau nom d'instrument s'ajoute à ceux déjà énumérés dans les couplets précédents;
on termine toujours par laire, laire, laire, etc.

Bonhomme, bonhomme, que savez-vous faire?
Savez-vous jouer de la mist' en flûte?
Flûte, flûte, flûte,
De la mist' en flûte,
Laire, laire, laire,
De la mist' en laire,
Ah! ah! ah! que savez-vous faire?

Bonhomme, bonhomme, que savez-vous faire?
Savez-vous jouer de la mist' en basse?
Basse, basse, basse,
De la mist' en basse,
Flûte, flûte, flûte,
De la mist' en flûte,
Laire, laire, laire,
De la mist' en laire,
Ah! ah! ah! que savez-vous faire?

11

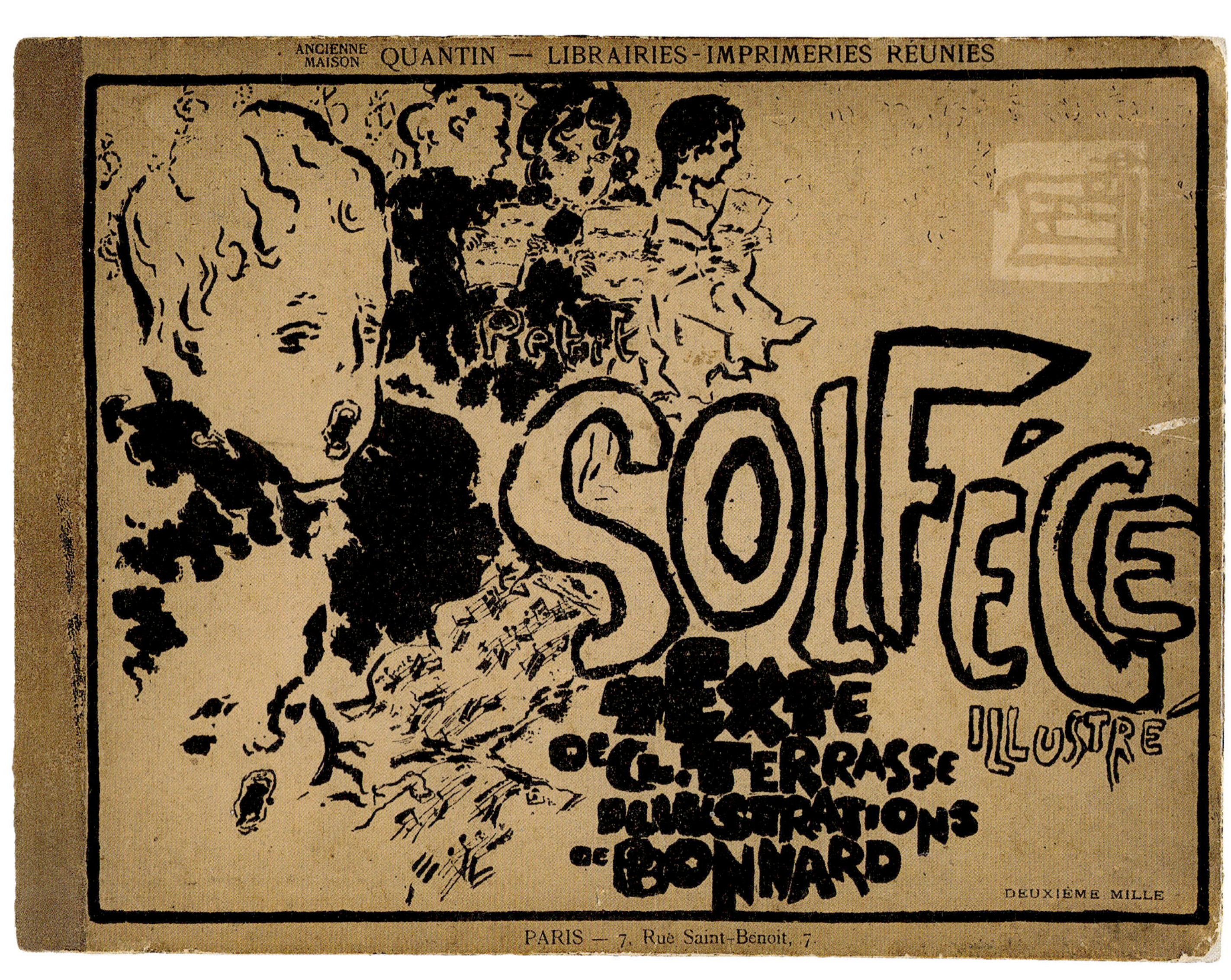

Cat. 80
**Claude Terrasse (1867–1923)
and Pierre Bonnard**
Petit Solfège illustré, Quantin,
Paris, 1893, 21.5 × 28 cm
Bibliothèque du musée
des impressionnismes, Giverny

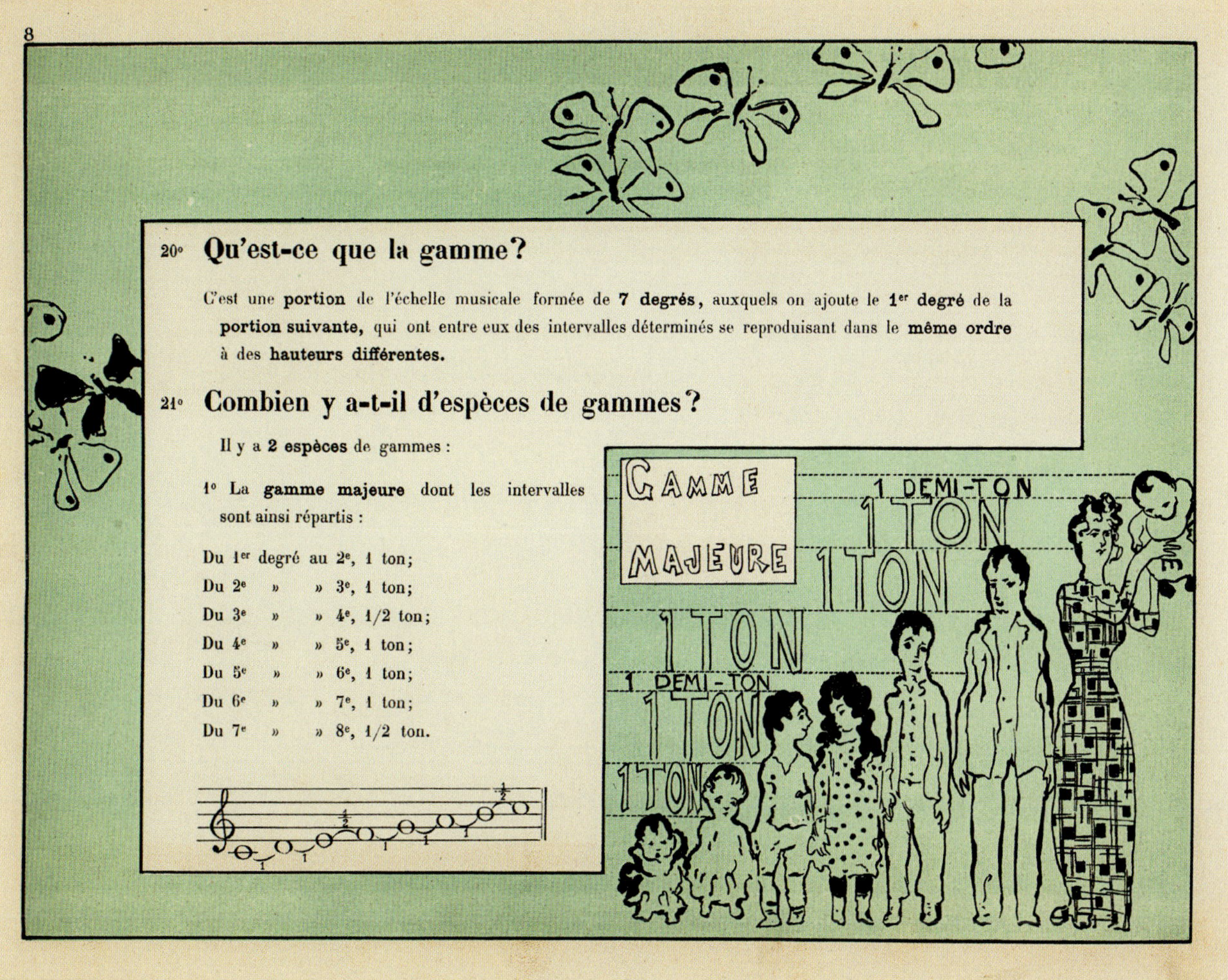
8
20° Qu'est-ce que la gamme?
C'est une portion de l'échelle musicale formée de 7 degrés, auxquels on ajoute le 1er degré de la portion suivante, qui ont entre eux des intervalles déterminés se reproduisant dans le même ordre à des hauteurs différentes.
21° Combien y a-t-il d'espèces de gammes?
Il y a 2 espèces de gammes :
1° La gamme majeure dont les intervalles sont ainsi répartis :
Du 1er degré au 2e, 1 ton;
Du 2e » » 3e, 1 ton;
Du 3e » » 4e, 1/2 ton;
Du 4e » » 5e, 1 ton;
Du 5e » » 6e, 1 ton;
Du 6e » » 7e, 1 ton;
Du 7e » » 8e, 1/2 ton.
GAMME MAJEURE
1 DEMI-TON
1 TON
1 TON
1 TON
1 DEMI-TON
1 TON
1 TON

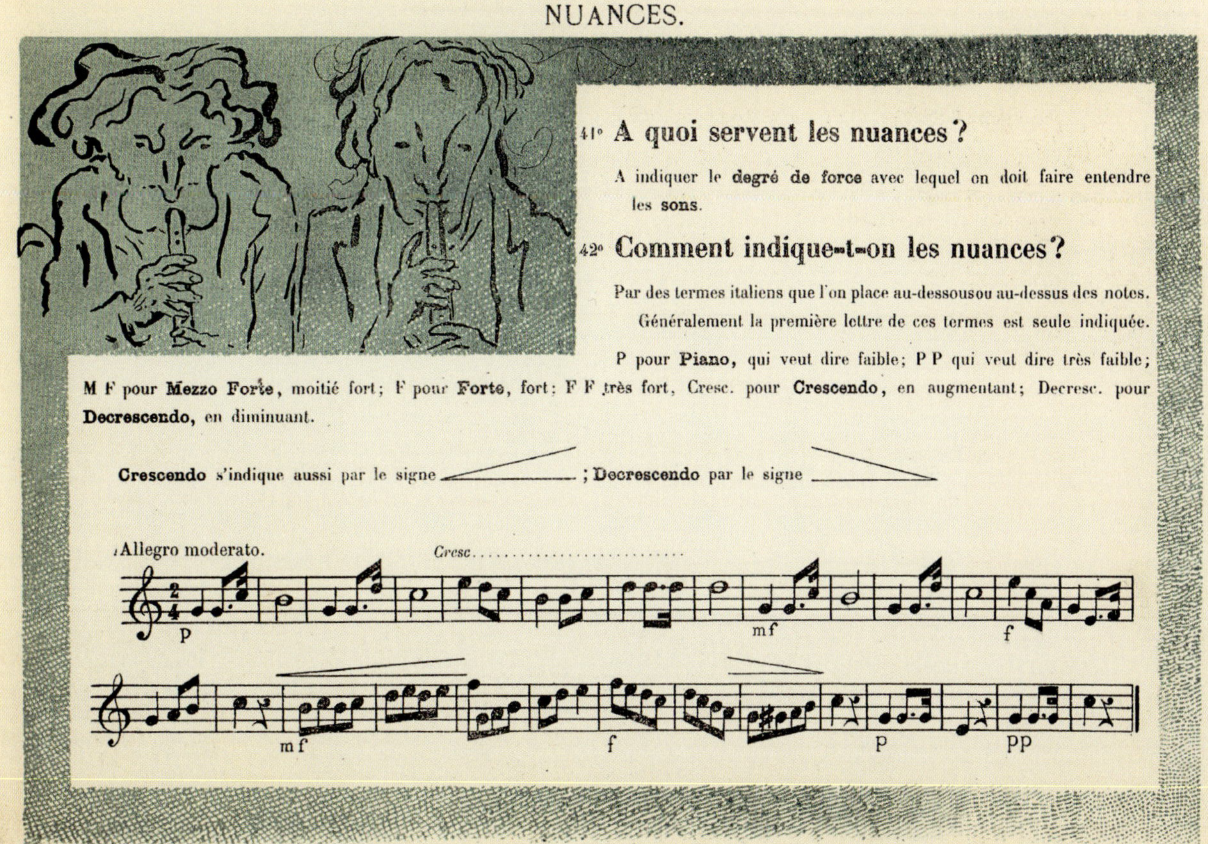
26
Chapitre VIII
NUANCES.
41° A quoi servent les nuances?
A indiquer le degré de force avec lequel on doit faire entendre les sons.
42° Comment indique-t-on les nuances?
Par des termes italiens que l'on place au-dessous ou au-dessus des notes. Généralement la première lettre de ces termes est seule indiquée.
P pour Piano, qui veut dire faible; P P qui veut dire très faible; M F pour Mezzo Forte, moitié fort; F pour Forte, fort; F F très fort, Cresc. pour Crescendo, en augmentant; Decresc. pour Decrescendo, en diminuant.
Crescendo s'indique aussi par le signe ____________ ; Decrescendo par le signe ____________
Allegro moderato.
Cresc
p
mf
f
mf
f
p
pp

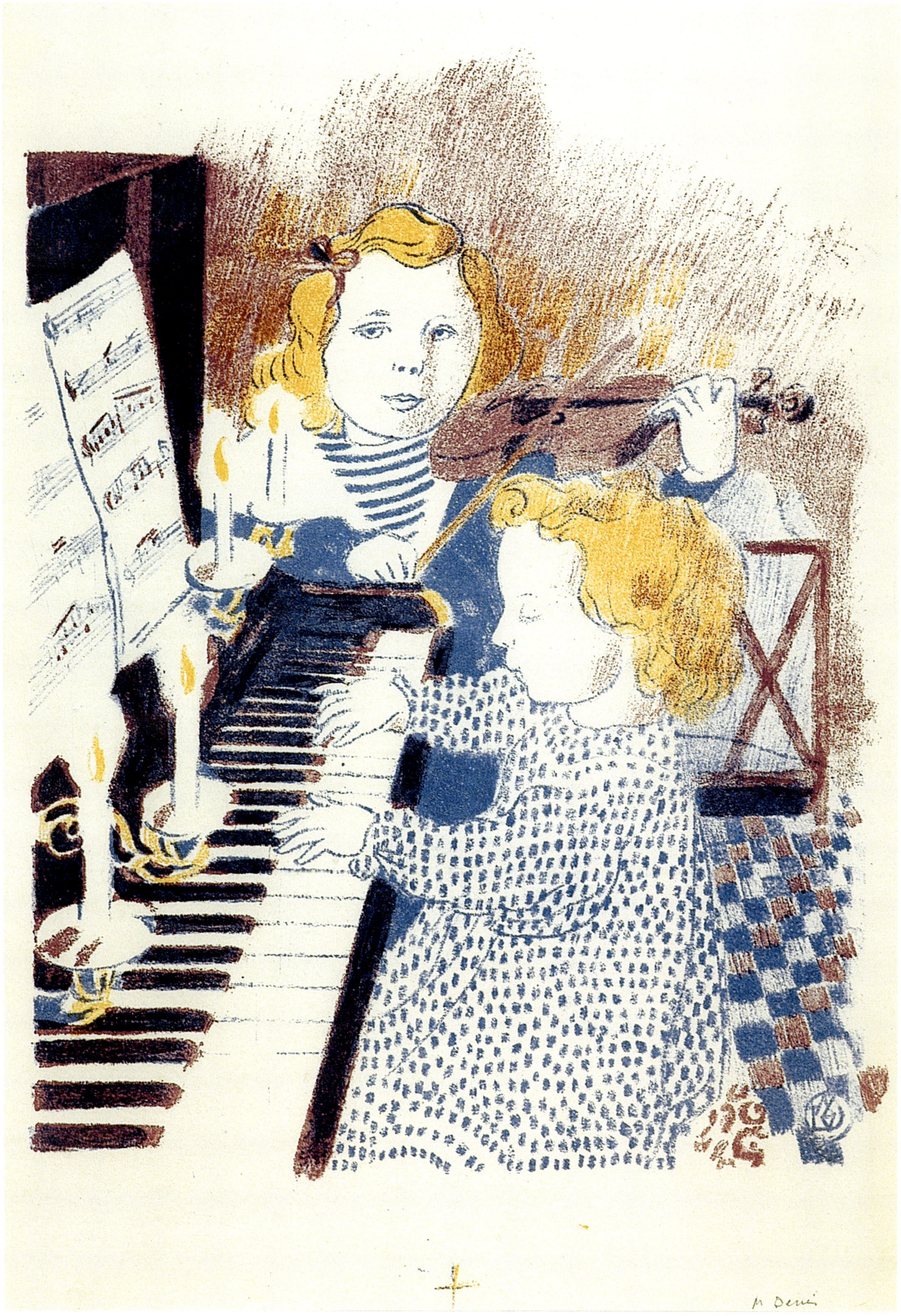

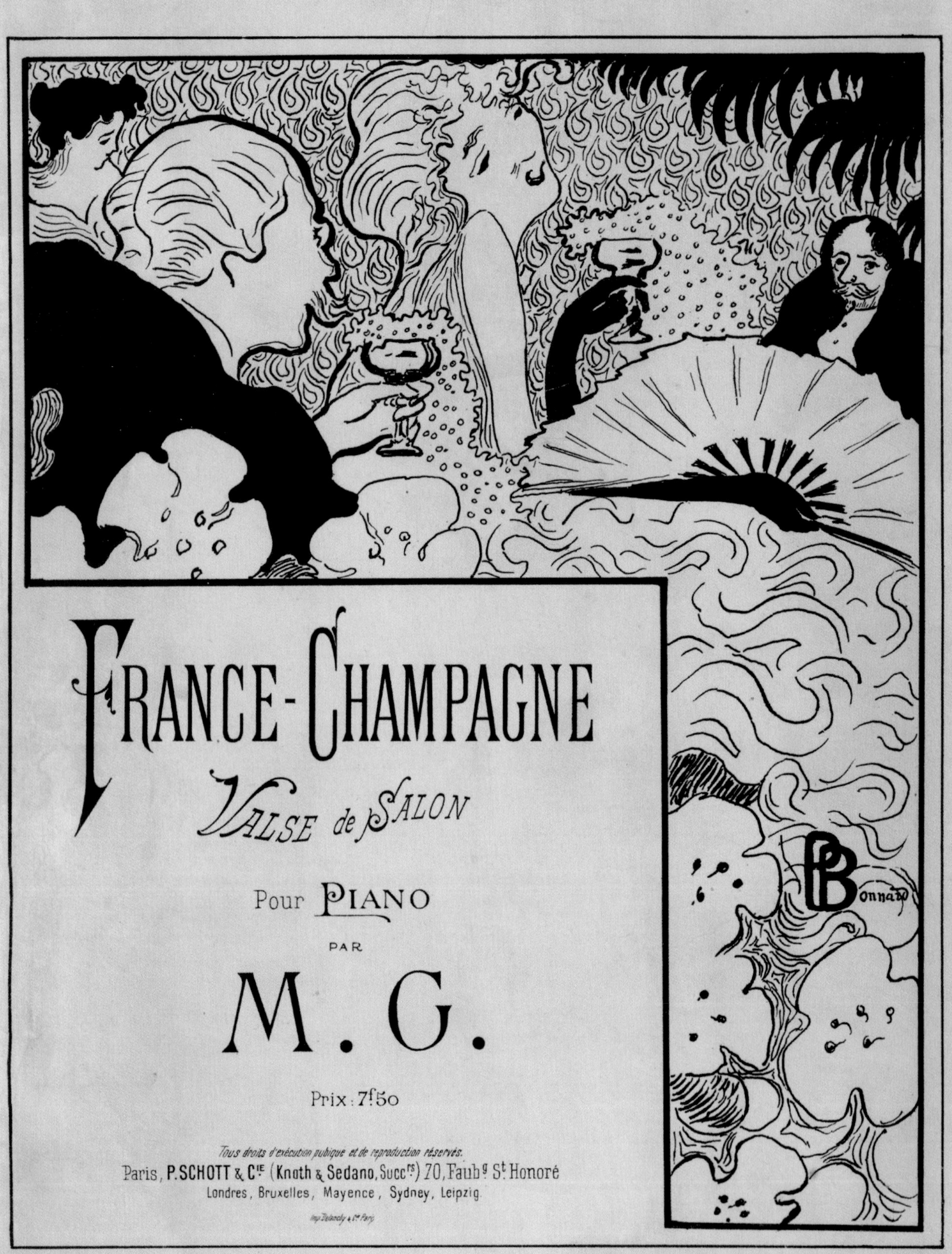

Cat. 82
Pierre Bonnard
France-Champagne, 'Valse de salon pour piano par M. G.' [Marie Gourat], P. Schott & Cie, Paris, March 1891
Cover for piano score, zincograph, 35.5 × 27.5 cm
Private collection

Cat. 83
Pierre Bonnard
Cover design for '*Suite for piano*', three pieces by Claude Terrasse op. 9, c. 1891
Pen and black ink over pencil, 31 × 24 cm
Private collection

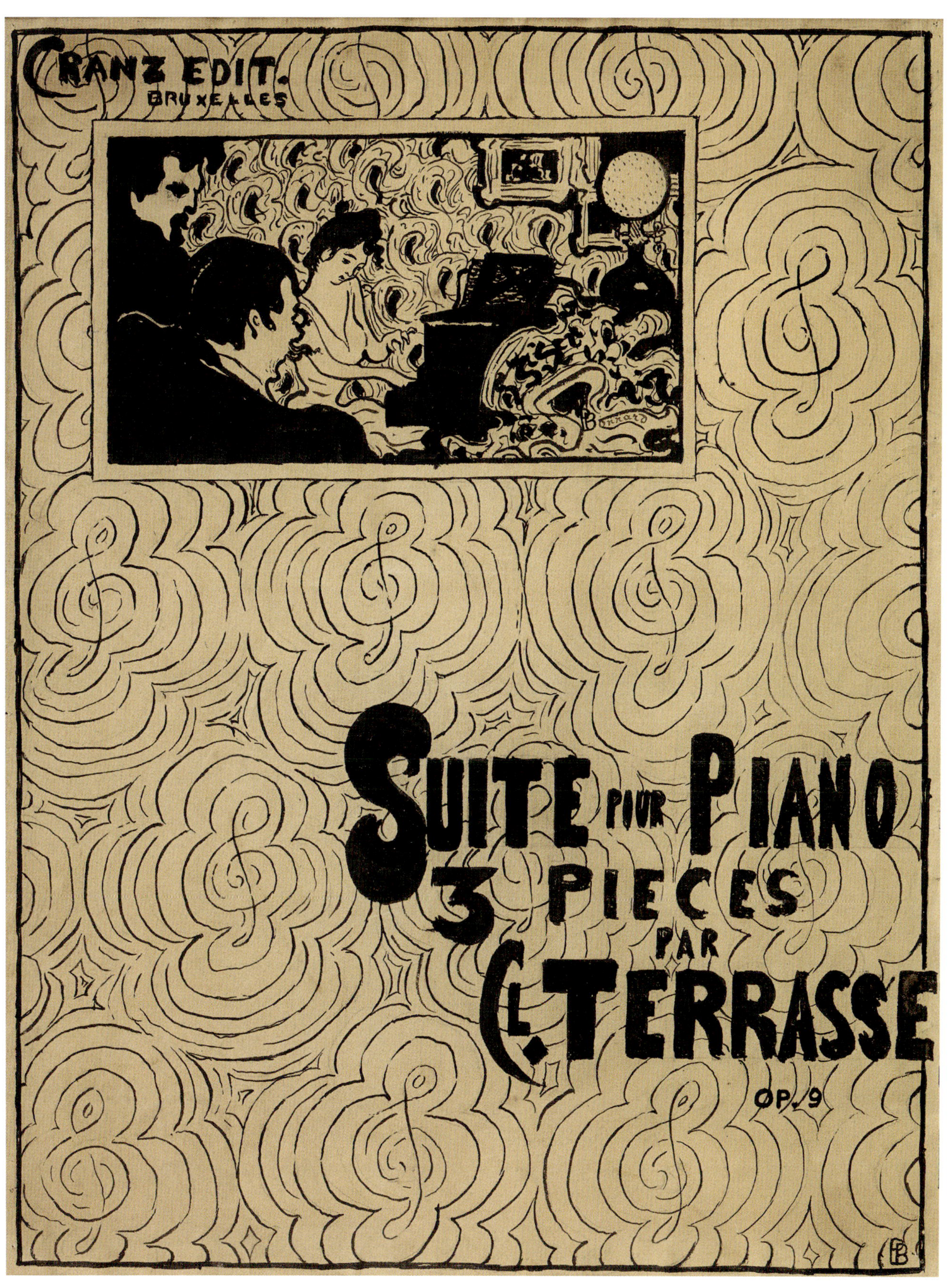
CRANZ EDIT.
BRUXELLES
SUITE POUR PIANO
3 PIECES
PAR
CL. TERRASSE
OP. 9

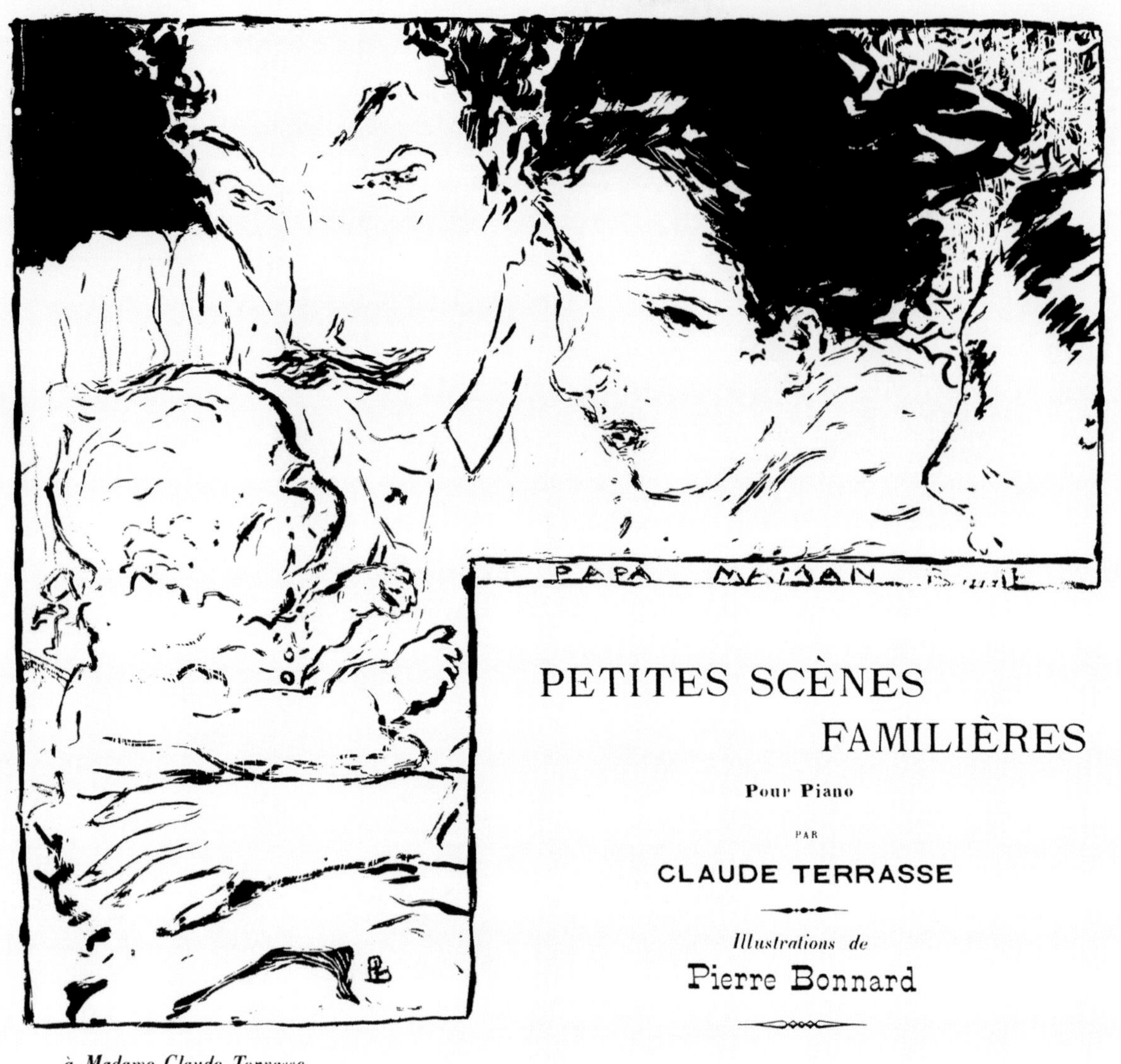

PETITES SCÈNES FAMILIÈRES

Pour Piano

PAR

CLAUDE TERRASSE

Illustrations de
Pierre Bonnard

à Madame Claude Terrasse

PAPA, MAMAN, Ie.^(MARIE)

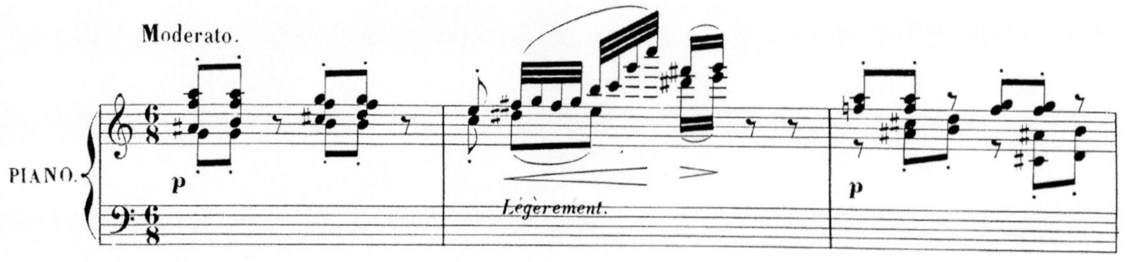

Paris. E. FROMONT Éditeur   E. 1140 F.   B.d Malesherbes. (40. rue d'Anjou.)

Cat. 84
**Claude Terrasse and
Pierre Bonnard**
*Petites Scènes familières for the
Piano*, illustrations by Pierre
Bonnard, Paris, E. Fromont, [1895]
Lithographs, 1893–1895
Daddy and Mummy, 35.5 × 27 cm
The Night Hours, 13.1 × 23.5 cm
Fair booth, 10.8 × 20.8 cm
Quadrille, 11 × 23.5 cm
Private collection

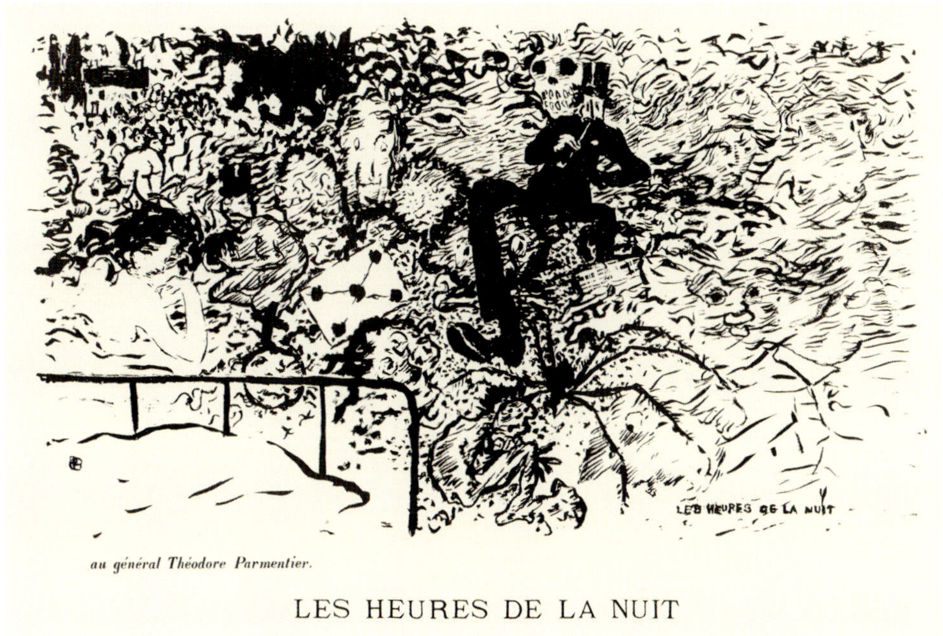

au général Théodore Parmentier.
LES HEURES DE LA NUIT

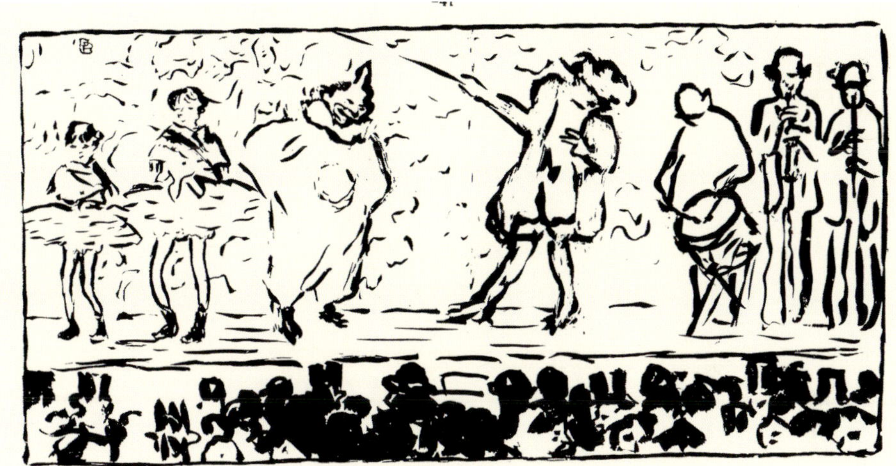

Nº 2.__La baraque.

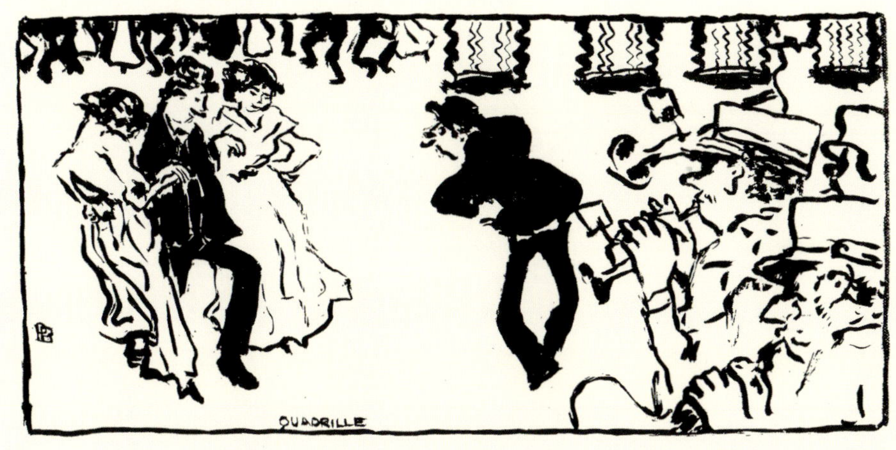

QUADRILLE
Nº 4.__QUADRILLE

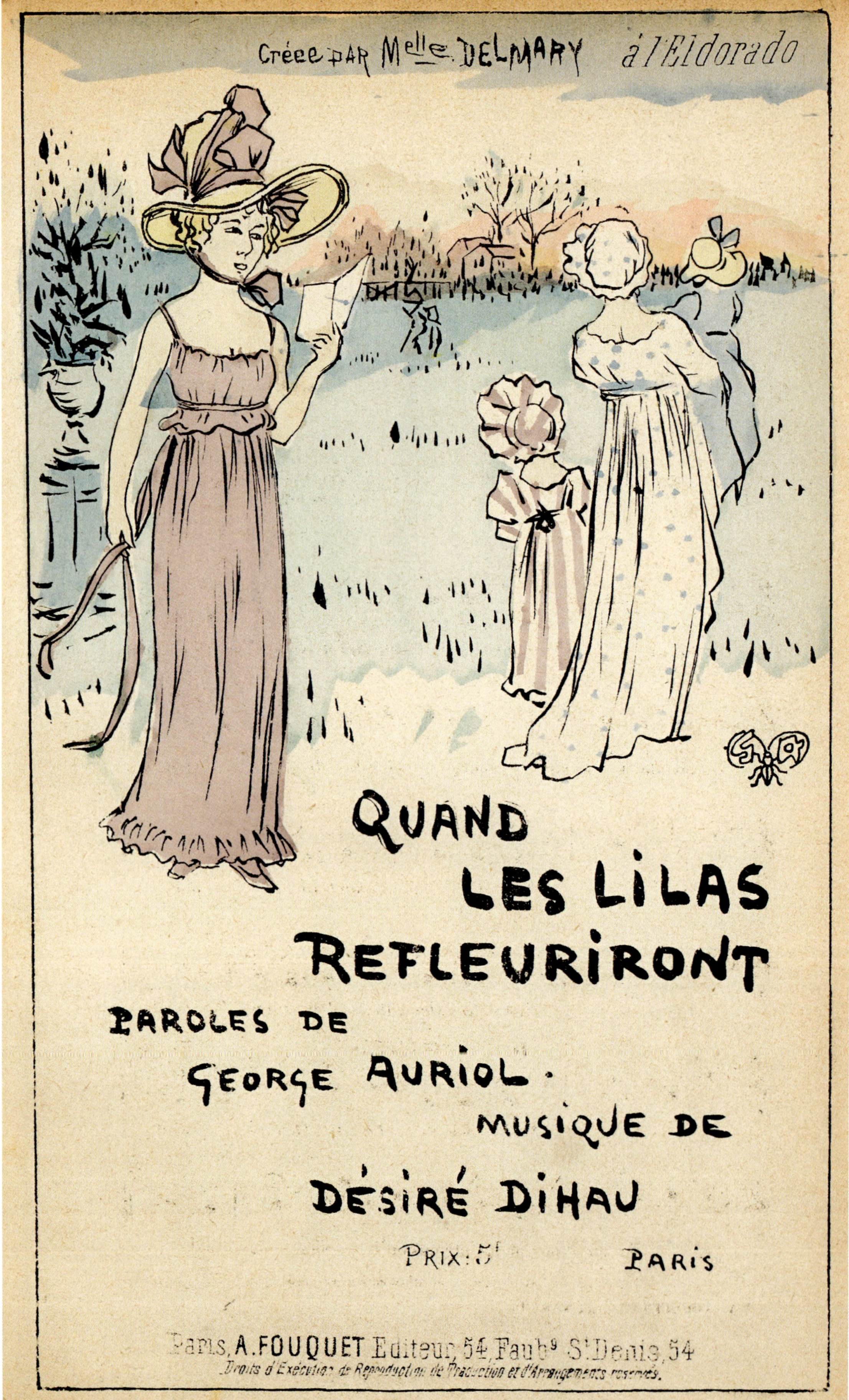

Cat. 85
George Auriol (1863–1938)
When the Lilacs Bloom again,
words by George Auriol, music by
Désiré Dihau, voice and piano,
Ed. A Fouquet, Paris, 1889
Printed in colours by
photomechanical process,
27 × 17.6 cm
Private collection

Cat. 86
Jacques Villon (1875–1963)
*Anxiety, Piano Waltz by
Gaston Roux*, Ed. A. Bosc, rue
Rouchechouart, Paris, 1901
Colour lithograph, 35 × 27 cm
Private collection

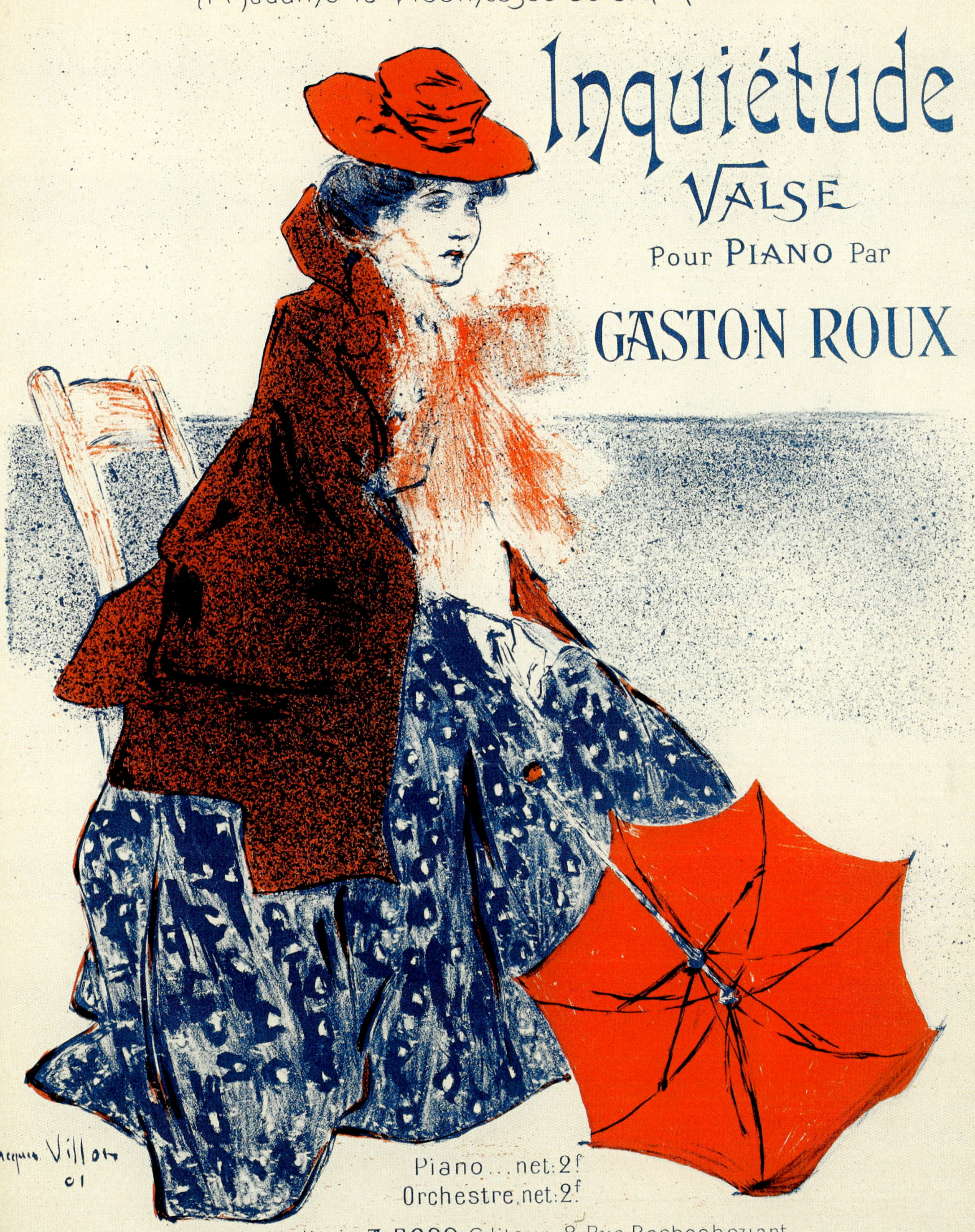

A Madame la Vicomtesse de CHARPIN.
Inquiétude
VALSE
Pour PIANO Par
GASTON ROUX
Jacques Villon
01
Piano... net: 2f
Orchestre. net: 2f
Paris, A. BOSC, Editeur, 8, Rue Rochechouart.
Tous droits d'exécution, de reproduction et d'arrangements réservés pour tous pays.
Imp. Chaimbaud & Cie Paris.

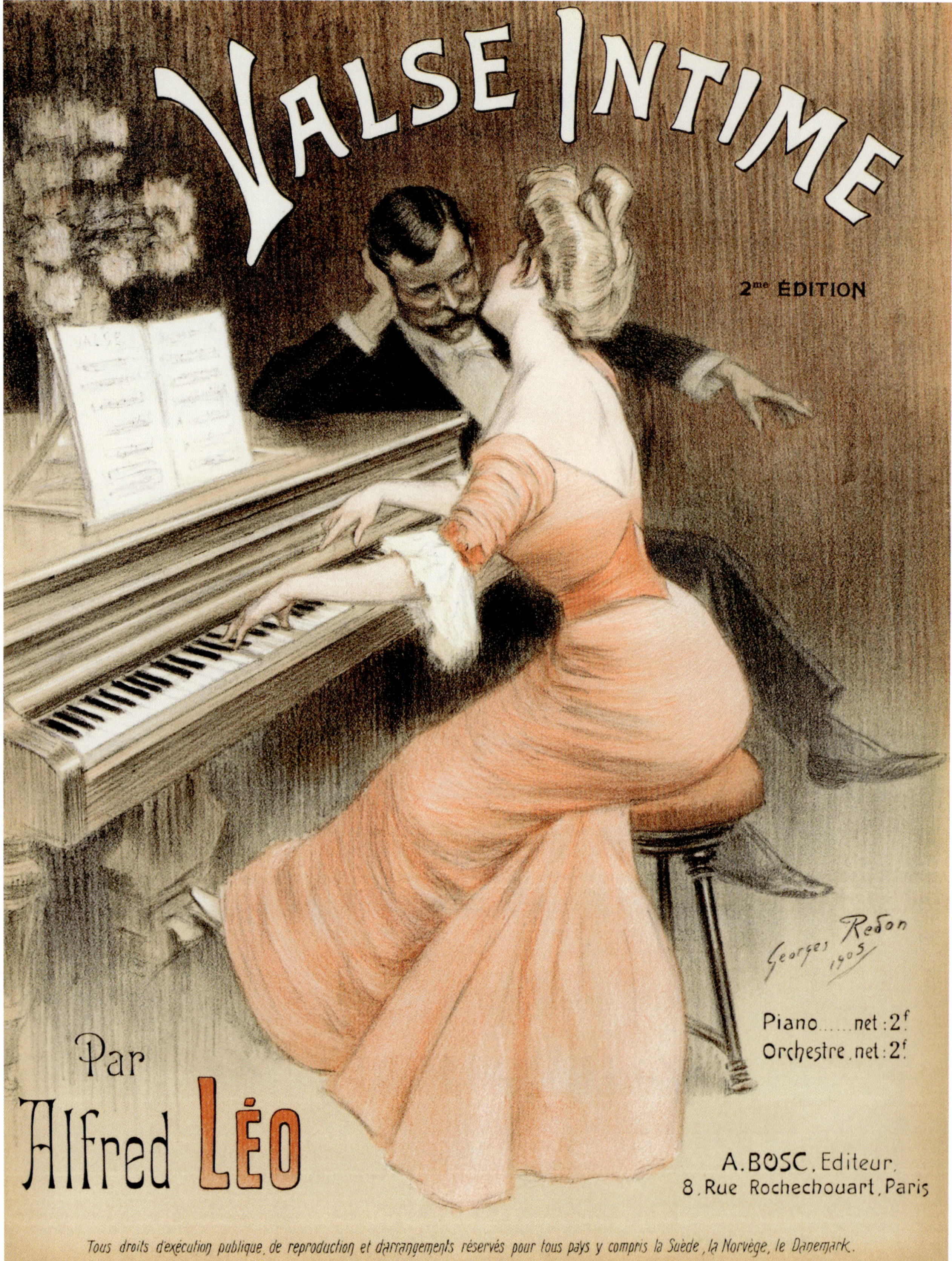

Cat. 87
Georges Redon (1869–1943)
Intimate Waltz, by Alfred Léo,
Ed. A. Bosc, rue Rochechouart,
piano version, 1905
Colour lithograph, 35 × 27 cm
Private collection

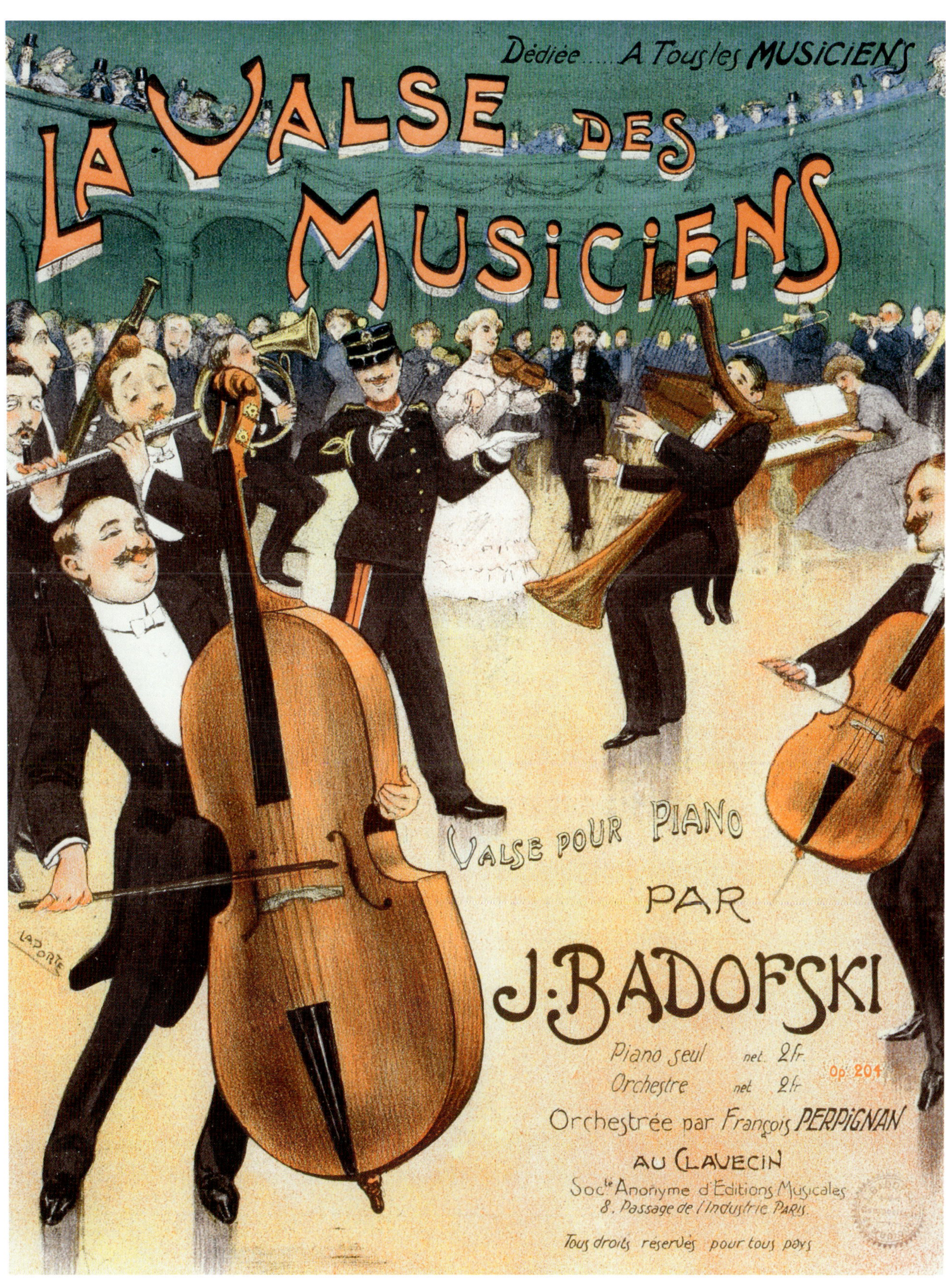

Cat. 88
Raoul Laporte
The Musicians' Waltz,
Piano Waltz, by J. Badofski,
Ed. Société anonyme d'Éditions
musicales, c. 1905
Colour lithograph, 35 × 27 cm
Private collection

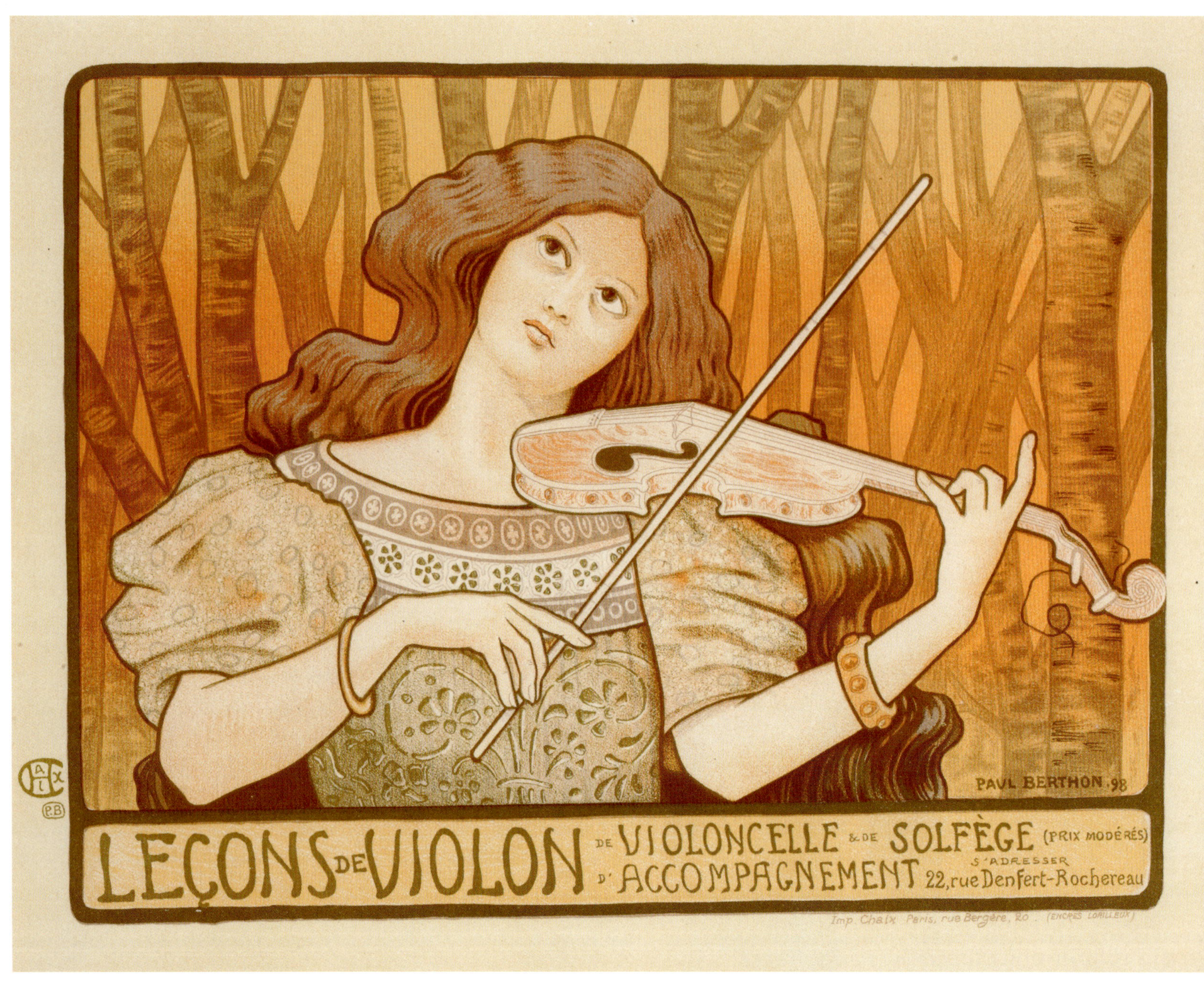

Cat. 89
Paul Berthon (1872–1909)
Poster for *Violin and Cello
Lessons etc.*, Paris, Chaix,
published in the album
Les Maîtres de l'Affiche, 1899,
vol. IV, plate 175, 1898
Colour lithograph, 29 × 39.5 cm
Private collection

Cat. 90
Georges Meunier (1869–1942)
Harmony, from *Le Rire*,
no. 417, 1 November 1902
Colour lithograph, 20.5 × 19.4 cm
Private collection

N° 417. — 9e Année. 1er Novembre 1902.　　　　20 centimes.

UN AN
Paris et Départements, **10** fr.
Étranger, **14** fr.

SIX MOIS
France, **5.50** — Étranger, **7.50**

Le Rire

JOURNAL HUMORISTIQUE PARAISSANT LE SAMEDI

Félix JUVEN, Directeur
122, rue Réaumur, 122
PARIS

VENTE ET ABONNEMENTS
9, rue Saint-Joseph, 9

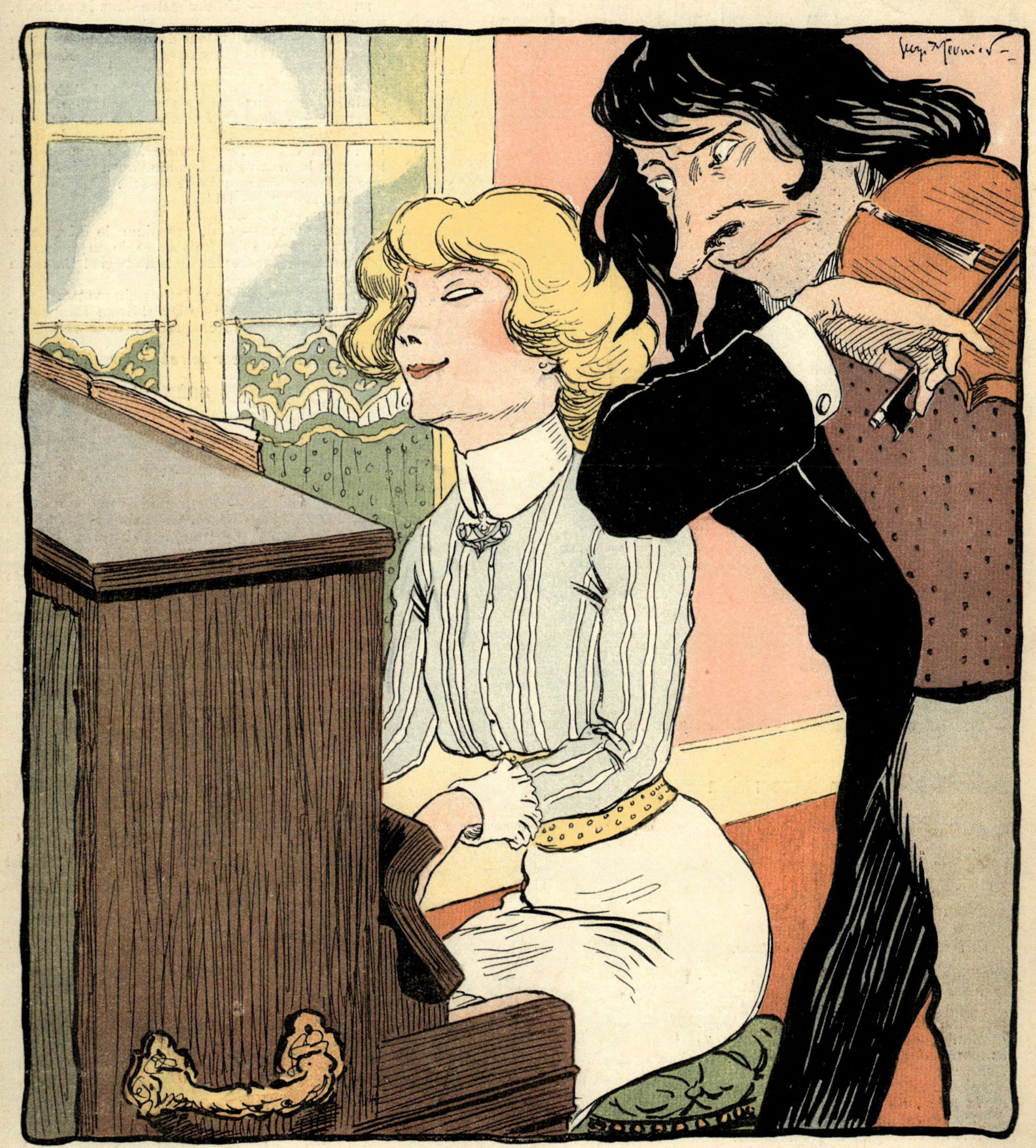

HARMONIE

— Attention, mademoiselle, glissez sur le do, pour finir ensemble par les deux soupirs.

Dessin de Georges MEUNIER.

milestones in the history of the guitar

Frédéric Frank

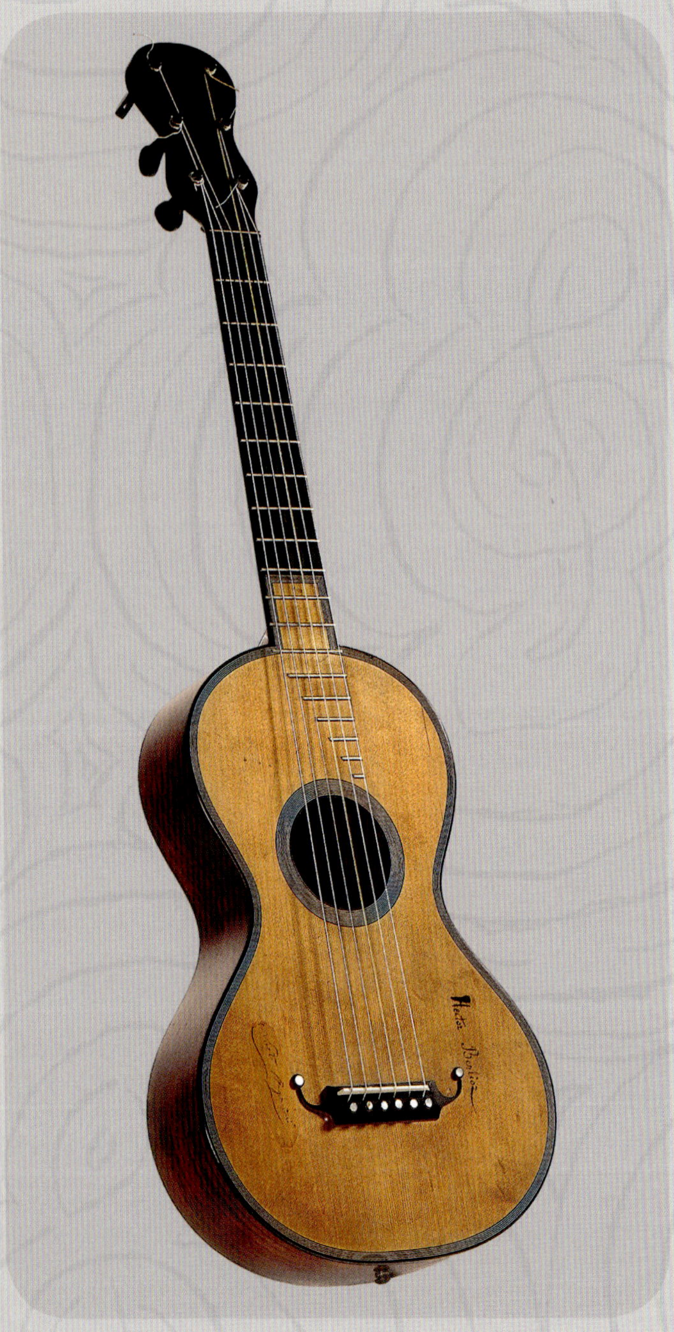

The guitar was the most popular instrument in the early nineteenth-century salon, before the piano took its place. The gittern, an instrument with four, then five strings, developed in the sixteenth century, in the wake of the medieval vihuela, and the first scores dedicated to this instrument with a 'figure-of-eight-shaped' body, whose strings were plucked with a plectrum or directly with the fingers, also date from this period. The seventeenth century was a veritable golden age for the so-called 'baroque' guitar. This ended at the start of the eighteenth, when the instrument attracted the attention of French luthiers such as Voboam, Du Mesnil and Bovin, and of musicians such as the guitarist François Campion, a contemporary of Bach and Handel. The luthiers of Cremona (Stradivari) also made a few guitars as, in Italy, did the Sellas and, in Germany, Tielke and Stadler.

In the early nineteenth century, the sixth string became standard for German, French and Spanish luthiers. Carulli, Giuliani, Paganini and Fernando Sor composed a considerable repertoire for the instrument, which was the object of a sudden vogue known as 'guitaromania'. The French school of instrument-making, including the luthiers of Mirecourt and also those of Paris (Lacôte, Laprévotte, Maréchal), who dominated Europe, faced competition from innovative makers in Germany (Martin), Austria (Stauffer), Italy (Fabricatore, Panormo) and, increasingly, Spain (Pages). As a result, amidst inventions and oddities of all kinds (guitar-lyre, *guitare d'amour*, *guitarrón*, etc.), the main concern of luthiers was to strengthen this instrument that was considered fragile, to increase its sonorousness and to improve the quality of the strings and duration of notes. Patents abounded. The French-based Savaresse family from Italy, who Hispanicised their name as Savarez, developed strings comprising a core with one or several wires wound around it. In about 1850, Ashburn de Walcottville invented pivoting mechanisms that improved the stability of the strings on the headstock.

Between 1850 and 1874, Spanish luthier Antonio de Torres Jurado reworked and developed the bracing fan, an element already prefigured by Pages and Panormo. He also introduced longer strings (as made by Lacôte and Stauffer), invented the open headstock (sketched by Martin) and pivot mechanisms, and revived the principle of the glued bridge, which had been introduced and then abandoned in the Baroque period. Above all, he made the body bigger

than ever before. This synthesis
constituted the modern guitar, or
classical guitar, as we now call it.
Appearing just when the instrument's
popularity had been toppled by the
piano in northern Europe and France,
it gradually led, thanks to makers such
as Ramirez and Ignacio Fleta, to the
disappearance of romantic guitars in
Spain. But it was in the United States
– where, following C. F. Martin, makers
of mandolins, lutes and bouzoukis
from Germany, Ireland, Greece, Italy
and Spain settled between the 1850s
and the 1900s – that the instrument
developed in the most spectacular
fashion, both in terms of instrument-
making (nylon strings, glued neck)
and the creation of a whole new
popular repertoire that would be
decisive for its future.

Fig. 35
Jean-Nicolas Grobert (1794–1866)
Guitar, c. 1830
Cité de la Musique,
Philharmonie de Paris, Paris,
E.375

Fig. 36
Antonio de Torres Jurado (1817–1892)
Guitar, 1859
Museu de la Musica
de Barcelona, Barcelona,
MDMB 626

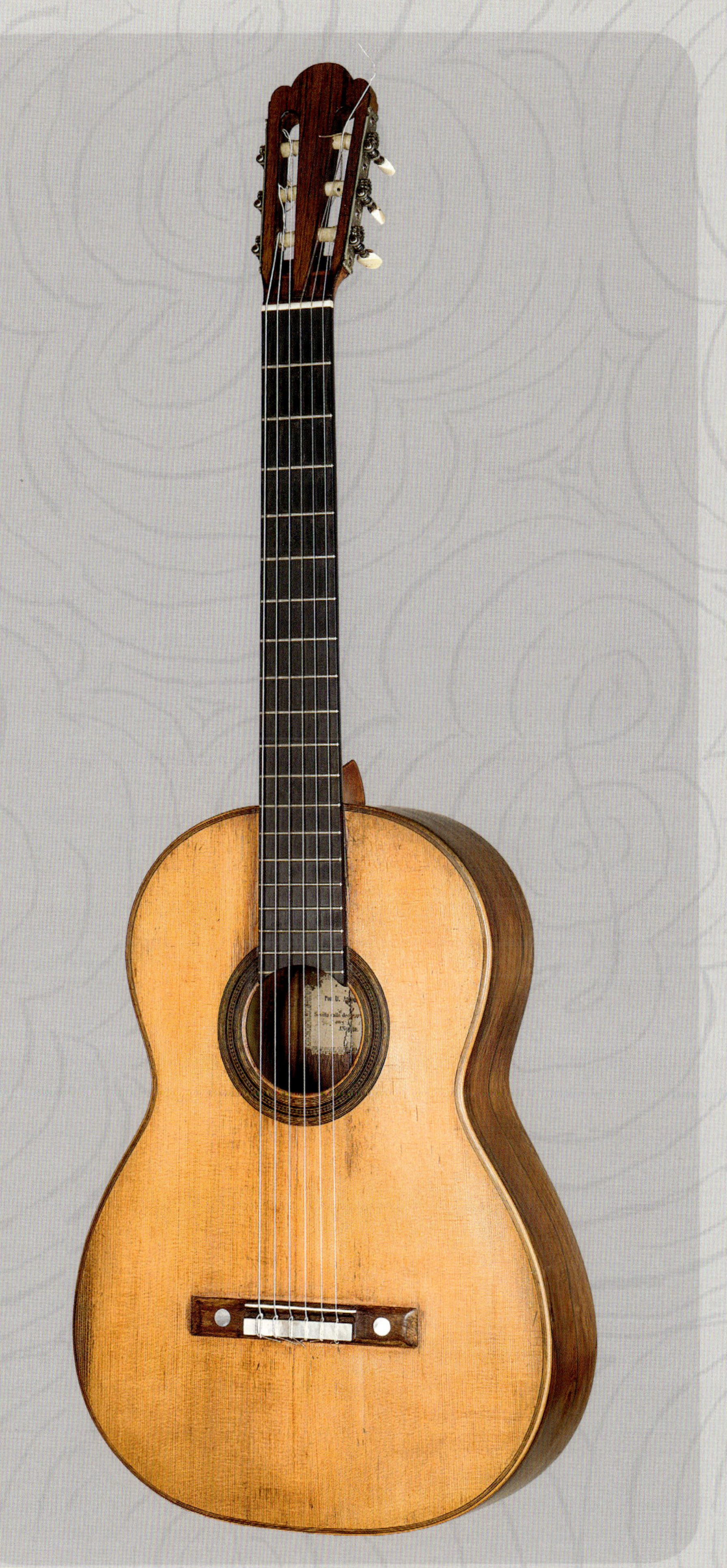

some aspects of piano history, 1860-1910

Belinda Thomson

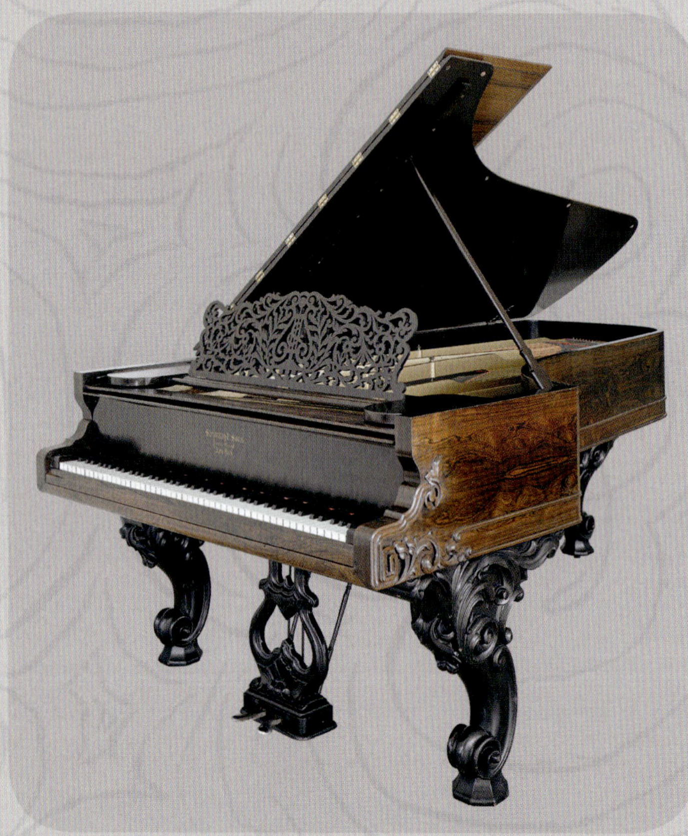

Fig. 37
*Grand Piano,
Steinway & Sons*, 1868
The Metropolitan
Museum of Art, New York,
Inv. 1985.407

Fig. 38
Maurice Biais
Poster for Érard Pianos, 1902
Bibliothèque Nationale
de France, Paris,
ENT DN-1 (BIAIS,Maurice,/2)-
ROUL, IFN-90055240

The piano's invention dates back to the early eighteenth century, when Italian harpsichord maker Bartolomeo Cristofori devised a new action whereby the strings were struck with hammers instead of quills. He dubbed the new instrument the pianoforte (literally, soft/loud) because of its conquest of the elusive goal of dynamic variation. Many improvements and refinements were introduced to the piano over the course of the nineteenth century. In France, in 1821, Sébastien Érard patented the 'double escapement' action, which allowed a note to be repeatedly and cleanly struck, opening the way to the revolutionary piano compositions of Chopin and Liszt featuring rapid arpeggios and brilliant cascades of notes. It was in the 1840s that 'Pianopolis', Théophile Gautier's mischievous nickname, caught on in Paris.[1] The Steinway firm registered no fewer than fifty-five patents between 1857 and 1887. Among the new industrial processes was the introduction of coiled wire for the bass strings, considerably increasing the instrument's sonority; another improvement was the Steinway system of overstringing, meaning space-saving upright pianos could achieve the same sound quality as grands; a third crucial improvement (resisted for a time by purists) was replacing the wooden frame, which tended to warp, with an iron one that stayed rigid, helping to keep the instrument in tune.

Initially, piano manufacturers were family dynasties working in artisanal workshops. Certain names stand out for the enduring quality of their instruments: Broadwood in England, whose pianos' strength and sonority were appreciated by Beethoven; in France, Pleyel, whose pianos had Chopin as advocate, and top of the range Érard, established also in London in the wake of the French Revolution; in Germany, Bechstein, Blüthner and Steinweg; and the latter firm's successful offshoot Steinway, established in America from 1849. But by the second half of the century, new piano factories had sprung up in all the major cities of Western Europe and America, instrument-making being one of the most competitive and profitable industries of the day. The story of the piano's rapid rise, boom and eventual bust as a commodity has fascinated economic historians, not least because its evolving manufacturing processes were so closely allied to the industrial revolution and its marketing methods (via World's Fairs and promotional concert tours) presage the rise in celebrity culture and the advertising industry.[2]

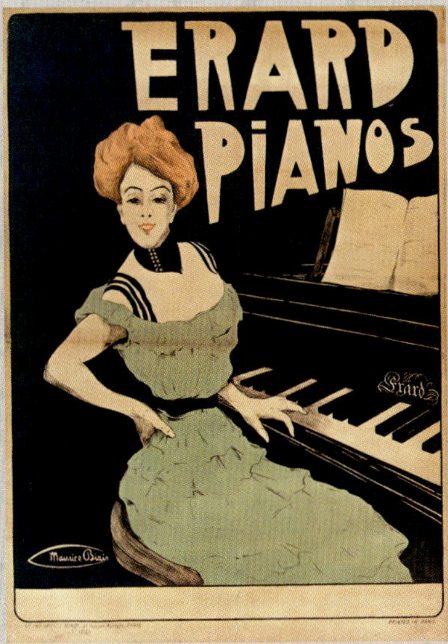

piano of the early nineteenth century, although the latter remained popular in America). Its very construction involved imported raw materials – ivory for the keys, mahogany or ebony for the case – available thanks to this prosperous and expansive era of colonisation. The well-known firms also turned out smaller numbers of grand pianos of varying sizes, to suit the wealthier customer or the professional musician. Once in a while a bespoke 'art piano' was made, combining the skills of the instrument maker for the action and an associated painter or sculptor to decorate the case.[3]

The year 1851, when the Great Exhibition in London was held, was an important one for the burgeoning piano industry. Hector Berlioz, no pianist himself, was sent by the French government as a member of the international commission examining musical instruments on display at Crystal Palace, where he would have encountered pianos manufactured in ten different countries, dominated by the thirty-eight makers from England, twenty-one from France and eighteen from Germany. Of the six American firms, Chickering, which made square pianos, was displaying the world's first iron-framed instruments. At the Expositions Universelles in Paris prizes and medals were not always distributed along unbiased lines. In 1878, for instance, following the 1870–01 Franco-Prussian war, German manufacturers were excluded and only by attending the London fairs could French critics judge their pianos. By the end of the century musicians were voting with their feet in favour of Steinways.

By the 1870s the aspiration of virtually every middle-class household was to own a piano, so it is scarcely surprising to find so many portrayed by artists. By this date a typical domestic piano of the kind affordable by households of modest income was a factory-made upright constructed of dark wood with candle sconces flanking the integral music stand (the upright largely replaced the square

In 1910, the year of the greatest production of pianos worldwide (much later than was previously thought), there were ten firms in Germany producing more than 2,000 pianos a year (alongside many smaller firms); in Britain eighteen firms producing between 1,000 and 2,000 pianos a year; and fourteen American firms producing at least 3,000 pianos a year. France, meanwhile, guilty perhaps of conservatism and complacency regarding the perceived superiority of its instruments, had seen a fall in productivity, with only three firms producing over a thousand instruments: in 1910, Pleyel produced 3,000 pianos, Bord (a manufacturer of robust cheap instruments) 2,000, and Érard and Gaveau 1,900 apiece.[4] This failure to keep pace with the international competition was the chief reason why a proposed piano tax in France was defeated in 1893, not for the first time.[5] In England, social emulation was one of the chief drivers of the piano's remarkable growth of popularity; there, even working-class families aspired to own a piano, egged on by advertisers of a hire system whose sales pitch asked: 'What is a home without a piano?'[6]

Pianos came in all shapes and sizes and at prices to suit different pockets. In France, whereas a second-hand upright by Pape typically changed hands for between 300 and 400 francs

in the 1870s – and such instruments could be found in all sorts of public and private contexts, not just domestic accommodation but in schools, bars and brothels – an Érard grand fetched tens of thousands of francs.[7] Érard was the undisputed watchword for quality, the pianos being famed for their exquisite touch and refined appearance. Despite France's protectionism and resistance to foreign imports, by degrees the 'American system' Steinway pianos with their iron frames and overstrung constructions began to prevail. The Polish concert pianist Jan Paderewski installed an Érard and a Steinway grand in his Swiss villa at Morges; when the composer Déodat de Séverac ordered a new upright piano for his house in south-western France, he sent to America for a Steinway; Marguerite de Saint-Marceaux bought herself a Steinway for 5,000 francs in 1896.[8] By 1912, the small-scale Paris piano manufacturer Édouard Moullé could make the proud claim that he was 'sole agent in France for Steinway & Sons pianos'.[9] Ironically, despite a letterhead listing royal dignitaries to whom he had supplied superior pianos, Moullé appeals to the popular composer Jules Massenet to accept an invitation to a recording session to have his playing captured for perpetuity onto piano rolls. Piano rolls were playable on the pianola, thanks to which fumbling amateur players could still impress assembled listeners without needing to conquer the keyboard themselves. With gramophone companies also being formed at this time, exploiting the technology patented by Edison in 1889, the writing was surely on the wall for the piano as status symbol and quasi ubiquitous domestic instrument.[10]

In the twenty-first century, piano making having shifted to Asia, piano-playing is arguably enjoying a resurgence in popularity, of which the phenomenon of free-to-play pianos located in public concourses such as stations and airports is a welcome sign.

[1] Gautier, writing in 1844, musing on how to rid Paris of the nuisance pianos were causing, devised the idea of a separate republic, Pianopolis, on the Butte Montmartre, led by Franz Liszt. See *Le Compilateur*, 25 April 1844, p. 370.

[2] Although he performed on behalf of Érard pianos at the Paris Exposition Universelle of 1889, on his hugely successful American tours the Polish virtuoso Jan Paderewski was under contract to promote Steinways. See Jean-Michel Nectoux in *Stars et Monstres Sacrés*, Paris (Les Dossiers du musée d'Orsay), 1986.

[3] Noted examples of art pianos: in England, by Edward Coley Burne-Jones (Victoria and Albert Museum, London); by Charles Robert Ashbee (Cheltenham Museum); in France by Albert Besnard and Alexandre Charpentier (Musée de Nice), Rupert Carabin; Victor Prouvé (Musée des Arts Décoratifs, Paris); in USA, by Lawrence Alma-Tadema (Clark Art Institute, Williamstown); Thomas Wilmer Dewing (Smithsonian Museum, Washington).

[4] These statistics for piano manufacture are from Cyril Ehrlich, *The Piano: A History*, London, Dent, 1976, an invaluable analysis of the rise and fall of the piano as an economic phenomenon.

[5] Earlier proposals for a piano tax had been mooted in 1861, 1874 and 1877, each time leading on the one hand to an upsurge of caricatures, on the other to an outpouring of reasoned argument for the democratic benefits of musical education.

[6] Charles Booth, *Life and Labour of the People in London: second series, Industry*, vol. 2, 1903, quoted in Ehrlich, *The Piano: A History*, p. 98.

[7] These figures were quoted by Edmond Tiersot in his 1877 report to the commission set up to look into the logistics of introducing a piano tax. Quoted in *Le Ménéstrel*, 12 March 1893, pp. 81–82.

[8] Information from Nectoux, *Stars et Monstres Sacrés*, 1986, p. 24; *Une famille d'artistes en 1900, Les Saint-Marceaux*, Paris (Les Dossiers du musée d'Orsay), 1992, p. 88.

[9] Letter from Édouard Moullé to Jules Massenet, 8 June 1912, Bnf. Gallica autographes. Moullé and his wife were close friends of the composer Emmanuel Chabrier, and of Édouard Manet. They inherited several paintings by Manet previously in Chabrier's collection. See Adolphe Tabarant, *Manet et ses œuvres*, Paris, Gallimard, 1947.

[10] The technology to produce recorded sound was invented simultaneously in the late 1870s by Charles Cros in France and by Thomas Edison in the United States.

wind instruments in the nineteenth century

Lolita Delesque

The nineteenth century was a key period in the development of the family of woodwind and brass instruments. Makes of wind instruments capitalised on the scientific and technical progress of the day[1] and improved understanding of the acoustic workings of instruments to make significant improvements. Instrument making gradually went from artisanal to industrial,[2] as production techniques were refined and materials evolved.

The gradual transition from the use of boxwood to that of ebony, starting at the turn of the century, marked the shift from ancient to modern instruments. Boxwood had been preferred by woodwind makers because it was dense, easy to turn, and looked good. However, as this kind of wood became scarce, they had to find another variety. Ebony was chosen for its remarkable qualities, combining great density with resistance to climatic change (temperature and humidity levels), to acidity and to saliva. Unlike boxwood, which grew in Europe, ebony came from Mozambique. The cost of this exotic material drove up instrument prices, which is why, until the 1920s, modern instruments were purchased mainly by professional musicians or by orchestras.
The rise of amateur orchestras and wind and brass bands impelled instrument makers to adapt their production to this new clientele. Where woodwinds had previously been limited to indoor performance, a new kind of vulcanised rubber, ebonite, made it possible for musicians to play outdoors without the risk of damaging their instruments.

Brass instruments also changed in the nineteenth century, with the development of the piston between 1815 and 1839, which revolutionised the trumpet and trombone and gave them the form they still have today (trumpet with the 'Périnet' system, the 'Sattler' valve trombone).

Woodwinds, too, saw numerous innovations. The invention of nickel silver, an alloy of copper, zinc and nickel, by Maillot and Chorier, two Lyonnais workers, at the start of the 1820s, made mechanisms more effective. This new alloy also enabled instrument makers to specialise in instruments made entirely of metal,[3] such as clarinets, flutes and the saxophone.

In the 1820s, the bassoon[4] was also refined, resulting in the modern instrument. Two very different systems emerged, the French bassoon, made by

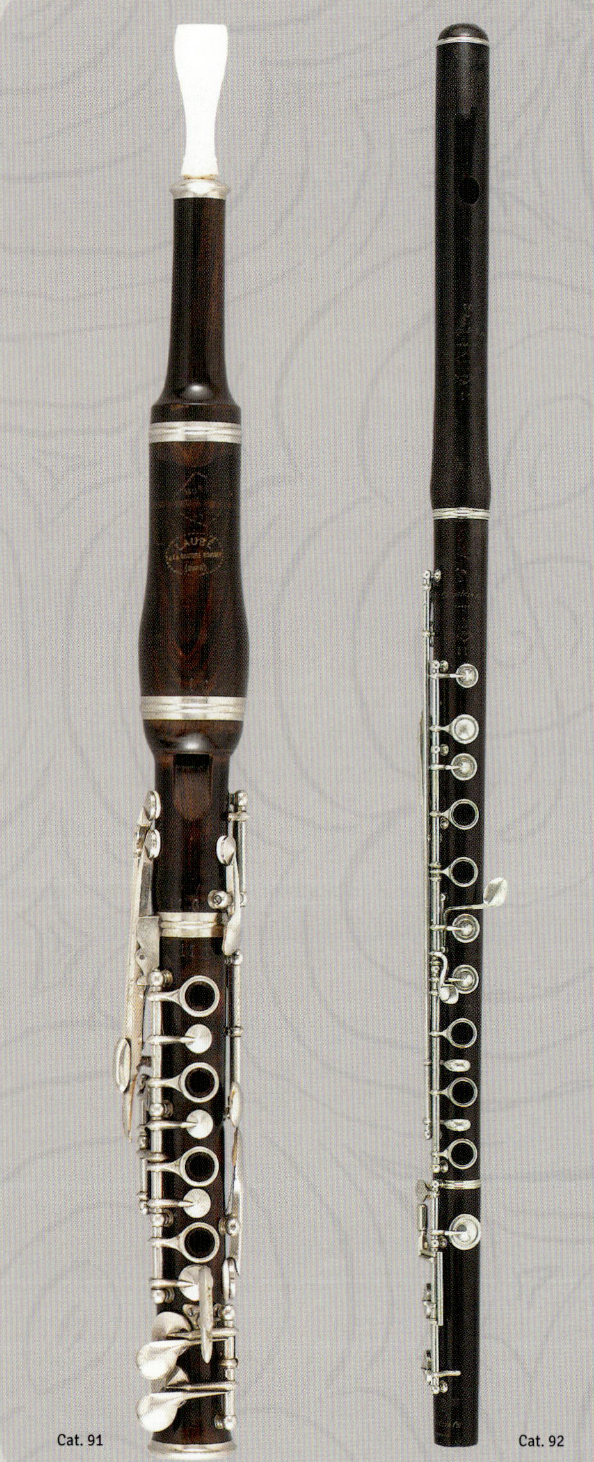

Cat. 91

Cat. 92

Jean Nicolas Savary (1823), Frédéric Triébert (1845) and Buffet (1880), and used mainly in France, Belgium and Switzerland, and the German 'Heckel' bassoon (1831). It was the latter that became the standard, and it is now used around the world.

In 1832, Theobald Boehm,[5] a Bavarian musician, composer, instrument maker and acoustician, marked the history of instrument-making by perfecting the flute. He discovered the correct position of the holes and recalculated their diameter, which was no longer based on the width of the player's fingers. He also invented a new system of keys that allowed the musician to open or close the fourteen holes simultaneously with his nine free fingers. By the end of the decade, the Boehm system was also being applied to the clarinet.

In 1847, the French instrument maker Guillaume Triébert adapted the Boehm system to the oboe,[6] redesigning the instrument's bore with his sons Charles Louis and Frédéric. In 1881 François Lorée, formerly the foreman at Triébert's workshop, founded his own oboe-making firm. His son, Lucien Lorée, invented the so-called 'conservatoire system' known as the plateau or French system, which is close to what we have today.

The nineteenth century also saw the appearance of new instruments such as the saxophone.[7] Its inventor, the Belgian instrument maker Adolph Sax, registered his patent in 1846. Although made entirely of metal, the instrument extended the range of woodwinds. Its simple, rational principles soon made it popular with musicians. It was adopted by the army in the late nineteenth century, but it was jazz that really gave the saxophone its musical prestige in the 1920s.

Despite the advocacy of instrument makers who, as of the 1850s, promoted the use of modern instruments at World's Fairs, musicians continued to resist new developments. It was not until the end of the century that they really took up the latest innovations.

[1] 'XIXe siècle. L'Europe romantique', in *Le Musée de la musique*, Paris, Cité de la Musique and Somogy, 2009, pp. 49–59.
[2] Jean-Yves Rauline, *Les Sociétés musicales en Haute-Normandie (1792–1914). Contribution à une histoire sociale de la musique*, Lille, ANRT Diffusion, 2000, p. 309.
[3] Virginie Allard, 'La Couture-Boussey, berceau français des instruments à vent', in *Trois petites notes de musique. Histoire de la facture et des pratiques instrumentales en Normandie*, exhibition catalogue, Château de Martainville, Musée des Traditions et Arts Normands, 2015–16, pp. 43–50.
[4] *Dictionnaire des musiques*, Encyclopédia Universalis France, 2016.
[5] Ludwig Boehm, 'Théobald Böhm, créateur de génie', *Traversières magazine* 90, 1st quarter 2007, pp. 46–67.
[6] *Dictionnaire des musiques*, Encyclopédia Universalis France, 2016.
[7] Ibid.

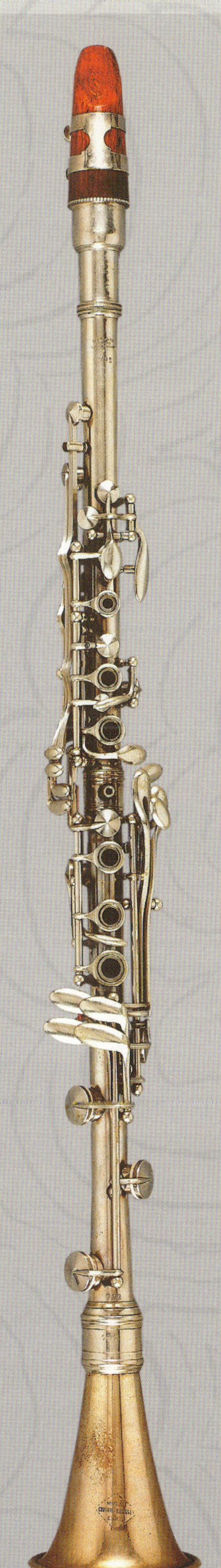

Cat. 91
Louis Laubé
Flageolet, 1897
Musée des Instruments à Vent,
La Couture-Boussey,
116

Cat. 92
Fernand Chapelain
Flute, 1897
Musée des Instruments à Vent,
La Couture-Boussey,
118

Cat. 93
Jules Boulland
Clarinet, late 19th century
Musée des Instruments à Vent,
La Couture-Boussey,
792

Cat. 93

selected bibliography

Theodor W. Adorno, *Philosophie de la nouvelle musique*, Paris, Gallimard, 1962.

Theodor W. Adorno, *In Search of Wagner*, London, NLB, 1981.

Jeanine Baticle and Gary Tinterow (eds.), *Manet-Vélasquez. La manière espagnole au XIXᵉ siècle*, exh. cat. (Paris, Musée d'Orsay, 2002–3), Paris, Réunion des Musées Nationaux, 2002.

Claire Bernardi (ed.), *Allegro Barbaro. Béla Bartók et la modernité hongroise 1905–1920*, exh. cat. (Paris, Musée d'Orsay, 2013–4), Paris, Hazan, 2013.

Richard Brettell, Françoise Cachin, Claire Frèches-Thory and Charles F. Stuckey (eds.), *Gauguin*, exh. cat. (Paris, Galeries Nationales du Grand Palais, 1989), Paris, Réunion des Musées Nationaux, 1989.

Françoise Cachin, *Gauguin*, Paris, Flammarion, 1988.

François Caradec and Alain Weill, *Le Café-concert (1848–1914)*, 2nd rev. ed., Paris, Fayard, 2007.

Laurence des Cars, Dominique de Font-Réaulx, Gary Tinterow and Michel Hilaire (eds.), *Gustave Courbet*, exh. cat. (Paris, Galeries Nationales du Grand Palais, 2007–8; New York, The Metropolitan Museum of Art, 2008; Montpellier, Musée Fabre, 2008), Paris, Réunion des Musées Nationaux, 2007.

Dennis Cate (ed.), *The Spirit of Montmartre: Cabarets, Humor and the Avant-Garde, 1875–1905*, exh. cat. (Rutgers, Jane Voorhees Zimmerli Art Museum, The State University of New Jersey, 1996; Palm Beach, The Society of the Four Arts, 1996–7; Gainesville, The Samuel P. Harn Museum, University of Florida, 1997), New Brunswick, N. J., Rutgers University Press, 1996; in particular Steven Moore Whiting, 'Music on Montmartre', pp. 159–97.

Philippe Cathé, *Claude Terrasse*, Paris, L'Hexaèdre, 2004.

Emmanuel Chabrier, *Correspondance*, edited by Roger Delage and Frans Durif with the aid of Thierry Bodin, Paris, Klincksieck, 1994.

Ernest Chausson, *Écrits inédits. Journaux intimes. Roman de jeunesse. Correspondance*, edited by Jean Gallois and Isabelle Bretaudeau, Monaco, Éditions du Rocher, 1999.

Myriam Chimènes (ed.), *Le Journal de Marguerite de Saint-Marceaux*, Paris, Fayard, 2007.

Guy Cogeval and Béatrice Avanzi (eds.), *De la scène au tableau*, exh. cat. (Marseille, Musée Cantini, 2009–10; Rovereto, Museo di Arte Moderna e Contemporanea di Trento e Rovereto, 2010; Toronto, Musée des Beaux-Arts de l'Ontario, 2010), Paris, Skira Flammarion, 2009.

Sidonie Gabrielle Colette, 'Un salon de musique en 1900', in *Maurice Ravel par quelques-uns de ses familiers*, Paris, Éditions du Tambourinaire, 1939.

François Daulte, *Frédéric Bazille et son temps*, Geneva, Pierre Cailler, 1952.

Peter Dayan, *Art as Music, Music as Poetry, Poetry as Art: From Whistler to Stravinsky and Beyond*, Burlington, VT, Ashgate, 2011.

Claude Debussy, 'Concerts Colonne' [review for the *Société musicale indépendante*, 15 May 1913], in *Debussy on Music*, New York, Alfred A. Knopf, 1977.

Claude Debussy, *Correspondance (1872–1918)*, edited by François Lesure and Denis Herlin, annotated by François Lesure, Denis Herlin and Georges Liébert, Paris, NRF, Gallimard, 2005.

Jill DeVonyar and Richard Kendall, *Degas & Music*, exh. cat., Glens Falls, NY, The Hyde Collection, 2009.

Dictionnaire des musiques, Encyclopédia Universalis France, 2016.

Claude Duneton and Michel Desproges, *Chansons sensuelles, le petit format illustré et la chanson à texte au tournant du siècle*, Paris, Les Éditions musicales Fortin, 2004.

Hippolyte Fierens-Gevaert, *La Tristesse contemporaine. Essai sur les grands courants moraux et intellectuels du XIXᵉ siècle*, Paris, Félix Alcan, 1899.

Paul Gauguin, *Oviri, cahiers d'un sauvage*, Paris, Gallimard, 1974.

Gilles Genty and Pierrette Vernon, *Bonnard Inédits*, Paris, Cercle d'art, 2003.

June Hargrove, 'Paul Gauguin: Sensing the Infinite', in Sally M. Promey (ed.), *Sensational Religion: Sensory Cultures in Material Practice*, New Haven, Yale University Press, 2014.

Colta Ives, Helen Giambruni and Sasha M. Newman, *Pierre Bonnard: The Graphic Art*, exh. cat. (New York, The Metropolitan Museum of Art, 1989–90; Houston, Museum of Fine Arts, 1990; Boston, Museum of Fine Arts, 1990), New York, The Metropolitan Museum of Art, 1989.

Vladimir Jankélévitch, *La Musique et l'ineffable*, Paris, Librairie Armand Colin, 1961.

Philippe Junod, *Contrepoints. Dialogues entre musique et peinture*, Geneva, Contrechamps, 2006.

Sylvia Kahan, *Music's Modern Muse: A Life of Winnaretta Singer, Princesse de Polignac*, Rochester (NY.), University of Rochester Press, 2003.

James Leggio (ed.), *Music and Modern Art*, New York, Routledge, 2010 (1st ed., 2002); in particular Charlotte N. Eyerman, 'Playing the Market: Renoir's Young Girls at the Piano Series of 1892', pp. 37–61.

Francine-Claire Legrand, 'Fernand Khnopff – Perfect Symbolist', *Apollo*, n. s., 85, April 1967.

Anne Leonard, 'To Themselves: Music in the Art of Henri Fantin-Latour and Odilon Redon', *Imago Musicae*, XXXVII–XXXVIII, 2014–5.

Richard Leppert, *The Sight of Sound. Music, Representation, and the History of the Body*, Berkeley, University of California Press, 1993.

Dominique Lobstein, 'Strettes', in *Honoré Daumier. Du rire aux armes*, exh. cat. (Saint-Denis, Musée d'Art et d'Histoire, 2008–9), Saint-Denis Musée d'Art et d'Histoire, 2008, pp. 105–14.

Edward Lockspeiser, *Debussy*, 3rd ed., London, Dent, 1951 (1st ed., 1936).

Julie Manet, *Journal (1893–99). Sa jeunesse parmi les peintres impressionnistes et les hommes de lettres*, Paris, Klincksieck, 1979.

Mena Marques (ed.), *Manet en el Prado*, exh. cat. (Madrid, Museo Nacional del Prado, 2003–4), Madrid, Museo Nacional del Prado, 2003.

Anne Martin-Fugier, *Les Salons de la IIIᵉ République. Art, littérature, politique*, Paris, Perrin, 2003.

Camille Mauclair, 'Le Symbolisme en France', in *L'Art en silence*, Paris, Ollendorff, 1901.

Camille Mauclair, *Servitude et grandeur littéraires*, Paris, Ollendorff, 1922.

Camille Mauclair, 'Eaux-fortes d'après l'orchestre', in *La Religion de la musique*, Paris, Fischbacher, 1928 (1st ed., 1909).

Kitti Messina, 'Mélodie et romance au milieu du xixe siècle. Points communs et divergences', *Revue de musicologie*, 94, no. 1, 2008, pp. 59–90.

Jean-Michel Nectoux, *Gabriel Fauré*, Paris, 1995 (1st ed., 1972).

Jean-Michel Nectoux (ed.), *Une famille d'artistes en 1900: les Saint-Marceaux*, Paris, Réunion des Musées Nationaux, 'Les Dossiers du musée d'Orsay' series, 1992; in particular Michel Delahaye, 'Marguerite de Saint-Marceaux 1850–1930', pp. 51–61.

Jean-Michel Nectoux (ed.), *Debussy, la musique et les arts*, exh. cat. (Paris, Musée de l'Orangerie; Tokyo, Bridgestone Museum of Art, 2012), Paris, Skira Flammarion, 2012; in particular Denis Herlin, 'Le Cercle de l'art indépendant', pp. 76–89.

Ader Nordmann, *Archives et souvenirs de la famille Heugel, éditeurs de musique*, Paris, Drouot Richelieu sale, room 9, 26 May 2011, Paris, T. Bodin, J. Izarn, A. Weill [2011].

Michelle Perrot (ed.), *Histoire de la vie privée*, Paris, Éditions du Seuil, 1987; *A History of Private Life. IV. From the Fires of Revolution to the Great War*, Cambridge, Mass., Harvard University Press, 1990.

Antonin Proust, *Édouard Manet. Souvenirs*, Paris, Éditions L'Échoppe, 1988 (1st ed., 1913).

Jean-Yves Rauline, *Les Sociétés musicales en Haute-Normandie (1792–1914). Contribution à une histoire sociale de la musique*, Lille, ANRT Diffusion, 2000.

Claudie Ricaud, *Francis Thomé*, Paris, L'Harmattan, 2013.

James Rubin, *Manet*, Paris, Flammarion, 2011.

James Rubin and Olivia Mattis (eds.), *Rival Sisters. Art and Music at the Birth of Modernism, 1815–1915*, Burlington, VT, Ashgate, 2014.

Antoine Salomon and Guy Cogeval, *Vuillard, Le Regard innombrable. Catalogue critique des peintures et pastels*, 3 vols., Milan, Skira, Paris, Le Seuil, Wildenstein Institute, 2003.

Michel Schulman, *Frédéric Bazille. Catalogue raisonné. Sa vie, son œuvre, sa correspondance*, Paris, Éditions de l'Amateur, 1995.

Paul Smith, *Seurat and the Avant-Garde*, New Haven and London, Yale University Press, 1997.

Paul Souriau, *La Suggestion dans l'art*, Paris, Félix Alcan, 1893.

Belinda Thomson (ed.), *Gauguin Maker of Myth*, exh. cat. (London, Tate, 2010–11; Washington, DC, National Gallery of Art, 2011), London, Tate Publ., 2010.

Natascha Veldhorst, *Van Gogh & Muziek: Symfonie in blauw en geel*, Amsterdam, Amsterdam University Press, 2015.

Martial de Villemoune, 'De l'imprécis en musique', *L'Art et la Vie*, 2, 1894.

Ricardo Viñes, 'Le journal inédit de Ricardo Vines', introduction, translation and notes by Nina Gubisch, *Revue internationale de musique française*, no. 2, June 1980, pp. 154–248.

Martha Ward and Anne Leonard (eds.), *Looking and Listening in Nineteenth Century France*, exh. cat. (Chicago, Smart Museum of Art, University of Chicago, 2007), Chicago, Smart Museum of Art, 2007; in particular Eleanor Rivera, 'Listening with your Eyes: *Le Petit Solfège Illustré* and French Children's Songbooks', pp. 61–71.

Francis Wolff, *Pourquoi la musique ?*, Paris, Fayard, 2015.

on the guitar

Manuel Cano, *La guitarra. Historia, estudios y aportaciones al arte del flamenco*, Cordoue, Universidad de Córdoba, Servicio de Publicaciones, 1986.

Alain Miteran, *Histoire de la guitare*, Paris, Éditions Zurfluh, 1997.

Harvey Turnbull, *The Guitar from the Renaissance to the Present Day*, New York, Scribner's, 1974.

on the piano

Robert Adelson, Alain Roudier, Jenny Nex, Laure Barthel and Michel Foussard (eds.), *The History of the Érard Piano and Harp in Letters and Documents, 1785–1959*, 2 vols., Cambridge (Great Britain), Cambridge University Press, 2015.

René Beaupain, *La Maison Érard, manufacture de pianos, 1780–1959*, Paris, L'Harmattan, 2005.

Cyril Ehrlich, *The Piano, A History*, London, Dent, 1976.

Charlotte Eyerman, *The Composition of Femininity: The Significance of the 'Woman at the Piano' Motif in Nineteenth-Century French Culture from Daumier to Renoir*, PhD. thesis, University of California at Berkeley, 1997.

Dieter Hildebrandt, *Pianoforte: A Social History of the Piano*, New York, G. Braziller, 1988.

Félix Le Couppey, *De l'Enseignement du piano, conseils aux jeunes professeurs*, 3rd ed., Paris, Hachette, 1874.

Thierry Maniguet, 'Pianopolis: Paris, capitale du piano romantique', *Revue de la Bibliothèque nationale de France*, no. 34, 2010, pp. 19–24.

James Parakilas, *Piano Roles: Three Hundred Years of Life with the Piano*, New Haven, Yale University Press, 2000.

James Parakilas *et al.*, *Piano Roles: A New History of the Piano*, New Haven, Yale Nota Bene, 2002.

Ronald V. Ratcliffe, *Steinway and Sons*, San Francisco, Chronicle Books, 1989.

Florence Gétreau, *Sébastien Érard ou la rencontre avec le pianoforte*, exh. cat., Luxeuil-les-Bains, [n.p.], 1993.

on wind instruments

'xixe siècle, l'Europe romantique', in *Le Musée de la musique*, Paris, Cité de la Musique and Somogy Éditions d'art, 2009.

Virginie Allard, 'La Couture-Boussey, berceau français des instruments à vent', in *Trois petites notes de musique. Histoire de la facture et des pratiques instrumentales en Normandie*, Château de Martainville, Musée des Traditions et Arts Normands, 2015.

photographic credits

Albi, Musée Toulouse-Lautrec: cat. 53

Amsterdam, Van Gogh Museum (Vincent van Gogh Foundation): cat. 49, 54, 62 and 65

Baltimore, The Baltimore Museum of Art / Photo: Mitro Hood: cat. 37 / Given by Hilda K. Blaustein, in Memory of her late Husband, Jacob Blaustein, BMA 1979.163: fig. 5, p. 25

Barcelona, Museu de la Música de Barcelona / Photo: Eduard Selva: fig. 36, p. 173

Barcelona, Museu Nacional d'Art de Catalunya, Barcelona 2016 / Photo: Jordi Calveras: fig. 18, p. 41

Boston, Museum of Fine Arts: detail p. 20, cat. 16

BPK, Berlin, Dist. RMN-Grand Palais / Elke Walford: cat. 11

Bridgeman Images: fig. 6, p. 27, fig. 12, p. 36, fig. 13, p. 37, fig. 16, p. 39, fig. 20, p. 43

Brussels, Belfius Art Collection: cat. 44

Brussels, Bibliothèque Royale de Belgique: cat. 55

Brussels, Musées Royaux des Beaux-Arts de Belgique / Photo: Guy Cussac, Brussels: detail pp. 2–3, cat. 32 / Photo: J. Geleyns - Ro scan: cat. 42

Cergy-Pontoise, Conseil Départemental du Val d'Oise – CAOA / Photo: J.-Y. Lacôte: cat. 33

Christie's / Bridgeman Images: fig. 15, p. 38

Chicago, Terra Foundation for American Art: cat. 31

Cincinnati, Taft Museum of Art / Photo: Tony Walsh, Cincinnati, Ohio: cat. 22

City of London, Guildhall Art Gallery: cat. 10

Classicalpaintings / Alamy Stock Photo: fig. 7, p. 27

Cleveland, The Cleveland Museum of Art: cat. 8

Courtesy HarpWeek: fig. 31, p. 62

Davis Museum and Cultural Center, Wellesley College / Bridgeman Images: fig. 25, p. 54

De Agostini / Bridgeman Images: fig. 2, p. 24

Dobra Collection: detail p. 32, cat. 30

Geneva, Association des Amis du Petit Palais / Photo: Studio Monique Bernaz, Geneva: detail p. 120, cat. 57

Giverny, Bibliothèque du musée des impressionnismes / Photo: Guillaume Onimus: cat. 80

Indianapolis, Indianapolis Museum of Art, Samuel Josefowitz Collection of the School of Pont-Aven / Photo: Bridgeman Images: detail p. 106, cat. 38

La Couture-Boussey, Musée des Instruments à Vent / Photo: Jean-Marc Anglès: cat 91, 92 and 93, pp. 176–7

La Rochelle, Musées d'Art et d'Histoire / Photo: Max Roy: cat. 3

London, The National Gallery, London, Dist. RMN-Grand Palais / National Gallery Photographic Department: fig. 8, p. 29

London, Tate: cat. 25

London, Tate, Dist. RMN-Grand Palais / Tate Photography: fig. 14, p. 37

Lukas – Art in Flanders VZW / Photo: Hugo Maertens / Bridgeman Images: fig. 34, p. 131

Madrid, Collection Juan San Nicolás / Photo: Katina Avgouloupis: cat. 43

New York, The Metropolitan Museum of Art, Dist. RMN-Grand Palais / image of the MMA: detail pp. 4–5, fig. 1, p. 22, fig. 9, p. 30, fig. 37, p. 174, cat. 29

Odense, Brandts Museum of Art & Visual Culture / Photo: Bent Hesby: cat. 34

Ostende, Mu.ZEE / Photo: Daniël de Kievith: cat. 14

Paris, Bibliothèque Nationale de France: detail p. 60 and 137, fig. 24, p. 52, fig. 27, p. 56, fig. 38, p. 175, cat. 68 to 73

Paris, Collection Musée de la Musique / Photo Giordan: fig. 35, p. 172

Paris, Institut National d'Histoire de l'Art, Bibliothèque, Collection Jacques Doucet: cat. 17, 39 and 74, fig. 3, p. 24

Paris, Les Arts Décoratifs / Photo: Jean Tholance: detail p. 48, cat. 12, 76 and 78

Paris, Musée Marmottan Monet / Bridgeman Images: cat. 20, 35 and 61

Paris, Petit Palais / Roger-Viollet: detail p. 1, cat. 4

Paris, RMN-Grand Palais (Château de Blérancourt) / Michel Urtado: cat. 40

Paris, RMN-Grand Palais (Musée de l'Orangerie) / Franck Raux: cat. 21

Paris, RMN-Grand Palais (Musée d'Orsay) / Michèle Bellot: cat. 28

Paris, RMN-Grand Palais (Musée d'Orsay) / Jean-Gilles Berizzi: cat. 13, fig. 28, p. 57

Paris, RMN-Grand Palais (Musée d'Orsay) / Photo: Thierry Le Mage: cat. 60

Paris, RMN-Grand Palais (Musée d'Orsay) / Hervé Lewandowski: cat. 5, 26, 47, 48, 50, 51 and 52, fig. 19, p. 42, fig. 21, p. 45

Paris, RMN-Grand Palais (Musée d'Orsay) / Patrice Schmidt: fig. 23, p. 51, fig. 26, p. 55

Paris, RMN-Grand Palais / René-Gabriel Ojéda: fig. 10, p. 34

Paris, RMN-Grand Palais / Benoît Touchard: cat. 56

Paris, RMN-Grand Palais / Fondation Bemberg / Photo: Mathieu Rabeau: detail p. 68, cat. 15

Richard and Mary L. Gray and the Gray Collection Trust: fig. 22, p. 50

Royal Academy of Music / Lebrecht Music & Arts: fig. 33, p. 126

Sarasota, The John & Mable Ringling Museum of Art: cat. 59

Stockholm, Nationalmuseum Stockholm: fig. 4, p. 25

Toulouse, Fondation Bemberg / Photo: JJ Ader: cat. 9

Ville d'Avignon, Musée Calvet / Photo: André Guerrand: cat. 1

Ville de Clermont-Ferrand, Musée d'Art Roger-Quilliot: cat. 6

Ville de Liège, Musée des Beaux-Arts de la Boverie: cat. 7

Villeneuve-sur-Lot, Collection Musée de Gajac: cat. 2

Washington, National Gallery of Art: detail pp. 6–7, cat. 45

Washington, Smithsonian American Art Museum: cat. 23

Washington, Hirshhorn Museum and Sculpture Garden, Smithsonian Institution / Photo: Cathy Carver: detail p. 84, cat. 27

All rights reserved: detail p. 12, cat. 19, 30, 41, 46, 50, 58, 81 and 90, fig. 32, p. 65

All rights reserved / Photo: Fabrice Lepeltier: cat. 36

All rights reserved / Photo: André Morin: cat. 18, 82, 83, 84

All rights reserved / Photo: Michiel Elsevier Stokmans: cat. 63, 64, 66, 67, 75, 77, 79 and 85 to 89

All rights reserved, Sotheby's, London: cat. 24

ADAGP, Paris, 2017: detail pp. 12 and 68, cat. 5, 15, 36, 44, 48, 50, 55, 80, 82, 83 and 84

Library of Congress Control Number: 2017932338

A catalogue record for this book is available from The British Library

ISBN: 9780300230093

Legal deposit: March 2017

Photoengraving: Litho Art New, Turin, Italy

Printed by Stamperia Artistica Nazionale, Trofarello, Italy